Studies in
Sardinian
Archaeology

Volume II: Sardinia in the Mediterranean

edited by
Miriam S. Balmuth

Ann Arbor
The University of Michigan Press

Published with the assistance of the J. Paul Getty Trust

*Camera-ready copy for this volume
has been provided by the editor.*

Library of Congress Cataloging-in-Publication Data
(Revised for volume 2)

Studies in Sardinian archaeology.

   Vol. 2 has special title: Sardinia in the
Mediterranean.
   Vol. 1 consists largely of selected colloquium papers
as they were presented from 1979 to 1982. V. 2 is based
on the proceedings of the First International Colloquium
on Sardinian Archaeology held at Tufts University,
Medford, Mass., Sept. 23–25, 1983.
   Vol. 2. edited by Miriam S. Balmuth.
   First vol. published without volume numbering.
   Includes bibliographies.
   1. Sardinia — Antiquities.   2. Excavations
(Archaeology) — Italy — Sardinia.   3. Italy — Antiquities.
I. Balmuth, Miriam S., 1925–   II. Rowland,
Robert J., 1938–   .   III. International Colloquium
on Sardinian Archaeology (1st : 1983 : Tufts
University)   IV. Sardinian archaeology.   V. Title:
Sardinia in the Mediterranean.
DG55.S2S78   1984   937'.9   84-3556
ISBN 0-472-10047-5 (v. 1)
ISBN 0-472-10081-5 (v. 2)

PREFACE

Miriam S. Balmuth

"Sardinia in the Mediterranean" is the name of the First International Colloquium on Sardinian Archaeology, held at Tufts University, Medford, Massachusetts on September 23, 24 and 25, 1983. With support from the National Endowment for the Humanities, the Samuel H. Kress Foundation, Tufts University and individual donors, the assembling of preeminent scholars in the field allowed for the presentation and exchange of ideas that are reflected in the papers as prepared for publication.

This book consists of a collection of articles given as papers in that colloquium. The title is meant to emphasize our newly acquired understanding of the relationship of Sardinia to the rest of the Mediterranean, and at the same time to illuminate those unique aspects of the island whose archaeological shape is just emerging. It was in recognition of the need to make the accelerating research on ancient Sardinia available to readers of English that the editor organized a continuing sequence of colloquia on the subject in 1979.

The first volume in this series, Studies in Sardinian Archaeology, co-edited with Robert J. Rowland, Jr. (University of Michigan Press: Ann Arbor 1984), was largely composed of selected colloquium papers as they were presented from 1979 to 1982. In this second volume, it is possible to benefit from the immediacy of a person-to-person exchange that shows up in the articles written after the initial papers were read, questions asked, and problems discussed. The subject matter of the papers was planned to be cumulative, so that aspects of the landscape and resources that appear in the first communication became a recurrent theme in other considerations. Likewise, the working of metals native to the island became the focus of several treatments, and the discussion of bronze figurines an indirect reference. An unusual feature of the colloquium that made it a genuine meeting of minds was the planning of colloquial discussions on some of the subjects. The one included here is on the oxhide ingots of copper. A few of the papers with a different focus, presented at the colloquium, have been collected for publication elsewhere under the title New Insights into Sardinian Society.

Some of the articles are syntheses, others present hypotheses. Still others are surveys or analyses, representative of the continuing study on the island, and centered either on the succession of cultures and civilizations, or on a medium of research such as epigraphy or obsidian. The spectrum is in itself a reflection of the quickening and widening interest in the island's archaeological history. Four catalogs present some hitherto unpublished material, ranging from the recently discovered and unexpected Nuragic stone statues, through Nuragic and Phoenician bronze figurines to Roman shipping amphoras. In place of an introduction to the book, there is a separate introduction to the six parts, designed to provide a brief background for the reader. A more substantive epilogue provides a catalog of the results of these opportunities for the exchange of both information and ideas, emphasizing the originality and importance of the contributions.

It is appropriate once more to remind the readers of the individuality of each contributor and the differences in the disciplines that they represent. This applies not only to ideas, but to ways of expressing and documenting them as well. People in different fields put colons or commas in different places; a 'stele' mentioned by a Classicist is traditionally a 'stela' to a Near Eastern specialist. It seems gratuitous to homogenize these perfectly understandable variations if they are clear to the reader. Inconsistencies extend to other usages of choice: one quotation mark or two; the manner of abbreviation; and some bibliographical conventions. Material presented for the separate catalogs was done in such a way that it was impossible to homogenize their appearance. Accents in Sardinian place names were submitted most fully by James Lewthwaite, and used sporadically elsewhere.

For the most part, each contributor defined his or her own type of bibliographical or dating convention and the need for strict consistency was felt to be necessary only within each article rather than throughout the book, so long as no confusion resulted. Perhaps the most divided (and divisive) case, after the use of accent marks, is that of the compass points, and the decision whether to capitalize or not seems to approach an almost philosophical dimension. While 'b.c.' should consistently refer to radiocarbon dates and 'B.C.' to others, the convention was, like the periods in the abbreviations, inconsistently submitted.

Abbreviations are those found in the American Journal of Archaeology, those presented by contributors and those invented by the editor. One abbreviation new to readers of English is 'AA.VV' used in Italian to identify a work that contains the contributions of several authors with no significant or substantive addition by a single editor.

The Chicago Manual of Style gave some assistance. Other help came from Elizabeth Gardner who did preliminary editing, even translating from the original Italian when necessary, and Robert H. Tykot added his skill at word-processing to combine with his growing knowledge of Sardinian archaeology. Aviva Weiss did some proof-reading, and so did Helen Arevalo, Sarah Hood and Amber Somes. Marilyn Beaven checked abbreviations and illustrations, and Michael Kelley drew diacritical marks. Other aid from colleagues and students was eagerly sought and cheerfully given.

In contrast to the first volume in this series, the production of this one was expedited by the use of a word processor generously supplied by the Provost of Tufts University.

This book is dedicated to Norman because and despite...

CONTENTS

ILLUSTRATIONS

Figures

Tables

ABBREVIATIONS

AA	Archäologischer Anzeiger
AASOR	Annual of the American Schools of Oriental Research
AA.VV	References of collections of essays by various authors, without editors listed
AIIN	Annali del Istituto Italiano di Numismatica
AJA	American Journal of Archaeology
AJP	American Journal of Philology
AmAnt	American Anthropology
AntK	Antike Kunst
ArchAustr	Archaeologia Austriaca
ArchSarda	Archeologia Sarda
AthMitt	Mitteilungen des deutschen Archäologischen Instituts, Athenische Abteilung
AttiLinc	Atti della Accademia Nazionale dei Lincei
BA	Biblical Archaeology
BAR	British Archaeological Reports. Oxford.
BAS	Bulletino Archeologico Sardo
BASOR	Bulletin of the American Schools of Oriental Research
BBSAJ	Bulletin of the British School of Archaeology at Jerusalem
BCH	Bulletin de correspondance hellénique
BdA	Bollettino d'Arte
BICS	Bulletin of the Institute of Classical Studies
BMOP	British Museum Occasional Paper
BPI	Bulletino Paletnologia Italiana
BSA	British School at Athens, Annual
BSPF	Bulletin de la Société préhistorique française

CAH	Cambridge Ancient History
CIL	Corpus Inscriptionum Latinarum
CIS	Corpus Inscriptionum Semiticarum
CNRS	Centre National de la Recherche Scientifique
CW	Classical World
DialAr	Dialoghi di Archeologia
Early Settlement	Early Settlement in the Western Mediterranean Islands and their Peripheral Areas. W.H. Waldren et al. eds. BAR International Series 229 (1984).
Ichnussa	Ichnussa: La Sardegna dalle origini all'eta classica. Milano: Libri Scheiwiller (1981).
IEJ	Israel Expedition Journal
IIPP	Istituto italiano di preistoria e protostoria
IJNA	International Journal of Nautical Archaeology
IOS	Israel Oriental Studies
JAS	Journal of Archaeological Science
JdI	Jahrbuch des k. deutschen archäologischen Instituts
JAOS	Journal of the American Oriental Society
JFA	Journal of Field Archaeology
JHS	Journal of Hellenic Studies
JNES	Journal of Near Eastern Studies
JRS	Journal of Roman Studies
Kunst Sardiniens	Kunst und Kultur Sardiniens vom Neolithikum bis zum Ende der Nuraghenzeit. Jürgen Thimme ed. Karlsruhe: Müller (1980).
MélRom	Mélanges d'archéologie at d'histoire de l'Ecole française de Rom
MonAnt	Monumenti Antichi

Niemeyer	Phönizier im Westen: Die Beiträge des Internationalen Symposiums über "Die phönizische Expansion im westlichen Mittelmeerraum" in Köln vom 24. bis 27. April 1979. H.G. Niemeyer ed. = Madrider Beiträge 8(1982).
NSc	Notizie degli Scavi di Antichità
NUR	NUR: La misteriosa civiltà dei Sardi. Dino Sanno ed., Milano: Cariplo (1980).
OpusAth	Opuscula Atheniensis
ParPass	La Parola del Passato
PCIA	Populi e civiltà dell'Italia antiqua, Roma: Biblioteca di Storia Patria (1974).
PPS	Proceedings of the Prehistoric Society
PZ	Prähistorische Zeitschrift
Quaderni	Occasional Publications of the Soprintendenza ai Beni Archeologici per le provincie di Sassari e Nuoro
RDAC	Report of the Department of Antiquities of Cyprus
RendLinc	Rendiconti della Accademia dei Lincei
Ridgway and Ridgway	Italy before the Romans: The Iron Age, Orientalizing and Etruscan Periods. D. and F.R. Ridgway eds. London-New York-San Francisco (1979).
RömMitt	Mitteilungen des deutschen archäologischen Instituts, Römische Abteilung
RSF	Rivista di Studi Fenici
RSP	Rivista di Scienze Preistoriche
RStLig	Rivista di Studi Liguri
RStO	Rivista degli Studi Orientali
SAM	Junghans, S., E. Sangmeister and M. Schröder, Metallanalysen kupferzeitlicher und frühbronzezeitlicher Bodenfunde aus Europa. Berlin: Mann (1960).
Sardaigne	Zervos, Christian, La Civilisation de la Sardaigne du début de l'Enéolithique a la fin de la Période Nouragique II° millenaire-V° Siècle avant notre ère. Paris: Cahiers d'Art (1954).

Sardegna Centro-Orientale	Sardegna centro-orientale dal neolitico alle fine del mondo antico, Nuoro, Museo Civico Speleo-archaeologico, Sassari: Dessì (1978).
Sardegna Centro-Settentrionalle	Nuove testimonianze archeologiche della Sardegna centro-settentrionale, Sassari, Museo Nazionale "G.A. Sanna" 18 luglio - 24 ottobre 1976, Sassari: Dessì.
Sardinia	Margaret Guido, Sardinia (Ancient Peoples and Places series 35). London: Thames and Hudson (1963).
SciAm	Scientific American
SIMA	Studies in Mediterranean Archaeology. Lund.
SMEA	Studi Micenei ed Egeo-Anatolici
SSA	Studies in Sardinian Archaeology. M.S. Balmuth and R.J. Rowland Jr. eds. Ann Arbor (1984).
StEtr	Studi Etruschi
StSar	Studi Sardi
StMisc	Studi Miscellanei, Seminario di Archeologia e Storia dell'Arte Greca e Romana dell'Università di Roma
TAPA	Transactions of the American Philological Association
TAPS	Transactions of the American Philosophical Society
UF	Ugaritische Forschungen
YCS	Yale Classical Studies

CONTRIBUTORS

Miriam S. Balmuth, Tufts University, Classics and Archaeology

Raniero Massoli-Novelli, University of Cagliari, Earth Sciences

David Trump, University of Cambridge, Archaeology

James G. Lewthwaite, University of Cambridge, Archaeology (1983)

Carlo Tronchetti, Archaeological Superintendancy for Cagliari and Oristano

Brunilde S. Ridgway, Bryn Mawr College, Classical and Near Eastern Archaeology

Larissa Bonfante, New York University, Classics

Francesca R. Serra Ridgway, University of Edinburgh, Archaeology

Moshe Dothan, University of Haifa, Archaeology

Frank Moore Cross, Harvard University, Near Eastern Languages and Literatures

Ferruccio Barreca, Archaeological Superintendancy for Cagliari and Oristano

David Ridgway, University of Edinburgh, Archaeology

Jean M. Davison, University of Vermont, Classics

Peter Wells, Harvard University, Anthropology

Patricia Phillips, University of Sheffield, Prehistory and Archaeology

Elizabeth Lyding Will, University of Massachusetts at Amherst, Classics

Fulvia Lo Schiavo, Archaeological Superintendancy for Sassari and Nuoro

R. F. Tylecote, University of London, Institute of Archaeo-Metallurgy
       (Communication published in SSA)

John F. Merkel, University of Pennsylvania, Museum Applied Science Center
       for Archaeology (1983)

PART ONE:
FROM THE EARLIEST SETTLEMENTS TO
THE FIRST APPEARANCE OF *NURAGHI*

Introduction

The first three articles in this collection treat the physiognomy of the island, the earliest settlements, and the subsequent pattern of settlements until the nuraghi. An account of the geological development of Sardinia by Raniero Massoli-Novelli is especially appropriate as a starting point, not only in view of the recent reports of paleolithic human presence on the island (Arca et al. 1982; Sondaar and Sanges 1984) but also to understand the environment and landscape, the mineral and metal resources, and the rock that constituted material first for overhangs and caves, and then for rock-cut tombs, built architecture and sculpture.

It is primarily the resource of obsidian that attracted the earliest documentable settlers and traders to the island (see chap. 14) and provided the industry for stable settlements, growth and continuity. The metal resources, principally lead, silver, and copper (and perhaps even tin) were also responsible for attracting other populations as traders and settlers (see chaps. 16-18), as well as furnishing material for the flourishing bronze industry that produced tools, weapons, jewelry, and the figurines that have become so important to the appreciation of the Nuragic culture. To this industry can be attributed the growing prosperity at the end of the Bronze Age that kept Sardinia prominent in the Mediterranean and altered the island society (see chap. 4).

Twenty years ago, 3000 B.C. was considered to be the date of the earliest known settlers in Sardinia. The very different picture today is largely a result of the work of David Trump and of Enrico Atzeni. Now five Neolithic cultures can be referred to in the 3000 years preceding that date (see table 16.1), and far earlier habitation is suggested as well. It is by combining clues from the landscape with excavated material that Trump has been able to read seven millennia of habitation in a cluster of sites in the Bonu Ighinu basin of the locality of Mara; he uses that area as a microcosm to project development elsewhere.

Further discussion of the periods from the Neolithic to that of the nuraghi (see table 16.1) is offered by James Lewthwaite, who warns against overemphasis on architectural details at the expense of such considerations as settlement patterns and their significance. He analyzes problems of chronology and space; his theoretical approaches and the use of models from elsewhere provide some ideas for speculation on aspects of land-use and their social implications. The approach to the material in these two articles is that of prehistorians or anthropologists and differs from that of other scholars who might choose to emphasize artifacts rather than ecofacts. In the absence of datable criteria, this treatment of pre-Nuragic Sardinia is necessary for, in Trump's words, "any answers we can squeeze from the archaeological material."

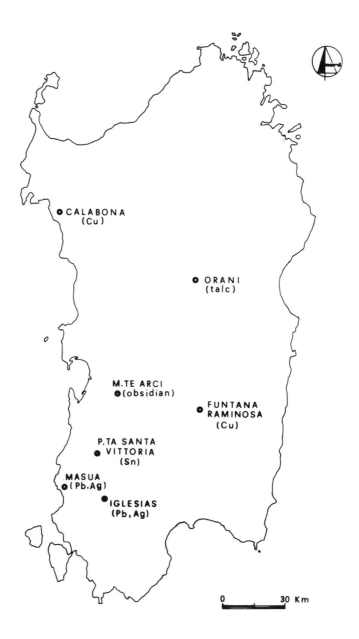

CALABONA
(Cu)

ORANI
(talc)

M.TE ARCI
(obsidian)

FUNTANA
RAMINOSA
(Cu)

P.TA SANTA
VITTORIA
(Sn)

MASUA
(Pb,Ag)

IGLESIAS
(Pb,Ag)

0   30 Km

Figure 1.1   Map of Sardinia showing sites of mineral and metal
resources mentioned in text of chapter 1

1. THE GEOLOGY, ENVIRONMENT, AND NATURAL RESOURCES OF SARDINIA

Raniero Massoli-Novelli

General Remarks

Sardinia and Corsica together form what is commonly known as the 'Sardo-Corsican Massif,' a very ancient geological unit, the formation of which began over 500 million years ago. The structure of this massif, from the southern part of the Sulcis in Sardinia to the mountains of Asco in Corsica, consists of a granite foundation that surfaces predominantly in the regions of Sarrabus, Nuoro and the Gallura, and in the major part of Corsica. The granites provide typical morphologies and landscapes both inland and on the coastlines; the beauty of much of the coastline of eastern Sardinia, with its huge rounded rocks and crystal clear seawater, is in fact due to the predominance of a hard and compact granite (fig. 1.1).

After the end of the Hercynian magmatic and tectonic events ca. 250 million years ago, a long period of quiescence began in Sardinia, with movements of slow subsidence and deposition of limestones in the Mesozoic sea. During the Miocene period, about 20-25 million years ago, the Sardinia-Corsica microplate began its counter-clockwise rotation, from the French-Spanish continental margin to the actual position it has now, with many analogies (geophysical, geological and paleontological) between the two regions (Cocozza 1975). Intense volcanic activity, with lavas and tuffs, is visible today along the western coast of Sardinia. The intense Alpine tectonic cycle affected Sardinia only with movements of essentially epeirogenetic character (movements of blocks up and down). These movements continued up to recent times and are still perceptible today.

Recent Geology

About the animal population of Sardinia, which has vertebrates both of European and African origin, there are various geological interpretations: the problem is open and we need more research. A land connection must have been present during the Upper Miocene/Lower Pliocene (ca. 5 million years ago), in coincidence with the so-called 'salinity crisis' of the Mediterranean, when a closure of geological origin in Gibraltar (the only important water input in this sea) might have lowered the actual level some hundreds of meters, probably accompanied by a eustatic change of sea level. As a result two landbridges might have formed: one is the 'Corse-Elba-Tuscany' bridge, which permitted the arrival of European species of animals to the island; another one may have been in a southern direction, connecting with North Africa, but the position and the size of this bridge is still debated. Sturani (1976) calculated that a level drop of about 500m of the Mediterranean, after the already-mentioned closure of the Gibraltar input, might possibly happen in only 400 or 500 years. In this way, considering that the maximum depth today between Sardinia and Libya is just a few hundred meters, a large bridge might have allowed the entry of animals of African species.

3

Other groups of vertebrates might have reached Sardinia during a regression during the Pleistocene, about 700,000 years ago (Kotsakis 1980). Sondaar (1977) suggested that many animals in Mediterranean islands in recent geological times like deer and elephants, with the capacity to swim, might have had the ability to cross a small sea barrier. Since there is no paleontological evidence to date, we must suppose that man introduced to Sardinia the moufflon, the fallow-deer, the wild boar, the horse, the donkey, the ox, and perhaps the deer, the fox and the wild cat. The arrival of the Sardinian red deer (Cervus elephus corsicanus) on the island may have been natural, i.e., via a landbridge, or artificial, i.e., introduced by man. Whether any of this occured before the Nuragic Age is still to be discussed. In any case, the first representation of animals in Sardinian bronze figurines is of deer, moufflon, wild-boar and fox.

The Climate
Sardinia is characterized by a hot-temperature climate; the scant rainfall (about 600mm throughout the year) and the regime of rains, concentrated in a short period time, along with the modest altitude, create conditions for strong erosion and are the bases of the tremendous problem of summer fires.

Sardinia is in the center of an area of almost steady low pressure and is therefore blasted by the winds, especially the 'maestrale,' a strong, dry wind blowing from the NW, that in winter can reach 120 km/h. The blowing of the wind contributes to the creation of particular landscapes, with deformation and bent trees, eroded rocks, the piling of dunes along the western coast, and the recent, tragic forest fires.

Flora
During the course of the last century the woodlands of Sardinia were, for the most part, completely deforested; the timber, which, from the descriptions of eighteenth and nineteenth century travellers, still covered all the island, was used to make charcoal and to build railways. At the same time forest fires and unchecked, widespread grazing of sheep contributed to the process of stripping the land bare. Hence Sardinia no longer has the lush forest that still characterizes Corsica; the few forests left intact, however, can give us an idea of what Sardinia once was, of that beautiful green cloak that covered the island over a century ago. The most beautiful forests left to us consist mostly of giant holm-oaks: and they are, from north to south: Monte Limbara (Tempio), Supramonte (the Funtana Bona Forest Rangers' outpost), Seui (the Monte Arbu Forest Rangers' outpost), Gennargentu (the Desulo Forest Rangers' outpost). Also remarkable are the large yew trees and hollies of the Marghine region at Bolotana, the forest of chestnut groves at Aritzo and Tonara, and the woods of 'macchia mediterranea' located to the west and to the east of Cagliari.

Fauna
Insularity favored the conservation and/or evolution of particular species of fauna which do not exist anywhere else. Beginning with the large mammals we can list: the Sardinian red deer, which inhabit the woods near Cagliari and are very difficult to observe for fear of poachers; the Sardinian fallow-deer, which are now extinct, because of the ferocious hunting by poachers that exterminated the last ones about twenty years ago; the European moufflon, a magnificent wild mountain sheep, which still inhabit the Gennargentu and Supramonte mountains; and the Sardinian boar, still widespread because of their natural strength and fertility. It is not difficult to observe small Sardinian wild horses on the basalt 'plateau' of the Giara di Gesturi.

Among the many colorful species of birds populating Sardinia we can name the great birds of prey, the griffon-vulture and the Sardinian royal eagle; their number is fast decreasing because of outside disturbances. In the coastal lagoons of Cagliari and Oristano can be found a large variety of migrating and nesting waterfowl: rare pink flamingoes, the purple gallinule, and thousands of ducks and coots.

Because of the absence of parks and the scarcity of natural conservation areas, Sardinian wildlife, and generally all the environment, suffer greatly from the negative effects of modern man and 'progress.'

From an archaeological-geological point of view, we can divide the mineral resources of Sardinia into 'non-metallic' and 'metallic' (fig. 1.1).

Non-metallic resources
Sardinia ranks among the Mediterranean regions of most ancient renown, thanks to its great variety of minerals and rocks useful to man. It is sufficient to specify obsidian from Monte Arci (Oristano), talc-steatite from Orani (Nuoro), and jasper from various localities, as well as sandstones, clay, granites, limestones and basalt, to demonstrate the importance of these substances in the cultures of past times. These constitute a link between archaeology and geology in Sardinia that justifies more extensive investigation and research.

Metallic resources
The mineralizing of Sardinia offers one of the finest examples of the variety of phenomena and the richness of ore deposits in the Mediterranean area. From the Neolithic Age on, man was attracted by the great outcrops of galena (PbS), silver, copper and other metals, in addition to other minerals of 'non-metallic type. Most of these de-

posits are in the Palaeozoic foundation. Three main metallogenic epochs are recognizable in this foundation:

(A) Pb-Zn-Ba strata bound ore bodies in Cambrian limestones, in the southeastern area of the island (mines at Masua and Monteponi).

(B) Fe-Cu-F-Pb-Zn ore bodies in the thick Ordovician-Silurian series in the central part of Sardinia (mine at Funtana Raminosa).

(C) Several groups of metal (Pb-Zn, Cu-Mo, Sn-As, etc.) in the veins and dikes associated with granites, in every part of the island (for example, the S. Vittoria vein in Fluminimaggiore (Iglesias) - a Sn deposit). It is interesting to observe that until the 18th century there was no interest in zinc, which is commonly present in about 500 small deposits as well as in deposits mixed with lead (galena).

Conversely, man in the Bronze Age was very much interested in copper; recently Lo Schiavo and Vagnetti (1980) found more findspots of ingots of 'oxhide' type in Sardinia (see below, part VI) than anywhere else in the Mediterranean. The distribution of at least 12 find-spots on the island suggests internal mining areas more persuasively than coastal depots for importation (Tylecote, Balmuth and Massoli-Novelli 1984).

From a geological point of view the two most important deposits for copper in Sardinia are: 1) the mine at Funtana Raminosa (Gadoni, Central Sardinia) and 2) the mine at Calabona (Alghero, NW Sardinia).

1) Mine at Funtana Raminosa: Funtana Raminosa may be the site of the earliest exploitation of copper on Sardinia; ore is linked to a 'skarn' rock with silicified limestones. Recent studies have pointed out the importance of volcanism in the Silurian sedimentary sequence and

the possible connection between the volcanism and the ore deposits. The ore actually exploited yields 1% Cu, 1.5% Pb, 3.5% Zn.

2) <u>Mine at Calabona</u>: The ore is disseminated in a porphyritic intrusion in Mesozoic limestones. The Calabona deposit is mainly known for the high-grade but scanty copper ore bodies at the contact with sedimentary rocks. The production of 9,000 tonnes of high-grade ore (average 9% Cu) between 1911 and 1921 has been reported. A recent study (Tylecote, Balmuth and Massoli-Novelli 1984) of the smelting of copper ore from Calabona, with a full analysis, shows that the refined metal from Calabona cannot be distinguished from any other copper available in the Mediterranean area during the Bronze Age by present techniques.

'Oxhide' and plano-convex ingots (see Lo Schiavo, chap. 16), usually of copper, may not be as widely known as the bronze figurines (<u>bronzetti</u>). Analyses show that the figurines are tin-bronzes with relatively little lead (Balmuth and Stodulski 1975-77). Tin is also present in some plano-convex copper ingots (Birocchi 1934). Tin is generally extracted from cassiterite (SnO_2), which is a typical mineral of high temperature genesis in the granitic complex with the more famous examples in Cornwall; but it

also occurs in Sardinia, where its use in antiquity is still uncertain.

Recent geochemical studies show that the Monte Linas area (Iglesiente) is the most important in Italy for Sn-Mo-W mineral deposits. The most important deposit for cassiterite in Sardinia is a vein-system at Punta Santa Vittoria, in the southwestern part of the Monte Linas granitic complex, between Fluminimaggiore and Gonnosfanadiga, on the watershed at an altitude of 700m. The principal vein is directed northeast-southwest and shows an interesting paragenesis: the SW part of the vein has mainly arsenopyrite, the NE part mainly cassiterite in a quartz gangue, a transition that symbolically recapitulates the apparent development of bronze-making in the Mediterranean area, from a copper-arsenic alloy to a true tin bronze. It is not clear whether or not there were earlier attempts at exploitation, but it is possible that cassiterite from this area was used in Nuragic times.

The brevity of this account is an indication of how much more we need interdisciplinary studies in the future, as well as more sophisticated methods of analysis. One of these must be on lead isotopes, a study that is just now beginning in Sardinia (Swainbank et al. 1982).

REFERENCES

ARCA, M., F. MARTINI, G. PITZALIS, C. TUVERI, AND A. ULVEGA
    1982   Il Paleolitico dell' Anglona: Ricerche 1979-80.
                Quaderni 12.

BALMUTH, M.S. AND L. STODULSKI
    1975-77   Sardinian Bronzetti in American Museums. StSar 24:
                145-156; pl. 1-9.

BALMUTH, M.S. AND R.F. TYLECOTE
    1976   Ancient Copper and Bronze in Sardinia: Excavation and
                Analysis. JFA 3:195-201.

BIROCCHI, E.
    1934   I ripostigli nuragici e le panelle di rame grezzo.
                StSar 1:37-108.

COCOZZA, T.
    1975   Structural pattern of Sardinia. Quaderni di Ricerca
                Scientifica, Consiglio Nazionale delle Ricerche. Roma.

KOTSAKIS, T.
    1980   Osservazioni sui vertebrati quaternari della Sardegna.
                Bollettino della Società Geologica Italiana 99:151-165.

LO SCHIAVO, F. AND L. VAGNETTI
    1980   Micenei in Sardegna? RendLinc 35.

MASSOLI-NOVELLI, R.
    1972   Contributo allo studio genetico del talco di Orani
                (Nuoro). Rendiconti della Associazione Mineraria Sarda
                74:1-31.

SONDAAR, P.Y.
    1977   Insularity and its effect on mammal evolution. Major
                Patterns in Vertebrate Evolution. Plenum Publishing
                Corporation, NY.

SONDAAR, P.Y. AND M. SANGES
    1984   First Report of a Paleolithic Culture in Sardinia.
                Early Settlement 29-46.

STURANI, G.
    1976   Messinian facies in the Piedmont basin. Memorie della
                Società Geologica Italiana 16:11-28.

SWAINBANK, I.GG., T.J. SHEPHERD, R. CABOI, AND R. MASSOLI-NOVELLI
    1982   Lead isotopic composition of some galena ores from
                Sardinia. Periodico di Mineralogia 51:275-286. Roma.

TYLECOTE, R.F., M.S. BALMUTH AND R. MASSOLI-NOVELLI
    1984   Copper and Bronze Metallurgy in Sardinia. SSA.

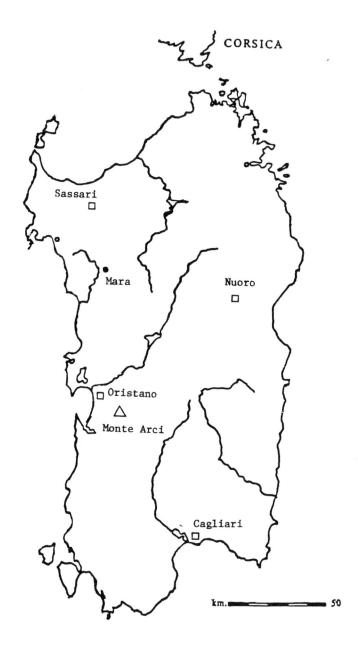

Figure 2.1 Map of Sardinia showing provincial capitals,
Monte Arci and the Mara locality

2. BEYOND STRATIGRAPHY - THE BONU IGHINU PROJECT

David Trump

There is no need to go over the ground covered at the first Sardinian colloquium at a meeting of the Archaeological Institute of America in Boston in January of 1979, nor that published in Loria and Trump (1978), and Trump (1983), but nevertheless some introduction before striking out 'beyond the stratigraphy' will be necessary.

The Bonu Ighinu valley in northwestern Sardinia (fig. 2.1) attracted no archaeological attention until Don Renato Loria explored the cave of Su Tintirriolu in 1969. It was the stalagmitic formations deep within it which appealed to him as, it turned out, they seem to have done to prehistoric man. But it was in the outer passage and hall that he noticed sherds of pottery and some human bones. The entrance passage is only 65cm high while further in, the height of the ceiling can be as much as 12m. His preliminary discoveries were followed by a proper investigation in 1971, a collaboration between Don Loria, the writer, and the Sop-

rintendenza alle Antichità per le Provincie di Sassari e Nuoro. The question being asked was simply: 'what is there to be found here'?

The answer, briefly, was a 50cm thick deposit of almost pure charcoal ash, with an extraordinary quantity of broken pottery, finely flaked points of flint and obsidian, terracotta figurines and shaped stones, the last apparently once used as stelai to flank the entrance. But it is many years since an archaeologist would be content with an answer like that. The next question was: 'to what period does this material belong'?

The deposits in trench C gave an invaluable stratigraphy (fig. 2.2). Leaving aside a scatter of Roman material, sherds of Monte Claro pottery overlay the Ozieri level, much the richest, and below that a pure deposit, though thin, enabled us for the first time to recognize Bonu Ighinu as a distinct and earlier material. Radiocarbon dates from the

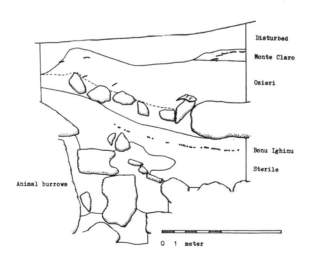

Figure 2.2 Sa Ucca de Su Tintirriolu, trench C

Rome laboratory added greatly to the value of the information. The Bonu Ighinu level gave a date of 3730+160 bc, and the Ozieri level three dates, 3140, 2980 and 2900, all ± 50 bc Full references are quoted in Lorìa and Trump (1978). The new phase of Bonu Ighinu and the new date for the Ozieri complex, at that time conventionally placed a millennium later, necessitated a profound re-appraisal of the Sardinian Neolithic.

Less spectacular in its immediate results was the third necessary question: 'what does this site mean'? The pure ash of the deposits, the richness of the contents, the figurines, and above all the difficulty of access, seemed to point inescapably to a ritual use. The human bones present, if in small quantity, did not contradict this. Certainly no one could or would have wished to live in such incommodious quarters. The search for their home led us to the next, and equally exciting, phase of the research.

In 1979 and 1980 we dug in the Grotta Filiestru, 350m downstream from Su Tintirriolu (fig. 2.3). The steep and rocky nature of the coun-tryside is clearly apparent. This cave had a spacious, light and airy entrance, and a perennial spring just outside the door. It had to be the settlement. Indeed, the trenches descended through 3m of well-strati-fied deposit (fig. 2.4), showing con-tinuous occupation through six cul-tural levels from Early Neolithic with Cardial Ware to Sa Turricula, an Early or proto-Nuragic phase, tran-sitional between the Middle and Late Bronze Age.

What was there? 3m of deposit containing, in one 3 x 4m trench, over 8000 sherds of pottery, 4000 pieces of flaked stone, 2000 iden-tifiable animal bones. When was it put there? Over 3000 years or more, from 4760+75 bc to 1510+40 bc (according to Cambridge radiocarbon dates, supported by obsidian hydra-tion dates from the Pennsylvania State University). And how did it get there? As domestic rubbish, obviously. The quality of the ma-terial was far below that of Su Tintirriolu, and must imply habita-tion. For example, in the periods when a direct comparison is possible, 97% of Bonu Ighinu phase pottery from Su Tintirriolu was decorated, yet

Figure 2.3   Monte Traessu and the Filiestru valley from the southwest. Grotta Filiestru in trees at center left, Su Tintirriolu mid-right.

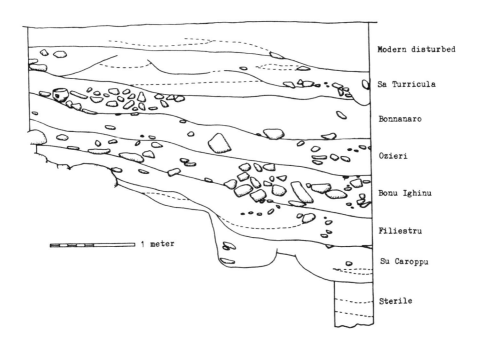

Figure 2.4 Grotta Filiestru, the section in trench D

only 7% at Filiestru. In the succeeding Ozieri phases, the figures
were 15.8 and 0.8%. And yet there is
no doubt that they were the same
people. Two very distinctive Bonu
Ighinu vessels with handle knobs
turned into little faces, one from
each cave, must surely have been made
by the same hand.

But it gradually became clear
that there were differences in this
accumulation. We had habitation, but
in two distinct varieties. The low-
est levels contained carbonized
grain, both emmer and einkorn,
querns, many awls and coloring
matter. A jar was found to contain
2kg of pure red ochre, and two others
a dried black paste. All these
suggest a complete community, including womenfolk. However, the rate
of accumulation, as shown by the

carbon-14 dates, decreased sharply
around 4000 bc. It was at this point
that the decline in quality, though
not in quantity, of potsherds became
noticeable. Awls and querns almost
disappeared, and Dr. Marsha Levine,
who studied the animal bones, noted a
sharp decrease in 'prime joints'
compared with other parts of the
skeleton. These certainly, and the
replacing of sheep by goat possibly,
suggest that the community had moved
elsewhere, leaving Filiestru to
temporary occupation by shepherds
only. In any case, it was obviously
too small a site, with space for only
two to three families, for its surplus production to have equipped Su
Tintirriolu so lavishly. Somewhere
there had to be a larger open village
settlement. We had to stand back
from the sites, and find a more
distant viewpoint from which to
survey the whole area.

What we found was a territory, with clearly defined limits, marked by craggy hills, a steep gorge and other natural features. The area is best called after the attractive 17th century rustic chapel of Bonu Ighinu at its center, now rarely used except for special occasions like marriages or a first communion service, and its annual _festa_. Immediately behind it rises Monte Noe, which gives an uninterrupted panorama of the whole basin (fig. 2.5).

Starting at the northeast, there are the precipitous cliffs of Monte Traessu, rising to an altitude of 717m, with the valley containing the caves in a fold in its flank (fig. 2.6). Moving to the right, Tuva e Mara is a limestone dolina behind those cliffs, with caves, sherds, but no intact deposits. To the right again, the missing village was found as a scatter of worked flint and obsidian and abraded sherds across a terrace flanking Monte Noe. Very sadly, erosion had left no deposit over bedrock. In the distance, the open country leads east into the Torralba plain, the only side on which the territory's limits are not clearly marked. But to the south, a deep gorge cuts off the hills in the middle distance, with the modern villages of Pozzomaggiore, Mara, and Padria hidden behind them. In clear conditions, Monte Ferru can be made out 35km off. In the foreground lies the rich agricultural basin of Bonu Ighinu, well-watered and dotted with sites, with three _nuraghi_ in view and as many again tucked out of sight in side valleys.

The southwestern view, however, is the finest, dominated by the 510m high peak with the 13th century Castello dei Bonvei on its summit. Prehistoric rock-cut tombs were chipped from its western saddle. The Riu de Badeda, which drains the valley, cuts through at its foot at 221m above sea level to join the Fiume Temo in the blue valley beyond. Two _nuraghi_ on inaccessible peaks, and a third on the shoulder between guard the western approach. To the northwest, the boundary hills rise steadily, and we begin to pass from cultivable fields back to rocky scrub, where the most prominent feature today is a kaolin quarry above the mouth of the Filiestru valley, the point where we started. The area enclosed by these boundaries measures 4km by 2.5km in round figures.

Figure 2.5 The heart of the Bonu Ighinu basin from the south. Monte Noe, the village site, Monte Traessu and Tuva e Mare above, _Nuraghi_ Sant'Andria, Salaserru and Salighentosa below.

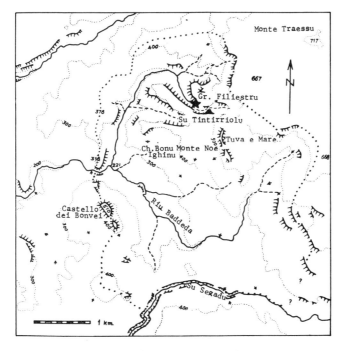

Figure 2.6   The Bonu Ighinu Basin in the Early Neolithic

There is time here to pick out only a few of the other sites within this area. Above the gorge to the south is a prominent rock-shelter, still occupied by stock, as prehistoric sherds suggest has been the case for a very long time. The river leaves the valley by a picturesque defile to the southwest, dominated by a nuraghe on the near-inaccessible Monte Peidru above. The nuraghi of the valley, though usually easily recognizable, are none of them the fine upstanding monuments that appear in book illustrations and on picture postcards. There is the Nuraghe Sant'Andria from close to, and from across the valley, on its spur below Monte Noe (fig. 2.7). There is another on the next ridge to the right, Salaserru. The earlier village overlooks both, and a big Roman site occupied the valley between. This gives some idea of the density of sites in this favored part of the basin. Finally, from a group

of a dozen or so rock-cut tombs (domus de janas) on the shoulder below the Castello, one is well-preserved, with ochre still on its walls. All are now devoid of archaeological content.

We are approaching the point, though I should be the first to agree that there is a lot to be done yet, where we could try to trace the changing pattern of settlement throughout past time within this single, clearly defined territory. In the first period, Filiestru was the village and Su Tintirriolu the ritual site (fig. 2.5). There is no sign yet of activity in the open country between the Traessu cliffs, Su Segadu gorge and Castello peak to the south. In period II covering a much longer time span, the village moves to Monte Noe, with minor activity at Filiestru and other caves, Su Tintirriolu at peak importance during Ozieri times but visited only

Figure 2.7 <u>Nuraghe</u> Sant'Andria from the northwest

sporadically thereafter (fig. 2.8).
The villages marked outside the
valley belonged to the next territory
to the west, and were successive, not
contemporary with one another.

Period III is in many ways the
most interesting. Instead of a
single village, there is now a
scatter of more or less equal sites,
the <u>nuraghi</u> (fig. 2.9). Of these
there are six within the territory -
only 10 square kilometers - and
another four on its borders. I have
added three to the west for the
additional information they give.
One, the <u>Nuraghe</u> Noeddos, investi-
gated in 1982, was founded and
abandoned early, hinting that not all
are necessarily contemporary. This
suggestion is reinforced by the two
at Pirasta, barely 100m apart. It is
difficult to see how these could have
been occupied by separate and probably hostile communities at the same
moment in time. At the center of the
Bonu Ighinu basin, Sant'Andria and
Salaserru are uncomfortably close
too.

Restricted length of occupation
may be part of the answer to the
quite extraordinary number of <u>nuraghi</u>
within the valley, and indeed
throughout the island. Difference of
function may be another. Where many,
like Sant'Andria, are admirably
placed to exploit the farming potential of their immediate neighbor-
hoods, and others, like Cuguruntis,
could have been supported by the
scanty productive land adjacent, two
here at least, Monte Peidru and Pedra
e Multa, both on crags of, to say the
least, difficult access, make far
more sense as strongholds or guard
towers than as farming establish-
ments, whether for agriculture or
stock-raising. But how they could
serve such a function within the
social organization of the Bonu
Ighinu valley at the time, as yet we
can hardly guess.

Equally importantly, we can only
speculate at this stage how the
social and economic change from
nucleated village to dispersed and
fortified farmstead - if that is what

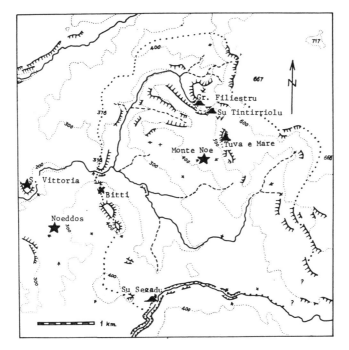

Figure 2.8 The Bonu Ighinu basin in the Late
Neolithic to Middle Bronze Age

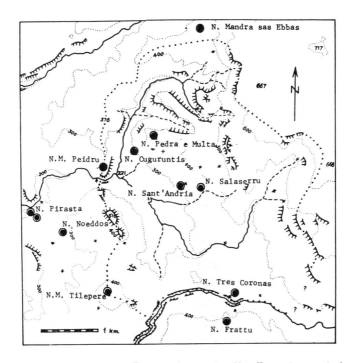

Figure 2.9 The Bonu Ighinu basin in the Nuragic period

the nuraghe really represents as seems probable - came about. Many problems undoubtedly remain to be answered.

Occupation in the Roman period was general, at least over the agricultural zone as one might expect. There is no sign of nucleated settlement within the valley at this period, and it was probably dependent on a small market town at Padria, 4km in direct line to the south. There is, as yet, no evidence of activity in the preceding Punic period, though detailed work on Nuragic survival or Roman farm antecedents could yet produce it. Complete abandonment seems unlikely. In medieval times, we find only the castle and chapel, with a village at Santa Vittoria way downstream. Today, there is a wide scatter of farms, naturally in the southern basin, and none of them permanently occupied. Their owners all come out daily from Mara, a pattern of exploitation which probably goes well back into the medieval period, but contrasts with all earlier ones.

I would end with several general points. There is always danger in interpreting past activity in terms of the modern landscape uncritically, and I am well aware of this. For example, tumbled walls show that cultivation was far more extensive in the quite recent past than it is today, when thistles appear to be the principle, or even only, crop. More drastically, a number of areas in the basin - the Monte Noe village site is a good example and the Piano Giuale, overlooking the Grotta Filiestru another - are now virtually bare rock but could once have been, almost certainly were, fertile fields. Around the Nuraghe S'Emis, 2km to the northwest, a fine group of corbelled field huts is associated with a large number of remarkable tidily constructed stone clearance cairns, again over practically bare rock. Runoff is carried down to the Temo by

side streams, with upwards of 3m of hillwash showing in their banks. Evidence from the Italian peninsula would place this phase of serious soil erosion in the post-Roman period. The S'Emis field huts, like the Piano Giuale threshing floors, must be more recent than that, if not exactly 'modern'; the huts, in part, are still used by shepherds, at least on occasion.

What has changed much less, however, is the general topography. The steep slopes with frequent outcrops of volcanic rock in the northern part of the Bonu Ighinu territory can never have supported cultivation like that of the southern and larger basin. The numerous small springs today, themselves often the result of the complex intercalation of volcanic and calcareous rocks in the area, are likely to have been more, rather than less, frequent and strongly flowing in the past.

Above all, the 4 by 2.5km territory is defined by natural features of some permanence, at least on a human time scale. Its present boundaries were there before the first farming settlers moved in. It is worth noting, incidentally, that this 10 square kilometer territory is substantially smaller than the area usually assumed in theoretical discussions of site catchment, territorial exploitation, etc.

Indeed, though this is a remote and unimportant corner of the island of Sardinia, its archaeology is neither of those, and may have lessons of much wider application. Quite apart from what it has already told us of the culture sequence and chronology of Sardinia, it offers a neatly defined sample of a single community and its activities over some seven millennia, and that community was not an eccentric and isolated one. The quantity of obsidian from the Grotta Filiestru, all imported from Monte Arci, 75km to the south, shows that its occupants were fully in touch with the outside world from the start. And some time early in the Nuragic period, one sherd found its way to the Grotta Su Guanu, just outside Mara village, from much farther off, the Aegean of the Mycenaeans.

We have dug through the stratigraphy into much richer deposits of information and understanding. Any answers we can squeeze from the archaeological material in the Bonu Ighinu valley will be of value over a far wider area than its modest 10 square kilometers.

REFERENCES

LORIA, R. AND D. TRUMP
    1978   Le scoperte a Sa 'Ucca de Su Tintirriolu e il neolitico sardo. MonAnt II-2.

TRUMP, D.
    1983   La Grotta di Filiestru, Mara, Sassari. Quaderni 13.

    1984   The Bonu Ighinu Project and the Sardinian Neolithic. SSA: 1-22.

1. <u>Nuraghe</u> Albùcciu (Arzachena)
2. <u>Nuraghe</u> Majori (Tempio)
3. <u>Nuraghe</u> Agnu (Calangiánus)
4. Monte Ossoni (Castelsardo)
5. Monte D'Accòddi (Sassari)
6. Monte Ruina = Cabula Muntones (Sassari)
7. Monte Baranta (Olmedo)
8. <u>Nuraghe</u> Peppe Gallu (Uri)
9. Rock-cut tombs of Sa Figu (Ittiri)
10. <u>Grotte</u> Sa'Ucca de Su Tintirriòlu e Filiestru, Bonu Ighinu (Mara)
11. San Giuseppe, Pàdria
12. <u>Nuraghe Túsarí</u> (Bortígari)
13. <u>Nuraghe</u> S'Ulivera (Dualchi)
14. <u>Tomba di Giganti</u> Soronna (Paulilátino)
15. <u>Nuraghe</u> Brunku Màdugui (Gésturi)
16. <u>Nuraghe</u> Su Nuraxi (Barùmini)
17. Nuragic village Santa Vittoria (Serri)
18. <u>Nuraghe Capanna</u> Sa Korona (Villagreca)
19. Biriai (Oliena)
20. Nuragic village Serra Orrios (Dorgali)

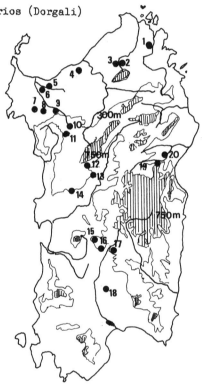

Figure 3.1 Map of Sardinia showing principal sites mentioned in text of
chapter 3

3. NURAGIC FOUNDATIONS: AN ALTERNATE MODEL OF DEVELOPMENT IN SARDINIAN PREHISTORY CA. 2500-1500 B.C.

James Lewthwaite

Introduction

The late David Clarke (1976: 449), in the preamble to a celebrated essay on the economic base of Mesolithic Europe, warned against the uncritical repetition of traditional interpretations based on partial data, vulnerable to bias and sample errors, particularly when compounded by persistent stereotypes. Clarke's exhortation to compare the interpretative models that arise as a consequence of the analysis of the data, with models of expectation derived from other sources and which take account of the sampling problems of the data under analysis' is, I believe, highly pertinent to our conventional model of the prehistory of Sardinia, based as it is on the polarization between static images of, on the one hand, the Ozieri culture and on the other, the Nuragic (Lilliu 1975). The Ozieri stereotype used to be that of a homogeneous population of peaceful, egalitarian village farmers of ultimately East Mediterranean origin whose religious ideology found its expression in collective burial in domus de janas and in stylized female figurines and standing stones (Lilliu 1975:41-77; 105-57). The attributes assigned to the Nuragic culture formed a complete contrast: warring, hierarchical clans with a pastoral and patriarchal orientation, whose social differentiation and militarism were mirrored in the familiar bronzetti and in the dominance by the Nuragic bastion of the surrounding capanne (Lilliu 1975:208-356).

Unfortunately, this static stereotype-pair corresponds only too well to the extant data sample. The numerous Ozieri villages of the Campidano can be dated by from materials in the stratified sequences of the Grotta del Guano (Oliena), Sa 'Ucca de Su Tintirriòlu (Mara) and the Grotta Filiestru (Mara) to between ca. 3300 and ca. 2800 B.C. despite the lower dating envisaged in earlier typologically based schemes (Castaldi 1972; 1980; Lorìa and Trump 1978:210; Trump 1982; 1983; 1984). The earliest dates for classic nuraghi such as Su Nuraxi (Barùmini) and Pizzinnu (Posada) fall into the middle of the second millennium B.C., a terminus post quem supported by the early Nuragic level in the Grotta Filiestru, recently dated to 1490 + 40 B.C. (Q-2031) (Trump 1983; 1984). The intervening 1300 radiocarbon years are occupied by a motley host of 'cultures': Filigosa, Abealzu, Monte Claro, Beaker, Bonnaro (Contu 1980: 15-20). David Trump (see above, chap. 2) has suggested that the term pre-Nuragic, on the analogy of the pre-Talaiotic in Balearic prehistory, be applied to the intermediate period on the grounds that the classic paradigm of named cultures may be counterproductive. There is a striking disparity between the relative duration of the Ozieri and pre-Nuragic periods and the models assigned to each: while the former is regarded as a relatively stable and enduring tradition, the cultures of the Copper and Early Bronze Ages are modelled as a rapid, overlapping succession of

19

historical-scale events bridging the gulf between the established poles (Lilliu 1975:78-105; 158-207).

The Effects of Bias and Sample Error on the Cultural and Economic Developments of the Intermediate Period (2800-1500 B.C.)

The weakness of the current methodology is evident in the confusion which pervades the cultural sequence (Contu 1980:16, n. 4) which is no more than a seriation of decorative ceramic styles, the only independent control being provided by Beakers and Beaker-derived or associated artifacts, which can be compared with neighboring areas where finer chronological resolution has been achieved. The general consensus favors the following order: Ozieri - Abealzu/Filigosa - Monte Claro - Beaker - Bonnanaro, terminating in the facies of Sa Turricula (Muros) which is indistinguishable in date from the earliest nuraghi, although associated with a Beaker-derived vessel (R-963a, 1510 + 50 B.C.) (Ferrarese Ceruti 1978:69-70). This ordering runs into temporal and spatial anomalies which are a product of the deficiencies in the data-base. First, although the Monte Claro culture is regularly encountered in stratigraphies below the Beakers present (Contu 1980:15-17), a number of sites have, it is claimed, yielded admittedly 'atypical' Monte Claro assemblages dated to the early second millennium B.C. - the cave of S'Acqua Calda (Nuxis), the proto-nuraghe of Brunku Màdugui (Gésturi) and the village of Noeddos (Mara) (Contu 1980:20, Trump 1984). Second, the findspots of Abealzu-Filigosa, Beaker and Bonnanaro cultures are concentrated in the north and peripheral areas of the south (Sulcis, environs of Cagliari, etc.) leaving the greater part of the Campidano, Marmilla and Trexenta blank (fig. 3.2). In the open sites of the latter region, the Ozieri culture is succeeded either directly by Monte Claro or through the medium of an atypical Abealzu-like plain Ozieri phase (Atzeni 1966:123; 1967: 175; 1980:33) and the Monte Claro in turn by the Nuragic culture (Atzeni 1967:177). Indeed, the proximity of open villages of the Monte Claro culture to nuraghi was formerly held to imply that this was in fact a Nuragic facies belonging to the end of the second millennium B.C. (Lilliu and Ferrarese Ceruti 1958-9; Lilliu 1975:182-201).

Santoni has attempted to solve at least part of this puzzle, suggesting that the Abealzu-Filigosa culture was confined to the north and that the Monte Claro culture first developed in the south (Santoni 1976: 5; 33). Although the existence of actual villages of the Abealzu-Filigosa culture at San Giuseppe (Pàdria) and Monte Cabula Muntones/Monte Ruina (Sassari) (Santoni 1976:35; Basoli 1984) lends some credibility to this suggestion, a more generally useful explanation has been provided by Contu in the specific case of the Bonnanaro-Early Nuragic overlap of the mid-second millennium B.C. Contu has suggested that Bonnanaro materials must have continued in use in the ritual context of the earliest giants' tombs (e.g. Goronna, Paulilatino) and in the domus de janas with similar facades (such as the group of Sa Figu, Ittiri) long after Bonnanaro ware had ceased to be used in domestic contexts (Contu 1980: 20-21).

In effect then, this allows much of the regional discrepancy to be reduced to no more than a persistent contextual differentiation between sepulchral and habitational sites which Trump has found occurring within a radius of no more than 3.5km in the Bonu Ighinu Valley (Trump, see chap. 2); thus within any given pairing or further qualifying (Abealzu-Filigosa: plain Ozieri, Beaker-Bonnanaro: plain Monte Claro or Early

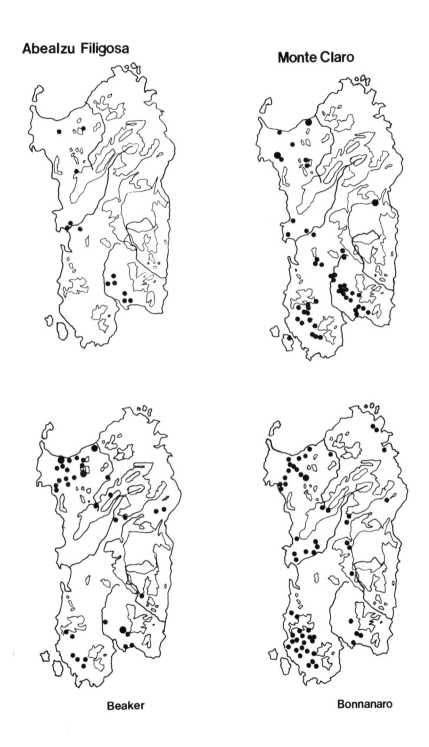

Abealzu Filigosa

Monte Claro

Beaker

Bonnanaro

Figure 3.2 Distribution of Intermediate Period Sites

Nuragic), the more distinctive element occurs in the tomb or ritual cave rather than the village or cave used only by the odd shepherd. The lack of attention to intra-cultural variation has had the further effect that innovations in the form of great functional significance have been regarded as no more than stylistic developments. In particular, the ceramic innovations of the later pre-Nuragic which can be interpreted as devices with specific functions such as the storage or processing of dairy products (the bollitoi, calefattoi, scrematoi) and the preparation of griddle cakes (tegami, spiane) which in Sardinian ethnographic contexts have been manufactured from acorn mush and clay as well as more orthodox ingredients (Ferrarese Ceruti 1962:188-96 esp. 188 n. 55; Contu 1959:140-142, 1964-5:224-6 esp. 225 n. 74; Lilliu 1975:197; Camps and Rostan 1980:4-5, 1982:247; Lewthwaite 1982:225) persist into the first millennium B.C., forming a high proportion of Nuragic assemblages. The introduction of the platter (tegame) has been recently dated in the course of the continuing excavation of the

Noeddos site (Mara) to the interface of the Noeddos I/Noeddos II facies, estimated to lie at ca. 1840 B.C. (Trump 1984).

A more important corollary is the need to reassess the spatial distribution of the cultures of the Ozieri and subsequent periods. The known villages of the Ozieri period occur mainly in the plains - the Campidano - contrasting markedly with the pattern of Nuragic settlement (Brandis 1980; 1982). Rowland (1982) has convincingly argued that the relative absence of Nuragic settlements in the lowlands is not a result of recent peasant destruction. If so, then the intermediate period is the obvious context in which to look for a major reversal of zonal settlement preferences. However, the Monte Claro settlement distribution (Atzeni 1980:16) shows only relatively marginal retouches: the disappearance of village settlement on the lower Sulcis, a contraction to a few major, long-surviving sites in the Oristanese, a slight drift towards the margins of the plains revealed by the thickening of sites in the

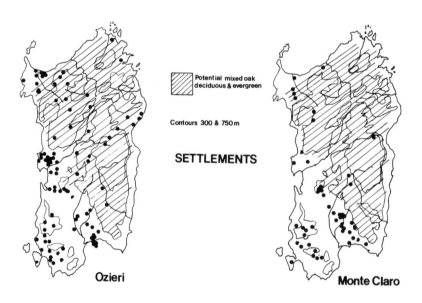

Potential mixed oak deciduous & evergreen

Contours 300 & 750 m

SETTLEMENTS

Ozieri

Monte Claro

Figure 3.3 Changing settlement patterns on Sardinia

Mogorese, around Nuràminis and Monastìr and in the Campidano Minore (fig. 3.3).

It is legitimate, however, to ponder the reliability of the village settlement pattern as the only or the best guide to the distribution of population. Santoni's seriation of the plans and various attributes of domus de janas suggests a penetration into the middle Tirso Valley and the Barbagia during this period (Santoni 1976:9) which Lilliu's discoveries around Ovodda and Fonni (Lilliu 1981) might be said to sample (fig. 3.4). However, when the distribution of domus de janas and Ozieri or Monte Claro settlements are compared, the most obvious conclusion is the lack of congruence, despite the unchallenged assumption that necropoleis and villages are the two most characteristic features of later Neolithic and pre-Nuragic culture. While it is easy to explain away the relative lack of villages in the center and north as the result of the comparative lack of research, accidented topography, vegetation cover and so forth, the absence of cemeteries in the region of dense village settlements cannot be ex-

plained similarly in terms of a lack of suitable rock outcrops. Why are there no necropoleis of simple earth graves as in contemporary Catalunya (fosa tombs) or during the Remedello period on the Po Plain? Is it not possible that the domus de janas became elaborated precisely where settlement was relatively dispersed, acting as a communal focus roughly along the lines of the hypogée in the context of the 'expanded village' in the S-O-M culture of northern France as modelled by Howell (1982; 1983)?

In the same way, the dolmens of the northern and central plateau (Atzeni 1980:35) might be regarded not as the products of a pastoral grouping of Pyrenean origin to be contrasted with the Ozieri agriculturalists (Lilliu 1975:98-105), but as an aspect of Ozieri culture in a particular geographical milieu in which the pastoral sector of a mixed economy might have been more prominent than elsewhere. That would confirm Santoni's suggestions of a close relationship between the builders of the two traditions (Santoni 1976:10; 21). Ferrarese Ceruti has, in any case, discovered Ozieri sherds among the later material in the dolmen of

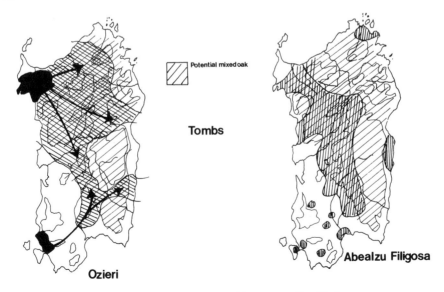

Figure 3.4 Colonization patterns on Sardinia

Motorra (Dorgali) one of the few not to have been voided in antiquity (Ferrarese Ceruti 1980:83-4).

There is a conclusion which may be drawn from such an admittedly speculative overview: that is that the model of Ozieri and Monte Claro settlement provided by the well-known agglomerations of capanne on the cùccurus of the Campidano is not likely to have been typical of Sardinian pre-Nuragic settlement overall. Furthermore, the apparent stability of this tradition may mask much greater dynamism elsewhere. In accordance with Clarke's suggestion, it is advisable to begin with 'a model of expectation derived from other sources' (Clarke 1976:149).

Sherratt has proposed a general, deductive model on the stadial development of European food production, which has found much empirical verification in the widely quoted research of Kruk in Little Poland (Sherratt 1980; 1981; Kruk 1973; 1980). Sherratt contrasts an early phase of horticulture practised on alluvium with a high groundwater level, with a later complex including agriculture based on the use of the ard (scratch-plow), and carried out on interfluvial areas dependent on rainfall and specialized, perhaps transhumant, pastoralism. The predilection for riverine and lagoon-edge locations evident in the Ozieri distribution is compatible with the postulated early horticulture; indeed, the practice of cultivating especially fertile, humid soils 'a rokku' recorded on the island as late as 1820 (Cherchi Paba 1974:351-354) may provide a useful model. According to Sherratt's prediction, the diffusion of the ard through the Mediterranean should have occurred between ca. 2700 and ca. 2500 B.C. (Sherratt 1981:271); Mezzena's discovery of ard-marks dated to 2650/2600 B.C. at St. Martin-de-Corléans (Aosta) provides a minimum of con-

firmation (Mezzena 1982:33). Neither ards nor ard-marks nor yoked cattle burials are known from Sardinia, so the adoption of advanced cultivation would have to be inferred from changes in the settlement pattern which cannot be demonstrated. The lack of dramatic change in the settlement patterns on the Campidano is no litmus test, as this is precisely the region in which the horticultural pattern would be expected to have persisted longest.

Sherratt's is not the only model available for developments in the third millennium B.C. in the western Mediterranean. I have suggested that the most logical manner of exploitation of the pristine oak forest would have been the collection of the acorn crop both for direct human consumption and for the mast-based rearing of swine (Lewthwaite 1981, 1982). Extensive cereal cultivation based on swidden (narboni) or the use of plots fertilized by small stock (cuilarza), as historically attested (Le Lannou 1941:56 n. 1, 2) would be compatible with this, as would the raising of cattle and goats, rather than sheep. The familial polyculture of the Gallurese stazzu provides an obvious model (Le Lannou 1941:222-30; Spano 1958:171-203). Archaeozoological, paleobotanical and palynological data are almost entirely lacking for this period in Sardinia, although the solitary faunal analysis carried out at the Grotta Filiestru (Mara) is at least in agreement with this proposition (Trump 1983; 1984). Acorns, swine and cattle appear to have been of considerable economic importance to the later Neolithic inhabitants of Terrina IV (Aléria) in eastern Corsica, a region not unlike the Campidano in many respects (Camps 1979:13, 17; Jehasse 1980:553). In effect, rather than the Gallurese or Corso-Gallurese pattern of settlement and subsistence forming a peripheral isolate in sharp contrast to the Ozieri norm inferred from the villages of the Campidano (Puglisi and Castaldi 1964-5; Contu 1964-5; Lilliu 1966-7) the latter may have been in reality the exception rather than the rule. The artefactual evidence for this argument has already been noted.

In summary the most fundamental commonplace assertions concerning pre-Nuragic cultural, settlement and economic developments can and should be questioned. I suggest that progress will be achieved through, first, widening the range of hypotheses and, secondly, generating the empirical evidence to test these hypotheses - most urgently, through systematic regional surveys, excavation as much for bioarchaeological as for artefactual evidence, and further stratigraphic excavation yielding sequences of Carbon-14 determinations.

The Foundation of Nuragic Architecture: Form and Function

The great controversy which has dominated the discussion of the development of the nuraghe has been that of the relative chronology of the majority class of corbelled nuraghi compared with the far less numerous, less uniform and structurally simpler corridor-variant. The polarized positions of Contu (1959:110-118), who once upheld a high relative dating for the corridor form and Lilliu (1962:30-35; 1966:58-60), who argued the converse case - regarding this variety as a guerrilla hide-out and a booby-trap for unwary Romans have converged in recent years on the consensus that, while the corridor form is the simpler and earlier, both forms coexisted throughout the Nuragic era (Contu 1974:156, 1980:35; Lilliu 1975:299-303, 1980:49). Each class can be derived from a Copper Age prototype: for the false-vaulted form, the capanna of Sa Korona (Villagreca); for the corridor-variant, the 'proto-nuraghe' of Brunku Màdugui (Gèsturi) (Atzeni

1966; Lilliu 1966: 62-4, 1975:91-4, 1980:48-9; Contu 1980:32).

On purely architectural grounds, Contu's original hypothesis seems preferable. The major flaw in the conventional wisdom is surely the assumption that the highly restricted internal space (corridors, cells, stairways, niches) of the surviving stone structures constituted the totality, or even the major function of the original habitation. On the contrary, the presence on the upper surfaces of the corridor-nuraghi Albùcciu (Arzachena) and Brunku Màdugui (Gèsturi) of the bases of capanne built with organic materials which have perished (Ferrarese Ceruti 1962:167; Lilliu 1966:figs. 66-9; Contu 1974:pl. 115) make it clear that the function of the stone mass was no more than that of a platform for a complex of upper quarters (fig. 3.5). Furthermore, a group of corridor-nuraghi are known in which these capanne are replaced by stone-built torrette, a miniature corbelled nuraghi in one case: these are the Nuraghi Agnu (Calangiánus), Majori (Tèmpio), Tùsari (Bortigàli) and S'Ulivera (Dualchi) the last being the best preserved (Ferrarese Ceruti 1962:185-6; Lilliu 1962:79, 179-80, fig. 2(8), pl. 85; Tanda 1975:404). It is therefore possible to postulate a developmental sequence from simple capanna through a platform supporting one or more capanne, reached by ladder or internal stairway (corridor!) to platform crowned with torrette. The final step in the genesis of the classical nuraghe would consist of the suppression of the platform in favor of the elaboration of the upper element into a free-standing tronco-conic tower housing the corbelled habitation chamber. Although this sequence cannot be validated from the available data, and perhaps never will be, it at least is not in conflict with the evidence available. Clearly, it is only the earliest material which is of interest, not

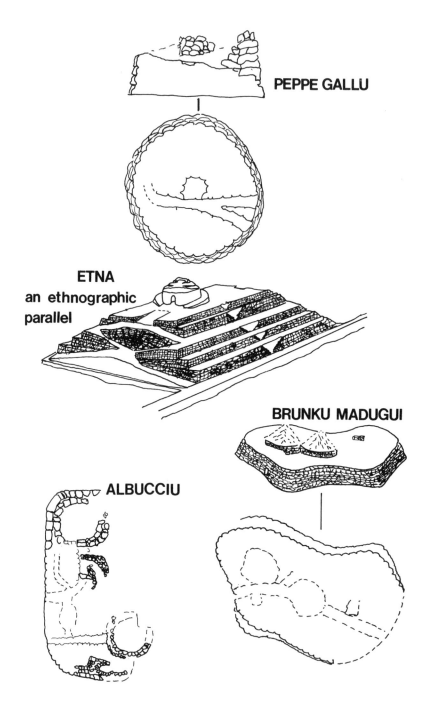

PEPPE GALLU

ETNA
an ethnographic
parallel

BRUNKU MADUGUI

ALBUCCIU

Figure 3.5 Proto-Nuraghi

the subsequent reuse and perhaps the rebuilding of the capanne.

In effect, the archaeological evidence at least does not contradict the model in that nothing earlier than Nuragic combed ware has yet been found within a corbelled nuraghe, while Brunku Màdugui has yielded atypical Monte Claro ware (Lilliu 1975:92-4, 1980:48-9) and Sa Korona some Abealzu (Atzeni 1966:122-3; Lilliu 1980:48). Moreover the same sequence appears valid for developments in the neighboring islands, with Contu's proviso (1959:113) that these never reached the level of sophistication of the nuraghe. The Baleares lacked the corbelling technique, their talaiots consisting either of a solid base or at best a hollow form with a central column taking the weight of radial roofing-stones, a technique only a little advanced beyond the megalithic (Rossellò Bordoy 1973:51-9). The southern Corsican torri are not only corbelled, but possess a curious vestigial platform or skirting wall outside the external stairway (Virili and Grosjean 1979:25) suggesting that they failed only to develop the Nuragic innovation of the troncoconic facade and internal stairway.

A more serious consequence of the fixation with the corridor-corbel controversy has been the lack of interest in the hierarchical and functional differentiation of nuraghi and Nuragic villages prior to the first millennium B.C., as if the perfectly valid assumption of an architectural development from simple to complex within a given structure in some way inhibited the evolution of settlement patterns. If so, Sardinia would have been practically unique within the West Mediterranean during the period concerned (later third and earlier second millennia B.C.).

J. Morais Arnaud has recently suggested that a three-level site hierarchy characterised the southwest Iberian Copper Age (Morais Arnaud 1983). The highest level comprised sites with an extent of 50 - 100 hectares, inhabited by 1,000 - 1,500 people, such as Ferreira do Alentejo, Valencina de la Concepción (Sevilla) and la Pijotilla (Badajoz); the middle by unenclosed povoados some 1 - 5 ha. in extent, with a population of 150 - 350, accounting for the great majority of Copper Age sites; finally, the small fortified sites of Monte da Tumba (Alcácer-do-Sal) and the Cerro do Castelo (Santa Justa) seem to have served some specialized purpose.

Recent and continuing excavations at the famous site of Los Millares (Santa Fe, Almeria) have revealed the complexity of a single 'site': the settlement was protected on its landward side by three successive defensive walls: the outermost, in addition to the long-known bastions, sported a sophisticated barbican gateway, while the middle bulwark incorporated five towers. Moreover, a further line of defense comprised at least ten forts, each the size of small nuraghi. Excavation of one has revealed a central tower girdled by dual concentric bastioned walls. This second level of the hierarchy was in turn served by a third, a humble watchtower (Arribas et al. 1979; Arribas and Molina 1984).

At a regional scale, the settlement hierarchy of final Neolithic, Chalcolithic and Early Bronze Age Languedoc and Provence comprises a wide variety of elements. The bulk of the population appears to have lived in villages, such as the three hectare site of Collet Redon near la Couronne (Martigues) (Escalon de Fonton 1980) or the agglomeration of hamlets, each consisting of a cluster of longhouses, which made up the village of Cambous (Viols-en-Laval) in the heart of the Garrigues (Canet and Roudil 1978: Roudil and Canet 1981).

In addition to these open settlements, there are a number of sites known which are wholly or partly enclosed, varying in size and sophistication from the 700 square meter pastoral camp of La Citadelle (Vauvenargues), a promontory blocked off with a crude stone and cob wall, to the 15,000 square meter Camp de Laure (Le Rove) near Marseille, a plateau defended by a double rampart 145m long, furnished at intervals and on the flanks of the gateway with bastions (Gutherz et al. 1982). On Mallorca, walled villages (poblats talaiòtics) were not anticipated before 1000 B.C., 300 years after the first talaiots (Pericot Garcia 1972:41, Rossellò Bordoy 1973:185). The discovery of a large settlement including an enclosure at So'n Ferrandell-So'n Oleza (Valldemossa) occupied between 2000 and 1400 B.C. (Waldren 1982:308-20) implies that several types of habitational site coexisted during the second millennium B.C.: longhouses (navi-formes), villages, stepped monuments and talaiots (Lewthwaite 1984). On Corsica, the period in question is poorly enough known at the cultural level, let alone from the perspective of settlement archaeology. Nevertheless, the model of a Bronze Age settlement pattern consisting, apart from the super site of Filitosa (Sollacaro), of small population nuclei inhabiting Torri, has been filled out by the discovery first of numerous Middle Bronze Age castelli on the Alta Rocca plateau (Lanfranchi 1978:266-7; Jehasse 1980: 558-9) and more recently of a triple enclosure at Castellucciu (Pila-Canale) at the center of which lay a monumental structure, built in ca. 2000 B.C. (Césari and Jehasse 1978; Jehasse 1978: 529-30; Lewthwaite 1983).

Comparable sites ought to occur in the Copper Age context of the Monte Claro culture, thereby focusing into a single stereoscopic frame the incompatible monofocal images of this culture conjured up by partial data: on the one hand, of a long post-Ozieri afternoon of the villages of the plains (Atzeni 1967); on the other, of the beginnings of Nuragic civilization as we know it (Lilliu and Ferrarese Ceruti 1958-9). Recent surveys in the provinces of Sassari and Nuoro have brought to light several Monte Claro settlements which in their partial or total enclosure and/or their ceremonial as well as domestic structures foreshadow the Nuragic sites of Serra Orrios (Dorgali) or Santa Vittoria (Serri): these comprise Monte Baranta (Olmedo), Monte Ossoni (Castelsardo) and Biriai (Oliena). Still earlier manifestations of this class of site occur at San Giuseppe (Pàdria) and Monte Ruina or Cabula Muntones (Sassari) with Filigosa-Abealzu associations (Basoli 1984; Castaldi 1979, 1984; Contu 1962, 1974:265, 1980:32; Lo Schiavo 1979:343; Moravetti 1979:332-4; Santoni 1976:35-6).

Although the enigmatic semicircular structure at Monte Baranta may very well have functioned as a watchtower or citadel, and while many of the sites are walled, there is no way in which any of these settlements could be described as being on the point of evolving into a nuraghe. Again, the presence of an elevated ritual structure at the center of Biriai, reminiscent in a sense of the great ramped pyramid of Monte d'Accòddi (Sassari) (Contu 1966, 1984) invites further consideration of the function of the 'platforms' among the proto-nuraghi, particularly Brunku Màdugui, in view of its Monte Claro associations. Did the six meters of stonework beneath the capanne really afford the occupants any practical protection against the slings and arrows of Copper Age warfare? Were the proto-nuraghi perhaps some sort of ritual focus?

The suggested architectural seriation need not imply a functional continuity. Or does the elevation of what appear to be otherwise unremarkable domestic structures signify the symbolic assertion of superiority with regard to the mass of the populace on the part of some nucleus of higher rank? However intuitive and impressionistic we may feel them to be, Lilliu's references to 'il padrone del nuraghe ed il signore (un ricco armentario) del prossimo villaggio'...'un massiccio e rustico palazzotto signorile d'un capo di pastori'...'La dimora rurale di un reuccio pastore' (Lilliu 1966:63-4; Contu 1974:198) draw attention to the social transformations which may have occurred in the Copper Age.

Social Foundations: ex occidente grex?

It is, on reflection, only through a series of historical accidents that the Monte Claro culture, unlike the Iberian and Aegean equivalents, has not been explained, in the first instance, through ex oriente lux diffusionism, since the tombe a forno of the hills of Cagliari (Atzeni 1967) and the still enigmatic citadel of Sa Urècci (Gúspini) (Lilliu 1962:180-1, pl. 36-2; Arnal 1973:174-5, fig. 59(7)) offer footholds for such speculation at least as secure as the spiral meander motifs and female figurines of the Ozieri culture formally assigned to this period (Castaldi 1972). Instead, the catalytic role in the transmutation of the Ozieri base-culture into the Nuragic Bronze Age has been ascribed, on the testimony of megalithic tombs and Beaker assemblages, to an irruption of bellicose Pyrenaean shepherds (Lilliu 1965). Anachronistic as the hypothesis of an exogenous warrior-herder culture may be, the premise that the later third and early second millennia B.C. witnessed an expansion of the pastoral sector closely accords with the model of a Secondary Products Revolution advocated by Sherratt (1981; 1983) and deserves further consideration.

In recent years the discussion of the development of ranked societies has become polarized: on the one hand, Renfrew (1972) advocates a model of a managerial elite organizing production and distribution pro bono publico; on the other, Gilman (1981) advances the 'nonfunctionalist alternative,' that parasitical dominant groups were tolerated by the toiling masses only because the latter were unwilling to sacrifice the long-term benefits accruing from past investment in 'capital intensive subsistence technology,' particularly fixed facilities. The sylvan and pastoral sectors receive scant attention in this debate compared with such agricultural developments as the scratch-plow, the cultivation of the olive and vine, and irrigation and terracing, because of the specific associations of the case study areas, Almería and the Aegean. However, the same question of the relationship between the intensification of food production and the development of social ranking must take into account those aspects in the Sardinian case. For instance, a fundamental oversight in Gilman's model is his failure to consider one capital resource essential to the working of an advanced farming system which could be all the more easily monopolized and manipulated by an ambitious segment through being, not a fixed facility which the rest of the population could ill forego, but one with a limited lifespan which few could afford to keep or renew. I refer of course to plow oxen. Delille has calculated that utilization of animal traction multiplies the productivity of the peasant by a factor of 3.5 (Delille 1977:128) permitting a nuclear family to subsist in marginal regions, where it could not through practising hoe cultivation (Delille 1977:130). This is an argument of critical importance if, as I have argued, the Copper Age population was concentrated largely in the hill zone of the center. Each ox, however, requires as much land again (10-12 ha. under southern Mediterranean conditions) as the entire family for its upkeep (Delille 1977:132, 135-6). Moreover, since cattle cannot reproduce until two years of age and are not fully mature until six, require intensive training and finally are fit for only ten years' service, to quote a modern Sardinian account (Angioni 1976: 100-10), it is hardly surprising that they are beyond the means of the peasant, who must have recourse to the latifundist patron, i.e. the large unit of production which can stand the cost (Delille 1977:135-6). Although I have previously derided Gilman's model of social differentiation as a scenario of e mafia dux it is perhaps worth noting that the feudal class in Sicily have been periodically renewed precisely from the ranks of the gabelotti, the cattle-raisers (Delille 1977:136, Rochefort 1961:47, 110-1). The introduction of the plow into the West Mediterranean at ca. 2600 B.C. cannot, therefore, be regarded as simply a technological advance without social ramifications.

In the same way, the contrast between the forest-raised pig and the sheep as the most numerous objects of animal husbandry in Copper Age contexts may indicate important differences in the form of social organization. Howell has suggested (1982) that the regions of western Europe which specialized in sheep during the later third millennium B.C. were in effect engaged in the production of a 'cash crop' (wool) which was being exchanged for copper in regional interaction spheres, while those regions which raised pigs remained at a subsistence level of production. Unfortunately, given the existing dearth of archaeozoological analyses from within Sardinia, we cannot begin to describe even the gross outlines of the animal husbandry sector, let alone consider looking for such subtleties as the possible social implications of eventual regional or site-level differences in the proportions of the major species.

Conclusions

Sardinian archaeology in the Copper Age, as elsewhere, operates on two levels: on the lower, the diligent accumulation of artefactual, art-historical and architectural data fulfills the perceived goal of narrative historiography, which might unkindly be called 'anecdote plus chronology'; on the upper, a corpus of received stereotypes fills out the culture-historical skeleton with economic and social detail. There is not, however, a true dialectic either between fieldwork and controlling models, or between the latter and the theoretical advances which have been made in other regions of Europe in recent years, or even between archaeology and closely related disciplines such as historical geography or social anthropology. If the past of Sardinia has a future, then it surely lies in the establishment of precisely these channels of communication.

Acknowledgments

I am most grateful to Prof. Miriam S. Balmuth for inviting me to the International Colloquium on Sardinian Archaeology and for her manifold hospitality, and to the National Endowment for the Humanities for generously defraying the costs of travel hither. I would also like to express my thanks to the many scholars who have, over the years, kindly provided offprints and valuable information in litteris: A. Arribas, E. Atzeni, P. Basoli, P. Brandis, E. Castaldi, A. d'Anna, M.L. Ferrarese Ceruti, J. Gascó, A. Gilman, X. Gutherz, J.M. Howell, J. Jehasse, F. Mezzena, J.

Morais Arnaud, P. Phillips, R.J. Rowland Jr., A.G. Sherratt, D.H. Trump and W.H. Waldren. I am indebted to Mrs. Robin Gould-Zvelebil for her

skill in deciphering and typing the manuscript, and to Dr. J.M. Howell for preparing the illustrations at short notice.

REFERENCES

ANGIONI, G.
1976   Sa Laurera. Il Lavoro Contadino in Sardegna.
         Cagliari: Editrice Democratica Sarda.

ARNAL, J.
1973   Le Lébous à Saint Mathieu-de-Tréviers (Hérault).
         Gallia Préhistoire 16(1):131-200.

ARRIBAS, A., F. MOLINA, L. SAEZ, F. DE LA TORRE, P. AGUAYO AND T. NAJERA
1979   Excavaciones en Los Millares (Sante Fe, Almeria).
         Cuadernos de Prehistoria de la Universidad de Granada
         4:61-96.

ARRIBAS, A. AND F. MOLINA
1984   Los Millares: Las recientes excavaciones y sus
         resultados. Early Settlement.

ATZENI, E.
1966   'Il Nuraghe' Sa Corona di Villagreca. Atti del XIII
         Congresso di Storia dell'Architettura:119-26.

1967   Tombe a forno di cultura Monte Claro nella Via
         Basilicata di Cagliari. RSP 22:157-79.

1980   Vornuraghenzeit. Kunst Sardiniens:15-44.

BASOLI, P.
1984   L'Insediamento preistorico di M. Ruina o M. Cabula
         Muntones (Sassari). Early Settlement.

BRANDIS, P.
1980   I fattori geografici della distribuzione dei nuraghi
         nella Sardegna nord-occidentale. Atti della XXII
         Riunione Scientifica IIPP:359-428.

1982   Problemi metodologici sulla geografia dei nuraghi.
         IGU Symposium on Historical Changes in Spatial
         Organization and its Experience in the Mediterranean
         World. Sassari.

CAMPS, G.
1979   La préhistoire dans la région d'Aléria. Archeologia
         Corsa 4:5-21.

CAMPS, G. AND E. ROSTAN
1980   Les poteries à perforations en ligne à propos du
            faciès terrinien du Chalcolithique corse. Travaux
            LAPEMO.

1982   Les poteries à perforations en ligne à propos du
            faciès terrinien du Chalcolithique Corse. BSPF
            79(8):240-9.

CANET, H. AND J.L. ROUDIL
1978   Le village chalcolithique de Cambous à Viols-en-Laval
            (Hérault). Gallia Préhistoire 21(1):143-81.

CASTALDI, E.
1972   La datazione con il C-14 della Grotta del Guano o
            Gonagosula (Oliena-Nuoro).   Considerazioni sulla
            cultura di Ozieri. Archivio per l'Antropologia e la
            Etnologia 102:233-75.

1979   Biriai (Oliena, Nuoro): il villaggio di cultura Monte
            Claro. RSP 34:231-42.

1980   Relazione preliminare sullo scavo della Grotta del
            Guano o Gonagosula (Oliena, Nuoro). Atti della XXII
            Riunione Scientifica IIPP:149-60.

1984   La cultura Calcolitica di Monte Claro nel sito di
            Biriai (Oliena-Nuoro-Sardegna). Early Settlement.

CESARI, J. AND O. JEHASSE
1978   Le site archéologique de Castellucciu (Pila-Canale-
            Corse du Sud). Archeologia Corsa 3:55-70.

CHERCHI PABA, F.
1974   Evoluzione Storica dell'Attività Industriale Agricola
            Caccia e Pesca in Sardegna 1. Cagliari: Regione
            Autonoma Sarda. Assessorato alla Industria e
            Commercio.

CLARKE, D.L.
1976   Mesolithic Europe. Problems in Economic and Social
            Anthropology. G. Sieveking, I. Longworth, and K.
            Wilson eds. London: Duckworth.

CONTU, E.
1959   I più antichi nuraghi e l'esplorazione del Nuraghe
            Peppe Gallu (Uri-Sassari). RSP 14:59-124.

1962   Il nuraghe Monte Baranta in località su Casteddu o
            Pala Reale (Olmedo, Sassari). StSar 17:630-1.

1964-5   Considerazioni su un saggio di scavo al nuraghe 'La
            Prisciona' di Arzachena. StSar 19:149-260.

1966   Elementi di architettura prenuragica. <u>Atti XIII</u>
               <u>Congresso di Storia dell'Architettura</u> 1:93-100;
               2:81-6.

1974   La Sardegna dell'età Nuragica. <u>PCIA</u> 3:143-203.

1980   La Sardegna preistorica e protostorica. Aspetti e
               problemi. <u>Atti della XXII Riunione Scientifica IIPP</u>:
               13-43.

1984   Monte d'Accòddi-Sassari. Problematica di studio e
               ricerca di un singolare monumento preistorico. <u>Early</u>
               <u>Settlement</u>.

DELILLE, G.
1977   <u>Agricoltura e Demografia nel Regno di Napoli nei</u>
               <u>Secoli XVIII e XIX</u>. Naples: Guida Editori.

ESCALON DE FONTON, M.
1980   Informations   archéologiques: circonscription de
               Provence-Alpes-Cote d'Azur.   <u>Gallia Préhistoire</u>
               23(2):525-47.

FERRARESE CERUTI, M.L.
1962   Nota preliminare alla I e alla II campagna di scavo
               nel Nuraghe Albucciu (Arzachena-Sassari). <u>RSP</u> 17:
               161-204.

1980   Le domus de janas de Mariughìa e Canudedda e il
               dolmen di Motorra. <u>Dorgali Documenti Archeologici</u>:
               57-69. Sassari: Chiarella.

FERRARESE CERUTI, M.L. AND F. GERMANA
1978   <u>Sisaia. Una Deposizione in Grotta della Cultura di</u>
               <u>Bonnanaro</u>. <u>Quaderni</u> 6.

GILMAN, A.
1981   The development of social stratification in Bronze
               Age Europe. <u>Current Anthropology</u> 22(1):1-23.

GUTHERZ, X., A. COLOMER, J. COULAROU, J. COURTIN, R. COUTEL, A. D'ANNA
1982   Les enceintes en piérre sèche du Nèolithique à l'age
               du Bronze dans le Sud-Est de la France. <u>BSPF</u>
               79(2):36-8.

HOWELL, J.M.
1982   Neolithic settlement and economy in Northern France.
               <u>Oxford Journal of Archaeology</u> 1(1):115-8.

1983   <u>Settlement and Economy in Neolithic Northern France</u>.
               British Archaeological Reports S 157. Oxford.

JEHASSE, J.
1978   Informations Archéologiques: circonscription de la
            Corse. Gallia Préhistoire 21(2):723-34.

1980   Informations Archéologiques: circonscription de la
            Corse. Gallia Préhistoire 23(2):549-65.

KRUK, J.
1973   Studia Osadnicze nad Neolitem Wyzyn Lessowych.
            Krakow.

1980   The Earlier Neolithic of Southern Poland. Eng.
            trans. ed. J.M. Howell, N.J. Starling. BAR S 93.

LANFRANCHI, F. DE
1978   Capula. Quatre Millénaires de Survivances et de
            Traditions. Levie: Centre Archéologique.

LE LANNOU, M.
1941   Patres et Paysans de la Sardaigne. Tours: Arrault.
            Ital. transl. ed. M. Brigaglia, Cagliari: della
            Torre 1979.

LEWTHWAITE, J.G.
1981   Plains tails from the hills: transhumance in
            Mediterranean archaeology. Economic Archaeology
            A. Sheridan and G. Bailey eds. BAR S 66:57-66.

1982   Acorns for the ancestors: the prehistoric
            exploitation of woodland in the West Mediterranean.
            Archaeological Aspects of Woodland Ecology. M. Bell
            and S. Limbrey eds. BAR S 146:217-30.

1983   The Neolithic of Corsica. Ancient France 6000-2000
            b.c.   C.J. Scarre ed.   Edinburgh: Edinburgh
            University Press:146-83.

1984   Social factors and economic change in Balearic
            prehistory 3000-1000 b.c. Beyond Subsistence. G.
            Barker and C. Gamble, eds. New York: Academic Press.

in press   Works and days: archaeological implications of recent
            settlement and subsistence activities in marginal
            regions of the Western Mediterranean. Progress in
            Mediterranean Studies. J.L. Bintliff ed. Bradford:
            Bradford Archaeological Publications.

LILLIU, G.
1962   I Nuraghi. Torri Preistoriche della Sardegna.
            Cagliari: La Zattera.

1965   Apporti Pirenaici e del Midi alle culture Sarde della
                prima età del Bronzo. Arquitectura Megalítica y
                Ciclópea Catalano-Bealear. Barcelona: Consejo
                Superior de Investigaciones Científicas.

1966   L'Architettura nuragica (relazione generale). Atti
                del XIII Congresso di Storia dell'Architettura 1:
                17-92; 2:9-77.

1966-7   Rapporti tra la cultura 'Torreana' e aspetti pre e
                protonuragici della Sardegna. StSar 20:3-47.

1975   La Civiltà dei Sardi[2]. Turin: RAI.

1980   Die Nuraghenkultur. Kunst Sardiniens.

1981   Monumenti Antichi Barbaricini. Quaderni 12.

LILLIU. G. AND M. FERRARESE CERUTI
1958-9   La 'facies' nuragica di Monte Claro. StSar 16:
                3-266.

LORIA, R. AND D. TRUMP
1978   Le Scoperte a Sa' Ucca de su Tintirriòlu e il
                Neolitico Sardo. MonAnt ii-2:115-253.

LO SCHIAVO, F.
1979   Notiziario. Neolitico e Metalli. Sardegna. RSP 34:
                334-43.

MEZZENA, F.
1982   Archeologia in Valle d'Aosta. Aosta: Regione Valle
                d'Aosta. Assessorato del Turismo, Urbanistica e Beni
                Culturali.

MORAIS ARNAUD, J.
1983   O povoado calcolitico de Ferreira do Alentejo no
                contexto da Bacia do Sado e do Sudoeste peninsular.
                Arqueologia (Porto) 6:48-64.

MORAVETTI, A.
1979   Notiziario. Neolitico e Metalli. Sardegna. RSP 34:
                332-4.

PERICOT GARCIA, L.
1972   The Balearic Islands. London: Thames and Hudson.

PUGLISI, S. AND E. CASTALDI
1964-5   Aspetti dell'accantonamento culturale nella Gallura
                preistorica e protostorica. StSar 19:59-148.

RENFREW, A.C.
    1972   The Emergence of Civilisation: The Cyclades and the
                    Aegean in the Third Millennium B.C. London: Methuen.

ROCHEFORT, R.
    1961   Le Travail en Sicile. Paris: PUF.

ROSSELLO BORDOY, G.
    1973   La Cultura Talayotica en Mallorca. Palma: Ediciones
                    Cort.

ROUDIL, J.L. AND H. CANET
    1981   Cambous Village Préhistorique.   Viols en Laval
                    Hérault. Guide no. 1.   Société Languedocienne de
                    Préhistoire.

ROWLAND, R.J.
    1982   Where did all the nuraghi go? Observations on the
                    distribution of Nuragic bronze.   Fourth Annual
                    Colloquium   on   Sardinian   Archaeology,   Tufts
                    University, Medford MA.

SANTONI, V.
    1976   Nota preliminare sulla tipologia delle grotticelle
                    artificiali funerarie in Sardegna. Archivio Storico
                    Sardo 30:3-49.

SHERRATT, A.G.
    1980   Water, soil and seasonality in early cereal
                    cultivation. World Archaeology 11(3):313-30.

    1981   Plough and pastoralism: aspects of the secondary
                    products revolution. Pattern of the Past: Studies in
                    Honour of David Clarke. I. Hodder, G. Isaac, and N.
                    Hammond eds. Cambridge: CUP.

    1983   The secondary exploitation of animals in the Old
                    World. World Archaeology 15(1):90-104.

SPANO, B.
    1958   La Gallura. Memoria di Geografia Antropica 13.
                    Rome: Consiglio Nazionale delle Ricerche.

TANDA, G.
    1975   Notiziario.   Neolitico e Metalli.   Sardegna.
                    Provincie di Sassari e Nuoro. RSP 30:399-406.

TRUMP, D.H.
    1982   The Grotta Filiestru, Bonu Ighinu, Mara (Sassari).
                    Le Néolithique Ancien Méditerranéen Actes du Colloque
                    International de Préhistoire Montpellier 1981. Sète:
                    Fédération Archéologique de l'Hérault.

1983   La Grotta di Filiestru, Mara (SS). Quaderni 13.

1984   The Bonu Ighinu Project - results and prospects.
                Early Settlement.

VIRILI, F.L. AND J. GROSJEAN
    1979   Guide des Sites Torreéns de l'Age du Bronze Corse.
                    Paris: Editions Vigros.

WALDREN, W.H.
    1982   Balearic Prehistoric Ecology and Culture. The
                    Excavation and Study of Certain Caves, Rock Shelters
                    and Settlements. BAR S 149 (3 Vols.).

PART TWO:
THE ART OF NURAGIC SARDINIA

Introduction

Perhaps the most extraordinary find in the realm of art history in this century in Sardinia is the group of large-scale sculptures of male figures in soft white sandstone that may have stood on a generation's span of tombs. These warriors, boxers and archers, appropriately dressed, evoke the iconography of the well-known Nuragic bronze figurines, but are otherwise unlike anything else in the central Mediterranean at this time (7th century B.C.). Some of them are shown for the first time; the discussion of their function by their excavator, Carlo Tronchetti, is also a premiere.

Assessing these sculptures for their time and place requires the expertise of scholars who are familiar with any similarities both nearby and in other parts of the Mediterranean. Brunilde Ridgway discusses the uniqueness of the statues both before and after she evokes possible parallels in material, style and subject matter. These come from Crete and Cyprus as well as Greece; she points out the essential disparities with Egyptian and Phoenician sculpture as well. Larissa Bonfante surveys Etruscan and Italic production of monumental sculpture, primarily from Vetulonia, Murlo and Capestrano, with the resulting analogies limited to the archaic interest in magnifying miniaturistic work. Both of these treatments put the Monte Prama statues into their time and place in a way that emphasizes their own uniqueness.

Until very recently, bronze figurines were the only widely recognized product of artistic creation from the Sardinia of the nuraghi. At first, the fact that they were neither Greek nor Roman meant that they were considered 'primitive' in contrast. As more and more appeared, however, they began to be appreciated on their own terms as reflections of the society that produced them. They have been studied as well for historical and cultural information, with the resulting interpretation of a pastoral society, warlike and religious, with metalworking as one of its widespread crafts. The structure of that society is being discussed on the basis of the objects found and read. For the art historian, however, the material betrays a number of different styles and conceptions with an aesthetic of varying origins, both local and foreign.

There is still a great deal about the bronze figurines, 'bronzetti,' that we do not know. Using the publication of bronzes from the British Museum as a point of departure, Francesca Ridgway has been able to add some unpublished pieces in their study and give some dates and relationships for at least one specific group. Her acute analysis allows her to make some chronological definitions and distinctions; she calls for a timely re-examination and reassessment of all Sardinian bronze figurines.

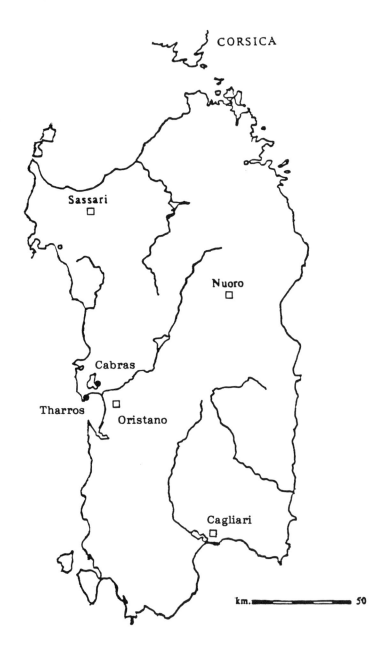

Figure 4.1   Map of Sardinia showing provincial capitals and sites
near Monte Prama mentioned in text of chapter 4

4. NURAGIC STATUARY FROM MONTE PRAMA

Carlo Tronchetti

The excavation from which the fragments of Nuragic statuary came took place on the eastern side of the hill named Monte Prama, in the Sinis area of Cabras (fig. 4.1), at the edge of the plain next to the Cabras lagoon (fig. 4.2). The fragments covered a necropolis that had been placed in a natural depression of the ground extending from south to north. The eastern side of the depression had been cut in order to place the graves in a curved line of about 40m along the edge. The graves, dug into the sterile, compact red ground, are small pits 60 to 70cm in diameter at the mouth and 70 to 80cm deep, narrowing at the bottom to a small, off-center depression. Every small pit is covered with a big sandstone slab, measuring about 100cm square by 14 or 15cm thick. The upper border of the depression had small squared blocks of stone, triangular cut stones, unworked stones, or sometimes, nothing at all, as a result of plowing. In fact, the archaeological layer is covered by humus not more than 20 to 30cm high. Between the grave-slabs red earth was pressed up to the upper face and sometimes a step, made of earth and stones, was found on the slabs. Westwards, the necropolis is defined by sandstone slabs, placed vertically in a small trench excavated in the sterile ground or, where this ground descends, fixed in the yellowish earth placed on the bottom of the depression. The space between the graves and the vertical slabs was filled with red, pressed earth. The necropolis starts at the south, with a vertical slab supported by a square block of sandstone. At the north there are, instead, two vertical slabs; one of these is broken for the placement of a grave. East of the last three northern graves, there are three other graves, placed there because the space assigned to the necropolis was too small.

The depression west of the graves, 6 to 7m wide, is filled with small stones on the bottom, and is covered with yellowish earth, chiefly where the natural ground descends. The western border of the depression, badly damaged by the plows, shows occasional rows of big stones. The dead were placed seated into the small pits, without grave goods, and facing different directions, for the most part east. The small pits were filled with the same excavated earth, and almost from the middle of the row, the head of the deceased was covered by a fragment of a small slab.

A dump over the graves, extended from the upper eastern edge of the depression two meters west; its northern and southern limits are homogeneous with the necropolis. In the dump were almost 2000 fragments of statues mixed with stones, fragments of sandstone slabs, whole and broken sandstone baetyls (standing pillars), fragments of bronze, and pottery dating from the Nuragic to the Roman Age. The dump was covered with earth that filled the depression at one time. The grayish color of the earth in which the statues were found was caused by the decomposition of the surface of the statues. The dump was made after the necropolis was no longer in use; some fragments have been found in the settling trench of the vertical slab west of the necropolis, removed in antiquity.

The chronology of the dump is given by the pottery sherds found

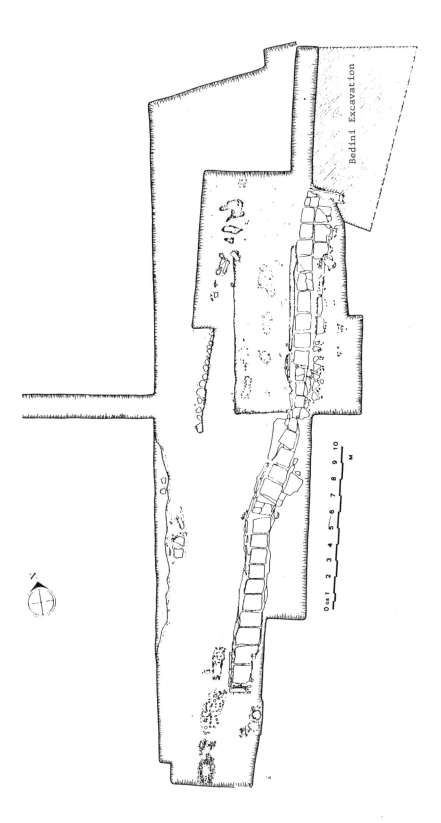

Figure 4.2 Plan of excavation at Monte Prama in Cabras

mixed with the fragments of statues since the upper level of the filling was disturbed by plows. The sherds belong to rims of Punic amphoras of the 4th to 3rd century B.C., and to small cups of the same period with oblique, straight walls and small, inward-turning rims.

The close association of the necropolis with the statuary is shown by their proximity. The fact that no traces of statues were found in another necropolis, a few meters north, with small pits lined with slabs, strengthens the hypothesis of relationship.

The alleged temple (Lilliu 1975-77) does not exist. The so-called columns are in reality baetyls, and the capitals are, as will be seen, large models of terraces belonging to nuraghi. There is no possibility that a temple is buried, because the sterile, compact red earth is covered by a low humus layer which often leaves the natural ground uncovered.

Near the necropolis a round Nuragic hut is visible, 20m southwest of the graves, a small squared construction with walls in opus caementicium, about 300m northwest on the slope, and a big Nuragic hut, 500m south, in which a late Punic and Roman Republican place for votive offerings can be seen. On the top of the hill is Nuraghe Monte Prama, and further south, Nuraghe Cann'e Fadosu.

The fragments of statues found in the dump, carved in chalky white sandstone, are very easily cut and decompose easily. These can be classified as: statues of boxers and warriors; models of Nuragic towers; and models of Nuragic fortresses.

Of the 25 over-lifesize statues, 17 represent boxers, bare-chested, with a belt holding a kilt that sometimes reveals the sex. The left arm holds a curved shield on the head, fixed to the arm with a decorated arm-band (fig. 4.3). The right arm is raised and the forearm and fist are covered by a leather sheath. On the edge of the hand is a projection, perhaps of metal. A cap covers the head, as we can see in some well preserved specimens, descending on the back under the nape and on the cheeks, with two long bands. Sometimes two or more braids descend from this cap which might be made of leather.

The form of the head is massive, especially in profile. The back is a compact spherical volume, on which the edge of the cap is modelled in very low relief. The profile view is marked by a hollow semicircular ear and the clean step of the eyebrows over a strong straight nose. Frontally, the head is characterized by a triangular face, Daedalic in aspect; the forehead and nose create a 'T' shape, with double-ring eyes (fig. 4.4). The measurements vary from head to head, but the outer ring is always double the inner. The torsos are large, with rather stiff modelling; the back is flattened and decorated only by a belt with two triangular points. Chests are barely modelled and the torsos are steeply tapered at the waist (fig. 4.6).

Although only eight warriors are preserved, there are many more types, as is the case with the small bronze figurines. Some figures wear a short cloth to the thighs, on which a plate with curved sides hangs, sometimes from a pectoral decorated with several patterns: straight horizontal, horizontal curved, or vertical stripes. On one torso is a grooved, triangular-patterned band. On another torso, unfortunately a fragment, the chest is covered with cloth with zones of vertical stripes, resembling leather armor. As in the boxers the backs are flattened and, on two specimens, we see a quiver and a sword, which probably has a lunate hilt. On a fragment of a torso, the lower part of a fringed stole, decorated with engraved patterns of triangles, is visible on the back.

The torsos have arms broken at the elbows, but we can recognize the iconography of the arms at the sides, flexed forward. Only one head is well preserved, and this shows the same style as the boxers' heads (fig. 4.5). It is covered by a horned and crested helmet, going back just at the nape. The mouth is marked with an angular groove. Another head has on the back chevron-patterned hair. All the heads have braids going to the chest. The warriors have narrower waists than the boxers.

Gloved hands with a brassard, holding a bow next to its lower end, belong to statues of archers (figs. 4.3, 4.8). A 50cm long fragment of a bow, curving in at its end, must be recognized as the upper part. Ends of small horns and a knob may belong to horned helmets. A hand-held shield made of strips arranged in multi-directional patterns, reveals characteristics of several typologies of warriors, well known in the small bronze figurines.

The calves of some legs belong to statues of warriors: two have chevron-patterned bands or greaves, whereas another has a plain figure 8-shaped greave. Some fragments of right hands stretched in the gesture of the worshipper-warriors survive. The patterns in the gloved hands, clothes, bands, and greaves are engraved in a linear technique, rather than a modelled one.

There are eight preserved bases, often with at least one foot broken off at the ankle (fig. 4.9). The bases are roughly square on the upper surface, and their dimensions vary, whereas the height is uniform. Since the bases are finished on all sides,

it appears that they were not set in a hole, but raised up in full view. The feet are parallel; their positions on the bases are all the same: closer to the front than the back edge, 19 to 20cm apart and 5.5 to 7cm from the side edges. The front parts of the feet are low, with flattened toes, and are narrower at the heels. The length of the feet is constant: 37 to 38cm. The malleoli are always represented. The relative slenderness of the egg-shaped ankles (11 x 16cm at the break), constantly broken at 8 to 12cm from the base, points out this part as the weakest.

There are some other fragments of statues of boxers or warriors: four heads and some calves, in which can be observed the angular shin. One calf joins with a fragment of a small foot.

There are also several fragments of models of Nuragic towers and Nuragic fortresses, the first in which the top terraces of the towers are shown. Three sizes are observed. The first consists of very few large specimens, previously called "capitals" (Lilliu 1975-77). In reality this interpretation fails both because of the close analogies with the smaller Nuragic models and because of the absence of the columned temple, as we have seen above. The upper part of these terraces is thoroughly polished, showing that they were not used for architrave supports. The dimensions of the two best preserved specimens are identical (ca. 70cm; parapet h. 21cm); the parapet is decorated with two patterns of triangles and the bastion with grooved lines, for rendering the supports.

This decoration is identical on the terraces of the smaller group (ca. 36/38cm; parapet h. 11/12cm) (fig. 4.10). The parapet has a concave section. On the upper part, the terraces have a central conical projection, explained as the covering of the inner stairs. It is very likely that these terraces belong to the large central towers of the Nuragic fortresses; the dimensions vary.

More numerous are the small terraces (ca. 13 to 19cm, parapet h. 7 to 8.5cm), divided into two typologies for the parapet patterns: one is decorated with triangles, the other with staggered vertical lines.

The models of Nuragic fortresses represent the central tower, surrounded by a square, eight-towered wall (fig. 4.11). The wall is horizontally divided by a bastion. The corner towers are integral, whereas the others are divided in the same way as the wall. The central tower is very tall, and we must suppose it was crowned by a second-level terrace. The bottom surface of these models presents nine small square projections, corresponding to nine towers, perhaps for placement on a base.

Several whole or fragmented baetyls, previously interpreted by Lilliu as columns (Lilliu 1975-77), have been found in the dump, together with the statue fragments. The baetyls are well finished on the upper surface as well, and show in their upper third the rectangular holes typical of the Oraggiana specimens (Lilliu 1982:97).

An examination of the statues shows that in style and technique, they are translations of the widely diffused and better known small bronze figurines. Large and heavy, they stand on relatively thin ankles; the limbs and the weapons stand out from the body very clearly, without any support; they make lively protrusions. The style of the statues shows us further their derivation from metal-working techniques. The faces have clear and rigid carving in the eyebrows and a straight nose. The calligraphic superficiality of the details, scantily scratched on the surface, are so obviously outlines, that they convince me that the statues were carved by craftsmen not used to working in this material (stone) in such dimensions. They have copied accurately some iconographic details (and we see the reasons for their choice below) of the bronze figurines, but the translation suffers because of the inappropriate size and the requirements of a different material.

The stone statues are exact counterparts of the bronze figurines. The boxers offer a very close comparison to the bronze boxer from Cala Gonone (Dorgali) (Tronchetti 1980). The posture is identical: the gloved right hand is raised while the left holds the shield on the head; the triangular skirt leaves the chest naked. The shape of the face is also similar in having a T-scheme created by the eyebrows and nose, and double-ring eyes. We must observe that stone statues of boxers are in the majority, whereas in bronze, the boxers are really very few. Here we can only formulate hypotheses, destined to remain open, as to how the boxers must be interpreted. I have written of this elsewhere, and shall return to it below, offering my interpretation of the Monte Prama context (Tronchetti 1980; 1981a).

The statues of warriors find stylistic comparisons in a group of bronze figurines from the sanctuary of Abini (Teti-NU). In this sanctuary, groups of bronze figurines were found in the second half of the nineteenth century; these groups were mixed and P. Bernardini is presently working to identify the separate styles. The group that is stylistically closest to the Monte Prama statues, consistently shows the triangular Daedalic face and the facial T-scheme with double-ring eyes, whereas others, like the Uta group, have cylindrical faces with

almond-shaped eyes. We can compare
the facial structures of the com-
militoni (fellow-soldiers) (Lilliu
1966:170) and of some worshipper-
warriors; one shows us a braid on the
chest and a shield, like some
specimens from Monte Prama (Lilliu
1966:239) but a better comparison is
with the figurine set between two
deer heads on a votive sword, also
from Abini (Lilliu 1966:367). The
archer wears a horned, crested
helmet, a short cloth on which the
pectoral plaque hangs, and greaves to
protect the legs. The left arm with
the brassard is flexed forwards and
holds the lower side of the bow; the
right hand is stretched in a worship-
ping gesture. On his back is a
quiver. The hair is chevron-patterned at the nape; the Daedalic face
has great rounded eyes and the familiar T-scheme. The flat feet are
parallel. As is the case with the
boxer from Dorgali (Tronchetti 1980),
the worshipper-archer from Abini is a
model for a literal translation to
large-stone statuary. Passing on to
single details, we can compare the
swelled calves and although to a
lesser degree, the chevron patterns
on the statues with those on the
bronze handles with animal figurines
or heads from Abini.

The bronze figurines are the
only comparison for the Monte Prama
statues. Apart from these, Nuragic
stone statuary is almost nonexistent; only a bull's head from S.
Vittoria di Serri and few models of
nuraghi, discussed below, are known.
However, one piece very close to the
Monte Prama heads survives. It is a
fragment of a head with the T-scheme
and double-ring eyes, found among the
objects recovered in a pit destroyed
by robbers, near Narbolia, about 15km
from Monte Prama, and now being
studied by R. Zucca. The objects,
unfortunately without stratigraphic
context, are from the Nuragic to the
Late Punic Age. The close resemblance of style and material link

this head to the Monte Prama statues,
and is perhaps an indication of their
geographical distribution.

The comparisons for the models
of Nuragic towers and fortresses are
much more widespread, both in bronze
figurines and in stone sculpture
recently studied (Moravetti 1980;
Ugas 1980). The fortresses recall
the bronze models from Ittireddu and
Olmedo (Lilliu 1966:383-385). In
both, the walls have four taller
towers in corners, crowned by terraces with concave parapets. In the
Olmedo specimen the walls have a
parapet also, with vertical lines.
In both models the central tower
stands out against the walls and the
corner towers. Among the stone
specimens, the better comparison is
with the limestone model from S.
Sperate (Ugas 1980), a Nuragic fortress with four corner tower walls
and a big central tower; the outward
sloping part of the walls and the
corner towers have cut grooves, like
the lines on the Monte Prama models.

Comparisons for Nuragic towers
can be found in specimens from the
Nuragic villages of Barumini and Palmavera. The one from Barumini has the
tower crowned by a terrace with a
straight parapet, on which is the
conical projection seen in the Monte
Prama models. Several other specimens of terraces survive, but their
sizes are so small that some seem to
be miniaturistic.

A triangular pattern is the more
common decoration of the parapets;
the vertical, staggered lines are
known only on one specimen, a model
of a Nuragic fortress with three
towers crowned by a terrace, found
near Nuraghe Cann'e Fadosu (Ugas
1980). This parapet has vertical,
staggered lines and three steps at
its top. In the relief panel, a man
is represented, poorly preserved. He
has been interpreted either as a wor-
shipper (Ugas 1980) or as a warrior

scaling the wall of the Nuragic fortress (Lilliu 1981:189-190). At the present, I can just point out the remarkable resemblance between the facial structure as well as the dress to those on the Monte Prama statues. This large (preserved height 87cm) model from Cann'e Fadosu, of the same material as those from Monte Prama, is very important for my attempt to reconstruct the significance of the Monte Prama context discussed below.

After outlining the iconographic and stylistic features of the Monte Prama statues, we must now consider the problem of chronology. As is well known, these are the two horns of the dilemma: The first (Lilliu 1975-77; 1981:190-192; 1982:200-204) fixes the statues in the eighth century, on the ground of stylistics limited to Sardinian production; this position, however, does not consider the origin and the manufacture of large-size stone statuary in the Mediterranean area. Furthermore the chronological data drawn from the necropolis have been passed over in silence, in the mistaken notion that the necropolis was violated in a time following its settlement and the carving of the statues. The excavation has shown that the graves were without doubt untouched; therefore there was no intrusion of later objects. The second position, before a hypothesis of the necropolis (Tronchetti 1978) was confirmed by the data (Tronchetti 1978; 1981a; 1981b), fixed the statues in the seventh century, inserting them in the Orientalizing cultural milieu. The chronological data drawn from the necropolis are not many, but are basic for the proposed dating. In the first place, we must remember that the necropolis goes from south to north, and was used for some time. The dead are always without grave goods, and the pottery sherds found in the earth filled in the graves and between the grave-slabs belong to types not exactly datable, being

mostly sherds of carinated bowls that date from the ninth to the sixth centuries B.C. (Lilliu 1982:110; 152). Only grave number 25 gives us an object of secure chronology. In the filling earth of the pit, some damaged bronze necklace-elements, one of rock-crystal, and one bone or ivory scaraboid seal in a pseudo-Hyksos style, datable from the very late 7th century downwards have been found (Gjerstad 1935:810-820). That gives us a precise fixed point for the chronology of the latest graves, and this is strenghthened by some fragmentary faience necklace elements in graves 24, 27 and 29.

The chronology is confirmed by the Daedalic features of the statues: the triangular face and the rigid frontal view (Ridgway 1977:19; Boardman 1978:13-17). The archer on the votive sword from Abini is dated by Lilliu to the Orientalizing period (Lilliu 1966:367). Lilliu (1941-42) places the fashion of the braids descending on the chest in the 7th century also, as well as the chevron-pattern handles from Abini, with animal figurines or heads, even if this has less value. In the case of the Nuragic models, the close comparisons with the Ittireddu and Olmedo figurines bring us to the same century (Pallottino 1950:52; Lilliu 1952). The triangular patterns on the Nuragic model parapets can be compared with the applied ones of some Nuragic bronze ships of the full Orientalizing period.

In contrast, Mediterranean life-size and colossal stone sculpture appears in the full Orientalizing period, with the earliest specimens appearing mostly in Crete, but in other parts of Greece too (Ridgway 1977:19; Boardman 1978:13-15), and diffuses very quickly to other Mediterranean countries like Etruria (Cristofani 1978:71) where the source seems to have been Oriental in one case at least (Cristofani 1978;

Colonna 1973:540), and in which other statues are translated from small figurines.

The Monte Prama area is placed in a very favorable geographical location for the growth of settlements and relations with both foreign countries and the interior of Sardinia (fig. 4.1). The large gulf of Oristano, into which the Tirso river flows, and the Cabras lagoon, both offer easy access and the right situation for hunting, fishing and agriculture; the Tirso valley is an easy pathway to the hinterland. Accordingly, the environs of the Cabras lagoon are very rich in settlements from the prehistoric to the Roman age. The density of nuraghi is very high; they are settled on almost all the hilltops, and of course there is the Phoenician settlement at Tharros (Capo S. Marco), not more than 10km from Monte Prama. Likewise the evidence of Orientalizing contacts and imports is remarkable, for example the bronze Cypriot candelabra from Nuraghe S'Uraki near S. Vero Milis, at the northern edge of the Sinis, and from Tadasuni, near the Tirso valley. They belong to a well known type, dated from the late 8th to the 7th century B.C. (Raubitschek 1978:649-707). The bronze figurines from Abini (on the way from the Tirso to the Taloro river valley), dated in the 7th century, have already been cited. Among the others are the above-mentioned archer on the votive sword, the bronze handles with animal figurines or heads (a similar specimen has been found in Tadasuni too), and a bronze dagger-hilt with a warrior in low-relief (Lilliu 1966:452); these are all significant.

From the data mentioned above, I shall now try to propose an interpretation for the Monte Prama context. The first difficulty is that the Monte Prama situation is unique in Sardinia. A necropolis of indi-

vidual pit graves has no comparisons. The one other sure example of an individual grave is the large chest-shaped grave from Senorbì (Taramelli 1931), where a warrior was buried with a sword and some bronze fragments, perhaps of a cuirass or such. This grave also can be placed in the Orientalizing period, whereas the situation and the background of some graves from Is Arutas, quite near to Monte Prama, are not so clear (Santoni 1977). It is interesting, however, to notice examples of individual burials, in contrast to the traditional collective burials in the giants' tombs; this provides evidence, even if we must be cautious because of scanty documentation, for the appearance of a new funerary ideology. It is also meaningful that the Monte Prama statues were not furnished with grave goods. This would perpetuate the tradition of the giants' tombs, strengthened by the presence, at Monte Prama, of the Oraggiana type of baetyls, always related to the giants' tombs in the former period. But whereas in the giants' tombs the collective burial was ennobled by the monumental view, in the Monte Prama graves the meaningful element is the large-size statuary.

The excavated area of Monte Prama, however, cannot be regarded as only a necropolis; this definition seems too restricting. In fact, all can be placed within political and social contexts: the baetyls are consistent with this aspect, the statues do not contradict it, and neither do the stone nuraghe models. The models from Barumini and Palmavera both come from particular huts, explained as the meeting place of the village chiefs. The one from Barumini is placed in the later sub-phase of Nuragic II, dated after the middle seventh century for the materials, among which is a Cypriot type fibula (Lilliu 1982:148). It is interesting to observe that the village at Barumini is rebuilt quite differently from the preceding village; even if it is still somewhat undeveloped, we nevertheless see some public works such as drains, wells, steps and even a street linking up the new houses with centripetal planning. Even if the comparison must be taken cum grano salis, these works remind us of the public works of the early sixth century in Rome (Pallottino 1977).

We have seen the Sinis rich in material (and undoubtedly cultural) imports during the Orientalizing period; we have also seen that these cultural influences elsewhere give rise to sometimes remarkable changes. How can we set Monte Prama against this background, and what kind of ideology does the statuary express? For this attempt at reconstruction we were helped by the bone analysis made by Dr. F. Mallegni of the Anthropology and Human Palaeontology Institute, University of Pisa, and Dr. F. Bartoli of C.A. Blanc Museum in Viareggio. Of the twenty-eight graves, from which the bones could be tested, fourteen are definitely male, three female, three possibly male, three possibly female, and five are children; the adults whose sex is uncertain may be all female. The age at death ranges from fourteen to fifty years, with a very rough average of twenty-seven years. We are in the presence of the burial of the members of a family group in a prearranged and distinct area. I speak of a prearranged and distinct area, because just at the northern end of the necropolis, another necropolis, cited above, lies, excavated by Dr. A. Bedini (cf. fig. 4.2).

I think the Monte Prama area must be interpreted as a funerary area with a particular social, cultic and political purpose, in which prearranged spaces were assigned to designated families and where, in one case at least, we find a heroic cult of the family which now, we can call aristocratic. The idealization of the 'gens' is shown by the typical values of the aristocratic class, as are known elsewhere in the Mediterranean area. The statues approximate the bronze figurine iconographies which can be related to these values. Concepts of valor, 'arete,' are shown by the statues of warriors: the family members are political and military chiefs. If, as I think, my interpretation of the boxers is right (Tronchetti 1980) - men performing in sacred games - the statues of boxers are related to the religious aspect of the community, in which the family has a leading role. The nuraghe models fit easily into this background. We have seen their arrangements in politically significant rooms in the villages, and we must add that they seem to have been objects of private cult too. A large, centripetally planned house, like those at Barumini from the second half of the seventh century, comes from the sanctuary of S. Vittoria di Serri, and has a larger and better-finished room, in which an object stands on a base. This can be explained as a model of the front of a building, with two side towers linked by a parapet with panels, and on the center, perhaps a bull's head. The models from Monte Prama can be explained as the symbolic representation of the political power of the family, shown in its most meaningful monument, namely the Nuragic fortress. The ideological link between the statues and the models, is physically expressed by the above-mentioned model from Cann'e Fadosu.

The proposed reconstruction presupposes a new phase in the economic and social structure of Nuragic society, at least in the area cited; this new view now has been offered by Dr. Paul Bernardini (1982).

The creation of such a large number of statues during such a short time, shows an advanced stage in the division of labor; some families are able to hoard a surplus, which may then be used in exchange and in making their wealth conspicuous.

A significant example of this economic and social change is found in the Sinis; I have mentioned above its rich contacts with foreign peoples at this time. The Phoenician settlement of Tharros, preceded by pre-colonial visits, provides the chief avenue for these contacts. It is appropriate here to remember that among the earliest specimens of large-size stone statues in Etruria, we find those in high-relief in an Orientalizing Caeretan tomb (Colonna 1973). According to Colonna, the types have their sources in the North Syrian art styles of the second quarter of the 7th century; the appearance of these statues may be associated with the presence in Etruria of eastern stone workers who were employed by an aristocratic class. That notion has many simi-larities to my reconstruction of the Monte Prama context; yet there are obvious differences.

The iconography of the statues is closely derived from bronze figurines that are Nuragic in context. The ideology of the statues, however, which are large in size and cultic in function, can only have come from contacts with the Phoenician and/or Italic world. This ideology found fruitful soil in a society in which the aristocrats, controlling the means of production, possessed the surplus that could afford glorification, employed craftsmen, and so accentuated the division of labor inside the community. We are now in the presence of a definable proto-urban society; but this society never developed, both for internal reasons and because strong-armed Punic intervention at the middle of the sixth century broke off the growing process at its very beginning.

CATALOG OF NURAGIC STATUARY FROM MONTE PRAMA

1. Head of boxer (fig. 4.3)

2. Head of boxer (fig. 4.4)

3. Head of warrior (fig. 4.5)

4. Torso of boxer (fig. 4.6)

5. Torso of archer (fig. 4.7)

6. Hand with brassard holding bow (fig. 4.8)

7. Base (fig. 4.9)

8. Terrace of nuraghe (fig. 4.10)

9. Model of Nuragic fortress (fig. 4.11)

Figure 4.3 HEAD OF BOXER COVERING HIS HEAD WITH SHIELD
Preserved ht. 62cm; face ht. 31cm; temples w. 18cm; outer eye diam.
6.1cm, inner 3.1cm. Preserved: the head to the base of the neck; the
left arm holding the shield; a fragment of the shield. Daedalic
triangular face. T-scheme of the eyebrows and nose. Double-ring eyes.
Strong, straight nose with two grooves for the nostrils. The ears are
hollow semi-circles. From the low ears the braids descend. The shield
arm-band is decorated with three patterns of grooves (h. 8.5cm). From
Monte Prama.

Figure 4.4 HEAD OF BOXER

Preserved ht. 45cm; face ht. 30cm; temples w. 16cm; outer eye diam.
5.4cm, inner 2.7cm. Preserved: the head, in fine condition. Daedalic
triangular face. T-scheme as the previous entry, without the braids.
Engraved mouth. On the right cheek hangs the band of a leather cap.
From Monte Prama.

Figure 4.5 HEAD OF WARRIOR
Preserved ht. 36cm; temples w. 15.5cm; outer eye diam. 5.8cm, inner
2.9cm. The cap helmet, horned and crested, goes to the nape over the
ears. From the helmet descends the braids. Stylistic features of the
face as the first entry. The mouth is an angular groove. From Monte
Prama.

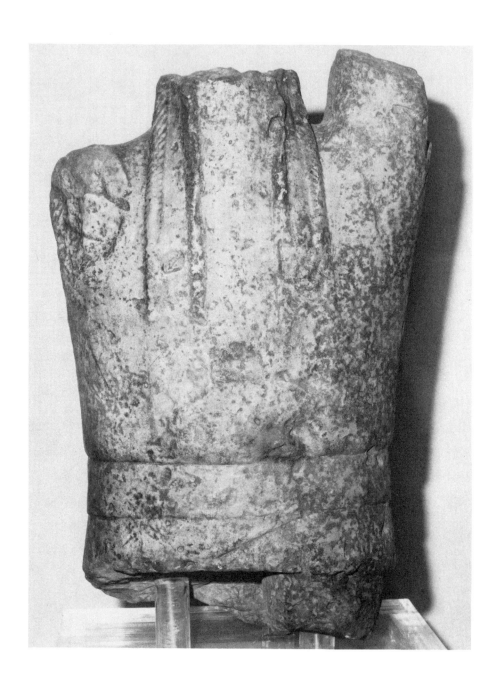

Figure 4.6 TORSO OF BOXER
Preserved ht. 94cm; shoulders w. 63cm; waist w. 50cm. Preserved: the
torso from the shoulder to the waist. The torso is bare. Left arm
raised, for holding the shield. A belt holds the triangular skirt. On
the breast, a pair of long braids. From Monte Prama.

Figure 4.7 TORSO OF ARCHER
Preserved ht. 88cm; shoulders w. 70cm; waist w. 40cm. Preserved: the
torso from the shoulders to the waist. The archer wears a cloth on
which a plate hangs from a decorated pectoral. On the breast a pair of
braids. Arms broken; the left is flexed at the elbow. On the back is
the quiver and the sword with a moon-shaped hilt. From Monte Prama.

Figure 4.8 HAND WITH BRASSARD, HOLDING BOW
Preserved arm l. 26cm; arm diam. 14cm; preserved bow l. 26cm; bow diam.
9cm. Preserved: the arm to the wrist and the lower part of the bow.
The inner left arm wears the brassard; the gloved hand holds the bow.
From Monte Prama.

Figure 4.9 BASE
W. 49cm; preserved l. 30cm; ht. 12cm. Preserved: part of the base with
the fore feet with flattened toes. From Monte Prama.

Figure 4.10 TERRACE OF NURAGHE
Diam. 38cm; preserved ht. 29cm; parapet ht. 12cm. Concave bastion with
grooved lines. Concave parapet with
two rows of triangle patterns. The
upper face is polished, and has a
conical projection.   From Monte
Prama.

Figure 4.11 MODEL OF
NURAGIC FORTRESS
Preserved ht. 95cm; central tower
preserved ht. 60cm; w. 47cm; preserved l. 40cm. Preserved: part of
the wall and of the central tower.
The wall has three towers on each
side.   The corner towers are
straight, whereas the central ones
are divided by a bastion as is the
wall. From Monte Prama.

REFERENCES

BERNARDINI, PAOLO
1982   Le aristocrazie nuragiche nei secoli VIII e VII a.C.
                 Proposte di lettura. ParPass 203:81-101.

BOARDMAN, JOHN
1978   Greek Sculpture. The Archaic Period. London.

COLONNA, GIOVANNI
1973   Cerveteri. StEtr 41:538-541.

CRISTOFANI, MAURO
1979   The Etruscans. New York: Galahad.

GJERSTAD, EINAR
1935   Finds and Results of the Excavations in Cyprus
               1927-1931 (The Swedish Cyprus Expedition, II).
               Stockholm.

LILLIU, GIOVANNI
1941-2   Bronzi preromani di Sardegna. BPI 5-7:179-196.

1952   Modellini bronzei di Ittireddu e Olmedo. StSar
                10-11:67-120.

1975-77   Dal betilo aniconico alla statuaria nuragica. StSar
                24:73-144.

1981   Bronzetti e statuaria nella civiltà nuragica.
                Ichnussa.

1982   La civiltà nuragica. Sassari.

MORAVETTI, ALBERTO
1980   Nuovi modellini di torri nuragiche. BdA 7:65-84.

PALLOTTINO, MASSIMO
1950   La Sardegna nuragica. Roma.

1977   Servius Tullius, à la lumiere des nouvelles
                découvertes archéologiques et épigraphiques.
                CompteRendusAIBL:216-235.

RAUBITSCHEK, I.K.
1978   Cypriot Bronze Lamp Stands in the Cesnola Collection
                of the Stanford University Museum of Art.
                Proceedings of the 10th International Congress of
                Classical Archaeology. Ankara - Izmir September 27 -
                30, 1973:699-707.

RIDGWAY, BRUNILDE SISMONDO
1977   The Archaic Style in Greek Sculpture. Princeton.

SANTONI, VINCENZO
    1977   Osservazioni   sulla   protostoria   della   Sardegna.
                    MélRom 89:447-468.

TARAMELLI, ANTONIO
    1931   Senorbì (Cagliari) - Tomba di età preromana scoperta
                    presso l'abitato. NSc:78-82.

TRONCHETTI, CARLO
    1978   Monte Prama. StEtr 46:589-90.

    1980   Bronzi figurati dal Dorgalese. Dorgali. Documenti
                    archeologici. Sassari:195-198.

    1981a   Monte Prama. StEtr 49:525-28.

    1981b   Prima Italia. L'arte italica del I millennio a.C.
                    Roma:40.

UGAS, GIOVANNI
    1980   Altare modellato su castello nuragico di tipo
                    trilobato con figura in rilievo dal Sinis di Cabras
                    (OR). ArchSarda:7-32.

5. MEDITERRANEAN COMPARANDA FOR THE STATUES FROM MONTE PRAMA

Brunilde Sismondo Ridgway

My assigned task - to provide comparanda within the sphere of Mediterranean sculpture for the Sardinian statues from Monte Prama - might be discharged very rapidly: there are no true parallels. I have nevertheless taken my mandate to include a brief review of other works in monumental sculpture which appear throughout the Mediterranean area, with the exception of the Etruscan examples which will be treated by Larissa Bonfante (chap. 6). I shall therefore present some of this material, and will stress in turn, where appropriate, medium, technique, style and iconography, in an effort to provide general background and possible sources of inspiration for the Sardinian sculptures, given their anomalous appearance within their own island.

Any such attempt must be governed by two main considerations: the civilization reviewed must have had the potential for contacts with Sardinia, and the time span must be compatible with the chronology of the Monte Prama sculptures. Since their date has been variously given in preliminary publications as ranging from the eighth to the sixth century B.C. (Lilliu 1982:200; 204; 8th c.; Tronchetti 1978:589; 1st half of 7th c.; Tronchetti 1981:527: terminus ante quem non at the end of the 7th c., at least for the end phase), I have covered approximately the same period, collecting only examples of sculptural productions that could theoretically have been known to the Sardinians or have influenced them in some fashion. I have therefore omitted the colossal statues from

Neo-Hittite territory, for instance, or Assyrian and Egyptian monuments, as unsuitable for comparison either with respect to medium (the hard basaltic stone of the Palanga (Özgüç 1971:pl. 39)) and Kululu statues (Özgüç 1971:102-109), the alabaster of the Assyrian reliefs, the granites and diorite of Egypt) or with respect to style (there is nothing Egyptian in the statues from Monte Prama). I shall, however, consider sandstone and limestone as virtually interchangeable. They are equally soft stones, easy to cut when freshly quarried, and comparable to wood in their potential for piecing and carving into flat surfaces and decorative detail. Their tendency to split and break may have also influenced the choice of subject matter and the specific style of sculpture (Adams 1978:134-140).

Geographically, I have taken into account the North Syrian and Phoenician coast, Cyprus, the Greek islands of the Aegean including Thasos, Samos, Crete and the Cyclades, Greece proper and, in Italy, South Italy and Sicily, the Apulian and Picene regions, as well as the area of Luni. Spain and North Africa, although potentially quite influential, have yielded nothing that I could consider comparable. The Iberian production in soft stone seems to be too late for our purposes. As for Punic North Africa, sculpture in the round is similarly late; the sole kouros-like torso in limestone, at present on display in the Utica Antiquarium, is - to my knowledge - unpublished and could be considerably later than the Archaic date its appearance suggests. It is, moreover, under clear Greek influence in style.

Not much sculpture is extant from the eighth century B.C., but some evidence leads us to believe that more might have existed, although it has not come down to us. Ancient Greek sources mention wooden statues of "remote antiquity" and perhaps of more or less aniconic appearance, around which entire sanctuaries grew. We no longer have such statues, but the architectural remains from the sites can be dated with a fair degree of approximation and attest to their existence. An obvious example is the Heraion at Samos, where the earliest Hekatompedon is dated around 750 B.C. (EAA s.v. Legno; Herrmann 1975:35-48; Ohly 1953:25-50).

Closely related to wood carvings were the Greek sphyrelata, made of hammered bronze sheets around wooden cores. It has, in fact, been recently argued (Neumann 1982) that the shape of the exterior must have followed closely that of the interior figure, since the nails fastening the bronze plates would have been useless without an immediate backer. The earliest examples come from Crete: one male and two female figures from the Late Geometric temple at Dreros, probably representing Apollo, Leto and Artemis (Boardman 1978:11; fig. 16). The structure which housed the sphyrelata has been traditionally dated to the late eighth century B.C., but the figures themselves had been considered as late as the mid-seventh century. Comparison with similar material from a datable tomb context has reasserted their eighth century manufacture, perhaps under Oriental influence and contemporary with the temple (Boardman 1967:61).

The Dreros sphyrelata are considerably larger than statuettes, but cannot rank as monumental sculpture:

the male figure is 0.80m, the taller female 0.40m. It is nevertheless well known that larger sphyrelata existed; for instance, the colossal Apollo Amyklaios near Sparta mentioned by Pausanias (3.18.9-19.5). More important is the issue of style. Despite some stylization, the Cretan figures are anatomically articulated, with relatively soft transitions from feature to feature, and are thus in no way comparable to the abrupt plane changes and decorative patternization of the Sardinian sculptures.

Closer in style is a limestone head from Cretan Amnisos, also dated to the second half of the eighth century, although found in an unstratified context (Adams 1978:5-8). It is half life size and carved almost in relief technique, the facial features lying only on the frontal plane, with virtually no depth to the head. This effect is partly caused by a possible split in the limestone, which tends to break along vertical, well-defined surfaces and may have removed the rear portion of the sculpture; it could also, however, be due to Oriental influence. It has been pointed out, in fact, that the receding chin, the prominent nose, the elongated proportions of the face of the Amnisos head have strong affinity to North Syrian renderings. A cogent comparison, although considerably removed in time, is the seated statue of King Idrimi from Alalakh (Strommenger and Hirmer 1964:figs. 174-175), ca. 1500 B.C. Since we know that Oriental artisans established workshops in Crete, having fled their homeland to avoid the Assyrian threat, it is logical to assume that the Amnisos head was produced by such immigrant carvers.

The Cretan sculpture resembles the Sardinian figures only in its overlarge and rounded eyes, but present appearance may be misleading. Found in the same context were several eyes made of bone, one of which is said to fit exactly into the orbital cavities of the Amnisos head. The practice of inlays is common in Oriental sculpture but has, to my knowledge, not been postulated for the Sardinian figures.

One final piece may be mentioned, although its attribution to the eighth century is disputed and may be erroneous: a peculiar limestone stele from Kimolos, an island near Melos, part slab and part human torso provided with arms and once, presumably, also with a head (Kontoleon 1970:49-53, pl. 23; Andronikos 1961-2:152-210; Kurtz and Boardman 1971:220). Although the piece has been cited to suggest that funerary statues developed from slab-like grave markers, through progressive anthropomorphism, other interpretations are possible: stelai and freestanding sculptures may be completely independent in their development, and the Kimolos "stele" could even be an extreme form of compression of a seated figure which was therefore conceived as fully anthropomorphic despite its apparent plank-like appearance.

Anthropomorphism, or rather naturalism as opposed to stylization, is a major issue in discussing the statues from Monte Prama. Although their human appearance is unmistakable, their degree of stylization and simplification of forms is so high that few other sculptures can be profitably compared, even when we come down into the seventh century, the period that saw the acknowledged beginning of monumental Greek statuary in stone.

Large-scale figures in limestone occur in seventh century Cyprus, an island of particular interest because its history may be considered similar to that of Sardinia in terms of openness to outside influences. The earliest seem to be the votaries from the sanctuary at Arsos: figures of

women or perhaps priestesses carrying symbolic images of bulls and adorned with elaborate jewelry (Gjerstad et al. 1937:585-586; pls. 185-186). Similar beads and necklaces have been found in tomb contexts and provide reliable evidence for a late seventh-century date. Except for some affinities in technique conditioned by the medium, the Arsos statues have little in common with the Monte Prama warriors, not only because of subject matter but also because of their style, which resembles Egyptian and Phoenician renderings and is therefore much less abstract.

To find Cypriot warriors we must turn to the numerous terracottas (approximately 2000) found around the open-air altar at Aghia Irini (Gjerstad et al. 1935:777-783; pls. 189-223). They have been dated to the final phase of the sanctuary, which was abandoned around 500 B.C., after the last of several floods, but which goes back into the Bronze Age. Most of the terracotta offerings were however set up between the end of the seventh century and the time of the last destruction. The warriors differ from the Sardinian figures both in their kouros pose and in the details of their attire, since their conical helmets cannot compare with the tight cap of the Sardinian boxer or the horned headdress of the archer. Yet Cyprus has produced an often-quoted example of a horned headdress, on the bronze statuette from Enkomi dated to the twelfth century B.C. (Dikaios 1962). We have to assume that the horns on the bronze have ritual and religious symbolism, and accept that the gap in time is too great to allow meaningful connections with the Sardinian figures.

Seventh century Crete sees a considerable production of sculpture in limestone, but again female figures predominate and many of them come from architectural contexts.

The seated lady from Gortyn (Adams 1978: 25; pls. 10-11; Boardman 1978: fig. 30; preserved height 0.80m) is useful as an example of decorative carving - the pattern on her skirt - probably made with the cutting compass, a tool that might have been used for the eyes of the Monte Prama statues. It also shows the abruptness of transitions typical of the medium, but it is impossible to judge how much of this rendering is due to the natural stylization of a seated pose and a heavily robed subject. The same comments apply to the architectural figures from Prinias dated around 620 B.C., both the seated women and the standing woman carved in relief on the soffit of the lintel (Adams 1978:65-78; pls. 17-18; Boardman 1978:figs. 32.1-4).

One more Cretan statue, important because no architectural context exists for it, is the colossal upper torso (pres. H. 1.04m) of a female figure from Astritsi, variously reconstructed as seated or standing (Davaras 1972; Adams 1978:35-40; Boardman 1978:fig. 29; Sipsie-Eschbach 1982). Here too, the limestone has been exploited for its engraving possibilities, but the figure's abundant hair and damaged face make her hardly comparable to the Sardinian statues with their rounded cranium and sharp features. I may also cite the well-known "Dame d'Auxerre" (Boardman 1978:fig. 28; Adams 1978:32-34), plausibly attributed to a Cretan workshop, because on a much smaller scale (H. 0.65m) it reproduces the type of the Astritsi colossus, thus documenting iconographic consistency regardless of scale; it may therefore support the possibility that the Monte Prama figures parallel the repertoire of the Sardinian bronzetti.

Limestone found only relative use in Greece which had access to plentiful sources of good statuary marble. Although limestone as a

medium was never abandoned, especially for architectural compositions, the true expression of Greek sculpture should be sought among marble statues, carved under strong influence from Egypt, both iconographic and technical. The kouros type - the naked male figure standing with one foot advanced and arms down the sides - finds its beginnings in the second half of the seventh century, some of the earliest examples coming from the island of Thera. Note that at least one of them, when complete, would have been over life size, ca. 2.50m in height (Boardman 1978:fig. 61; Kontoleon 1958). In their abundant long hair and lack of movement in their poses, they differ from the Sardinian figures; on the other hand, the aligned feet of the latter do not have the suggestion of striding implicit in the kouros' posture. The feet of a kouros at Thera were found embedded in the rock near an ash urn hidden on a rockshelf, thus attesting to the funerary use of the statue as early as the late seventh century B.C. (JHS-AR 12 (1966):18, fig. 31). Whether the kouroi could be considered depictions of the deceased or, as I believe, images of Apollo in his capacity as protector of corpses (Ridgway 1977: 49-59; 149-150; Simon 1973), is irrelevant in this context, since similarity in appearance and function need not reflect identical symbolism in Greece and in Sardinia.

Other kouroi of the late seventh century are such, both in scale (triple life size) and iconography (the presence of attributes, such as a belt and perhaps other ornaments) that a special identity can be postulated. Inscriptions also support the theory that a colossal male figure in Delos represented the god Apollo donated by the Naxians (pres. H. of upper torso: 2.20m, total H. probably 10.0m). The head and many parts of the statue are missing, but the stylization of the shoulder blades and the simplification of other parts of the anatomy (a large hand is still extant) indicate an abstract approach to the human figure somewhat comparable to that of the Monte Prama statues (Boardman 1978:fig. 60; Ridgway 1977:45; bibl. on 78). On the island of Thasos another monumental statue carrying a ram could represent either a human votary bearing an offering, or the god Hermes a protector of herds and domesticated animals. The piece has been dated to the early sixth century, but its unfinished state, without articulated facial features, makes precision impossible (H. 3.50m; Boardman 1978:fig. 69; Ridgway 1977: 73; 82).

Few kouroi in limestone are known, and these somewhat late in date; the requirements of the type - such as the removal of the Egyptian backscreen which could serve as a support, and the opening of the legs in stride - made it unsuitable for the relative brittleness of limestone, so that kouroi in that medium, rather than the predecessors of their marble brothers, are likely to be daring imitations produced in areas without local marble quarries and where sculptors were more familiar with the carving properties of wood and terracotta, akin to soft stone (Ridgway 1975).

Marble was also, however, used to render the female figure, despite its more compact appearance engendered by the presence of a long costume. Although the kore type does not seem to have the same stylistic derivation as the kouros, some of the earliest Greek statues represent women (or rather goddesses) and are now taken to be approximately contemporary with the limestone sculptures from Crete, an area without marble quarries where the harder stone was never properly exploited (Boardman 1978:24-25; Ridgway 1977:85-112). The well-known "Nikandre" (ca. 650 B.C., H. 1.90m)

from Naxos, dedicated to Artemis in Delos, probably depicted Apollo's divine sister (Boardman 1978:25, fig. 71; Ridgway 1977:86-87). Other early female images (e.g., from Thera and Samos) are less clearly identifiable. The same uncertainty exists for the perirrhanteria supporting large water basins, a form of sculpture which had been thought earlier than the first free-standing marble statues but which may in fact constitute once again a parallel if short-lived development (Ridgway 1977:88-89; Boardman 1978:25-26). Of these, the most elaborate known so far is the large and varied stand from Isthmia, dated ca. 675-650 B.C. (Boardman 1978:fig. 74). A new restoration and publication of all the Isthmia sculptures from the sanctuary of Poseidon (Sturgeon 1984:262) will reveal the greater complexity of the work; in addition, traces of color have been noticed, which indicate elaborate attire for the supporting korai. Other perirrhanteria are considerably smaller and therefore should not be ranked as free-standing statuary, but rather as functional products of the "minor arts."

Some female figures were also made in the sphyrelaton technique continued from the previous (eighth) century. At Olympia, an almost life sized face in bronze was clearly meant to be fastened to a wooden core and may depict a divinity (Mallwitz 1972:56-57, fig. 59). Another, better preserved figure shows a one-winged "monster" of uncertain identification, which may be as late as ca. 580 (Boardman 1978:fig. 134; JHS-AR 12 (1965-66):9, fig. 12); because of her human features it can be properly described as almost life size. A smaller bronze kore from Samos can nonetheless be reconstructed to an original total height of ca. 1m (Buschor 1961:73-74, figs. 313-316). Also in Samos, a wooden statuette now destroyed has been dated around 630 B.C. (Boardman 1978:fig. 49), but is likely to reflect the earlier cult image or other monumental wooden sculptures of Hera adorned with real clothing, as was traditional for several Oriental statues like the Artemis of Ephesos, the Artemis of Perge and the Aphrodite of Aphrodisias.

By the end of the seventh century, therefore, sculpture in large or natural scale was widespread in the Aegean area: in wood, hammered bronze (sphyrelaton), limestone and marble. The Greek types - the kouros, the kore, the seated figure - were well established and were especially popular in marble, the medium par excellence, which was supplanted by bronze only when the technique of hollow casting was mastered, toward the end of the Archaic period. During the sixth century B.C. many more statues were produced, and proportionately more have survived, so that a survey would be impossible within the limits of my assignment. On the other hand, Cretan production virtually stops, and Cypriot sculpture acquires a character of its own which marks it as different indeed from the Sardinian figures. For this final period I have therefore decided to concentrate solely on those examples, from both Greece and Italy, that may bear some resemblance to the Monte Prama statues, despite the fact that a tendency toward increasing naturalism characterizes most Greek works. The similarities are therefore to be sought in specifics, rather than as a whole: in the use of the same medium, in the employment of certain tools, in the depiction of a related subject or in the purpose of the sculpture.

Beginning with Greece, we may consider for the medium of limestone the colossal female head from Olympia, generally identified as Hera but possibly from a sphinx, since attribution of the piece to the cult image within the Heraion seems highly

dubious (Boardman 1978:fig. 73; Sinn 1984). The date given to this head has varied, from the late seventh century (in imitation of Orientalizing ivories, or because of the association with the specific building) (Ridgway 1978:124, n. 2) down to as late as ca. 560 B.C. (EAA s.v. Olympia:643). Not only is the head in limestone, but the iris and pupil of each eye have been marked with a cutting compass, although not with the emphasis given to the Monte Prama heads.

Also in limestone are the two brothers Dermys and Kittylos, from Tanagra in Boiotia (Boardman 1978: fig. 66; H. of figures 1.47m). Although the inscription on the monument reads like a votive offering, the purpose of the sculpture may have been funerary, and the typology is a cross between a stele in high relief and statuary in the round with a supporting backscreen. The geometry of the male torso, the engraved treatment of the hair flanking the face and descending onto the chest, and the stylization of the knee muscles bespeak some of the same approach visible on the Sardinian sculptures, although facial features are too damaged to be compared.

A seated statue from Haghiorghitika in Arkadia (Adams 1978:130, pl. 34) has been alternatively considered male or female; in favor of the first hypothesis speaks the costume, which includes a triangular tip of a mantle flung back over the left shoulder; for the latter speak the undifferentiated lap and the findspot in a sanctuary of Demeter. The eyes, which would seem to provide a parallel to the Sardinian warriors, should be disregarded because they are a later vandalism now filled in to repair the damage. In all three cases it is useful to note that higher dates have been traditionally assigned to each piece, and that only greater stylistic understanding has allowed us to place them, correctly, in the sixth century. It would seem that limestone, because of its very nature, tends to encourage conservative renderings and decorative engraving, which seem chronologically out of place among more highly modelled contemporary sculptures in marble or bronze. The Arkadian seated figure has even been attributed to the Daedalic period! (Ridgway 1977:123).

Another limestone work differs from all those previously examined because it is in high relief and part of a gable: the pedimental sculptures from the Temple of Artemis at Corfu (Boardman 1978:153; figs. 187.1-6). They too have been dated high, around 590 B.C., on both architectural and sculptural grounds, but they may come down one or two decades. The male figure near the Gorgon - Perseus or Chrysaor according to different opinions - has overlarge eyes and pupils cut with the compass, and so has Medusa; but in both cases, I believe, the effect was intentional and the magnification can be ascribed to the apotropaic function of the feature rather than to normal canons of human renderings. The same engraved circles are found on the large animals flanking the central composition, an additional example of the ease with which limestone can be decorated.

In terms of iconography and funerary purpose, I have not included the marble Kroisos whose epitaph declares him killed in battle (Boardman 1978:fig. 107), because nothing in its rendering differs from the standard kouros type and helps identify it as a warrior. I have rather selected a votive hoplite, from the sanctuary of Hera at Samos (Boardman 1978:fig. 176), although as late as ca. 530 B.C. It is over life size and fragmentary (preserved H. of upper torso 0.86m), but what remains of its greaved leg shows some of the

sharpness of rendering of one Monte Prama fragment (Freyer-Schauenburg 1974:pl. 67.78C). The torso, however, and the helmeted head, are much more naturalistic, despite their relative stylization. An earlier example of a man in armor has been found in Sparta, but it is too ill preserved for proper analysis; its damaged state may also be responsible for its tentative assignment to the seventh century (Delivorrias 1969: 131-132, no. 2; pl. 121a-b).

Funerary statues, as we have mentioned, are largely uncharacterized, but far more distinctive are gravestones, which identify the deceased as an athlete, a warrior or a man of status. A fragmentary relief from the Kerameikos cemetery in Athens has retained one of the earliest representations of a boxer, with bandaged wrist, broken nose and cauliflower ears (Boardman 1978:fig. 233). Although the stele can be dated around 560 B.C., its naturalism is well beyond the stage of the Monte Prama pugilist. Another Attic gravestone, the well-known Aristion stele (Boardman 1978:fig. 235), shows a warrior in armor, but here again the affinity with the Sardinian statues is limited to subject matter.

Statuary coming from Italy falls into distinct categories. In Sicily and South Italy we have many monuments from the Greek colonies, and it would be useless to review them in this context since their affinities are definitely with the Greek or the Asia Minor world rather than with the Sardinian sculptures. Of interest is what is perhaps a Phoenician product found in the "stagnone di Marsala," the lagoon in front of ancient Lilybaion; but the dating of the statue to the mid-sixth century or somewhat earlier would exclude provenience from that city, which was founded only in the early fourth century B.C. (Falsone 1970:esp. n. 9). The statue, today in the Palermo museum, probably comes from Motya, a Phoenician colony since the late eighth century B.C., and may have fallen into the sea while being salvaged from the island destroyed by Dionysios of Syracuse in 397 B.C. Comparison with the Monte Prama statues is invited by the fact that Sardinia too knew intensive Phoenician-Punic contacts and occupation, but this comparison functions rather as a contrast. The Sicilian piece is in hard volcanic stone, and all its details conform to Egyptian schemata of standing male figures, as adopted by Cypriot and Phoenician sculpture. This juxtaposition almost serves, therefore, to highlight the non-Punic character of the Monte Prama statues.

Northern Italy has produced over fifty stelai from the territory of Luni (Anati 1981:30-31; 34), which have proven difficult to date. Some of them may go back to the third and second millennium before Christ, but several should come from the seventh/ sixth centuries B.C., as part of a tradition that probably continued until considerably later. Three types have been distinguished on the basis of the head shape:

1) the head is carved together with the slab-like body (Pontevecchio type);

2) the head is separate from the body and looks like a "chapeau de gendarme" (Malgrate type); and

3) the head assumes a rounded form closer in width to the neck than to the body (Reusa type).

This last type bears some resemblance - like a primitive cousin - to the rounded shapes of the Monte Prama figures. In addition, the weapons incised or carved in low relief on the surface of the stelai (and which are a major criterion for typology and chronology) ensure that most

among the males represented are warriors. Yet it is important to note that the stelai from the Lunigiana territory never developed into completely anthropomorphic renderings; since the Sardinian statues have been, at least implicitly, connected with the baetyls of Sardinian prehistory (Lilliu 1977), this consideration may be relevant here.

Moving southward in the Italian peninsula, we find several important monuments in soft stone coming from the Picene region. Some of them, like the sixth century stele from Guardiagrele (H. 0.83m; Cianfarani 1969:76, no. 178; pls. 84-85), consist of a slab-like body to which a head in high relief has been applied against the background. That the total composition represents a warrior has been made clear through the engraved indication of disc armor, the kardiophylakes which appear both in front and back. The same type of armor occurs on the famous Capestrano Warrior (Cianfarani 1969: 78-80, no. 182; pls. B; 89-93; dated to the mid-sixth century), colossal in size (H. 2.53m with plinth) and perhaps having a funerary function, not so much because of the two spears, one on either side, which seem to support the figure upright, but because extensive traces of red coloring have been brought out by the latest restoration. The practice of painting funerary statues in red (the life-giving color of blood) is well attested even in Greece and in many other non-related areas. The Capestrano Warrior (fig. 6.1) shares with the Monte Prama statues the general iconography (although not the details of specific weapons or the active pose), the strong stylization of the human form, the sharpness of the shins combined with the rounded contours of legs and thighs which look almost inflated, the abrupt emergence of the nose from the facial plane, the relative roundness of the eyes, the abbreviated indication of ears and mouth (note however that the Warrior is taken to be wearing a mask). Armor and ornaments carved in low relief against the surface of the body, as if without volume of their own, reveal also a somewhat similar approach.

Attributed to the Picene culture, but coming from Numana (Marche) rather than from Abruzzo, is the intriguing head in the Ancona Museum which so resembles the Capestrano Warrior as to need no separate description or justification for inclusion (H. 0.42m, limestone, 6th century B.C. Bianchi Bandinelli and Giuliano 1976:fig. 108). Much more primitive, yet dated to the fifth century B.C., is a limestone head from Pietrabbondante (near Campobasso) now in the Chieti Museum (Bianchi Bandinelli and Giuliano 1976:fig. 135), which suggests the continuation and perhaps even the provincialism of some patterns, such as the overlarge, rounded eyes crowding the massive nose.

Finally, one more Italic culture and one more sculptural production should be considered: the Daunian stelai from the region of Manfredonia (the so-called Beccarini area in Puglia), which have recently received thorough cataloguing and illustration (Nava 1980). Their actual function is uncertain, since they were mostly found out of context and in highly fragmentary state, but in at least two or three cases a funerary connection seems likely (Nava 1980:10). Chronology (which is given as ranging from the seventh to the fifth century B.C.) has to depend largely on typology, which is complex and based on the ornamentation engraved on both sides of the stone slabs; only one of these stelai has preserved its head (total H. 1.13m; Nava 1980:27, no. 122; pls. 64-65), and in this case the "finial" is aniconic and abstract in shape. Yet single heads have also been recovered, some of which still retain traces of back braids or neck decoration, thus ensuring connection with certain types of stelai. In a few instances it was possible to note that the head had been carved separately and attached to the "body" by a tenon. If the typology established at present is correct, however, the stelai became progressively more abstract and stylized, from initial renderings which included a plastic indication of the arms against the torso, through a more linear and schematic treatment, to an abstract stylization of the shoulders in lunate form, ending in the total elimination of arms and hands. Aniconic heads may be concurrent with more articulated types and represent both men and women; likewise, the bodies engraved on the slabs, from their ornaments, can be separated into female figures and warriors with shield and other weapons.

Among the relatively few heads preserved, some have a rounded headdress, like a horizontal disc, which recalls the helmet of the Capestrano Warrior (Nava 1980:no. 1179; pl. 387); others wear a conical hat which may also represent armor (Nava 1980: no. 727; pl. 233; pres. H. 0.215m, attributed to type I). One more face belongs to the spheroid type and sports incised bangs and back braid (pres. H. 0.18m; Nava 1980: no. 950; pl. 316, type II). All these heads are characterized by the sharpness of their features and the roundness of the eyes, which are cut with a compass. In this respect, they show true affinity to the Monte Prama sculptures, although they certainly do not resemble them in the stylization and decoration of the body.

To summarize this long review, I can repeat my initial statement that I could find no true parallel to the Sardinian statues. Although sculptural production begins in earnest throughout the Aegean and even the wider Mediterranean area during the seventh century B.C., the approach to the human form does not assume such high degrees of stylization; on the other hand, poses seem more static and less expressive. It is only in Italic territory that stylistic affinities can be detected, strongest perhaps in the heads crowning the Daunian stelai, but also in some Picene works. The Monte Prama figures appear almost as a cross between the two trends - the naturalistic Aegean current and the stylized Italic approach - but do not seem clearly indebted to either influence. They are a most exciting discovery that needs to be evaluated in its own terms.

Notes on the Bibliography

In supplying documentation for the monuments cited in my presentation, I have attempted to provide, whenever possible, an easily accessible and comprehensive source of illustration, especially if of relatively recent date of publication - hence my many references to Boardman 1978 as a convenient handbook of early Greek art. In that book, captions to the figures are particularly extensive and informative, although text commentary is brief. More extended discussion and bibliography can usually be found in Ridgway (1977) and, for the limestone pieces, in Adams (1978). Although my discussion of Anatolian, North Syrian and Palestinian monuments supplies minimal references - since I find that sculptural production unrelated to the Sardinian - useful illustrations can be found in H. Frankfort, The Art and Architecture of the Ancient Orient (The Pelican History of Art, rev. ed. 1970), especially pp. 290-322. See also E. Akurgal and M. Hirmer, The Art of the Hittites (Harry N. Abrams, New York 1962) pp. 124-143 and pls. 103-150. Note especially pls. 106-107, illustrating the statue of a king from Malatya, limestone, H. 3.18m, dated to the end of the eighth century B.C. but definitely Assyrian in style and therefore not comparable to the Monte Prama figures. Finally, in citing sources of illustrations and within my main text, I have attempted to give either the preserved or the calculated height of the monuments mentioned, whenever useful for proper assessment.

REFERENCES

ADAMS, L.
    1978   Orientalizing Sculpture in Soft Limestone from Crete and Mainland Greece. BAR Suppl. Series vol. 42.

ANATI, E.
    1981   Le statue-stele della Lunigiana. Milan: Jaca Book.

ANDRONIKOS, M.
    1961-2   Hellēnika epitaphia mnemeia. Deltion 17.1:152-210.

BIANCHI BANDINELLI, R. AND A. GIULIANO
    1976   Etruschi e Italici prima del dominio di Roma. 2nd Italian ed., Milan: Rizzoli.

BOARDMAN, J.
    1967   The Khaniale Tekke Tombs II. BSA 62:57-75.

1978   Greek Sculpture. The Archaic Period. London: Thames
               and Hudson.

BUSCHOR, E.
1961   Altsamische Standbilder 5. Berlin.

CIANFARANI, V.
1969   Antiche civiltà d'Abruzzo. Rome.

DAVARAS, C.
1972   Die Statue aus Astritsi = AntK Beiheft 8. Bern.

DELIVORRIAS, A.
1969   Chronikà, Lakonia. Deltion 24.2:131-132.

DIKAIOS, P.
1962   The Bronze Statue of a Horned God from Enkomi. AA
               1-39.

FALSONE, G.
1970   La statua fenicio-cipriota dello Stagnone. Sicilia
               Archeologica 10:54-61.

FREYER-SCHAUENBURG, B.
1974   Samos XI: Bildwerke der archaischen Zeit und des
               strengen Stils. Bonn.

GJERSTAD ET AL.
1935   Swedish Cyprus Expedition II. Stockholm.

1937   Swedish Cyprus Expedition III. Stockholm.

HERRMANN, H.-V.
1975   Zum   Problem   der   Entstehung   der   griechischen
               Grossplastik. Wandlungen, Studien zur antiken und
               neueren Kunst = Festschrift für E. Homann-Wedeking
               35-48. Waldsassen-Bayern.

KONTOLEON, N.
1958   Theräisches. AthMitt 73:117-139.

1970   Aspécts de la Gréce préclassique. Paris.

KURTZ, D. AND J. BOARDMAN
1971   Greek Burial Customs. Oxford.

LILLIU, G.
1975-77   Dal "betilo" aniconico alla statuaria nuragica.
               StSar 24:73-144.

1982   La civiltà nuragica. Sassari.

MALLWITZ, A.
1972   Olympia und seine Bauten. Munich.

NAVA, M.L.
    1980   Stele Daunie I. Sansoni: Florence. 2 vols, text
                    and plates.

NEUMANN, G.
    1982   Lecture   on   the   beginnings   of   Greek   sculpture,
                    delivered at Bryn Mawr College in December 1982.

OHLY, D.
    1953   Die Göttin und ihre Basis. AthMitt 68:25-50.

OZGUÇ, T.
    1971   Kültepe and its vicinity in the Iron Age. Ankara.

RIDGWAY, B.S.
    1975   A Poros Kouros from Isthmia. Hesperia 44:426-30.

    1977   The Archaic Style in Greek Sculpture. Princeton.

SIMON, E.
    1973   Die Tomba dei Tori und der etruskische Apollonkult.
                    JdI 88:27-42.

SINN, U.
    1984   EKTYMON. Der sog. Hera-Kopf aus Olympia. AthMitt
                    99:77-87.

SIPSIE-ESCHBACH, M.
    1982   Bemerkungen zum Torso aus Astritsi. AA 487-91.

STROMMENGER, E. AND M. HIRMER
    1964   5000 Years of the Art of Mesopotamia. New York: H.N.
                    Abrams.

STURGEON, M.
    1984   AJA 88:262 (abstract).

TRONCHETTI, C.
    1978   Monte Prama. StEtr 46:589-90.

    1981   Monte Prama. StEtr 49:525-27.

6. THE ETRUSCAN CONNECTION

Larissa Bonfante

At first sight these fragments of statues, hands and heads and torsos, all larger than life, are startling and somewhat upsetting, but Carlo Tronchetti's careful, plausible reconstruction of their chronology, iconography, function and significance allows us to deal with them by placing them in a world familiar to us, the Orientalizing period of the seventh century B.C. This was everywhere a rich new world of exchange, experiment, invention and local adaptation. All over the Mediterranean the unexpected is the rule, diversity and surprises the order of the day. In Italy we are just beginning to be able to say something about the development of monumental sculpture in reference to material which is only recently coming to light.

Much of what we know about large size sculpture in Italy is a recent acquisition. Gone are the days when the Capestrano Warrior (fig. 6.1) stood in strange and splendid isolation - he has brothers and sisters all over Italy, and beyond. More surprises surely await us in this area. Meanwhile, a survey of the large-scale sculpture from Etruria will not take long. Dating from the seventh century are the following monuments:

1. The fragmentary statues (figs. 6.2, 6.3) from the Tumulo della Pietrera, in Vetulonia, were excavated in the 1880's. Dating from the mid or late seventh century B.C., the fragments may have belonged to some twelve statues, six male and six female. They are just under life size. Bust of best preserved female fragment: h. 64 cm. Male fragment, waist to knee: h. 44 cm.

2. In 1971 were found two seated male figures carved in high relief as guardians on either side of the door in the antechamber of a seventh-century tomb at Ceri, near Cerveteri. They have not yet been fully published. Near Eastern influence is clear from their beards, and their seated pose with folded arms holding the symbols of their rank and status (swords, or a lituus?).

3. Another recent discovery, from archives rather than in the field, restores to us the original setting of three well-known terracotta statuettes. They are large scale, though not nearly life-size (47 cm). Originally there were five, three males and two females, seated at a banquet table in a tomb in Cerveteri, the Tomba delle Cinque Sedie. (Nineteenth-century restorers, anxious to provide "complete" statuettes, combined various fragments to form the two hybrids, with female heads and male bodies, in the British Museum; and another, correctly restored as a male, in the Conservatori Museum).

4. The only monument not to come from a funerary context is the life-size (149 cm) terracotta statue from Murlo (Poggio Civitate) near Siena, affectionately known as "The Cowboy." With its companions, some of whom were apparently female, it originally sat on the roof of a building, part of a monumental complex, a great palace or "sanctuary." These statues date from the early sixth rather than the seventh century B.C.; but they belong in the context of the local

73

Figure 6.1 Warrior from Capestrano, Abruzzo. Sixth century B.C.
Chieti, Museo Civico.

Figures 6.2-6.3 Fragmentary statues from the Tumulo della Pietrera, Vetulonia. Mid-seventh century B.C. Florence, Museo Archeologico.

craftsmanship and exhibit the same kind of independent, "primitive" quality as earlier statues, where the Near Eastern influence has been variously interpreted by each artist. The desire to bring forth large scale sculpture leads the Etruscan artist to turn his special abilities and training to the task, and to "invent" in this way something outside any consistent tradition. Here, we see craftsmen trained as potters, using their special skills to make these large, outsize figures, quite outside their usual range of small pots decorated with mould-made heads and other figures.

Elsewhere in Italy, outside Etruria, the desire to produce monumental sculpture resulted in some strange figures.

1. In 1934 the discovery of the impressive (209cm) statue of a warrior (fig. 6.1), from Capestrano in the Abruzzo (now in the Chieti Museum, it is soon expected to move into a new museum in Capestrano), created a sensation. It was thought to be unique. It actually turns out to be one, though certainly the most outstanding, of a group of large stone statues from the middle Adriatic region, all of funerary origin. With the Warrior were found a smaller female figure (his wife?), whose torso alone has been preserved (26cm); and a number of fragmentary companions. In the last few years a number of statues of this type, scale and destination have been found. One, known as the "Devil's Legs," from the vicinity of L'Aquila (70cm), is close to the Warrior in form. The torso of another warrior, perhaps originally armed, from nearby Atesa was discovered in 1971 (86cm). Then there is a torso from Guardiagrele (83cm) wearing the same kind of armor as the Capestrano Warrior; and a helmeted head of another warrior, found farther north, near Ancona (45cm). In spite of the Oriental-

izing decoration on his armor, the Capestrano Warrior is now dated to the sixth century B.C. rather than the seventh.

Elsewhere in Italy, anthropomorphic series of statues are based on their earlier form of funerary stelai. Chiefly under Etruscan influence were added some more "modern" features, occasionally even writing.

2. Stelai from Liguria, in northwest Italy, stele lunigiane, are plentiful in the seventh century. There is a male model, shown with belt and armor (an axe and two spears; the same armament was placed in the warriors' tombs), and a female version, with dress, breasts and necklace.

3. Somewhat wilder are the stele daunie, recently pubished, and exhibited in the Castello at Manfredonia. These also represent men and women, with gloves, decorations, figures and scenes incised directly on the body.

Beyond Italy, to the north, in an area influenced by Greek culture mediated by way of Etruria, has come to light (1962) a figure halfway between a stele and a kouros. A reconstruction (fig. 6.4) shows this life-size statue (150cm; 170cm with base) in its original position, crowning the mound of a tomb in Hirschlanden, Germany. Armed and belted, it protected the grave and memorialized its owner as a hero. Today, it is in the Stuttgart Museum.

Yet nothing that we have seen speaks for an Etruscan connection for the sculpture from Sardinia elaborated by Carlo Tronchetti. So far, there are no real links. of the kind that might be expected, and perhaps will be found, for there was contact and exchange between Sardinia and Etruria. That the Etruscans liked Sardinian bronzes is clear, for a

Figure 6.4 Reconstruction of funerary mound with Hirschlanden warrior.
Seventh century B.C.

bronze boat was buried in the seventh-century Tomba del Duce at Vetulonia (Gras 1980); and a handsome bronze statuette came to Vulci (Camporeale 1967).

Be that as it may, there are no Etruscan comparanda for the statues we have seen; nor is there evidence for any direct contact. There are, however, parallels, similar responses to the problem of producing monumental sculpture from scratch.

The statues from the Pietrera Tomb in Vetulonia, the Cowboy from Murlo, and the Capestrano Warrior illustrate these parallels. For they too, like the Sardinian sculpture, are related to small-size statuettes known to the local artist, rather than to large scale models imported from the outside.

Scholars agree that the models for the female statues from Vetulonia must have been something like the ivory caryatid supports on precious footed cups found in the seventh century Barberini tomb at Praeneste. Made in southern Etruria, of ivory or in cheaper bucchero imitations (figs. 6.3-6.4), they were exported, and could easily have been available to the sculptor who carved the Vetulonia statues. In these small figurines we find the same hairdress, the so-called Hathor lock or curl in front, the back braid falling over a long back mantle and the dress with tight belt. The tight-lipped face of the Pietrera head (fig. 6.2) has also

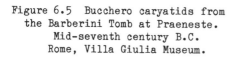

Figure 6.5 Bucchero caryatids from the Barberini Tomb at Praeneste. Mid-seventh century B.C. Rome, Villa Giulia Museum.

Figure 6.6 Bucchero vase from the Regolini-Galassi Tomb, Cerveteri. Mid-seventh century B.C. Vatican, Museo Etrusco.

been thought to show the influence of terracotta techniques. The delicate relief decoration of the belt resembles the Orientalizing tracery on the body of the cup.

The fragments of the kouros-like male statues seem closer to small bronze statuettes made in northern Etruria than to contemporary, large-scale Greek models. Certainly the perizoma or shorts which they are wearing is no longer found on Greek sculpture at this late date. Unfortunately the fragmentary condition of the Pietrera statues does not permit us to make close comparisons. We can see the same distant, indirect relation to the kouros type on the Warrior from Capestrano. The influence is that of the Greek kouros; a life-size, standing figure. But this is indirectly, by way of Etruria, rather than directly. To this kind of figure has been added the Etruscan perizoma, and, very carefully represented in all its details, the local

type of armor. The artist is fascinated by the idea of a colossal statue. He had visual models, but they were not Greek.

As long as the figure was unique, seemingly unrelated to any tradition, scholars turned to literature to explain its strange, stiff pose. But there is no need to recall Polybius' account of setting out the corpse in public, propped up on two spears. The statue is now no longer unique; there are others, similarly moving awkwardly towards an impressive, colossal appearance. Brendel (1978:101) has shown, by means of convincing stylistic parallels, that the influence at work on the statue was that of small-scale bronzes, the so-called "skirted kouroi" of northern Etruscan art (fig. 6.7). Though Cianfarani has denied the possibility of such influence, it does seem, at this point, the most plausible way for the provincial artist to have created his monumental statue, which

Figure 6.7   Bronze statuette of kouros with perizoma, from northern Etruria.
Seventh century B.C. Paris, Louvre Museum.

is not only life-size, but realistically dressed with the uniform and armor of a real warrior.

We have seen that the life-size statues crowning the roof of a building at Murlo (Gantz 1972) are also made by enlarging, "blowing up" the features of smaller terracotta figurines: it is clear that it is this change of proportion that accounts for much of their strangeness.

In conclusion we can perhaps agree that the statues from Vetulonia, Murlo and Capestrano share the following features with the Sardinian statues from Monte Prama:

1. Their development as monumental sculpture from small-scale statuettes. Usually, as has been pointed out, the opposite is true: it is small sculpture that tends to reflect large, important works.

2. Form and decoration; these are adapted to the local iconography. Details of dress, armor, gestures are all carefully rendered because of their importance in expressing status, rank, etc..

3. The stylization of the linear surface decoration, more appropriate to metalworking or ceramics than to stone carving.

4. The contrast between rounded, three-dimensional head and flat body.

5. The funerary function of the statues (except for those from Murlo).

6. The absence of any direct influence of Greek art.

7. The adoption of the idea of monumental art.

8. The aristocratic context of this new "ideology," the importance of the family and the honors given to them after death.

There are differences, however, some of which seem to be significant, in spite of the small number of pieces available to us and their scrappy condition:

1. In Etruria the proto-urban phase gives way to the development and growth of real cities. The innovation of monumental sculpture is accompanied by other features characterizing the growth of a city: the technique of writing, and monumental architecture. Elsewhere in Italy, the city never came to its full flowering. In Sardinia, we have seen, this development was cut short by the Carthaginians.

2. No women are represented in the group from Monte Prama.

3. The subject matter, in the Sardinian group, is limited to warriors, boxers, and fortifications. The Capestrano Warrior and his companion apparently all represent armed warriors, except, of course, the woman. The Etruscans include, from an early period, the aristocratic sport of hunting in their iconography, ritual scenes, and soon, under Greek influence, banquet scenes and mythological figures.

4. I do not know what to make of the architectural models. Are the earlier terracotta models of hut urns from south Etruria and Latium to be thought of as having a similar significance? A later tower model, from Vulci, has recently been interpreted as a lighthouse.

In conclusion, we are beginning to see how, for a while, the excitement of the changes taking place in the Orientalizing period stimulated artists and patrons in many places to create for the first time brave new forms of monumental sculpture. In doing this they followed their own local traditions, and expressed their native customs, religion and society. The Greeks were the ones to bring to the attention of all these people touching the Mediterranean such life-size sculpture. We have seen, however, the deep difference between the Greek concept of such sculpture and these western, native interpretations. Should the idea of "blowing up" small-scale sculpture to large size perhaps be considered a typically "barbarian" response to this Greek innovation, one which presupposes less a sharp break with the past than the adaptation of former ways to fit a new fashion?

Acknowledgments

Photo credits: 2-3. Soprintendenza alle Antichità, Firenze. 4. From Zürn. 5. Villa Giulia Museum. 6. Gall. Mus. Vat. 7. Museum photo, Paris, Louvre.

REFERENCES

Etruscan-Sardinian Relations

CAMPOREALE, G.
1969   I commerci di Vetulonia in età orientalizzante 94-97. Florence.

GRAS, M.
1980   Sardische Bronzen in Etrurien. Kunst Sardiniens 126-133.

LO SCHIAVO, F.
1978   StEtr 46:25-46.

1980   NUR.

1981   Ichnussa.

MARRAS, L.A.
1981   ...Monte Sirai. RSF 9:187.

ZUCCA, R.
1981a   Ceramica etrusca in Sardegna. RSF 9:31.

1981b   Nuove acquisizioni... ArchSarda 31.

Statues from the Pietrera Tomb, Vetulonia

BONFANTE, L.
1975   Etruscan Dress 25; 32; 35; 116; 138; figs. 28; 57. Baltimore.

CAMPOREALE, G.
1963   Gnomon 35:289-98.

1967   La tomba del Duce 94-96. Florence.

FALCHI, I.
1893   NSc 152-153., 509-514.

1894   NSc 335-339.

1891   Vetulonia e la sua necropoli antichissima.

HANFMANN, G.
1936   Altetruskische Plastik I:37-53.

HUS, A.
1961   Recherches sur la statuaire en pierre étrusque archaïque
          97-134. Paris.

LEVI, D.
1926   NSc 176-188.

PINCELLI, R.
1943   StEtr 17:47-113.

Other Monumental Sculpture in Etruria

BIANCHI BANDINELLI, R.
1972   Qualche osservazione sulle statue acroteriali di Poggio
          Civitate (Murlo). DialAr 6:236-47; reprinted in L'arte
          etrusca (1982)315-25. Rome.

BONFANTE, L.
1975   Etruscan Dress figs. 14-16; 121. Baltimore.

CRISTOFANI, M.
1978   L'arte degli etruschi. Produzione e consumo.   Turin:
          70-72; 131-135; figs. 32-35; 104.

COLONNA, G. AND F.W. VON HASE
in   La tomba delle statue. StEtr.
press

GANTZ, I. EDLUND
1972   The Seated Statue Akroteria from Poggio Civitate (Murlo).
          DialAr 6:167-235.

PRAYON, F.
1974   Zum ursprünglichen Aussehen und zur Deutung des Kultraumes
          in der Tomba delle Cinque Sedie bei Cerveteri. Marburger
          Winkelmann-Programm:1-15.

1975   Zur Datierung der drei frühetruskischen Sitzstatuetten aus
          Cerveteri. RömMitt 82:165-79.

1975b   Frühetruskische Grab- und Hausarchitektur.   Heidelberg:
          108, pl. 60; with refs. for Tomba delle Cinque Sedie,
          Tomba delle Statue.

SPRENGER, M., AND G. BARTOLONI
1983   The Etruscans nos. 47-48; 55. New York.

Capestrano Warrior and Related Statues

BRENDEL, O.J.
    1978   *Etruscan Art* 100-101. Harmondsworth.

CIANFARANI, V. (ED)
    1969   *Antiche civiltà d'Abruzzo*. Rome.

    1976   Culture arcaiche dell'Italia medio-adriatica. *PCIA* 5:
               61-63; 71-92.

    1978   *Culture adriatiche antiche di Abruzzo e Molise*. Rome.

ORLANDINI, P.
    1978   L'arte dell'Italia preromana. *PCIA* 7:252; 279; pl. 36.

Other Monumental Sculpture in Italy

AMBROSI, A.
    1972   *Corpus delle statue-stele lunigianesi*. Bordighera.

LANDAU, J.
    1977   *Les représentations anthropomorphes mégalithiques de la
               région méditerranée*. Paris.

    1974-8   *PCIA* 3; 5; 7.

    1981   *Prima Italia* 40-46. Rome.

PALLOTTINO, M.
    1981   *Genti e culture dell'Italia preromana*. Rome, with new
               maps.

Hirschlanden Warrior

ZÜRN, H.
    1970   *Hallstattforschungen in Nordwürttenberg* 67-72. Stuttgart.

    1980   *Die Hallstattkultur*. Steyr: Schloss Lamberg.

Proto-urban Civilization

BONFANTE, L.
    1981   *Out of Etruria: Etruscan Influence North and South*. *BAR*
               S103, with refs.

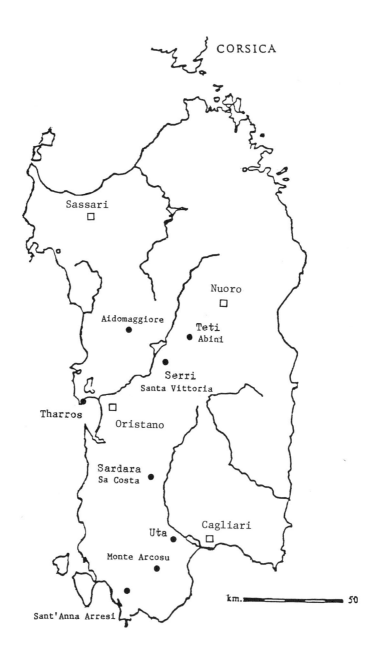

CORSICA

Sassari □

Nuoro □

Aidomaggiore ●

Teti
● Abini

● Serri
Santa Vittoria

Tharros □
Oristano

Sardara
Sa Costa ●

Uta ● Cagliari □

Monte Arcosu ●

● Sant'Anna Arresi

km. ▬▬▬▬▬▬ 50

Figure 7.1 Map of Sardinia showing provincial capitals and sites of
some workshops and finds mentioned in text of chapter 7

7. NURAGIC BRONZES IN THE BRITISH MUSEUM

Francesca R. Serra Ridgway

The purpose of this paper is to present the few Sardinian Nuragic bronzes in the British Museum, London, except for the hoard from Santa Maria in Paulis (Macnamara et al. 1984). There are six in all, kept in the Department of Greek and Roman Antiquities, although for two of them this fact raises some problems. The bronzes are: one chain with spear-shaped pendant (no. 1, below); two miniature sheaths with daggers (nos. 2 and 3); and three figurines of warriors (nos. 4 to 6). The three warriors and one of the sheaths have no known context or provenance; the other sheath and the chain were found in graves 5 and 10, respectively, of the Punic cemetery at Tharros (fig. 7.1), some fifty tomb groups from which were acquired in 1856 by the British Museum from Mons. Barbetti for the total sum of £1000. Most of this material was recently transferred from the Greek and Roman Department to the Department of Western Asiatic Antiquities, where R. D. Barnett is working on their publication. He has confined his selection to the "real Punic" objects, leaving out, at least for the moment, - all the "classical" pieces like black-glaze pottery, unguentaria, etc., and these two bronzes, which are not only of certain Nuragic origin, but were surely found in Punic graves. I suspect we shall never be able to discuss the real significance of this fact, if the final publication of the Tharros groups does not include these pieces.

The catalog that follows will list the specific dimensions and information with the photograph, while the fuller description with comparisons will remain in the text.

1. CHAIN WITH SPEAR-SHAPED PENDANT (figs. 7.2a-b).

The long, heavy chain is made up of fifteen 8 (or S) shaped links of thick cast bronze ribbon, slightly ribbed lengthwise; the pendant is made of hammered sheet bronze, decorated with punched dots and rosettes.

This kind of heavy chain with pendants is well known among Nuragic bronzes, both from tombs and votive deposits (Pinza 1901:cols. 144, 269, pl. 17:11; Lilliu 1966:no. 339 p. 448 ff.). They are usually found in groups of three hanging from a large bronze ring with loops and since two of them were apparently found in a tomb at the dead man's shoulders, they were thought to be ceremonial arm-rings, but the interpretation as personal ornaments has been more recently rejected (Lo Schiavo 1981: 327; fig. 371). Lilliu (1966) pointed in general terms to Etruscan, Picene and Atestine parallels, proposing a date in the 7th century. In fact, many parallels can be found in continental Italy, from at least the 8th century onwards, if not for the particular shape, certainly for the technique of hammered sheet bronze with punched decoration often very close to our example. This technique appears to be a later development in Sardinia when compared with the earlier and more widespread methods of casting, either in moulds or with the lost wax process. But the chains themselves, with their heavy cast rings, are totally unlike any of the innumerable examples from the Italian peninsula, usually made up of smallish circular rings of bronze wire, doubled and linked together in a very simple and characteristic way (the "loop-in-loop" method), and assembled in very different types of pendants and ornaments.

The context in the Tharros cemetery where our example was found is in any case a secondary one; this is not an unknown occurrence, as other similar chains were found in hoards, mixed with Punic and Roman material (Lilliu 1966).

2. MODEL SHEATH WITH DAGGER AND THREE STILETTOS (figs. 7.3a-b).

The shape is triangular, with two small suspension rings (now broken) at the top and middle of one long side. One side shows in high relief three large pins or stilettos with reel-shaped head, each inserted in a strap and possibly made of leather, like the whole real object this miniature piece reproduces. The other side is extremely worn, and only shows a vague shape, apparently of a dagger with wide triangular blade and round pommel.

3. MODEL SHEATH WITH DAGGER AND STILETTO (figs. 7.4a-b).

Triangular shape, with one upper corner rounded, and bottom ending in a globular expansion. Along the straight side are two suspension rings (one broken) with small studs at their sides. They appear to be cast together with the main piece, and not "soldered" as Lilliu states for similar examples (1966:456ff, no. 347ff). On one side a stiletto is reproduced in high relief; it has a globular head followed by three mouldings, and appears as if inserted in a strap. A narrow raised border

decorated with a braid motif runs around the three sides of the plate. On the other side is a dagger inserted into a sheath with horizontal ribs; it has a wide triangular blade with central rib, clearly riveted to the oblique shoulders of the T-shaped hilt; the field around it is plain. Two small sharply bored holes to the left appear to be ancient, since they are covered with a green patina.

Model sheaths of this kind are not uncommon in Sardinian votive deposits of Nuragic age as about thirty are known; they also found their way into Etruscan tombs at Populonia (seven are in the Florence Archaeological Museum), and - like our no. 2 - into Punic tombs at Tharros where there are seven examples. These occurrences must be regarded, at least for chain no. 1 above, as a secondary reuse of the model, possibly as a personal ornament (a pendant). They are improperly called, in the Italian literature, "faretrine" = miniature quivers, which they clearly are not. They are all very similar to one another, but no two are identical, as is of course the case with objects produced with the lost-wax method. Our no. 2 belongs to the most common type with three "pins" or stilettos on what can be considered as side A (Lo Schiavo 1981:figs. 377-378); it is particularly simple in the apparent absence of a decorated frame, while the stiletto heads find their closest parallel in the second example from the right in the cited illustrations (also much like our piece for the very flat relief of the dagger on face B).

This piece is unique in the representation of a single stiletto: two are shown in Lilliu (1966 nos.348-349, both of unknown provenance); the latter also has the raised cordon frame, rounded corner and bottom pommel as our example; round corner and frame also appear on

Lilliu no. 347, where the stiletto is replaced by a thin, long gamma-hilted dagger. The same ribbed "pocket" on side B, bottom pommel, and rings with lateral studs appear in the example in the center of Lo Schiavo (1981: figs. 377-378), whereas the second from left (ibidem) has one neat round hole through the plate in the top corner. Wholly unusual is the example on the extreme left in the cited illustrations, which is larger than average and reproduces an empty sheath, with three large oval holes, to which perhaps three real model pins would be fastened on the side of fig. 378, while a real, small dagger was put in the pocket of fig. 377.

These sheaths correspond most probably to the ones only partially visible in the equipment at the back of the bronze archers (no. 5 below). Similar model weapons are not known, as far as I am aware, either in Near Eastern or Italian votive deposits of the Bronze and Iron Ages, although tiny model weapons are found, together with miniature pottery and sometimes human figurines, in some of the hut-urns of the Early Latial Culture. Both the daggers and the stilettos reproduced in these models correspond to types well attested as real examples in many Nuragic contexts: Pinza (1901:pls. 16:6; 17:14, 15, 18, 19, 23) and Lo Schiavo (1981: fig. 372), for "pins" with variously moulded heads; and again Pinza (1901: pl. 15:12, 24, 31) and Lilliu (1982: fig. 136), for daggers with a large blade. The hilts, made of perishable material, are obviously lost. The type of our no. 3 might in fact be the same as the small example with cast bronze and decorated hilt from Santa Maria in Paulis, which has parallels dated 10th-9th century or earlier (Macnamara et al. 1984:no. 6; 10 n. 68).

4. FIGHTING WARRIOR (figs. 7.5a-c).

The man is standing on straight, slightly parted legs; his right arm is lowered behind, straight, the hand holding a sword pointing slightly above the horizontal, in front; the left arm is stretched frontally at shoulder level, and was probably holding a shield, now lost. The large head, tilted back, has the usual elongated features, with projecting eyebrows marked by oblique incisions; eyes rendered as oval bulges surrounded by a ridge (the lids); very long straight nose; small mouth with lightly marked lips; short square chin; high, projecting naturalistic ears. The head is covered with the usual horned cap, from which the hair emerges in two triangular raised and striated bands on his temples in front of the ears, and two more just behind the ears: the back of the head appears shaven, as are cheeks and chin. The long neck is protected by a wide collar with raised edges, and V-shaped at the back. The thin flat body wears a short tunic with double hem, over which a ribbed corselet, possibly made of leather or sheepskin, and fastened at the back, is on the chest. There are two large shoulder-pieces whose fastening at the back forms a horizontal ring; another ring is slightly below the first one. Two vertical fringed bands hang over the tunic, the right one overlapping a third wider piece of fringed material. Buttocks and genitals are lightly indicated under the tunic. On both shoulders is a projecting element which is higher on the left. The thighs are thin and cylindrical, and very short compared to the man's body; the thin legs are protected by the usual greaves or leg-guards with two back bands. The left arm, very thin and rod-like, appears to be naked; the right arm has a wide ribbed wrist-guard possibly made of leather with raised borders, to which is fastened a large hand-guard with similar edge; the fingers are clearly marked, with long overlapping thumb. The sword the man is brandishing had a long and narrow blade, while the hilt appears to be of the double-pommel or antenna type.

The figurine clearly belongs to the Uta-Abini style, as defined by Lilliu (1966), and can be counted among the finest examples of this fine group. Its closest parallels can be seen in the "warrior with sword and shield" and "warrior with sword and bow," Lilliu nos. 12 and 11 respectively, from the eponymous site of Monte Arcosu in Uta (CA), and now in the National Museum in Cagliari. These form a uniform group with the other figurines from the same site (Lilliu nos. 7 to 10). Considering that our warrior almost certainly held a shield, now lost, in his left hand which is also lost, the main difference between it and Lilliu no. 12 resides in the gesture; the latter has in fact his arms bent at the elbow, and the sword resting on his shoulder, while our example is caught in actual fight - in spite of the standing posture of his legs. This gesture is unusual but not unknown among the many Sardinian bronze soldiers: two examples, very close to ours, are the two fragmentary figurines Lilliu nos. 14 and 15, from Aidomaggiore (OR); whereas no. 103, from the Sulcis area, repeats the posture of the arms, but differs both in clothing and armor, as well as in general appearance and style, it is nevertheless still within the Uta-Abini Group. Also from Sant'Anna Arresi in the Sulcis region is the warrior now in the Museum of the Rhode Island School of Design, Providence, published by Balmuth (1978:no. 2) and cited by Lilliu (1966:63). The perizoma, with prominent phallus, and the style in general make him similar to Lilliu no. 103 (and see no. 6 below), but he wears the same corselet as our present example, still preserving a rod inserted in the rings at the back; his arms, though now broken very

short, show the same fighting position.

The warrior from Monte Arcosu (Lilliu no. 12 cited above) is certainly from the same workshop and possibly by the same hand as ours, shares with him the elongated flat body, big oblong head on a very long neck, and the treatment of the face, with the long straight nose forming a T with the eyebrows. Slight differences can be noted in the shape of collar and gauntlet; in the slightly longer corselet; in the absence of the third vertical band at the back, and of the projections on the shoulders; in the shape of the sword, both blade and hilt; and in the three rather than two rings at the back. To the same hand Lilliu would assign also his no. 13, from Sulcis in the Museo Preistorico L. Pigorini, Rome, which is perhaps the biggest and best of all the Sardinian "bronzetti" (39cm high), and among the oldest known: Winckelmann discussed it in his Geschichte der Kunst (1766). The general features are somewhat shorter, with a larger, rather triangular face; his garment shows three rather than two hems, while the collar has two bands like Lilliu no. 12. Otherwise, the parallels with our warrior extend to the three vertical bands and two rings at the back, the shorter corselet, the shape of the wrist and hand-guard, and apparently the shape of the hilts, both of the sword in his hand and of the dagger emerging from the shield; and more particularly the rendering of the eyes, oval and surrounded by a raised ring.

5. ARCHER DRAWING HIS BOW (figs. 7.6a-b).

The man is standing on slightly parted legs, his left one partly turned to the left and bent at the knee. The head is turned left in full profile; his left arm is stretched laterally to hold a large bow, while the right one, stretched and bent at the elbow, adjusts the arrow at shoulder height. The warrior's head is very similar to our no. 4, even in the horned cap and the hairstyle; it is only less refined in the rendering of the eyes and mouth. The thin elongated body wears the usual plain short tunic with double hem; over this is a rectangular breast-plate with a fringed border round the neck, and partly covering the typical Sardinian gamma-hilted dagger, which is suspended from a bandolier just visible at the back. The thin short legs wear the usual greaves. The left arm is protected by a wrist-guard; on his back, the man carries a quiver full of arrows, to the right of which is attached a dagger or short sword with slightly leaf-shaped blade and double-pommel or antenna hilt, while on the left is a small conical object usually interpreted as a container for the oil necessary to grease the bow; between the top and bottom of this and the quiver there are two projecting horizontal rings: just as for warrior no. 4, these are most probably part of the actual equipment - intended to carry the asta or javelin as seen in Lilliu no. 16 (an archer), or in the warrior in Providence mentioned above with our no. 4. The large bow and arrow are reproduced in all their details, despite the unnatural position and excessive length of both arms, particularly the right one.

This archer is rather unusual among his many Nuragic companions because, like the warrior no. 4, he is shown in actual fight, drawing his bow, and not just standing with his weapon on his shoulder. Here, it is not only the arms that have a different pose, but the whole body, with head in profile and left leg advanced sideways and slightly bent at the knee. The very same position is found in two "specular" figurines from Abini in Teti (NU), Lilliu nos. 17-18, the latter left-handed. They

both repeat, with minor differences (smaller bow, dagger less prominent on the chest, longer horns in no. 17) our archer's features, clothing, armor and arms; they might well come from the same workshop, even if by a different hand, showing in the less elongated proportions of the bodies and legs, with a very large, heavy head. The quiver and dagger at the back are the same, but without the rings. A more complex quiver, with no rings but with the addition of a long plumed asta (javelin), accompanies Lilliu no. 16, again from Abini, that is closer to our example in the slim proportions of head and body, and in the relative dimensions of the large bow. In spite of the distortion of his left arm with the residual bit of the bow, there is no doubt that his right arm has never been so unnaturally long as in the other three examples considered, and its position, together with the forward bending of the head, seems to suggest a moment shortly before the actual shooting, when the arrow is adjusted to the bow before aiming at the target. Also very close in all the details of elongated features, clothing, etc., is Lilliu no. 11 from Monte Arcosu, already mentioned above with our no. 4, that represents the more common type of the resting as opposed to fighting archer; his bow is held on his left shoulder, and a large sword is on the right one; he also has - like no. 12 and unlike our figurine and the three from Abini - the stola showing with two fringed bits in front and two long fringed bands at the back, and the double collar, also present in no. 16 mentioned above; the front dagger is completely covered by the larger breast-plate; the quiver is shorter, and has only one horizontal ring (the second possibly broken, as is part of the string of the bow).

Another resting archer of very similar style but probably by a different hand is Lilliu no. 26, again from Abini; the bow is held on the right shoulder in this case, while the left hand is raised in greeting – a very common feature in a number of these figurines. Other resting or praying archers (Lilliu nos. 27 to 36) are more or less different in details of clothing or armor, but most of all in their style and quality, generally coarser; particularly notable are no. 34 from Abini and no. 36 from Suelli (CA), both miscast and not finished after casting; the latter, with bow and sword as Lilliu no. 11 already mentioned, has a corselet like our no. 4.

Three more shooting archers, with the same stylization of the unnaturally long arms on a horizontal line, come from the sanctuary at Santa Vittoria in Serri (NU): Lilliu nos. 21 to 23; they differ from ours both in costume (tail-skirt, elaborated helmet, etc.) and style, with wiry body and legs, and pointed nose. Two more from a tomb at Sa Costa – Sardara (CA), closer to our no. 6 below in the distinctive round shape of the head covered by a skull-cap, wear a very peculiar 'eastern' armor (Lilliu nos. 24 and 25).

In spite of Walters' publication of 1899, this piece, together with no. 3 above and no. 6 below, was not entered in the Museum's inventory register until 1974 – by which time all information about acquisition and provenance had been lost. But their presence in the Museum before the end of the last century is in itself a strong argument in favor of authenticity.

6.   RESTING WARRIOR/CHIEF (figs. 7.7a–c).

The man is standing on slightly parted legs facing front. The large, rounded head, tilted backwards, wears a tight skull-cap with a longitudinal rib ending with a short tassel in front, and a small triangle at the back. Two triangular striated bands of hair cover the temples in front of the ears; no hair is indicated on the back of the head, nor on cheeks or chin. The arched eyebrows are lightly striated, the eyes rendered with two oval bulges marked by a central circular impression for the iris. The nose is straight, short and slightly snub. A neat horizontal line marks the mouth, with thin lips. The cheekbones are well marked, and the chin rounded. Rounded ears protrude sharply. There is a large, long neck. On the thin body the man wears a sleeveless tunic reaching his hips, under which is a sort of perizoma or short skirt, made of a round cloth overlapping diagonally, in front; from the hem of the tunic two fringed straps hang over the skirt. The naked legs, not too thin, have clear indications for knees, shins and calves, and anklebones, while the toes are not marked in the long, bare feet. The man is equipped with gamma-hilted dagger hanging on his breast from a diagonal strap; the long, thin, naked arms are bent forward, holding a huge knotted stick in the left hand straight in front and linked to the left foot through a bronze strip, while the right hand, resting on the left wrist, holds a large sword now broken with the edge on the left shoulder. The round modelling of the back, with marked buttocks, is in contrast with the flat backs of nos. 4 and 5 above.

This figurine clearly shares the same high quality and basic kind of stylization as nos. 4 and 5, although there are visible differences not only in the attitude and attributes of the warrior, but also in his garments and particularly in his features and style of representation. The latter have a number of parallels among the known Nuragic figurines, whereas the posture, combination of weapons and details of clothing are so far unique. Assuming the knotted stick as distinctive, and perhaps indicating a chieftain according to Lilliu's definition (Capotribu: his nos. 4 to 7), we find that the most obvious difference resides in the large square open mantle, which is as characteristic of the cited examples as it is absent from ours; likewise typical of these chieftains is the greeting gesture of the right hand, with the one exception of no. 7 from Monte Arcosu in Uta, stylistically very close to nos. 11-12, and thus to our nos. 4-5, featuring a large sword resting on his right shoulder. To-gether with Lilliu no. 4 from Santa Vittoria in Serri and no. 5 from Teti in Abini no. 7 wears a double tunic just reaching to his thighs, like all the warriors and archers mentioned with our nos. 4 and 5. The same gamma-hilted dagger hangs from a diagonal strap in front of all the figurines mentioned: only ours shows the strap at the back, otherwise hidden by the mantle; naked legs and bare feet are common to all of them. Only Lilliu no. 6, again from Santa Vittoria, shows a sort of skirt or tunic longer at the back and super-imposed in front like ours; but it is closed with a soft thin belt, knotted in front, and not covered with the short "jerkin" and fringed bands of our no. 6; his arms, even if broken, clearly have a position like the other examples, rather open and so possibly greeting, not superimposed in front as they are in our chief-tain.

But the most telling similarity between these two figurines resides in their heads, in both cases large, round, with full lips and a large neck tapering to the shoulders, and covered by the very peculiar tight skull-cap with a raised band in the center. These characteristic features recur in seven more "bronzetti," which can therefore be considered, together with these two, as a uniform group proceeding from one workshop and possibly by the same hand, within the more general Uta (Abini) style. They are: Lilliu no. 32 (provenance unknown), a praying archer with over-lapping skirt, but with the small

breast-plate, neck-band and horned cap typical of his specialty; no. 46 (from Abini), a soldier with sword and shield, with overlapping skirt and outer sleeveless tunic like ours; no. 47 (Santa Vittoria), a praying soldier, very like ours but for arms, and a longer outer tunic; no. 48 (same site), an offerer with shorter tunic, overlapping skirt and fringed bands, possibly no head-cover, usual gamma-hilted dagger in front; no. 49 (Aidomaggiore, OR), similar, broken and much worn; no. 59 (same site), also badly worn, wearing mantle and knotted belt on the over-lapping skirt like Lilliu no. 6 above, but carrying a double stick with offerings; no. 60 (Santa Vit-toria), another offerer with knotted belt on the overlapping skirt, and slightly different skull-cap.

We find a similar style, sug-gesting possibly the same workshop but a different hand, in the two shooting archers from Sardara (Lilliu nos. 24-25), already mentioned with our no. 5 above. They wear a skull-cap with raised border like no. 60 just mentioned, a sleeveless leather cuirass reaching to the waist (ap-parently on the naked chest), a bel-ted studded heavy "apron" probably fastened to the cuirass and opened at the back, over a skirt reaching from hips to knees (possibly shorter and overlapping in front). There is a peculiar studded face-guard with a band reaching to the back and thus protecting the left side (a sort of "kardiophylax") and double neck-band; the quiver has a different shape and position compared with all other archers. Similar, but coarser and presenting significant differences in his armor, is the fighting warrior, Lilliu no. 103 from Sulcis, mentioned above with our no. 4; to this we can add the warrior, also mentioned above, from S. Anna Arresi now in Providence, clearly belonging to the "round-head" group, but wearing the horned cap and ribbed corselet of our no. 4 and his companions (though, significantly, a short perizoma instead of the tunic, leaving back and belly naked). Another chieftain with long sword resting on his right shoulder and a heavy ringed club in his left hand is Lilliu no. 149 (provenance unknown): he wears a decorated tunic or skirt reaching to the knees, under a thick jacket with long sleeves and covering the hips; on his head is a sort of cylindrical turban (cf. "Barbetta": Lilliu no. 61), at his right ankle a ring. Technique and style assign this figurine to a mixed group, halfway between the more refined "aristocratic" Uta Group, and the coarser, "popular" Barbaricino Group. It is perhaps noteworthy that some of the above mentioned "bronzetti" (nos. 46, 60, 103, 149) have the same black patina as our no. 6, which is, in fact, more commonly found in the Barbaricino Group, in contrast with the bright or dark green patina typical of the Uta-Abini figurines. Close to Lilliu no. 59 above is no. 58 (another offerer, also from Aidomaggiore); and close to nos. 46-47 is no. 45 (provenance unknown; black patina; possibly an archer): they appear to mix features proper to the first group we have considered with our nos. 4-5, with others distinctive of this second "round-head" group.

Another soldier-chieftain, resting with stick and sword (from which the shield hangs on his back), is Lilliu no. 89 in Florence (provenance unknown); it is assigned rightly by Lilliu to the same hand as his no. 96 ("Miles cornutus" from Senorbi(CA): cf. Pinza (1901:pl. XIII:12)), belonging to the sword-and-shield type of his nos. 12 to 15 mentioned above. They both wear a tunic with triple hem and fringed bands, ribbed corselet without the ubiquitous gamma-hilted dagger in front, large oval greaves with longitudinal ridge and ribbed back bands, and a cap with very long horns. The face is small, round and delicate, framed with two braids or bands of hair coming down the sides. At the back the hair forms a triangular mass marked with the well-known leaf or herring-bone pattern. The general similarity in style and equipment relates these two warriors to our first group (nos. 4 and 5, together with Lilliu nos. 7 to 16 etc.), although the differences pointed out suggest a different hand; a link with our second group is offered by the peculiarity of having both stick and sword but no mantle.

Without embarking now in a detailed reappraisal - that would be inappropriate here - of the chronological, cultural and artistic place occupied by these "bronzetti" and their companions in the general framework of ancient Mediterranean civilization, I would like to stress the need for a fresh and careful re-examination of the whole question, starting with the corpus of the material itself.

In 1901, after discussing parallels and possible sources of inspiration for the Sardinian products, and noting the preference of many authors for Asian or Phoenician models while Reinach favoured a Mycenaean connection, G. Pinza remarked (cols. 214-215) how "these different opinions did not exclude each other ...," adding poignantly: "These parallels do not allow us to establish the chronological limits within which (the Sardinian figurines) were manufactured: on the contrary, the relative mastery with which some of the figurines are modelled and cast might induce one to believe that they belonged to a period artistically more advanced than that so called of oriental art (i.e. Orientalizing) ..." (which apparently he himself did not believe).

Recent studies have indicated for some of the Etruscan contexts containing Sardinian bronzes a date in the late 9th century (Bartoloni and Delpino 1975), which in turn has induced most authors to accept, albeit not without some apparent reluctance, a date before 800 B.C., at least for the beginning of the production, maintaining its pace for three centuries or more (Lilliu 1982). M. Gras (1980) has shown convincingly how the 7th and 6th century contexts for some of the model boats in tombs at Vetulonia or in the Greek sanctuary at Gravisca (Tarquinia) must be regarded as secondary, because the production of these bronzes cannot have gone on for too long, and the bulk of the evidence points to the second half of the 9th century as the time of closest contacts between Etruria and Sardinia. A logical extension of this argument might indeed lead us to accept even this date as indicative only of the terminus ante quem for the actual manufacture of the relevant Sardinian bronzes (which include the only human figure so far found outside Sardinia, from Vulci: Lilliu no. 111), without telling us precisely how long ante. I do not think this applies to the pottery jugs; nor to the bronze fibulas etc. imported from Etruria to the island. In other words, I suspect that the late 9th century must be accepted as the latest and not the earliest possible date for the production at least of the Uta-Abini style figurines.

In fact, with Pinza's sensible remarks in mind, I suggest that the whole of the Sardinian production, with special regard to human figures and model boats, must be re-examined and reassessed. Re-evaluation of contacts between Sardinia and Cyprus and the East Mediterranean (Lo

Schiavo 1979, with literature; Macnamara et al. 1984) had already prompted Bisi (1977), rightly in my view, to suggest the possibility of a direct Oriental, as opposed to Orientalizing, origin for some aspects of the Sardinian "bronzetti." Two main directions should be explored:

1) First, it is time to proceed to a systematic division and grouping into different workshops and hands of the many pieces (ca. 150 human and 150 boats, animals, etc.) assigned to the Uta-Abini style, developing the illuminating but only sporadic indications already provided by Lilliu (1966), thoroughly exploring and defining possible relationships -iconographic, formal, chronological etc. - of these groups with each other and with the external world. This will lead, inter alia, to recognizing, I suspect, a comparatively short time span for the whole production of this style.

2) Then I believe that a more definite distinction can and must be understood between this high quality, "aristocratic" Uta-Abini Group, and the fewer and undoubtedly coarser "popular" products of the so-called Barbaricino Group. I submit that the concept of derivation from Phoenician inspiration brought in by Phoenician colonization can only be applied to the latter group and not to the production of the former group as well, with all its cultural and especially chronological implications.

Acknowledgments
The photographs in this article are all reproduced through the courtesy of the British Museum.

The following table shows an analysis by atomic absorption spectrometry, with a precision of ± 1% for major elements and 20% for traces, done by Paul Craddock of the British Museum Laboratory.

Table 7.1   Chemical Analysis of the Sardinian Bronzes
in the British Museum

No.	Cu	Sn	Pb	Zn	Fe	Ni	Ag	Sb	As
2=429	88.50	9.80	0.45	0.03	0.11	0.12	0.07	0.25	0.10
3=430	88.50	11.80	0.38	0.03	0.09	0.01	0.02	-	0.01
4	89.00	10.80	0.07	-	0.07	0.05	0.02	-	0.20
5=337	94.00	5.00	0.40	0.20	0.42	0.04	0.07	0.25	0.10
6=338	88.00	10.00	1.00	-	0.04	0.03	0.02	Tr	-

CATALOG OF NURAGIC BRONZES IN THE BRITISH MUSEUM

1. Chain with spear-shaped pendant (fig. 7.2)

2. Model sheath with dagger and three stilettos (fig. 7.3)

3. Model sheath with dagger and stiletto (fig. 7.4)

4. Fighting warrior (fig. 7.5)

5. Archer drawing his bow (fig. 7.6)

6. Resting warrior/chief (fig. 7.7)

(British Museum is abbreviated 'BM' in the catalog that follows)

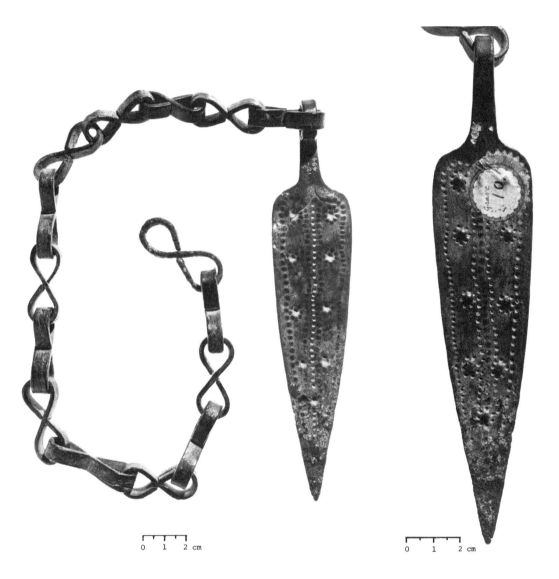

Figures 7.2a-b CHAIN WITH SPEAR-SHAPED PENDANT
BM Inv. 1856.12-23.494; from Tharros, Grave 10. Unpublished. Pendant
l. 18cm, w. 3cm; l. of each link 4cm, w. 0.7cm. Well preserved, with
green patina.

Figures 7.3a-b MODEL SHEATH WITH DAGGER AND THREE STILETTOS
BM Inv. 1856.12-23.664; from Tharros, Grave 5. Bibl.: Walters (1899:
59, no. 429) (not illustrated); Swaddling (1980:344 no. 244 (illustration); 418 (text)).   L. 7.3cm.   Complete, except for the suspension
rings; one side worn and corroded; dark green patina.

Figures 7.4a-b MODEL SHEATH WITH DAGGER AND STILETTO
BM inv. 1974.12-1.5; from Sardinia, provenance unknown. Bibl.: Walters
(1899:59 no. 430 (not illustrated); Swaddling (1980:344 no. 243 (illustration); 418 (text)). L. 8.5cm. Complete and well preserved; dark
green patina.

0 1 2 cm

Figures 7.5a-c FIGHTING WARRIOR
BM Inv. 1914.3-18.1; from Sardinia, provenance unknown. Unpublished.
Bought from Rev. H. Holden, St. Cross, Whitstable. Purchased by Dr. H.
Holden between 1845-1853. Preserved ht. 27.5cm. Complete, except for
feet and ankles, left hand, and part of sword; fine dark green patina.

0 1 2 cm

Figures 7.6a-b ARCHER DRAWING HIS BOW
BM Inv. 1974.12-1.2; from Sardinia, provenance unknown. Bibl.: Walters
(1899:52 no. 337) (not illustrated); Lilliu (1966:70f. no. 19; fig. 56);
Swaddling (1980:284 no. 111; 384f.). Preserved ht. 17.4cm. Complete,
except for missing feet; surface slightly corroded; dark green patina.

Figures 7.7a-c RESTING WARRIOR/CHIEF
BM Inv. 1974.12-1.1; from Sardinia, provenance unknown. Bibl.: Walters
(1899:52 no. 338) (no illustration). Ht. 19.3cm. Complete, except for
part of the sword missing; very smooth fine patina, black at front,
brown-yellow at back.

REFERENCES

BALMUTH, M.S.
1978   Sardinian Bronzetti in American Museums.   StSar 24
            (1975-77):145-156.

BARTOLONI, G. AND F. DELPINO
1975   Un tipo di orciolo a lamelle metalliche. Considerazioni
            sulla prima fase villanoviana. StEtr 43:3-45, pls. 1-4.

BISI, A.M.
1977   L'apport phénicien aux bronzes nouragiques de Sardaigne.
            Latomus 36:909-932, pls. 33-46.

GRAS, M.
1980   L'Etruria villanoviana e la Sardegna settentrionale:
            precisazioni e ipotesi. Atti XXII Riunione Scientifica
            IIPP 513-539.

LILLIU, G.
1966   Sculture della Sardegna nuragica. Cagliari: La Zattera.

1982   La civiltà nuragica. Sassari.

LO SCHIAVO, F.
1979   Osservazioni sul problema dei rapporti fra Sardegna ed
            Etruria in età nuragica. L'Etruria mineraria. Atti XII
            Conv. St. Etr. e Ital. 299-314, pls. 60-62.

1981   Economia e società nell'età dei nuraghi.   Ichnussa
            255-347.

MACNAMARA, E., D. RIDGWAY AND F.R. RIDGWAY
1984   The Bronze Hoard from Santa Maria in Paulis, Sardinia
            = BMOP 45.

PINZA, G.
1901   Monumenti primitivi della Sardegna = MonAnt 11.

SWADDLING, J.
1980   Entries in Kunst Sardiniens.

WALTERS, H.B.
1899   Catalogue of the Bronzes...in the British Museum. London.

PART THREE:
EAST AND WEST

Introduction

It has become a persistent practice to try to trace some aspects of ancient Sardinia to influence or visitors from eastern areas: the Aegean, Anatolia, or the Syro-Palestinian area known as the Levant, for example. In the following articles, suggestions are made about potential relationships with 'Sea Peoples' and clearer associations with Phoenicians from the East Mediterranean, and Carthaginians. The tribes of the so-called 'Sea Peoples,' are known primarily from Egyptian texts as a group of marauders from the 14th to 12th century B.C., where they are named. It is the appearance of one of the names, Šrdn, transliterated as Šardina (Albright 1950), that prompts further study with reference to Sardinia in the Mediterranean. Like a recurrent fashion, the very idea of the Sea Peoples has its moments of popularity and moments of dismissal. In a recent comprehensive book on Sardinia (Thimme, J. Kunst Sardiniens. Karlsruhe: Müller 1980), the notion of any connection of Sardinia with the Sea Peoples is summarily dismissed, but in the most recent comprehensive book on the Sea Peoples (Sandars, N. The Sea Peoples. London: Thames and Hudson 1977) there is a very different consideration of the possibility that these tribes existed, fought, traveled, and gave their names to the area in which they ultimately settled.

Trying to attach a specific geographical area to the name of the tribe has become almost a game in linguistics as well as in archaeology. Moshe Dothan adds ceramic identification to the exercise, pointing out the similarity of the Late Helladic pottery found in Sardinia to that found elsewhere in the East Mediterranean, especially along the coast of Canaan. He cites historical and linguistic evidence as well to suggest the possibility of a link between the name of the tribe and the name of Sardinia.

Linguistics and, to a greater degree, epigraphy figure largely in Frank M. Cross' treatment of the Phoenician inscriptions in Sardinia that enable him to suggest the presence of Phoenicians in the western Mediterranean as early as the eleventh century B.C. This early date, in turn, enables an early date for Phoenician figurines on Sardinian soil. Those catalogued by Ferrucio Barreca include previously unpublished pieces from the Nuragic village site of Santa Cristina (Paulilatino). Their presence there confirms the exposure of Sardinians to the craft traditions of the Phoenicians at the end of the second and the beginning of the first millennium B.C.

The comprehensive and timely account of Phoenician and Punic civilization in Sardinia by Ferruccio Barreca analyzes the extent to which some of the imported institutions were assimilated and others resisted. This badly needed information fills a long-standing void in that study in the English language.

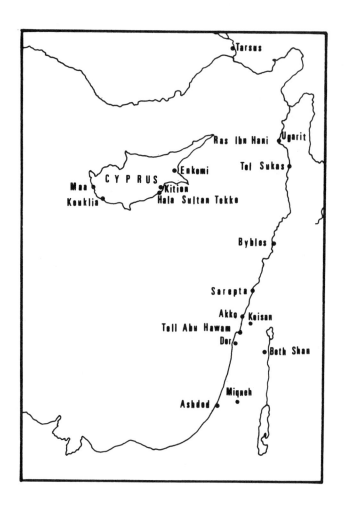

Figure 8.1   Map of the East Mediterranean showing sites mentioned in
text of chapter 8

8. ŠARDINA AT AKKO?

Moshe Dothan

New excavations and surveys in the Near East, especially in the East Mediterranean, have added substantially to our knowledge of the period of the great catastrophes at the end of the Late Bronze Age in the last quarter of the 13th century B.C. These catastrophes heralded the end of the period of the great Mycenaean civilization and of the Hittite empire, on the one hand, and the beginning of the decline of the Egyptian empire of the New Kingdom, on the other. We are dealing with a period of two generations at least, approximately from the days of Merneptah onward (ca. 1224 B.C., or 1213 according to the lower chronology). The absolute chronology of the Late Bronze period in the Near East is built mainly on Egyptian dates.

For relative chronology, we depend on the Mycenaean IIIB pottery found throughout the Mediterranean basin; after its disappearance around 1200 B.C., Mycenaean IIIC pottery seems to be the accepted criterion for the relative chronology of the next period in the area. The sites where it was found serve as evidence for the diffusion of this Mycenaean ware, primarily as a local product or as a result of emigration and resettlement and, perhaps, of minor trade, after the destruction of the main centers. In the East Mediterranean it is mostly found in the strata succeeding those destruction levels that many scholars attribute to the Sea Peoples ("Peoples of the Sea" as translated from the Egyptian account) and others to such natural causes as earthquakes or severe droughts fol-lowed by waves of emigration and changes of population around 1200 B.C. The destroyed areas in which Myc. IIIC pottery appeared along the coast of the East Mediterranean range from the great cities of Cilicia (Tarsus) in the north, to the cities of Philistia on the Egyptian border in the south and Cyprus (fig. 8.1). In the Aegean it flourished in many of the great cities of the Greek mainland and in her islands.

Mycenaean IIIC pottery appears in regional versions in the Mediterranean and is subdivided generally into three phases. Though the forms of Myc. IIIC:1 vessels are a direct continuation of those of Myc. IIIB, they show a varied character in details at the different sites. The regional variations are also pronounced in the pottery ornamentation and, of course, in the different clays.

The East Mediterranean variety is best attested in Cyprus. Some of the main sites with Myc. IIIC pottery are concentrated there, where it was found in the old harbor cities like Enkomi (Dikaios 1969:II 845-50), Kition (Karageorghis 1976:1-15), Hala Sultan Tekke (Åström 1983:115, 126, figs. 339-59), and Palaeopaphos-Kouklia (Maier 1967:88-93; 1969:33-42; 1976:92-97), in new, fortified, short-lived settlements like Maa (Karageorghis et al. 1982:105-08), and in inland sites like Sinda (Furumark 1965:99-116) and Athienou (Dothan and Ben-Tor 1983:115-117). In some of these Cypriot sites its appearance has been attributed to the Sea Peoples' invasion and settlement, although its final attribution is still being examined by some scholars. Along the Canaanite coast, it is sometimes associated with one of the earlier waves of attacks and raids of the Sea Peoples before the well-documented invasion of the 8th year of Ramses III. Similar raids had occurred before Ramses III, possibly already toward the end of Merneptah's rule and later, in that period of Egyptian instability that includes the interregnum years between the XIXth and XXth dynasties.

Myc. IIIC pottery and especially its subtype, 1b, was first recognized stratigraphically as a group in Israel in the excavations at Ashdod (M. Dothan 1971). Lately this ceramic phenomenon has been found at more sites and, as at Ashdod, in large quantities at Miqne (Ekron) (T. Dothan and Gitin 1982:150-153; 1983: 128). Another group is known as well from the coastal plain site of Tel Keisan and from Beth Shean in the Jordan Valley (Balensi 1981:399-401; Hankey 1966:169-171). These assemblages seem to be linked to the northern Canaanite coast at sites such as Ras Ibn Hani and Sarepta (Bounni et al. 1979:217-291; 1978:233-301; 1976:233-264; Herscher 1975:85-96), and to some of the sites in Cyprus, such as Enkomi and Sinda (Dikaios 1969:II 845-850; Furumark 1965:99-116).

Recently, a group of similar pottery was found in the excavations at Akko (Acre). The city is situated at the crossroads of the ancient coastal way leading north from Egypt through Canaan towards Syria where it meets with the road traversing the country from the east toward the Bay of Akko (M. Dothan 1981:100-102; 1983:132-143; 1979:227-228). The natural harbor of this bay, the only large one in the country, was extremely valuable as the terminus of international trade routes. Its importance for sea trade can be illustrated by one example: a large amount of Cypriot White-Painted ware of the first half of the second millennium was found in the excavations at Akko in Middle Canaanite (Bronze) 2a-b deposits. All of those sherds, which have been analyzed by neutron activation analysis, come from eastern Cyprus, about 250km away.

The areas of the ancient mound of Akko excavated to date are comprised mostly of well-preserved fortifications of the early second millennium B.C. and habitation quarters from the Israelite (Iron) II Age to the Hellenistic period (Areas A, B). Only in isolated areas have we succeeded in uncovering the strata of the last phases of the Late Canaanite (Bronze) Age and the beginnings of the Israelite (Iron) Age. These were mostly remains of workshops - and a possible cult place - situated directly above the Middle Canaanite (Bronze) ramparts and graves, or above the Late Canaanite (Bronze) destruction levels. The most prominent was an artisan complex in Area B with a well preserved pottery kiln and a stone floor for metal-reworking with at least two crucibles, fragments of pottery pipes, bronze fragments, and layers of ashes from a metal oven that did not itself survive. The most significant single pottery vessel was a small skyphos, found partly in the kiln and partly in the ashes outside it (waste). It was decorated in red with the typical antithetic wing motif of Myc. IIIC:1 (fig. 8.2). Other pieces, recognized as Myc. IIIC:1b ware found in Area B and in other areas of the tel (mainly in Area F), excavated under supervision of Dr. A. Raban, included, in addition to the bowls (fig. 8.3 Area K), a comparatively large number of fragments of closed forms. These fragments, most probably of stirrup jars, were decorated in the upper register-handle zone with hatched triangles (fig. 8.4). The lower register decoration consisted of a broad band, bounded by continuous geometric motifs, horizontal chevrons and rhomboids with net filling, all applied in monochrome (fig. 8.5). Among other motifs, semicircles and dotted scale patterns should be mentioned.

A fragment of an unusually large krater with an outturned rim came from Area F in the 1983 season (fig. 8.8). The decoration consists of three painted bands below the rim and four bands enclosing the central zone. This zone was divided into metopes of vertical lines enclosing a bird. The stylized bird (swan?) has a long neck with a forward-pointing head. The neck is decorated in parallel stripes (ladder motif). The head is unusual, small in proportion, and the beak is open. The body of the bird is closely related to the representation of the birds in Myc. IIIC such as those found at Perati (Iakovidis 1970:B 187, 569) and can be seen as a prototype of the Philistine bird.

In addition to the pottery and metal workshops which attest to a settlement of artisans - at least on the edge of the mound - we found nearby a probable cult place (Area H) excavated under the supervision of Dr. Michal Artzy, which has to be attributed to the same period as this settlement. On a small, mortar-like portable(?) altar a few incised drawings of ships - coasters with rounded ends - were incised. Their rendering is reminiscent of the representation of the ships on the ashlar walls of the temple of Kition in Cyprus of the 12th century B.C. (Artzy 1984:59-64).

We may conclude this section by stating that overall, the pottery forms and decorations from Akko are related to the Myc. IIIC:1b pottery of Greece (e.g., Perati, Tiryns, Mycenae) and of Cyprus (Enkomi, Sinda, Maa, Hala Sultan Tekke).

In Canaan itself, the local Mycenaean IIIC:1b assemblages from Ashdod stratum XIIIb-a and Miqne and the vessels from Tel Keisan stratum XIII and Beth Shean stratum VIb are closest to this pottery. The Philistine ware proper, e.g. in Ashdod stratum XII, though also a local branch of Myc. IIIC:1b ware, is stratigraphically and chronologically somewhat later than the Akko ware just described.

Historical Sources
As mentioned above, it is certain that one group of local pottery of the Myc. IIIC:1b type, found mostly in Philistia at Ashdod and Miqne, was made by the Sea Peoples. It may even include an early wave of the Sea Peoples before the main wave of the Philistines who appear most prominently in the Egyptian sources of Ramses III. The question arises: To whom may we attribute the other groups of this pottery, especially those found on the northern coast of Canaan?

Among the other Sea Peoples who took part in the great invasion of the time of Ramses III, the two who seem to be the most important are the Seqila (Tjekker) and the Šardina. The Seqila are well known from the Egyptian Wen Amon story (ca. 1100 B.C.), according to which they then lived in Dor. Their pottery, some of which is quite similar to the Philistine ware, was found there in the excavations conducted in the 1920's (Garstang 1924:35-45; 1925:80-82). New excavations at Dor (Raban 1983: 229-251) will, it is to be hoped, shed more light on the material culture of the Seqila.

For the geographical setting of the Šardina on the Canaanite coast we have only one source, but an important one: the Onomasticon of Amenope, ca. 1100 B.C. (Gardiner 1947:192, 194f). In its enumeration of the southern Canaanite coast, the towns of Gaza, Ashkelon, and Ashdod are listed. In the ethnic section it lists, from the north to the south, Šardina, Šeqila, Pelaštu. We know from biblical sources and from archaeological research that the Philistines settled mainly in the southern part of the coast, approximately up to the Yarkon River; the Šeqila, according to the Wen Amon story, covered the coast around their capital Dor and stretched to the north, most probably up to the Carmel Ridge. Since the Šardina was, according to the Amenope list, the northernmost group, they most probably inhabited the coastal area from the Carmel northward to Tyre. Curiously enough, the Biblical name of Asher, one of the twelve Israelite tribes to whose territory Akko belonged, appears nearby in the Amenope text. Though some scholars have suggested an alternative understanding "Assur" (Assyria), rather than "Asher" (Gardiner 1947:192f), this does not seem to fit the context. It seems that the list of Amenope reflects the ethnic distribution on the coast of Canaan before the conquests of David around 1000 B.C., listing from the north to the south the ethnica: Šardina, Šeqila, Pelaštu.

The Šardina

Having suggested their geographical location on the Canaanite coast, we have to ask, who were these Šardina and what was their history? Most scholars maintain that they came either from southern Anatolia or from the East Mediterranean and Aegean (Barnett 1973:368-9, 376-7; Daniel and Evans 1975:741-742). They are known first and primarily from the Egyptian sources; then later also from the Ugaritic sources and now most recently from the archives of Boghazköy (Personal information from Prof. Schachermeyr on the basis of a yet unpublished text from Boghazköy. For the Ugaritic sources see Drower 1973:496, n. 1; Liverani 1969: 194-

195; Dietrich-Lorentz 1972:39-41, 84f; Heltzer 1983:119-123).

At this point it is possible to give only a very sketchy story of the Šardina. They are the earliest known of the Sea Peoples and the only one known in the Egyptian sources from as early as the Amarna letters to the Onomasticon of Amenope, spanning the centuries from ca. 1370 to 1100 B.C. In the Amarna letters they appear as pirates, a foreign element in the Levant. Ramses II succeeded in restraining them to the Nile Delta and the Šardina are afterward depicted in the Abydos reliefs as his bodyguard and as fighting as warriors on the side of the Egyptians against the Hittites in the Battle of Kadesh. It is interesting to note that by that time (early 13th century B.C.), the Šardina were already living on the northern Canaanite coast at Ugarit, probably also in the king's military service.

Very significant for the later relations of the Šardina with the West Mediterranean is their appearance in Libya fighting against Egyptians in the fifth year of Merneptah (ca. 1220) (Breasted 1906:III, sects. 593-602). In order to participate in this war, some of the Šardina had to cross the Mediterranean Sea and land on the southwestern coast. This turn to the west of some of the Šardina may well have happened during or after the catastrophes and ethnic movements which occurred at that time in the East Mediterranean and in which the Šardina may have participated. Even more crucial for the later history of the Šardina was their participation in the great invasion of the Sea Peoples in the 8th year of Ramses III. In a depiction quite similar to their representation in the Battle of Kadesh at Abydos, the Šardina warriors carved on the walls of Medinet Habu one hundred years later appear cleanshaven with their distinctive long double-edged swords, horned helmets and round shields (Nelson 1930:pls. 32; 37). They are shown as <u>enemies</u> of the Egyptians in the sea battle but as Egyptian <u>allies</u> or mercenaries in the land battle (Nelson 1930:pl. 32). It seems that after these battles (ca. 1190) at least part of the "Šardina of the Sea," as they are called by the Egyptians, were among those who settled in the strongholds and in "their towns" (in Egypt or in Canaan?) (Breasted 1906:IV, sect. 123). The significance of the presence of Šardina as the northernmost of the Sea Peoples on the Canaanite coast a few generations later, as attested by the <u>Onomasticon</u> of Amenope, will be discussed below.

The question arises: Did the Šardina and Šeqila, who came possibly from southwestern Anatolia or from the Aegean, and lived by piracy and the sword, settle only on the Canaanite coast or also in other places? From Ugaritic sources we know about the previous presence of both Šardina and Šeqila on the sea and on land (Drower 1973:496, n. 1; Liverani 1969:194-195; Dietrich-Lorentz 1972: 39-41, 84; 1978:53-56; Heltzer 1983: 15; Lehmann 1979:481-483). The names of those peoples have been connected by some with the islands of Sardinia and Sicily (Guido 1963:32-35).

Archaeological Evidence

Because of the lack of historical evidence we have to go back to archaeology for some clues. We have already stressed that the material culture of the Philistines was very closely connected to Late Mycenaean civilization. The same seems to be true for the Šeqila and the Šardina, although research on the subject is only beginning. One obvious element common to all these peoples after the disintegration of Mycenaean civilization is the <u>koiné</u> of Myc IIIA-B ware, as represented during the peak of trade in the 14th-13th centuries. The Myc. IIIC style, for the most

part locally-made, is the hallmark of the end of the 13th and the beginning of the 12th centuries in the Mediterranean, and was recognized in small quantities by Lord Taylour in Italy in the fifties (Taylour 1958:184-190; pls. 6; 13; 14; 15). In the sixties and seventies, ever-growing quantities of Myc. IIIB ware, which had been brought to Magna Graecia either by trade or by settlers, were found there in excavations. Later, Myc. IIIC:1 ware was either brought to Magna Graecia or, more probably, made on the spot by people who were familiar with it back in the Aegean or East Mediterranean.

Mycenaean Pottery in Sardinia

The latest and most relevant evidence relating to the problem of the Šardina are the new finds from Sardinia. Until two or three years ago only a few stray Myc. IIIC sherds had been found on the island, at Barumini (Ferrarese Ceruti 1981:611) and Tharros (Lo Schiavo, chap. 16). The new finds from <u>Nuraghe</u> Antigori, in the Bay of Cagliari near Nora, may change the picture competely (Ferrarese Ceruti 1981:figs. M2; M7; M8). Here we have for the first time stratigraphical evidence from the floor deposits of a genuine Nuragic center. It is appropriate to emphasize the prominent position of this Nuragic site on a steep hill overlooking the southern coast of the island, and accessible to the metal sources of the Sulcis.

The pottery found in several levels of a room in <u>Nuraghe</u> Antigori was mixed with local Nuragic pottery. The Myc. IIIC:1 types included mostly bowls and some closed forms. Among the decorative patterns, one that should be especially stressed is the continuous rhomboid, or lozenge, filled with a net pattern on a krater with a flanged rim (Ferrarese Ceruti 1981:fig. M2). This vessel from Antigori has a flanged rim as do many of the Myc. IIIC:1 pieces from Ashdod. The same pattern appears in Akko (figs. 8.4-8.7), and Keisan (Balensi 1981:pl. XI), and in Beth Shean, on stirrup jars (T. Dothan 1982:pl. 20:3; fig. 70:5-6; 9). Other patterns include wavy lines below the rims, etc. Significant is the overall pattern of decoration which relates to the milieu of the early phase of the Myc. IIIC:1 of the Canaanite coast.

The Antigori finds are the first group of well stratified Myc. IIIC:1 pottery in Sardinia and we may expect more such finds to be forthcoming. These finds constitute the first firm archaeological evidence for the connections between the island and the East Mediterranean and Aegean in the period of transition between the 13th and 12th centuries B.C. It also supports the view of those scholars who argued for the possibility of links between the representations of the horned helmets of the Sardina warriors in the Egyptian depictions and those known from the "late" horned bronze figurines of warriors found in Sardinia (Ferrarese Ceruti 1981:605-612), although we still do not know of any direct connections between the wearers of these helmets on the Egyptian depictions and the horned-helmeted bronze statue from Enkomi (Dikaios 1969:III, pls. 38-44). The comparison, however, made by several scholars of these roughly contemporary representations, and especially of the male figurine standing on an ingot, is tempting (Schaeffer 1971:505-566, pls. I-VII); it is especially tempting when we are aware that Cyprus was conquered and destroyed by the Sea Peoples who may also have included the Sardina. In this context, the rich finds of identical ingots from Cyprus and Sardinia from this same period, discussed in this colloquium should again be mentioned. Here we should also stress the new discovery of ingots including the "oxhide" type identical with those with Cypro-Minoan signs, in the Mediterranean area south of the Bay of Haifa (Galili and Shmueli 1983).

Linguistic Evidence

And now let me mention that the long disputed link in the historical geography and in linguistics, a link between the name of the island and that of the Šardina, one of the most powerful and long existing among the Sea Peoples. It seems that this phenomenon is similar in a way to what happened in ancient Palestine. The ancient Greeks, most probably when crossing the sea to southern Canaan, met its coastal inhabitants - the Pelaštu or Philistines. Thus, all the southern coast of Canaan became to the Greeks, pars pro toto, Palaistine (Herodotus II.104). In Sardinia, part of the island (probably the south) settled partly by Šardina warriors or merchants, became known later to the Phoenician sailors, merchants, and, from the 9th century on, to the settlers also, as the land of Sardinia. For this, the name that appears on the Nora inscription (cf. Cross, chap. 9) seems to be the main evidence. Later, the name was probably adopted by the Greeks (Herodotus I.170; Skylax 7; Pausanias IV.23.5) as one of the names of the whole island of Sardinia, and remains the only one which is still preserved today.

Acknowledgments

I would like to express my gratitude to Dr. R.D. Barnett, former Keeper of Near Eastern Antiquities of the British Museum, for first drawing my attention to the recent finds from Sardinia and to Dr. M.L. Ferrarese Ceruti for graciously showing me the site and its finds. I especially wish to thank my wife and colleague, Prof. Trude Dothan, with whom I hope soon to publish an article on the recent Mycenaean IIIC:1b material found in Israel, for her insightful comments and analyses of the material.

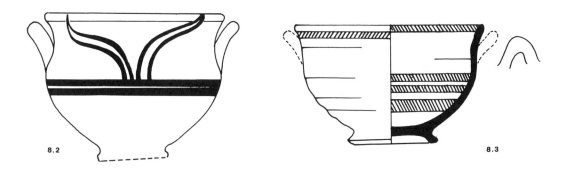

Figures 8.2-8.7   Mycenaean IIIC:1 pottery from Akko

Figure 8.8   Fragment of a Mycenaean IIIC krater

REFERENCES

AHARONI, Y.
    1979   The Land of the Bible: A Historical Geography.
                Philadelphia.

ALBRIGHT, W.F.
    1950   Some Oriental Glosses on the Homeric Problem. AJA
                54:162-76.

ARTZY, M.
    1984   Unusual Late Bronze Ship Graffiti from Tel-Akko.
                Mariners' Mirror 70:59-64.

ASTROM, P.
    1972   The Late Cypriote Bronze Age: Architecture and Pottery.
                The Swedish-Cyprus Expedition IV: Part 1C. Lund.

    1983   Hala Sultan Tekke VIII. SIMA. Lund.

BALENSI, J.
    1981   Tell Keisan: A Preliminary Source for the Appearance of
                Mycenaean IIIC:1a in the Near East. Revue Biblique 88:
                399-401.

BARNETT, R.D.
    1973   The Sea Peoples. CAH^3 II:359-378. Cambridge.

BOUNNI, A., J. AND E. LAGARCE, N. SALIBY AND L. BADRE
    1979   Rapport préliminaire sur la troisième campagne de
                fouilles (1977) à Ibn Hani (Syrie). Syria 56:217-291.

    1978   Rapport préliminaire sur la deuxième campagne de
                fouilles (1976) à Ibn Hani (Syrie). Syria 55:233-301.

    1976   Rapport préliminaire sur la première campagne de
                fouilles (1975) à Ibn Hani (Syrie). Syria 53:233-264.

BREASTED, J.H.
    1906   Ancient Records of Egypt III-IV. Chicago.

DANIEL, G. AND J.D. EVANS
    1975   Sardinia and Corsica. CAH^3 II:741-742. Cambridge.

DESBOROUGH, V.R.
    1975   The End of Mycenaean Civilization and the Dark Ages.
                CAH^3 II:ch. 36(a). Cambridge.

DIETRICH, M. AND O. LORENTZ
    1972   Die Shardana in den Texten von Ugarit in Antike und
                Universelgeschichte. Münster.

1978   Das Seefahrende Volk von Sikila (RS 34.129). <u>Ugarit</u>
              <u>Forschungen</u> 10:53-56.

DIKAIOS, P.
1969   <u>Enkomi Excavations</u>, 1948-1958 II; IIIa. Mainz am Rhein.

DOTHAN, M., F. ASARO AND I. PERLMAN
1971   An Introductory Study of Mycenaean IIIC:1 Ware from Tel
              Ashdod. <u>Archaeometry</u> 13:169-175.

DOTHAN, M. AND D.N. FREEDMAN
1967   <u>Ashdod</u> I. Jerusalem.

DOTHAN, M.
1983   Tel Akko: Some Clues to the Picture of the Great City,
              <u>The   Ruben   Hecht   Festschrift</u>:132-143   (Hebrew).
              Jerusalem.

1981   Akko. <u>IEJ</u> 31:100-102.

1979   Akko. <u>IEJ</u> 29:227-228.

1971   Ashdod II & III. (<u>Atiqot</u>' 9 & 10). Jerusalem.

DOTHAN, T.
1982   <u>The Philistines and their Material Culture</u>. New Haven:
              <u>Yale</u>.

DOTHAN, T. AND A. BEN-TOR
1983   Excavations at Athienou, Cyprus, 1971-1972. <u>Qedem</u> 16.
              Jerusalem.

DOTHAN, T. AND S. GITIN
1982   Tel Miqne (Ekron) 1981. <u>IEJ</u> 32:150-153.

1982   <u>Tel Miqne (Ekron) Excavation Project - Field Report</u> I.
              Jerusalem.

1983   Tel Miqne (Ekron) 1982. <u>IEJ</u> 33:127-129.

DROWER, M.S.
1975   Ugarit. <u>CAH</u>[3] II:417-519. Cambridge.

FERRARESE CERUTI, M.L.
1981   Documenti micenei nella Sardegna meridionale. <u>Ichnussa</u>:
              605-612.

FRENCH, E.
1975   A Reassessment of the Mycenaean Pottery at Tarsus.
              <u>Anatolian Studies</u> 25:53-75.

FRENCH, E. AND P. ASTROM
1980   A Colloquium on Late Cypriote III Sites. <u>RDAC</u>:267-269.

FURUMARK, A.
1965   The Excavations at Sinda.   Some Historical Results.
            OpusAth 6:99-116.

GALILI, U. AND N. SHMUELI
1983   Notes: Israel.   IJNA 12/2.

GARDINER, A.H.
1947   Ancient Egyptian Onomastica I-III.   Oxford.

GARSTANG, J.
1924   BBSAJ 4:35-45.

1925   BBSAJ 7:80-82.

GOLDMAN, H.
1956/63   Excavations at Gözlü Kule: Tarsus 2-3.   Princeton.

GUIDO, M.
1963   Sardinia.   London.

HANKEY, V.
1966   Late Mycenaean Pottery at Beth-Shan.   AJA 70:169-171.

HELTZER, M.
1983   Some Questions Concerning the Sherdana in Ugarit.   IOS
            9:9-15.

HERSCHER, E.
1975   The Imported Pottery.   Sarepta: A Preliminary Report on
            the Iron Age, J.B. Pritchard ed., 85-96.   Philadelphia.

IAKOVIDIS, SP.
1970   Perati.   Athens.   (Greek; English summary in Vol. B).

1979   The Chronology of LH IIIC.   AJA 83.

KARAGEORGHIS, V.
1976   Kition.   London.

1982   Excavations   at   Maa-Palaeokastro,   1979-1982.   A
            Preliminary Report.   RDAC:86-108.

KILIAN, K.
1980   Zum Ende der mykenischen Epoche in der Argolis, Jahrbuch
            des Römisch-Germanischen Zentralmuseums.   Mainz.

LEHMANN, G.A.
1979   Die Sikalaju ein neues Zeugnis zu den 'Seevölker' -
            Heerfahrten im späten 13 Jh.v.Chr.   Ugarit Forschungen
            11:481-483.

LIVERANI, M.
  1969   Il corpo di guardia del palazzo di Ugarit. RStO 44:
              191-198.

MAIER, G.
  1967   Excavations at Kouklia (Palaeopaphos). RDAC:86-93.

  1969   Excavations at Kouklia (Palaeopaphos). RDAC:33-42.

  1976   Excavations at Kouklia (Palaeopaphos). RDAC:92-97.

MAZAR, B.
  1964   The Philistines and the Rise of Israel and Tyre.
              Proceedings of the Israel Academy of Sciences and
              Humanities 1:1-22.

  1971   The Philistines and Their Wars with Israel. The World
              History of the Jewish People 3: Judges, B. Mazar ed.,
              164-179. New Brunswick: Rutgers.

NELSON, H.
  1930   Medinet Habu I.

NOUYGAROL, J.
  1956/7   Le Palais Royal d'Ugarit II; IV. Paris.

RABAN, A.
  1983   Recent maritime archaeological research in Israel. IJNA
              12:229-251.

SANDARS, N.K.
  1978   The Sea Peoples, Warriors of the Mediterranean.
              London: Thames and Hudson.

SCHAEFFER, C.F.-A. ET AL.
  1971   Alasia I. Paris.

TAYLOUR, LORD W.
  1958   Mycenaean Pottery in Italy and Adjacent Areas.
              Cambridge.

VAGNETTI, L. (ED.)
  1982   Magna Grecia e mondo miceneo. Nuovi Documenti =
              XXII Convegno di Studi sulla Magna Graecia, Taranto,
              7-11 ottobre 1982.

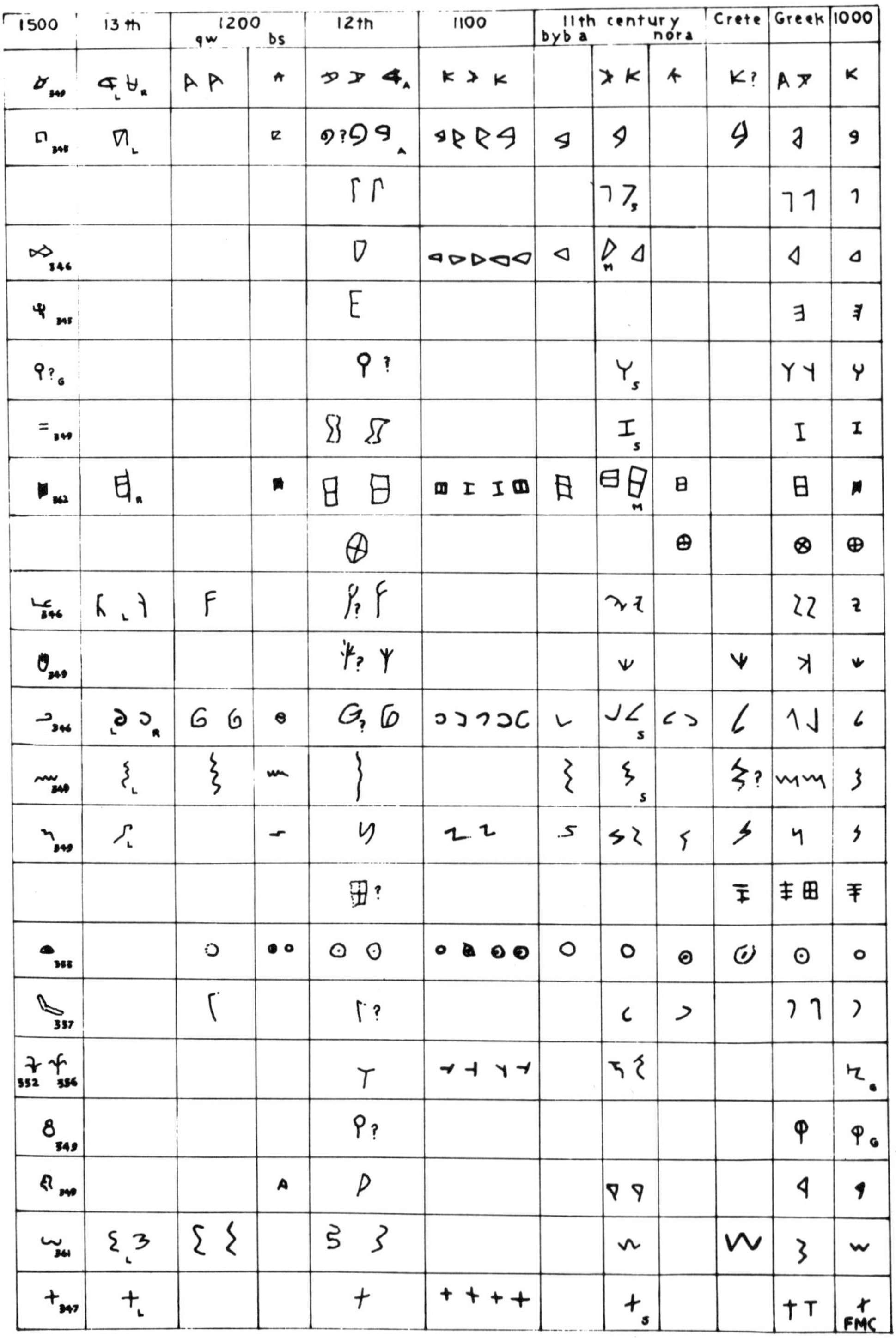

| 1500 | 13th | 1200 | | 12th | 1100 | 11th century | | | Crete | Greek | 1000 |
		qw	bs			byb a		nora			

Figure 9.1   A Chart of Old Canaanite and Linear Phoenician Scripts
ca. 1500-1000 B.C.E.

9. PHOENICIANS IN THE WEST: THE EARLY EPIGRAPHIC EVIDENCE

Frank Moore Cross

The discoveries of the past thirty years have transformed our knowledge of the palaeographical development of the Old Canaanite script and the emergence about 1100 B.C. of the early Linear Phoenician character. A turning point came in 1954 with the publication of three inscribed arrowheads from El-Khadr in Palestine dating to ca. 1100 B.C. This group of arrowheads provided easily deciphered texts from precisely the era of transition from pictograph to linear script and proved to be in some sense a missing link in the history of the alphabet (1). Today twenty inscribed arrowheads are known, published and unpublished, all stemming from the era between ca. 1100 and 950 B.C. (2). In addition some fifteen additional inscriptions, on pottery, bronze, and stone are now part of the corpus of mainland Phoenician inscriptions from the same period, twelfth to mid-tenth centuries, B.C. (3). Many of these inscriptions are closely dated from controlled archaeological contexts, or from the typology of the pottery or weapons upon which they were found. Moreover, they link up with closely-dated inscriptions of the late tenth and ninth centuries. Today the typology of Phoenician inscriptions of the twelfth, eleventh, and tenth centuries is firmly established, as is the development of the daughter scripts of Phoenician, Hebrew and Aramaic, of the ninth century B.C. (fig. 9.1).

These rich palaeographical data from the Syro-Palestinian mainland require reexamination of the dates of Phoenician inscriptions from the islands and western shores of the Mediterranean.

The dates of early inscriptions from Cyprus require very little revision. The Archaic Cyprus inscription (Donner and Röllig 1962-64:No. 30; Masson and Sznycer 1972:13-20; Müller 1975:104-132) must be dated to the second half of the ninth century, in the era of Pygmalion of Tyre (Phoen. pmytn, pmyytn < *p^{c}mytn) whose dates may now be calculated as ca. 831-785 B.C. (4). The Ba^{c}l Lebanon Inscription (Donner and Röllig 1962-64: No. 31) is dated to the reign of Hiram II named in its text. Hiram paid tribute to Tiglath Pileser III (744-727 B.C.) in 738, and died within the year to judge by the chronology of Menander (Peckham 1968:15). The inscription thus must be dated between 785 and 738. Belonging to the first half of the eighth century are also the ᵓntš jug and the Kition Bowl (5). The latter is generally dated to the end of the ninth century on archaeological grounds, but its script is typologically more developed than that of the Ba^{c}l Lebanon inscription.

The earliest extant inscription from Carthage is the so-called Gold Pendant. Typologically its script belongs to the second half of the eighth century B.C. The attempts of Ferron to raise its date to the ninth century founder on close palaeographical analysis (6). There is, I believe, no longer any reason to doubt that while the owner of the pendant may have been Cypriot in origin, it was placed in its Carthaginian tomb not many years after its manufacture (7).

From Spain comes an old Phoenician inscription dedicated to Hurrian Astarte (8). In the <u>editio</u>

princeps J.M. Solá-Solé dated the inscription to the eighth century, and preferred a date in the first half of the century. I have argued in some detail for a date in the second half of the eighth century, and most recently Puech has suggested a date in the mid-eighth century, more precisely in the third quarter (Puech 1977). In any case, its script falls between the scripts of the Ba^c l Lebanon inscription (mid-eighth century) and the Karatepe Bilingual (ca. 720 B.C.) (9).

A complex for metalworking on Pithekoussai (Ischia) has produced two graffiti in Phoenician. The industrial establishment and the graffiti belong to the eighth century B.C. (10).

The oldest of the Phoenician inscriptions from the West come from Crete and Sardinia. The oldest inscription from Crete (fig. 9.2) was found in a tomb at Tekke near Knossos; it is inscribed on a bronze bowl (Sznycer 1979; Catling 1977; Cross 1980:15d). The inscription reads: ks. šm^c bn 1bnn, "The cup of šama^c, son of Labanon" (11). The script includes the three-fingered kap, a form which disappeared after the tenth century, but is regular in both eleventh and tenth century scripts; an archaic mem in vertical stance; and an ^cayin with a large pupil, a form which disappears by the end of the eleventh century. The bets, in opposite stances, have their best parallels also in the eleventh century B.C. In short, detailed palaeographical analysis, in light of the new resources for dating inscriptions

of this period, requires that the Tekke bowl be dated to the end of the eleventh century B.C. (12).

We turn finally to the archaic Phoenician inscriptions of Sardinia. Three Phoenician inscriptions of very early date have been found in Sardinia, two from Nora, one from Bosa. Nora I, a stela of considerable size (105 x 57cm), is one of the most important monuments of Phoenician antiquity (figs. 9.3a, b; 9.4a, b). It has not been preserved intact, I believe; the top of the stela has been cut off to facilitate its later reuse. Eight lines of script remain. J. Brian Peckham succeeded in establishing the material reading of the text (Peckham 1972). Despite the grumblings of scholars who have held out for a late date for Phoenician expansion to the west, there is a consensus among palaeographers that the inscription dates to the ninth century B.C., probably to ca. 825, contemporary with the great and long-lived king of Tyre, Pygmalion (See Cross 1972:13-18; Röllig 1982b:125-130).

The text of the inscription reads as follows;

1. btršš
2. wgrš h^o
3. bšrdn š
4. lm h^o šl
5. m ṣb^o m
6. lktn bn
7. šbn ngd
8. lpmy

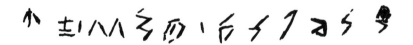

Figure 9.2   The Phoenician inscription from Tekke (Crete)

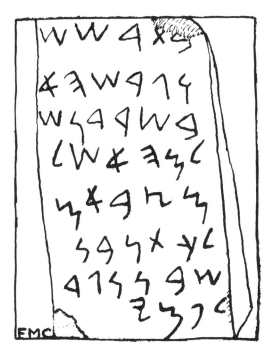

Figure 9.3a   Drawing of the Nora Stone

Figure 9.3b The Nora Stone. Chalking has distorted several
letters (see drawing in fig. 9.3a).

The first two lines complete a sentence cut off from the top of the stela, and hence are not entirely clear: "at Tarsis," or "from Tarsis, and he drove (the enemy?) out." I have suggested that a battle was the subject, and that the stela is a victory stela. Other interpretations are possible. The remaining lines are clear enough. "He is (now) at peace with the Šardina, and his army is at peace: Milkaton, son of Subna, the officer of Pummay."

The stela asserts that a Phoenician officer and his army are secure in the midst of pacified Sardinian tribesmen. This presumes, I believe, not merely the presence in Sardinia of Phoenician merchants or metal workers, but of Phoenician colonists with military forces capable of defending them. Or, at the very least, it presumes a Phoenician force in Sardinia establishing security for the purpose of the colonization in the island.

Crucial to the understanding of the stela is the title of Milkaton son of Šubna: nagīd la-pummay (13). The basic meaning of nagīd in early Hebrew and Aramaic, is "officer," and ordinarily a high military official, "commander" or "general" (14). Pummay, Greek Pygmalion, may be taken as a divine name - awkward in the present context - or as the hypocoristicon for Pummayyaton, a personal name. I have taken it as the name of the Tyrian king, Pummayyaton, Pygmalion of Tyre. In this case Milkaton leads the expeditionary force of the king of Tyre who ruled precisely in the time the stela was erected (15).

The fragmentary stela from Bosa (CIS I:162) has only four letters preserved:]rm°n[, probably to be split up]rm °n[. The letters include, however, diagnostic forms, notably the large-headed reš, the "vertical" mem, and archaic °alep,

which place the inscription in the ninth century, roughly contemporary with the Nora Stone. Thus we have two monumental, ninth century inscriptions from Sardinia, one from the southern coast, one from the northwestern coast, some one hundred miles distant by sea. These inscriptions, particularly the Nora Stone, add support to the view that no later than the ninth century, Tyre was involved in the systematic colonization of the western Mediterranean. One may also argue that Pummay/Pygmalion's activities in Sardinia give us additional warrant to believe that the traditional date of Carthage's foundation in the seventh year of Pygmalion's reign is essentially historical, despite mythological and legendary elements in the surviving accounts of its founding.

The Nora Fragment (fig. 9.4a, b), or Nora II (CIS I:145) is the earliest Phoenician inscription found on Sardinia, and probably the earliest from the western Mediterranean, slightly older than the Cretan Bowl. As I pointed out in a recent paper (Cross 1974:490-493; cf. Cross 1980: 104 esp. fig. 8; Cross 1984), it was published upside down, and moreover, written boustrophedon, further confusing epigraphists unfamiliar with old Canaanite multi-directional writing and its impact on the stances of signs that persisted into the eleventh century.

Nine letters are preserved in two lines of script. The first line reads]°n.p°l[, written sinistrograde, the second line]lt.ḥṭ[written dextrograde.

The °alep of the first line, if I have correctly read the inscription, is a short-lived form appearing first in the twelfth century, flourishing (though not the exclusive form) in the eleventh century, and surviving into the tenth century, chiefly in Byblian texts. The nun is

Figure 9.4a Drawing of the Nora Fragment

Figure 9.4b The Nora Fragment. Chalking has distorted
some letters (see drawing in fig. 9.4a).

a characteristic eleventh century form. ᶜayin has a point in its center, the vestige of the eye's pupil. It is the standard, but not exclusive form - "undotted" ᶜayins appear in all periods of Linear Phoenician - in the twelfth century and is frequent in the eleventh. Its latest appearance is in the Cretan Bowl and in the archaizing Phoenician script of the Aramaic Tell Fakhariyeh Bilingual. •

The ḥet too is diagnostic. Three types of ḥet are used in the twelfth-eleventh centuries, the "box-form" of the Nora Fragment, a "ladder-form" with the vertical strokes extending below the bottom horizontal line, and frequently above the top horizontal, especially the left horizontal, and finally a rare ēta form. The box form belongs almost exclusively to the twelfth and eleventh centuries. Its latest occurrence is a sporadic usage along-side the ladder form in the tenth century Gezer Calendar. Two word dividers appear in the text, one on each line, a usage documented as early as the twelfth century. In short, the palaeographic evidence is consistent, and along with the boustrophedon style, points to a date no later than the end of the eleventh century.

My analysis of the Nora Fragment has been attacked recently by Wolfgang Röllig (1982b:125-130). Röllig wishes to lower my dates, and to argue against a boustrophedon decipherment. I find his palaeographic arguments weak, and at several points demonstrably false.

His primary attack is upon the reading of lamed in line 2 (his line 1). His drawing in Abb. 1 (but not Abb. 2) actually shows the clear two lines which I read as lamed, and faint traces on the surface above the top of (my) lamed. These traces to my eye look pocked, with high ridges between, which, were a line incised, should have been cut through. Even

if one concedes that the line exists - which I do not - the three lines form no letter - unless it be a nun of twelfth-eleventh century type, and one quite different from the nun of 1.1. Röllig adds another stroke, which Röllig concedes does not exist, to form a bet. I do not believe it can be a bet; if so the form (as drawn in Abb. 1) would be twelfth-eleventh century with its short lower stroke emerging from the angle of the head. Dalet, his only plausible alternate reading, is not impossible. The left (Röllig's right edge) is abraded, and a line, completing a triangle with the sides forming an acute angle (giving it a characteristic, slender form) can be reconstructed, though not a trace now exists. In this case, once again, the proposed dalet is a characteristic 12th-11th century form which gave way to the "fat" dalet of the tenth century. It should be noted too that if one reads dalet, it conforms well to a boustrophedon reading (16). In short, I reject Röllig's main argument, and note that if he were correct, it would supply further palaeographical evidence for an eleventh-century date.

His other arguments can be dealt with more briefly. Röllig questions the existence of a "pupil" in the ᶜayin. "Vielmehr scheint es sich um eine natürliche Pore des Steines zu handeln." Such an argument is plausible, only if the "pupilled" ᶜayin is contradicted by all other evidence. It shows even more clearly in newer photographs than the old. Röllig comments that "Das Het (of Nora II - the Fragment) ist leides in den anderen vergleichbaren Inschriften nicht belegt." This statement is simply false. It is found in the ᶜIzbet Ṣarṭa Ostracon, on El Khaḍr I and IV, on the Ruweiseh arrowhead, on the ᶜbdny arrowhead, on the Manahat sherd. In fact, it is the dominant late 12th and 11th century form (17). Röllig apparently was so intent on looking for comparable forms in the ninth century (in conformity with his views of the western expansion of the Phoenicians (Röllig 1982) that he failed to look at 12th and 11th century inscriptions. Similarly the parallels to the Nora Fragment's ᵓalep are to be found on the arrowheads in vogue in the late twelfth and eleventh centuries (18). Finally, Röllig proposes to read ᶜayin for ṭet on l. 2 (Röllig 1.1). While I must agree that there are only faint remains of cross-marks within the circle, it must be noted that the "circle" is large (larger than ᶜayin in line 1). Furthermore a word divider separates ṭaw and ḥet (clearer in newer photographs than in the old). This forces Röllig to read the sequence ḥet-ᶜayin (or ᶜayin-ḥet), a phonemic sequence not permitted in Semitic. The letter must be ṭet.

The massive increase in inscriptions in Old Canaanite and in Early Linear Phoenician, and the consequent increase in our knowledge of the detailed evolution of these scripts in the thirteenth through the ninth centuries B.C. has shed light, not only on the date of the Phoenician presence in the West, but also on the vexed question of the date of the borrowing of the alphabet by the Greeks.

Joseph Naveh was the first to perceive that the new data provide a solution to the debated issue of the antiquity of the Greek alphabet (Naveh 1973; 1982:175-186; McCarter 1975). Beginning with the writer's reconstruction of the early development of Old Canaanite and Linear Phoenician, Naveh noted that the earliest Greek inscriptions were written in multiple directions: sinistrograde, dextrograde, and boustrophedon, precisely as was the practice in Canaanite and Early Phoenician before the end of the eleventh century. Thus early Greek writing exhibits the same shift of stance and rotation of forms which characterize Old Canaanite (and the earliest Linear) writing and its other early descendant, Old South Arabic. A number of archaic Greek letter forms also are most easily explained as derived from the period of transition from Old Canaanite to Early Linear Phoenician: the ᶜayin/omicron with a dot in its center, the vestigial pupil of the pictographic eye, the symmetrical box-shaped ḥet/ēta. The legless five-stroke mem/mu, the legless (or short-legged) he/epsilon, the large-headed, short-legged reš/rho, and the short-legged samek/xi. One notes also the "I"-shaped ēta (El Khaḍr only), the "Y"-shaped vau/upsilon/waw. All these are eleventh-century Linear Phoenician forms which die out in Phoenician after the eleventh century. Greek also preserves the extreme "verticality" of Early Linear Phoenician. However, this trait survived longer than the multi-directional fashion, and longer than the listed letter forms. The shift of vertical strokes to slanted strokes begins at the end of the tenth century.

The form of the letter kappa was the one serious problem in Naveh's analysis. Kappa looks like the ninth-century kap of Nora, or the tenth-century kap of the Gezer Calendar. In "Early Alphabetic Scripts," I suggested that the tenth-century kap in "three-fingered" form, and the tenth-ninth century "K"-shaped kap were by-forms, and that an older trident form (with its middle shaft elongated downward) would be the common ancestor of both the Greek and the "K"-shaped kap. The anticipated trident form appears now in the ᶜIzbet Ṣarṭa sherd and in the Tell Fakhariyeh scripts as the regular form of kap. Thus the one troublesome element in Naveh's typology is removed. I should date the borrowing to the eleventh century, slightly later than Naveh's 1100 B.C. In any case it appears to me that Naveh's case is sound, and that newer finds have confirmed it.

In 1974 I suggested that there was some reason to believe that the "Phoenicians in the West (Aegean and further west) rather than Greeks in the East were the primary agents in the initial spread of the alphabet." Only in such fashion could one explain the marked concentration of archaic features in the alphabet of Crete, Thera, and Melos (Guarducci 1968). It was not a new suggestion, but was a view passed over by recent specialists in Greek epigraphy. The appearance of the verb poinikázen, "to write," and poinikastás "scribe" in an archaic Greek inscription from Crete, recently published, provides new evidence pointing in the same direction, (as acknowledge recently by Lilian H. Jeffery), as does the appearance of the Phoenician Bowl of the eleventh century from Crete (Morpurgo-Davies and Jeffery 1970:153; Edwards and Edwards 1976).

I should conclude that the epigraphic evidence now in hand gives us reason to believe:

1) that Phoenician merchantmen were plying the western Mediterranean in the metal trade no later than the eleventh century;

2) that contacts between the Phoenicians and Greeks in Crete and nearby islands were equally early; and

3) that no later than the ninth century, the Phoenicians had commenced systematic colonization in the West Meditereranean.

Postscript
    After this manuscript went to press, two papers have come into my hands which treat the Tekke (Knossos) Bowl. E. Lipiński (1983:129-165), especially 129-133 complains (with polemical flourishes) that my dating of the Tekke inscription to the end of the eleventh century is too high, and then proceeds to propose a date ca. 1000 B.C. Literally taken, this puts us a year apart, at most a scribal generation. I am taken aback therefore by the vehemence of Lipiński's attack. In fact Lipiński dates the bowl contemporary with the Ahiram Inscription. I should argue that it is slightly earlier typologically.

Emile Puech has also discussed the Tekke inscription (1983:365-395, especially 374-391). He dates the inscription to the third quarter of the eleventh century, very slightly earlier than my preferred date. He reads ks sm bn l mn, in agreement with my reading save for the patronymic. I still prefer lbnn.

Puech also treats an important new find from Hala Sultan Tekke in Cyprus, a silver bowl published by P. Åström and E. Masson (1982:72-76). The bowl is inscribed in the so-called reduced Canaanite cuneiform alphabet and is attributed to a LC IIIA:1 level usually dated to the early twelfth century B.C. It reads (with Puech) ks(!). ky. bn ypthd "The cup of Aky son of Ypthd." It will be noted that the inscription on both the Cretan bowl and the Cypriot bowl follow the pattern: ks PN bn PN.

NOTES

1. (Cross and Milik 1954; Cross and Milik 1956; Cross 1967). Two additional El-Khadr arrowheads - including the arrowhead with the longest text - were published in Cross (1980:4-7).

2. The published and unpublished pieces are enumerated in Bordreuil (1982:188-190).

3. These texts are surveyed and publication data listed in Cross

1967; Cross 1979; and Cross 1980. On the palaeographic character the Tell Fakhariyeh Inscription, an Aramaic text in Phoenician Linear script, see the writer's forthcoming paper in the Lambdin Volume.

4. See Cross 1972:155, n. 11 (with literature).

5. On the ᵓntš Jug, see Peckham (1968:115, m. 1); the Kition Bowl was published by Dupont-Sommer (1970:1-44); see now Amadasi and Karageorghis (1977:No. D21 (pp. 149-160 and references); Coote (1975); and Röllig (1982a:26).

6. See Ferron (1958/9, and 1968) (where he revises his views). Cf. Röllig (1928:27).

7. See the balanced and informed discussion of Peckham (1968:119-124).

8. See Cross (1971). Independently M. Weippert recognized the goddess ᶜstrt ḥr as Hurrian Astarte (Weippert 1971:431f.), and this identification has increasingly been accepted (Puech 1977). An excellent photograph may be found in Amadasi (1967:pl. LXI) (Spa. 16).

9. Garbini (1967:1-6) argues for a date in the seventh-sixth centuries. His arguments are unconvincing.

10. McCarter (1975); Buchner (1978); Garbini (1978); Teixidor (1979:387). Teixidor assigns the "Aramaic" graffiti to Phoenician. See also Drews (1979:45) and references.

11. This reading is new, a revision of my earlier reading which left the patronymic undeciphered following the initial l. I was, however, inclined to read the final letter as nun (as did Sznycer): l--n. The next to last letter also resembled nun. The problem has been with the second letter of the name, which I took as ᵓalep following Sznycer, but with consider-

able reserve. In fact it must be read b, not in its usual right-to-left stance (as is the first bet) but in the reverse (left-to-right) stance. Compare the left-to-right stances of bet found on El-Khaḍr Arrowheads II and III (over against the normal right-to-left stance on I, IV, and V). Mixed stances are frequent in the eleventh century before the final demise of multi-directional writing and the fixing of normative stances. Mary Joan Winn Leith first urged upon me the possibility of reading a name from the root lbn. Cf. bibl. lbn, lbnᵓ lbny; Ugaritic labnay, labnu, lbn, lbny, and lbnn (cp. the GN lbnn). However, the vertical stroke on the left of the letter seems to render the reading impossible - until it occurred to me that the stance was reversed.

12. Tomb J at Tekke is "Early Protogeometric in Cretan terms, equivalent to the late Protogeometric of Attica" (Catling 1977:14). Desborough's dates for this phase are ca. 950-900. If this chronology is followed it may be concluded that the bowl is an heirloom left in the cave, a half-century or so older than the main deposit in the tomb. A Late Minoan lentoid seal (LM III) was also found in the tomb. However, there is strong pressure on the part of archaeologists trained in both Near Eastern and Mediterranean ceramics of this period to raise the date of the beginning Early Geometric and the end of Protogeometric on the basis of Near Eastern data. It will be remembered that the chronology of both Protogeometric and Geometric depend entirely on Near Eastern data for absolute dates. In a recent dissertation, D.L. Salz (1978) has argued that the transition from Protogeometric to Geometric in the East must now be dated to the mid-tenth century. Desborough himself - if not his nepotes - was aware that his chronology would be shifted upward a half century if Tell Abu Hawam III

fell to Shishak (Šešonq) in ca. 926 (Desborough 1951:294). Reexamination of the stratigraphy of Tell Abu Hawam now makes this date highly probable if not certain. Further, Anita Yannai-James in her Oxford dissertation "Studies on Trade Between the Levant and the Aegean in the 14th to 12th centuries B.C." (unpublished dissertation, Linacre College 1983 ; I owe my knowledge to a symposium she held at Harvard University) argues on unrelated grounds that the end of Protogeometric must also be raised by a half century or more above the Desborough date. It may be that the Tekke Bowl gives epigraphic support from an unsuspected direction for at least a modest raising of the "low" chronology.

13. It is interesting to note that Wilhelm Gesenius in 1837 already read the sequence of letters correctly: ngd lpmy.

14. ngdᵓ znh in 1.8 of the Adon Letter refers to the commander of the Babylonian expeditionary force. See most recently B. Porten (1981:36-52).

15. For a detailed discussion of the name, see Cross (1972:17-19). I have also rejected the interpretation of 1.8 as dedicatory. Normally in a votive or dedicatory inscription, the formula lDN comes at the beginning, or early in the text, not as an "afterthought."

16. Also arguing against reading pᶜl in line 2, rather than reversed in line 1, is the stance of the sign read lamed. It is very low, rather than above the ceiling lie as it is regularly in scripts of the ninth century.

17. Röllig compares the Kilamuwa ḥet with the Nora form: "Noch in der Kilamuwa-Inschrift kommt neben der Form mit zwei Querstrichen dieser Type vor, wenn auch etwas trapez- förmig verzogen." First of all the Kilamuwa inscription is written in characteristic late ninth-century Aramaic script, although the language is Phoenician (see Cross 1969:15, legend to line 7). It is always dangerous to compare different national scripts even if they have diverged only a century or so (as is the case with the ninth-century Aramaic scripts). Archaisms as well as innovations are preserved in daughter scripts. However, the comparison has no merit in any case. The Kilamuwa Inscription has more than a dozen ḥets. All are in "lad- der-form," and show the shift of stance from the vertical (vertical strokes shifted slightly to the dia- gonal; horizontal strokes also slant- ing downward to the left), a ninth- century innovation. The "vertical legs" break through downward below the lower horizontal always; the left vertical also regularly if not always breaks through above the top hori- zontal. I am not sure what ḥet in Kilamuwa, Röllig wishes to compare: certainly not the standard forms in ll. 3, 6, 9, 11 (tris), 12 (bis), 14, 15, 15. Perhaps he has in mind the ḥet in l. 1 where the relief is chipped away, but examination of this ḥet on a good photograph makes clear that it is a "ladder-form," not com- parable to the Nora ḥet. Incidental- ly the ḥet in the Šipṭi-baᶜl Inscrip- tion is a normal "ladder-form," not the form drawn in Röllig's script chart, as an examination of the stone (not the script charts of Dunand) will demonstrate.

18. Röllig perceives a ninth-century kap in my ᵓalep. Some comment is appropriate on the development of kap. The kap had by-forms in the twelfth-tenth century: a trident- shaped kap ("three fingers and wrist") found in the Izbet Sarta Ostracon and the Tell Fakhariyeh Inscription, a short-lived three- fingered form (Cyprus Bowl, the Byblian texts of the tenth century, and the Ruweiseh Arrowhead), and a

kappa form, which survived in Greek, and is found in the Nora Stone and the Gezer Calendar (and is the ancestor of later kap in Phoenician, Hebrew, and Aramaic). The last-mentioned developed from the trident-form, and its precise evolution awaits further epigraphic data.

REFERENCES

AMADASI, MARIA GIULIA GUZZO
    1967   Le Iscrizioni fenicie e puniche delle colonie in Occidente. Rome: Istituto di Studi del Vicino Oriente.

AMADASI, M.G.G. AND V. KARAGEORGHIS
    1977   Fouilles de Kition III. Inscriptions phéniciennes. Nicosia: Department of Antiquities, Cyprus.

ASTROM AND E. MASSON
    1982   A Silver Bowl with a Canaanite Inscription from Hala Sultan Tekké. RDAC 72-76.

BORDREUIL, PIERRE
    1982   Epigraphes phéniciennes sur bronze, sur pierre et sur céramique. Archéologie au Levant: Recueil R. Saidah. Collection de la Maison de l'Orient Mediterraneen No. 12, Serie archéologique, 9. Lyon.

BUCHNER, GIORGIO
    1978   Testimonianze epigrafiche semitiche dell'VIII secolo A.C. Pithekoussai. ParPass 179:130-142.

CATLING, H.W.
    1977   The Knossus Area, 1974-76. Archaeological Reports for 1976-77. No. 23:11-15.

COOTE, R.B.
    1975   The Kition Bowl. BASOR 220:47-53.

CROSS, FRANK MOORE
    1954   The Evolution of the Proto-Canaanite Alphabet. BASOR 134:15-24.

    1967   The Origins and Early Evolution of the Alphabet. Eretz Israel 8:1*-24*.

    1969   Epigraphic Notes on the Amman Citadel Inscription. BASOR 193:13-19.

    1971   The Old Phoenician Inscription from Spain Dedicated to Hurrian Astarte. Harvard Theological Review 64:189-195.

1972   An Interpretation of the Nora Stone. BASOR 208:13-19.

1974   Leaves from an Epigraphist's Notebook. Catholic Biblical Quarterly (The Skehan Volume) 36:486-494.

1979   Early Alphabetic Scripts. Symposia Celebrating the Seventy-Fifth Anniversary of the Founding of the American Schools of Oriental Research, ed. F.M. Cross Cambridge: ASOR, 97-123.

1980   Newly-Found Inscriptions in Old Canaanite and Early Phoenician Scripts. BASOR 238:1-20.

1984   Phoenicians in Sardinia: The Epigraphical Evidence. SSA 53-65 (reprints of Cross 1972 and Cross 1974).

CROSS, F.M. AND J.T. MILIK
1954   Inscribed Javelin-heads from the Period of the Judges. BASOR 134:5-15.

1956   A Study of the El-Khadr Javelin- and Arrowheads. Annual of the Department of Antiquities of Jordan 3:15-23.

DESBOROUGH, V.R. D'A
1951   Protogeometric Pottery.   London: Oxford University Press.

DONNER H. AND W. ROLLIG
1962-64   Kanaanäische und aramäische Inschriften.   3 vols. Wiesbaden: Harrassowitz.

DREWS, R.
1979   Phoenicians, Carthage and the Spartan Eunomia. AJP 100: 45-58.

DUPONT-SOMMER, A.
1970   Une Inscription phénicienne archaïque récemment trouvée à Kition (Chypre). Mémoires de l'Académie des inscriptions et belles-lettres 44:1-28.

EDWARDS, G.P. AND R.B.
1976   The Meaning and Etymology of POINIKASTAS. Kadmos 16: 131-140.

FERRON, JEAN
1958-59   Le Médaillon de Carthage. Cahiers de Byrsa 8:45-60.

1968   Les Problémes du Médaillon de Carthage. Le Museon 81: 255-261.

GALLING, KURT
1972   Der Weg der Phöniker nach Tarsis in literarischer und archäologischer Sicht. Zeitschrift des Deutschen Palästina-Vereins:1-18; 140-181.

GARBINI, GIOVANNI
    1967   Note di epigrafia punica: II. 6 Sull'iscrizione de
                Siviglia 'Hispania 14'. RStO 42:2-6.

    1978   Un iscrizione aramaica a Ischia. ParPass 179:143-150.

GUARDUCCI, MARGHERITA
    1968   Der Geburtsort des griechischen Alphabets. Das
                Alphabet, G. Pfohl ed. 197-213. Darmstadt: Wissen-
                schaftliche Buchgesellschaft.

LIPINSKI, E.
    1983   Notes d'épigraphie phénicienne et punique. Orientalia
                Lovaniensia Periodica 14:129-165.

MASSON, O. AND M. SZNYCER
    1972   Recherches sur les Phéniciens à Chypre. Geneva and
                Paris: Librarie Droz.

MCCARTER, P. KYLE
    1975a   A Phoenician Graffito from Pithekoussai. AJA 79:140f.

    1975b   The Antiquity of the Greek Alphabet and the Early
                Phoenician Scripts. Missoula, Montana: Scholars Press.

MORPURGO-DAVIES, A. AND LILIAN H. JEFFERY
    1970   Poinikastás and poinikázen: A New Archaic Inscription
                from Crete. Kadmos 9:118-154.

MULLER, H.P.
    1975   Die phönizische Grabinschrift aus dem Zypern-Museum: KAI
                30 und die Formgeschichte des nordwestsemitischen
                Epitaphs. Zeitschrift für Assyriologie 65:104-132.

NAVEH, JOSEPH
    1973   Some Semitic Epigraphical Considerations on the
                Antiquity of the Greek Alphabet. AJA 77:1-8.

    1982   Early History of the Alphabet. Jerusalem: Magnes.

PECKHAM, BRIAN
    1968   The Development of the Late Phoenician Scripts. Harvard
                Semitic Series 20. Cambridge: Harvard University
                Press.

    1972   The Nora Inscription. Orientalia 41:457-468.

PORTEN, B.
    1981   The Identity of King Adon. The Biblical Archaeologist
                44:36-52.

PUECH, E.
    1977   L'Inscription phénicienne des trone d'Astart à Séville.
                RSF 5:85-92.

1983   Présence phénicienne dans les iles a la fin du IIe
              millenaire. Revue Biblique 90:365-395.

ROLLIG, W.
1982a   Die   Phönizier   des   Mutterlandes   zur   Zeit   der
              Kolonisierung. Niemeyer 15-30.

1982b   Paläographische Beobachtungen zum ersten Auftreten der
              Phönizier in Sardinien. Antidoron Jürgen Thimme
              125-130. Karlsruhe: Verlag C.F. Muller.

SALZ, D.L.
1978   Greek Geometric Pottery in the East: The Chronological
              Implications.   (unpublished   dissertation,   Harvard
              University).

SZNYCER, M.
1979   L'Inscription phénicienne de Tekke près de Cnossus.
              Kadmos 18:89-93.

TEIXIDOR, J.
1979   Bulletin d'épigraphie sémitique 1978-1979.   Syria 56:
              353-405.

WEIPPERT, M.
1971   Abraham der Hebräer? Biblica 52:407-432.

YANNAI-JAMES, A.
1983   Studies on Trade Between the Levant and the Aegean in
              the 14th to 12th centuries B.C.   Unpublished
              dissertation, Linacre College.

Addendum

JOHNSTON, ALAN
1983   The Extent and Use of Literacy: The Archaeological
              Evidence. The Greek Renaissance of the Eighth Century
              B.C.: Tradition and Innovation, R. Hägg ed., Proceedings
              of the Second International Symposium at the Swedish
              Institute in Athens, 1-5 June 1981. Skrifter utgivna av
              Svenska Institutet i Athen. Acta Instituti Atheniensis.
              Regni Sueciae 4, XXX. (Stockholm). This paper, which
              touches on the Pithekoussai graffiti, was called to my
              attention by David Ridgway to whom I am grateful.

10. PHOENICIANS IN SARDINIA: THE BRONZE FIGURINES

Ferruccio Barreca

Two basic styles can be distinguished among the bronze figurines of ancient Sardinia: the "geometric" style in which there is a stiff, coherent composition of the figure and the "Barbaricino-Mediterraneizzante" style, characterized by a lively, uninhibited aesthetic. Examples typical of the first style can be found in the bronze figurines from Uta near Cagliari. The second style is represented by those found in the Nuorese, mostly in the Barbagia and the Ogliastra. The difference in styles reflects a basic difference between two opposing social contexts: the first is the artistic production of a formally organized society emerging from the small monarchies around the coast and flatlands; the second shows the gusto of the shepherds who dwelled in the mountains of the interior.

Without trying to diminish the value of local production, it is nevertheless possible to perceive indisputable similarities with those from Urartu from the 9th/8th centuries, those from Syro-Palestine from the 7th/6th centuries, and those from Luristan. In the case of the last-mentioned, it is possible to explain the similarities by suggesting the presence of artists from Luristan in Sardinia within the 8th/7th century B.C. period. This, however, must remain a mere speculation for the present; a supposition with firmer documentation can be presented with respect to the Phoenician arrival on the island of Sardinia (Barreca 1979:25-26, 29-60; Barreca 1981: 351-353). By 1000 B.C., they were already visiting the coasts in sporadic landings, some of which were to become permanent settlements around 800 B.C., and only then true colonies.

It is important to point out that the Phoencians introduced the products of their bronze industry to Sardinia before their actual presence on the island, as we know from the figurines (figs. 10.1-10.2) found in the Nuragic "sacred well" at Santa Cristina (Paulilatino) and at Nuraghe Flumenelongu (Alghero), both datable to about 1000 B.C. and contemporary with the earliest Phoenician inscription from Nora, recently redated by Cross (1974:486-494; see above, chap. 9. The production of the Sardinian bronze figurines is considered to have begun around 800 B.C., or 1000 years after the commencement of the culture of the nuraghi (Lilliu 1982: 9-12), and after about 200 years of sporadic visits by the Phoenicians when they began to found their first cities along the coasts of Sardinia.

Since the Nuragic bronze figurines reflect some eastern stylistic elements, the chronological framework requires that we consider to what extent the presence of Phoenicians in Sardinia was responsible. It is clear in the case of the aforementioned bronze figurines in Paulilatino and Alghero that Nuragic craftsmen were aware of Phoenician metalwork at the same time that they began their own production, and that they were able not only to comprehend a new artistic expression, but also to grasp completely the technology, and to develop it further in style and content. Phoenician bronze sculpture

(Moscati 1972:435-444), however, appears to differ from Nuragic production; yet, two fundamental stylistic currents may be documented as well: a formal one, and a folk type, both present at the same time, as early as the 2nd millennium B.C. The first of these two currents (often marked by a certain soft quality) is characterized by a generalized realism, especially in respect to the proportions of the body and anatomical details. In contrast, the second trend (which always uses a sketchy artistic vocabulary) tends to bypass realism in favor of an abstract representation of the figure, a simple human form, flat and wiry, with a head on which the distinguishing traits are scarcely scratched; a disproportionate figure in which everything appears to be subordinated to the head, and which is attenuated for exaggeration so that it looks deformed. It is probable that this individual tendency reveals an effort to express the personality of the subject portrayed, emphasizing those elements that would aid this intention without troubling to achieve an accurate naturalism, but revealing in the details of the figure a certain decorative taste, in accord with the tendency generally shown in Semitic art. Finally, it is worth mentioning the common characteristics of the two opposing Phoenician styles: namely the frontality and static posture expressed in the bronze figurines that show influence from Egyptian, Hittite and Syrian sources, reflecting the complex and changing political scene in the Phoenician region at that time.

Both male and female Phoenician figurines represent divinities, worshippers or priests. The divine masculine figures are seated or standing, hands down at the side, or right hand bent out in a gesture of benediction or power, or raised to hurl a staff, while the left hand is held forward, perhaps brandishing a scep-

tre; or else both hold a disk to the chest and lean on something, now lost, in front. The divine feminine figures hold their arms to their breast as a divine nurse or else, like the male figures, may be seated on a throne and sometimes grip a sceptre, now lost. The ritual performed by the worshippers or priests, in contrast, is done seated, with a patera or other liturgical objects in their hands. There are echoes of these types in the iconography of the Nuragic figurines, such as the bronze from Ittiri of a double-flute player (Lilliu 1966:298-301, no.183, figs. 408-409; here below, fig. 10.9), which can be compared to a Phoenician figurine of a seated cithara player found at Monte Sirai (Carbonia)(fig. 10.7). Another possible stylistic comparison can be made with the "Lottatori" - 'wrestlers'- from M. Arcosu (Uta) (Lilliu 1966:56-57, no. 10, figs. 25-28; here fig. 10.10); the fluid outline is reminiscent of the tubular, wiry Phoenician bronze of a seated female (fig. 10.1) found at S. Cristina (Paulilatino), which, like other bronzes from the "Barbaricino-Mediterraneizzante" type, also has a pellet-shaped head.

In general, however, the Nuragic style is both different from and superior to the Phoenician, especially in the rendering of proportion and motion, and for the capability of representing a coherent structure; and another reason it is undoubtedly different and superior is the variety and liveliness of motifs in Nuragic iconography. If we see a cause and effect relationship attached to the arrival of Phoenicians in Sardinia, we must also see that the Sardinian production cannot be called derivative or artistically dependent.

It seems to me that it is preferable to think in terms of bronze figurines brought in from abroad and perhaps also produced by Phoenicians on the island, as providing the impetus and desire on the part of the Nuragic people for local production of figurines similar in conception and execution, to a certain extent, but widely divergent in style and subject matter. In these respects, they rarely correspond to the Phoenician models; there is usually a profound difference between them because of the artistic vocabulary belonging to the larger, ancient pan-Mediterranean cultural sub-stratum of the Nuragic population in Sardinia.

There is, in fact, a double Phoenician contribution to the rise of Nuragic bronze sculpture: the impetus or inspiration from their own production is one; the other is as conveyor of influences from other bronze sculpture produced in Urartu and Luristan, influences already acknowledged in Nuragic bronze sculpture between the 9th and 7th centuries B.C. by Lilliu (1967:332-333). To be more specific, I maintain that material from Urartu reached the Phoenician cities along the Lebanese coast with the caravans that descended along the natural roads made by the river valleys along the Euphrates, Orontes, Leontes (Nahr el Litani) and Eleutheros (Nahr el-Kebir). Craftsmanship from Luristan, in contrast, arrived at the same cities either directly as objects, or in the presence of the craftsmen themselves, by way of the passes of the Zagros Mountains and then by re-ascending the Tigris or Euphrates and descending to the sea along the same valleys of the Orontes, the Leontes and the Eleutheros (Contenau 1949: 237). These are the traditional, unchanging passages in use for thousands of years in the Near East by shepherds, merchants and soldiers. Phoenician naval trade could act as a vehicle for the diffusion of the cultural ferment of the Mediterranean, ultimately bringing it to Sardinia. As a consequence, the Phoenicians must have brought to Sardinia, as they did to all the other areas that they colonized or visited, not only their own art, but also that of all the other people with whom they had some kind of trade relationship, such as, in this case, those of Urartu and Luristan.

There are still some unanswered questions in the matter of whether the ideas, the works of art themselves, or even, as Lilliu has suggested in the case of Luristan emigrants, the very artists are responsible for their presence on the island of Sardinia. All of these possibilities exist in the current state of research, but with varying probability.

Only future research, combined with future finds, will be able to give a clear and coherent picture to what will undoubtedly turn out to be a complex explanation for the miraculous appearance and flowering of ancient Sardinian bronze sculpture.

The catalog and photographs that follow present a representative selection that illustrates the points made in this narrative.

1. SEATED FEMALE (fig. 10.1).

Description: Seated female figure; pellet-shaped head with prominent nose and deep eye sockets; at the top of the head, a crest surmounts a cap or the hair; short neck attached to a wiry body and decorated with a torque that ends in a braid on the chest; finely modelled arms stretched out in front with hands clasped; legs fused together, divided by a groove in front and back; feet joined in a single squared volume with rounded corners; the figurine is placed on a small, rectangular base, provided with a depression, with remains of a bronze nail used in the attachment.

Bibliography: F. Barreca, Civiltà fenicio-punica e antichità romane. Sardegna, AA.VV., Milano 1971:140, fig. 131; Sardegna. L'espansione fenicia nel Mediterraneo, AA.VV., Roma 1971:13-14, pl. 60; Moscati 1972:439-440; A.M. Bisi, La civiltà fenicio-punica in Sardegna, Urbino 1975:112-113; Lilliu 1975:376; A. Parrot, M.H. Chehab and S. Moscati, Les Phéniciens - L'expansion phénicienne-Carthage, Paris 1975:224, fig. 244; Bisi 1977:910; 916; 918, pl. 33:2, with bibliography cited above; Barreca 1979:35, 198, pl. 4; 1980: 122-123, pl. 88; Tore 1981:23; Barreca 1981:372; 405-406.

2. STANDING MALE (fig. 10.2).

Description: Male statue standing wearing a short skirt; globular head; semicircular face with arched eyebrows, eye sockets with tiny lozenges, a triangular nose, a scantily incised mouth with a minimal beard; neck distinct from chest; long body, convex in front, flat in back with a vertical groove, broad shoulders, arms parallel to body; right forearm raised obliquely, lower limbs narrowing below the knee; right leg further back than left;

trapezoidal feet placed on a fragmentary quadrangular base.

Bibliography: Unpublished. For a general notice of the four bronze Phoenician figurines found at Santa Cristina (Paulilatino), see G. Tore, Elementi sulle relazioni commerciali della Sardegna nella prima età del Ferro, Atti del I Convengno Internazionale di studi geograficistorici, "La Sardegna nel Mondo Mediterraneo," Sassari 1981:262, n. 13.

3. WALKING MALE (fig. 10.3).

Description: Male figure wearing short skirt. Elongated head; triangular face with large eyesockets which define a thin, curved nose; mouth implied by a slight depression; small painted beard at end of chin; ears rendered by two vertical reliefs; tapering neck distinct from the head; chest sketchily shaped with shoulders emphasized; flat back; arms parallel to body; right forearm raised obliquely; missing hand probably had palm extended outward; lower limbs slightly separated.

Bibliography: Unpublished. See bibliography in catalog no. 2 above.

4. BUST OF MALE (fig. 10.4).

Description: Bust of male figure provided with small discoidal base; pellet-shaped head; triangular face ending in a pointed beard; semicircular eye sockets with bulbous eyes applied; pointed nose; horizontal slash for mouth; neck inserted on bust without transition; flattened upper limbs bent toward the head; left forearm ends in a distorted hand turned inward; bust damaged; ancient hole on the bottom of the base for the insertion of a pin.

Bibliography: Tore 1981:15, n. 14.

5. **WALKING MALE** (fig. 10.5).

Description: Male figure wearing a high conical hat with a rounded tip, arched eyebrows and a modelled nose can be identified on a triangular face; wide auricles of the ear, eye sockets and mouth indicated by an oblique incision; fairly small neck attached to a somewhat damaged bust with sturdy shoulders; arms parallel to bust; right forearm diagonally raised with palm turned outward; left forearm extended forward with closed fist perhaps originally wielding some unknown thing; lower part truncated; a slight twist of the stump on right with respect to the left suggests that the figure was walking.

Bibliography: V. Spinazzola, I bronzi sardi e la civiltà antica della Sardegna, Naples 1903:86, fig. 40; E. Pais, Sulla civiltà dei nuraghi e sullo sviluppo sociologico della Sardegna, Archivio Storico Sardo 6, 1910:158, n. 4; G. Porro, Influssi dell'Oriente preellenico sulla civiltà primitiva della Sardegna, Atene e Roma 18, 1915:160; 100, fig. 1; ns. 199-201; C. Albizzati, Sardus Pater, Il convegno archeologico in Sardegna, Reggio Emilia 1927:105; 109, n. 22; 107, fig. 14; A. Taramelli, Tempietto protosardo del Camposanto di Olmedo (Sassari), BPI 53, 1933:115; G. Lilliu, Modellini bronzei di Ittireddu e Olmedo (nuraghi o altiforni?), StSar 10-11, 1950-51:78, n. 15; G. Pesce, Sardegna punica, Cagliari 1961:94, fig. 87; S. Moscati, Il mondo dei Fenici, Milano 1966:276, pl. 104; Lilliu 1966:181; 287-288; S. Moscati, Considerazioni sulla cultura fenicio-punica in Sardegna, RendLinc 22:1-2, 1967:143, pl. IIb; S. Moscati, Fenici e Cartaginesi in Sardegna, Milano 1968:144; 45, pl. 41; S.M. Cecchini, I ritrovamenti fenici e punici in Sardegna, Roma 1963; F. Barreca, Civiltà fenicio-punica e antichità romane in Sardegna, Venezia 1969:140, fig. 132; F. Barreca, Ricerche puniche in Sar-

degna, Ricerche puniche nel Mediterraneo centrale, Roma 1970:34; F. Barreca, Sardegna, L'espansione fenicia nel Mediterraneo, Roma 1971:2; 13; 15; 18; Moscati 1972:441; 440, fig. a; J. Bouzek, Syrian and Anatolian Bronze Age figurines in Europe, PPS 38, 1972:158, n. 20; L. Vagnetti, Syrian and Anatolian Bronze Age figurines in Europe: an addendum, PPS 39, 1973:467; F. Barreca, La Sardegna fenicia e punica, Sassari 1974:17-22, 24, 180; V. Tusa, La civiltà punica, PCIA 3:70, pl. 68; F. Barreca, La colonizzazione fenicio-punica in Sardegna alla luce delle nuove scoperte, Simposio de Colonizaciones (Barcelona-Ampurias 1971), 1974:2; S. Moscati, Les Phéniciens en Sardaigne, Les Phéniciens, A. Parrot, M.H. Chehab, and S. Moscati eds., Paris 1975:223, fig. 243; F. Lo Schiavo, Il ripostiglio del Nuraghe Flumenelongu (Alghero-Sassari), Quaderni 2, 1976:15; 19, n. 38; Bisi 1977:912; 915-919; 924; 931, pl. 33:1; Tore 1981:11-13; 15-25, with bibliography above; Barreca 1981:372, 405.

6. **WALKING MALE** (not illustrated) H. 10.4cm.

Provenience: Camposanto (Olmedo).

Details of Find: Nuragic well-temple. Excavated by A. Taramelli, 1926.

Present Location: Sassari, Museo Archeologico Nazionale "G.A. Sanna" inv. 893.

Technical Data: Cast by lost-wax process.

Description: Walking male figure wearing short skirt; head covered by a wig; triangular face; eye sockets and mouth vaguely shown; prominent nose; round-tipped beard; fairly short neck; broad shoulders; bust tapers downward; arms parallel to bust; right forearm raised with palm turned outward; left forearm extended forward with bent elbow; lower left leg forward of right leg; the figurine is provided with a parallelopiped base.

State of Preservation: Fair; corroded.

Date: 8th-7th centuries B.C.

Bibliography: A. Taramelli and E. Lavagnino, Il Museo "G.A. Sanna" di Sassari, Roma 1933:8; A. Taramelli, Tempietto protosardo del Camposanto di Olmedo (Sassari), BPI 53, 1933: 114-115, pl. 1:1; G. Lilliu, Modellini bronzei di Ittireddu e Olmedo (nuraghi o altiforni?), StSar 10-11, 1950-51:77-79, n. 15; Lilliu 1966: 287-289, n. 175; E. Contu, La Sardegna nell'età nuragica, PCIA 3:193; Bisi 1977:913; 920-924; 931-932, pl. 33:3; Tore 1981:14-25 (with bibliography cited above); Barreca 1981: 375; 406.

7. STANDING? MALE (fig. 10.6)

Description: Globular head with just hints of eyes; curved nose, very small neck distinct from head; cylindrical chest with pellet-like breasts; vertical groove in back; arms parallel to body; right forearm bent up diagonally with palm turned outward; traces of a short skirt encircles the waist.

Bibliography: G. Spano, Bullettino Archeologico Sardo 3(1857):114-115; G. Spano, Catalogo della raccolta archeologica sarda del Canon. G. Spano, Cagliari 1860:69, n.3; G. Spano, Scoperte archeologiche fattesi in Sardegna in tutto l'anno 1876, Cagliari 1876:32; Lilliu 1966:279, no. 166; G. Tore, Le opere dell'arte, NUR:230, fig. 246.

8. STANDING NUDE FEMALE (not illustrated)

Provenience: Mandas.

Present Location: Cagliari, Private Collection.

Technical Data: Cast by lost-wax process.

Description: Flattened pellet-shaped head; elliptical face; eye sockets divided by pillar-shaped nose; mouth made by a diagonal incision; neck distinct from head, placed on a long body with a slight narrowing to mark the waist; arms a bastoncello, the right raised above the breast, the left parallel to the chest with a hand on the left hip; legs abstracted to two semi-cylinders, ending in two sketchily implied feet, there is a strong pin for insertion; a large torque, wound around the neck falls braided on the breast; the absence of male characteristics plus the similarity of female figurines with torques in the Syro-Palestinian area suggests that our bronze is the figurine of a female divinity.

Date: 9th-8th centuries B.C.

Bibliography: G. Tore, Gli scambi commerciali. NUR:244; 246, fig. 255; 1981:23, n. 73.

9. SEATED SMALL MALE PLAYING LYRE (fig. 10.7).

Description: Seated figure of cithara player wearing a close-fitting tunic; sketchy head with indication of nose and almond-shaped protruding eyes; bust block-shaped with a hint of a pectoral; flat back; cithara on a semicircular base with strings represented by a central plate, supported on the left arm; the right arm stretched out to play it; legs are abstracted to a semi-cylindrical volume; feet modelled together with a dividing line midway between; between the feet, a bronze nail is soldered for insertion.

Bibliography: F. Barreca, Il mastio, AA.VV., Monte Sirai-III, Roma 1966: 20-21, pls. 38-39; G. Garbini, Documenti artistici a Monte Sirai, AA.VV., Monte Sirai-III:113-115; Lilliu 1967:333; S. Moscati 1968: 143-144, fig. 40; Moscati 1972:440-441; Parrot et al. 1976:223-224, fig. 246; Barreca 1979:199, pl. 34; 1980: 123, pl. 93; 1981:407.

10. SEATED MALE MAKING AN OFFERING (fig. 10.8).

Description: Seated male figure with head bent forward; eyes represented by pellets in the eye sockets which are divided by a fairly well-defined nose; mouth made by a groove; short neck; flattened, unmodelled body; right arm rests on knee with a patera in the hand; left arm bent inward to pour a liquid into the patera from an askos-shaped base in the left hand; legs semi-cylindrical; separated in front by a vertical groove that also separates the feet; nail for insertion placed in a hole between the lower legs.

Bibliography: F. Barreca, L'acropoli, AA.VV, Monte Sirai-II, Roma 1965:53; 57-58, pls. 26-27; Moscati 1968:143; Moscati 1972:440; Parrot et al. 1976: 223-224, fig. 245; Barreca 1979:199,

pl. 35; 1980:123, pl. 92; 1981:406-407, fig. 410; G. Lilliu 1980:333.

11. DOG (not illustrated)

Provenience: Monte Sirai (Carbonia).

Details of Find: Fortress, casemate 3, stratum D, excavated by Ferruccio Barreca in 1965.

Present Location: Rome, Università degli Studi - Istituto del Vicino Oriente.

Technical Data: Cast by full lost-wax process.

Description: Running dog supported on a ring; long muzzle; body well modelled; forelegs advanced.

State of Preservation: Poor; strongly oxidized.

Date: 7th-6th centuries B.C.

Bibliography: F. Barreca, Il Mastio, AA.VV., Monte Sirai-III, Roma 1966: 21, pl. 39; Moscati 1972:440-441; Bisi 1977:199; G. Lilliu 1980:333.

Acknowledgments
    Thanks are due to my student, Dr. Raimondo Zucca, for his help in compiling this catalog.

CATALOG OF PHOENICIAN BRONZE FIGURINES FOUND IN SARDINIA

1. Seated female (fig. 10.1)

2. Standing male (fig. 10.2)

3. Walking male (fig. 10.3)

4. Bust of male (fig. 10.4)

5. Walking male (fig. 10.5)

6. Walking male (not illustrated)

7. Standing? male (fig. 10.6)

8. Standing nude female (not illustrated)

9. Seated small male playing lyre (fig. 10.7)

10. Seated male making offering (fig. 10.8)

11. Dog (not illustrated)

0   1   2 cm

Figure 10.1 SEATED FEMALE
From the Nuragic well-temple at Santa
Cristina (Paulilatino).   Ht. 8.6cm;
max. w. 2.55cm; thickness of bust
0.7cm.   Excavated by Enrico Atzeni,
1967; now in Cagliari, Museo Archeologico Nazionale.   Cast by lost-wax
process ca. 1000 B.C.

0   1 cm

Figure 10.2 STANDING MALE
From the Nuragic well-temple at Santa
Cristina (Paulilatino).   Right hand
and forearm missing.   Ht. 2.5cm; max.
w. 3.55cm; thickness of bust 1.2cm;
base 2.2 x 2.3cm.   Excavated by Enrico Atzeni, 1967; now in Cagliari,
Museo Archeologico Nazionale.   Cast
by lost-wax process, 9th-8th centuries B.C.

Figure 10.3 WALKING MALE
From the Nuragic well-temple at Santa
Cristina (Paulilatino). Left forearm
and right hand missing; lower limbs
broken off above the knee. Ht. 8.6cm;
max. w. 3.34cm; thickness of bust
1.43cm. Excavated by Enrico Atzeni,
1967; now in Cagliari, Museo Archeologico Nazionale. Cast by lost-wax
process, 9th-8th centuries B.C.

Figure 10.4 BUST OF MALE
From the Nuragic well-temple at Santa
Cristina. Right hand missing. Ht.
4.20cm; max. w. 4.2cm; thickness of
bust 0.6cm. Excavated by Enrico
Atzeni, 1967; now in Cagliari, Museo
Archeologico Nazionale. Cast by
lost-wax process, 9th-8th centuries
B.C.

Figure 10.5 WALKING (?) MALE
From Nuraghe Flumenelongu (Alghero).
Ht. 9.45cm; max. w. 5.10cm; thickness
of bust 1.4cm. Excavated by F. Nis-
sardi, 1882-1883? Now in Cagliari,
Museo Archeologico Nazionale. Cast
by lost-wax process, ca. 1000 B.C.

Figure 10.6 STANDING (?) MALE
From Rio Mulinu (Bonorva). Left
forearm and legs missing. Ht. 8.0cm.
Discovered in 1846 in a man-made
cave; now in Cagliari, Museo Archeologico Nazionale. Cast by lost-wax
process, 9th-8th centuries B.C.

Figure 10.7 SEATED SMALL
MALE PLAYING LYRE
From Monte Sirai (Carbonia). Ht.
5.85cm; max. w. 2.4cm; thickness of
bust 1.05cm. Excavated by Ferruccio
Barreca, 1965; now in Cagliari, Museo
Archeologico Nazionale. Cast by full
lost-wax process, 7th-6th centuries
B.C.

Figure 10.8 SEATED MALE
MAKING AN OFFERING
From Monte Sirai (Carbonia). Ht.
5.4cm; max. w. 2.6cm; thickness of
bust 0.9cm. Excavated by Ferruccio
Barreca, 1964; now in Cagliari, Museo
Archeologica Nazionale. Cast by full
lost-wax process, 7th-6th centuries
B.C.

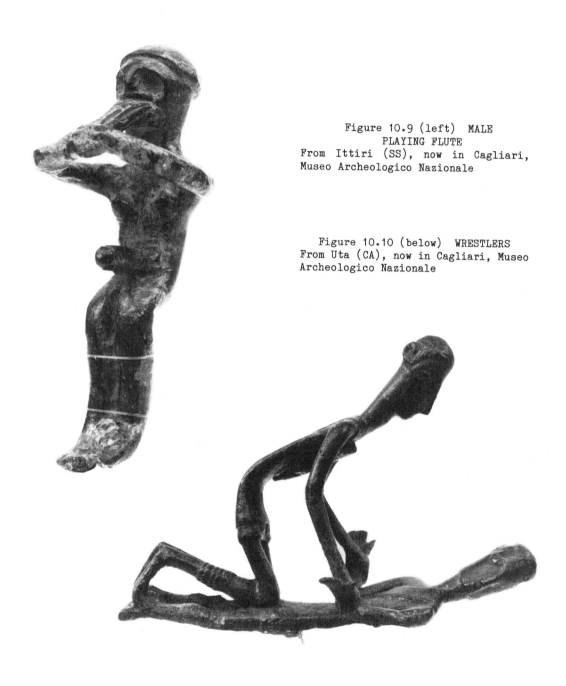

Figure 10.9 (left) MALE
PLAYING FLUTE
From Ittiri (SS), now in Cagliari,
Museo Archeologico Nazionale

Figure 10.10 (below) WRESTLERS
From Uta (CA), now in Cagliari, Museo
Archeologico Nazionale

REFERENCES

BARRECA, F.
    1979   La Sardegna fenicia e punica. Sassari: Chiarella.

    1980   Phönizischer Einfluss auf die Bronzeplastik. Kunst
            Sardiniens.

    1981   La Sardegna e i Fenici. Ichnussa.

BISI, A.M.
    1977   L'apport phénicien aux bronzes nouragiques de Sardaigne.
            Latomus 36:909-932.

CONTENAU, G.
    1949   La civilization phénicienne. Paris: Payot.

CROSS, F.M.
    1974   Leaves from an Epigraphist's Notebook. The Catholic
            Biblical Quarterly 36(4):486-494.

LILLIU, G.
    1966   Sculture della Sardegna nuragica. Cagliari-Verona: La
            Zattera.

    1967   La civiltà dei Sardi. Torino: E.R.I.

    1980   La civiltà dei sardi dal neolitico all'età dei nuraghi.
            Torino: E.R.I.

MOSCATI, S.
    1968   Fenici e Cartaginesi in Sardegna. Milano.

    1972   I Fenici e Cartagine. Torino: U.T.E.T.

PARROT, A., M.H. CHEHAB AND S. MOSCATI
    1976   I Fenici. Milano.

TORE, G.
    1981   Bronzetti fenici dalla Nurra. Bronzetti dalla Nurra.
            Quaderni 9. Sassari.

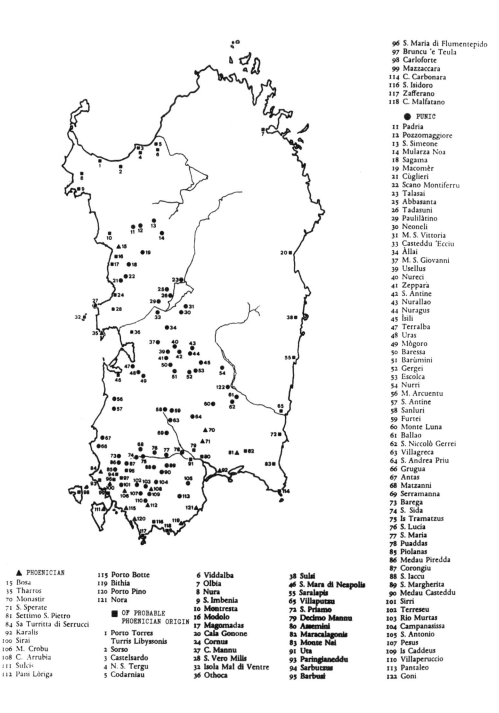

96 S. Maria di Flumentepido
97 Bruncu 'e Teula
98 Carloforte
99 Mazzaccara
114 C. Carbonara
116 S. Isidoro
117 Zafferano
118 C. Malfatano

● PUNIC
11 Padria
12 Pozzomaggiore
13 S. Simeone
14 Mularza Noa
18 Sagama
19 Macomèr
21 Cùglieri
22 Scano Montiferru
23 Talasai
25 Abbasanta
26 Tadasuni
29 Paulilàtino
30 Neoneli
31 M. S. Vittoria
33 Casteddu 'Ecciu
34 Àllai
37 M. S. Giovanni
39 Usellus
40 Nureci
41 Zeppara
42 S. Antine
43 Nurallao
44 Nuragus
45 Ìsili
47 Terralba
48 Uras
49 Mògoro
50 Baressa
51 Barùmini
52 Gergei
53 Escolca
54 Nurri
56 M. Arcuentu
57 S. Antine
58 Sanluri
59 Furtei
60 Monte Luna
61 Ballao
62 S. Niccolò Gerrei
63 Villagreca
64 S. Andrea Priu
66 Grugua
67 Antas
68 Matzanni
69 Serramanna
73 Barega
74 S. Sida
75 Is Tramatzus
76 S. Lucia
77 S. Maria
78 Puaddas
85 Piolanas
86 Medau Piredda
87 Corongiu
88 S. Iaccu
89 S. Margherita
90 Medau Casteddu
101 Sirri
102 Terreseu
103 Rio Murtas
104 Campanasissa
105 S. Antonio
107 Pesus
109 Is Caddeus
110 Villaperuccio
113 Pantaleo
122 Goni

▲ PHOENICIAN
15 Bosa
35 Tharros
70 Monastir
71 S. Sperate
81 Settimo S. Pietro
84 Sa Turritta di Serrucci
92 Karalis
100 Sirai
106 M. Crobu
108 C. Arrubia
111 Sulcis
112 Pani Lòriga

115 Porto Botte
119 Bithia
120 Porto Pino
121 Nora

■ OF PROBABLE PHOENICIAN ORIGIN
1 Porto Torres Turris Libyssonis
2 Sorso
3 Castelsardo
4 N. S. Tergu
5 Codarniau

6 Viddalba
7 Olbia
8 Nura
9 S. Imbenia
10 Montresta
16 Modolo
17 Magomadas
20 Cala Gonone
24 Cornus
27 C. Mannu
28 S. Vero Milis
32 Isola Mal di Ventre
36 Othoca

38 Sulsi
46 S. Mara di Neapolis
55 Saralapis
65 Villaputzu
72 S. Priamo
79 Decimo Mannu
80 Assemini
82 Maracalagonis
83 Monte Nai
91 Uta
93 Paringianeddu
94 Sarbutzus
95 Barbusi

Figure 11.1 Phoenician-Punic settlements in Sardinia

Ferrucio Barreca

Since 1958, there have been excavations, surface surveys and studies on material in museums, that all
relate to the ancient products of the
Phoenician and Punic civilization in
Sardinia. These have been so numerous
and careful that today, there is now
sufficient data to present a far more
complete and reliable view of that
civilization than in the past. Obviously, the time and space available
here do not allow for a critical exposition of these achievements; they
will have to be presented only in
brief synthesis, referring anyone to
the references at the end of this
communication for further information
and deeper insight into the impressive body of excavation and
research reports, analytical
catalogs, and the critical studies on
which our conclusions are based.

Phoenician and Punic Colonization in
Sardinia

Around 1000 B.C., the Phoenicians were already visiting Sardinia
in the course of their maritime trade
between the eastern and western Mediterranean. Proof of these visits can
be found in a fragmentary inscription
from Nora (Cross 1974:486-494; see
above, chap. 9), a bronze figurine
from Santa Cristina (Paulilatino)
(Barreca 1971:7-27, pl. 60; here,
fig. 10.1) and another from Flumenelongu (Alghero) (Barreca 1979a:35;
here, fig. 10.5); these need not mean
that at that time, there were
permanent Phoenician ports of call
along the coast of Sardinia. In
fact, it is certain that these
trading posts, first founded in the
ninth century B.C. all around the
island in indefinite number, became

regular settlements before 700 B.C.
(Barreca 1979a:37-39) (fig. 11.1).
Among these settlements are undoubtedly Karali (fig. 11.2), Sulci (fig.
11.3), Nora (fig. 11.4), Tharros
(fig. 11.5), Bosa, and perhaps Bithia
(Barreca 1979a:40-41).

In the seventh century B.C., at
least some of these settlements began
to spread towards the Sardinian hinterland with an average penetration
of about twenty kilometers from the
coasts, thereby originating the model
of the "polis" surrounded by territory on which smaller settlements
rose (Barreca 1979a:46-47).

Specific archaeological documentation of this territorial expansion
is confined at present to Karalis,
modern Cagliari, from which were
founded settlements at Settimo S.
Pietro and S. Sperate (Barreca 1979a:
42-48), and to Sulci, modern Sant'Antioco, which founded the famous military settlement of Monte Sirai near
Carbonia (Barreca 1979a:49-50) (figs.
11.6-11.7) and perhaps Pani Loriga
near Santadi (Barreca 1979a: 50-51).

It is possible and reasonable,
however, that all the major Phoenician coastal settlements in Sardinia
may have originated in a similar
spreading manner. In the second half
of the sixth century B.C., Carthage,
in order to prevent Greek colonization in Sardinia, and probably to
protect the Phoenician settlements
against the danger of native aggres-
sion of increasing intensity successfully achieved the armed conquest of
the island (Barreca 1979a:57-58;
Lilliu 1967:210-211).

1. Necropolis of S. Avendrace or of Tuvixeddu
2. Tophet?
3. Harbor
4. Temple-bouleuterion
5. Castello Hill (Acropolis?)
6. Southeastern necropolis of Bonaria

Figure 11.2   Cagliari (=Karali): Topographical map
of archaeological sites

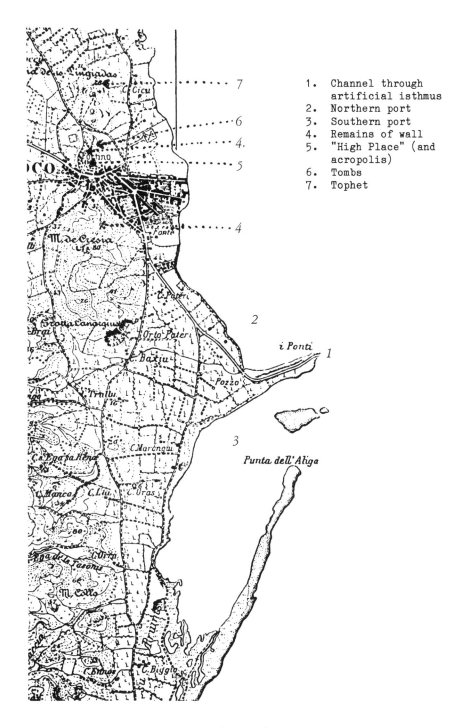

1. Channel through
   artificial isthmus
2. Northern port
3. Southern port
4. Remains of wall
5. "High Place" (and
   acropolis)
6. Tombs
7. Tophet

Figure 11.3 S. Antioco (=Sulci): Topographical map
of archaeological sites

1. Acropolis
2. Esplanade rocks near the harbor works
3. Remains of the city wall
4. Piazza
5. Northeastern port
6. Southeastern port
7. Northwestern port
8. Temple of Tanit
9. Roman theater
10. Sanctuary of health and oracles
11. Necropolis
12. Isthmus barrier
13. Punic aqueduct
14. Tophet

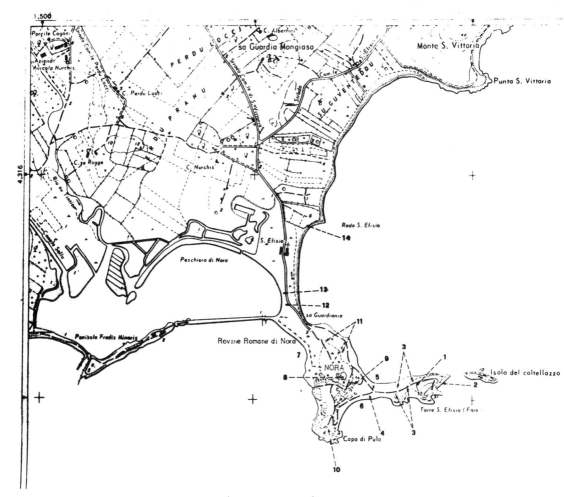

Figure 11.4 Nora (=Capo di Pula): Topographical map
of archaeological sites

1. Phoenicio-Punic necropolis of
   S. Giovanni di Sinis
2. Byzantine basilica of S.
   Giovanni Battista
3. Northern fortifications: first
   line (trench)
4. Northern fortifications:
   second line
5. Northern fortifications: third
   line; necropolis of the
   imperial age superimposed in
   ditch
6. Roman aqueduct
7. Nuragic Tophet
8. Temple of Demeter
9. Water works
10. Paleochristian basilica (S.
    Marco?) and Baptistry
11. Baths n. 1
12. Temple with semi-Doric columns
    and sacred area with a square
    portico
13. Baths n. 2
14. Temple with Punic inscriptions
15. Habitation quarter
16. Western fortifications
17. Southern fortifications
18. Roman necropolis
19. Phoenicio-Punic necropolis
    (reused in Roman period) of
    Capo S. Marco
20. Harbor piers
21. Fortification ruins
22. Phoenicio-Punic acropolis and
    Nuraghe Baboe Cabitza
23. Temple of Capo S. Marco
24. Access road to the acropolis

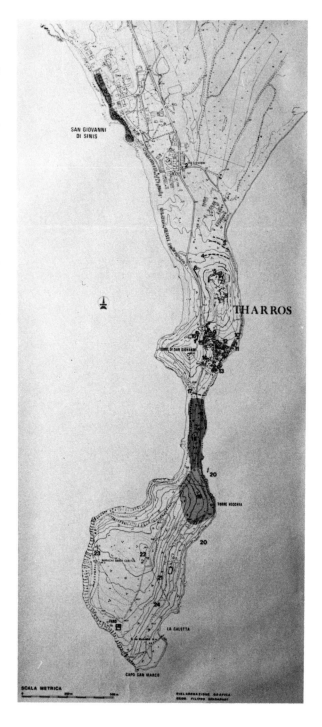

Figure 11.5 Tharros (=S. Giovanni di Sinis): Topographical map
of archaeological sites

1. Acropolis
2. Northeastern bastion
3. Southeastern fortifications
4. Southeastern access way
5. Natural bulwark, partially fortified
6. Fortifications on the southwestern access way
7. Necropolis
8. Tophet
9. Central-western fortifications
10. Fortifications on the northern access way
11. Fortifications on the plain
12. Typical rural house
13. Northeastern access way
14. Southwestern access way
15. Northern access way

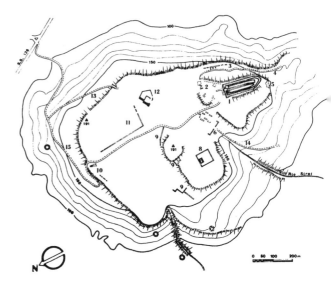

Figure 11.6 Monte Sirai (Carbonia): Topographical map
of archaeological sites

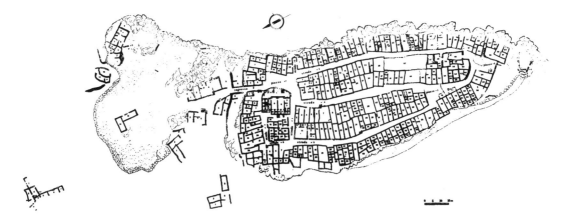

Figure 11.7 Monte Sirai (Carbonia): Plan of the acropolis

The scanty reports of the ancient historians about these facts (Moscati 1968:21-26) are today abundantly confirmed on the basis of archaeological finds along all Sardinian coasts and in the inner part of all four provinces; the documentation is particularly rich for the provinces of Cagliari and Oristano in which exploration has been carried out for a longer time and more extensively than in the other two.

In the light of our present knowledge, it seems possible to say that only in the innermost mountains of the Nuorese and the Gallura was there a lack of Punic presence, while in the fourth century B.C. all the remaining country was surely occupied and colonized by the Carthaginians (Barreca 1979a:73-76, fig. II; Barreca 1981a). The results of recent excavations in Senorbì (Costa 1980: 265-290; Usai 1981:39-47), Sanluri (Barreca 1982b:45-47; Paderi 1982a,b: 49-51, 63-66, pls. 28-31, 34; Tore 1982:53-58, pls. 32-33), Genoni (Guido, unpublished) and Padria (Tore 1973-74:374-379), moreover, prove this.

In the well-known treaty with Rome of 509 B.C. (Polybius *Histories* III:22, 8), the fact that Carthage could forbid the Romans and their allies from trading on any of the Sardinian coasts without the presence of Carthaginian heralds or scribes, is a reflection of their ability to guarantee for themselves the observance of this provision and gives graphic proof of their political influence along the whole coastal perimeter of Sardinia.

Many Punic tombs dated to the fourth and third centuries B.C. have been discovered in small groups scattered in agricultural, wooded or mining areas, away from major and minor urban settlements. These finds surely show that Carthage organized the occupied Sardinian territory by applying the notion of colonization through far-reaching settlements, with families living in isolation or small groups in the countryside near the smaller urban settlements, which tended to be closer to the major settlements (Barreca 1979a:77-82; 1981a:356-357).

Carthage's sovereignty on Sardinia ceased formally in 238 B.C., as is well-known; but the Phoenician and Punic civilization survived for a long time on the island, persisting in its last manifestations to the Constantinian age at least, as the archaeological finds in the temples have proven at Antas (Fluminimaggiore) (Barreca et al. 1969; Barreca 1975; 1981:384) and S. Salvatore (Cabras) (Barreca 1975; 1979a:20; 1981:384-5).

Such a long survival surely marks the presence in Roman Sardinia of a solid number of descendants from the old Punic settlers, but it can hardly be explained without the admission that Carthage's civilization was deeply assimilated by the native elements, not through an acculturation process as some say (Lilliu 1982:218), but rather, I think, through a true process of integration; not only ethnic integration (favored by colonization in outlying settlements), but also cultural integration, visible in the native component of the Punic civilization of Sardinia from at least the fourth-third centuries B.C. (Barreca 1980a: 475-486; 1981a:377-417).

With respect to this matter, it is sufficient to cite both the representations on Sardo-Punic bronze coins of the third century B.C., in a style clearly associated with native bronzework that reflects the obvious artistic congeniality of the indigenous artisans (Barreca 1979a:180-181), and also the substantial survivals of native worship of cults of fertility and salvation in the Punic-

Roman temples at Antas (Fluminimag-giore) (Barreca 1981a:380-381; here fig. 11.8), S. Jaci (S. Nicolò Gerrei) (Barreca 1979a:144; 1981a: 383), S. Salvatore (Cabras) (Barreca 1981a: 381-382) and Terreseu (Narcao) (Barreca 1981a:383-384); and more-over, generally, in the shrines nested within <u>nuraghi</u> and Nuragic "sacred wells," where during the Punic-Roman period Demeter, clearly the version of the most ancient Mediterranean "Dea Madre" was wor-shipped as the principal goddess by the Nuragic inhabitants (Barreca 1979a:139), another indication of this fusion with Phoenician/Punic elements.

The determinants of this cultural integration were not only the ethnic medley produced by such far-reaching settlement and the enrollment of Sardinian mercenaries in the Carthaginian army, but also, and especially, the integrity of the two cultures, lived by the two peoples simultaneously in the same territory and inevitably mutually encountered; this confrontation was encouraged by the circulation of men and goods in the territory lying between the cities, and also among the cities and the country, against the background of an open economy of

first a civic and then a national type, even though it was applied in colonial society (Barreca 1979a:177-180).

Phoenician and Punic Antiquities in Sardinia

1. Public, Civil and Military Institutions

Archaeology proves that the first cities to appear in Sardinia were the ones built by Phoenicians on the coast as well as inland (Barreca 1961a:27-47; 1979a:270-273). Coastal Phoenician settlements were primarily commercial in nature: ports of call on the routes of Phoenician ships coming into the western Mediterranean in order to transport metal to sell in the marketplaces of the Near East. The original core of the city was consequently centered on the market-place, next to the harbor which, in order to exploit the calm water in front of the most easily defensible ports, utilized the coasts of small peninsulas (Nora, Sulci, Tharros) with the isthmus acting as a double jetty, usable on both sides, depend-ing upon the winds; or else lagoons (Karali, Bithia) or estuaries (Bosa) guarded at the back by neighboring hills, were used.

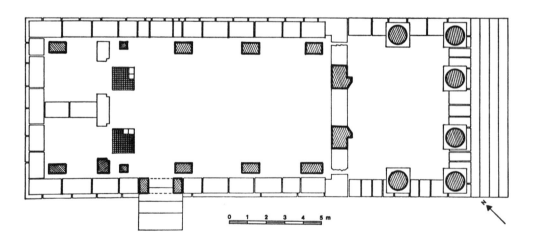

Figure 11.8 Fluminimaggiore (Antas): Plan of the Temple of Sardus Pater

The docks were made mainly by utilizing coastal rocks (Tharros), and also by newly excavating or adjusting inner basins to make round or straight channels (Capo Frasca and Porto Pino). It is possible to say of the archaeological topography of Karalis, Nora, Bithia, Sulci and Tharros, that the oldest buildings rose near the marketplace: houses, storehouses and a shrine, undoubtedly very important to settlement life, but surely very different from the tophet which always rose in the most decentralized area: the outskirts of the town or even outside the town walls. The necropolis obviously had to occupy a zone outside the inhabited area but not necessarily outside the perimeter wall which defended the site. It was also necessary to enclose within the perimeter walls the acropolis which contained the fortifications occupying the more easily tenable positions along the harbor such as Capo S. Marco at Tharros, Capo di Pula at Nora, and the Castello hill at Karali.

Sometimes the urban walls were supported by complicated and impressive fortifications, which show that some coastal settlements (Tharros, Sulci) were real maritime fortresses, used as well for important military aims without losing the original commercial function (Barreca 1976: 215-223, pls. 59-65, fig. 10; 1978: 116-128, figs. 27-36). The settlement then expanded to accomodate the population growth by filling in the empty areas within the town walls and constructing new buildings in a fan shape around the original core (Karali, Sulci), or along the road connecting the harbor with the hinterland. Further expansion added to the urban area outside the walls (Tharros, Karali). Obviously such urban enlargement would require the formation of a new necropolis, as well as an enlargement of the still-existing one, as at Karali, with the amplification of the Tuvixeddu necropolis

and the creation of the Bonaria one. The rebuilding overlap and modification of the following periods make it difficult to determine the network of the road system in the coastal settlement in the Phoenician/Punic Age. The anomalies of Roman roads, some excavation tests made here and there analogy the best known road system of an inner settlement (M. Sirai) suggest a functional road system, which managed to conform to the land, but also sought a straight, wide road system as well. Surely a main road existed that came from the marketplace, crossed the urban area and emerged from one of the gates, directing itself towards the back of the settlement, and serving the oldest necropolis and the tophet. Other roads radiating like spokes of a wheel connected the various urban area sectors with the marketplace, the gates and the acropolis, must have existed, but at present it is not possible to say anything about those roads.

The problem of the water supply was resolved with the creation of public and private cisterns (Karali, Nora, Tharros), but the use of artificial conduits (Nora), even though much restricted, was also known (Patroni 1904:17).

Civic buildings, like courts or the assembly of elders are not yet known, so it is reasonable to think that these functions may have been assumed by temples, usually endowed with small shrines (sacelli) and large courtyards (Barreca 1979a:241-242). To the well known data referring to Punic state administration (heralds and scribes) and municipal administration (sufeti and senators), and in addition to the three social classes (aristocracy, common people and slaves) that formed the urban population, and to particular components of such classes (princes of priests, craftsmen), other new elements can be added, furnished by some inscriptions from Antas documenting among citizens with complete political rights, the presence of persons using an unusual expression, declaring themselves "ba'am", namely "in (the name of) the people" of the city, emphasizing in their particular legal position, the status of foreigners (Sardinian natives?) brought into the urban population with full rights, apparently as a reward of some kind (Barreca 1981a:379).

The Phoenician inland settlements, unlike those on the coast, were surely of military origin. They were founded in order to assure rule over the hinterland by virtue of the presence of garrisons. The core was, therefore, always in a fortified position: a fortress occupied by a military contingent, around which the civil population lived, not in the fortress itself, but in an area reserved within the perimeter of an external fortification line. Thus the fortress rose: a military settlement, with its original fort on an acropolis, while the sector occupied by the civil population formed the lower town with a small urban area, necropolis and tophet. Basing our knowledge on the documentation provided by excavations at Pani Loriga (Santadi) (Barreca 1978:121-122, fig. 32), and especially at Monte Sirai (Carbonia) (Barreca et al. 1964-67; Barreca 1978:120-121, fig. 31; 1981a: 360-361, figs. 391-394), we can say that while the layouts of these areas are similar to those in the coastal cities, different criteria determined both the original arrangement of the settlement and its components, and also its expansion, as a clear consequence of their different functions.

Typical of the interior city is the location on the top of a secluded plateau, in a strategic position for surveillance of crossroads (M. Sirai, Pani Loriga), of river crossings (Senorbì - Monte Luna), and so on, or else in the heart of a particularly important territory (Uselis). Its fortifications, from the Archaic period on, are characterized, especially in the acropolis, by a plan of specifically connecting elements, responsible for the creation of many defensive lines, ideally concentric, of external towers, "railroad rack" curtain walls, "elbow bend" entrances, "entrance hall" doors, "pliers" doors and "advanced works"; and by an impressive accomodation to the contour of the ground. On the one hand these elements join a great functionality in defensive plan and its realization; on the other a decided predilection for the quadrilateral plan of the structures compatible with the requirements of the site and functionality (Barreca 1979a:12-14). As long as the interior city had a military function, its civil or religious areas (new quarters, tophet, necropolis) were entirely within the perimeter walls, since any use by the population of inadequately protected areas was obviously inconceivable. The acropolis (M. Sirai - see fig. 11.7, Pani Loriga) was always well developed and furnished with mighty fortifications for sheltering a whole garrison. It presented the look of a small urban center, with lodgings and storehouses collected in long blocks, with a good road system and with enough wide and straight carriage roads laid out upon the natural road bed, integrated by stones and covered by earth. There were also open areas, squares, located near the gates in order to facilitate the muster of troops for sorties or for the defense of these weak spots. Of all the buildings on the acropolis, the bastion dominated, placed in the most tenable sector (Pani Loriga, Genoni - S. Antini) or else near a gate (M. Sirai) to strengthen the defense. On the acropolis there was also a public shrine but today the only well known example is the bastion shrine in the Monte Sirai acropolis which appears like an adaptation of a military building (the _mastio_), made after the fortress was abandoned by the garrison (fig. 11.9); it is therefore not easy to specify today the original form and location. There are, however, indications of how worship was carried on both inside and in front of a movable sanctuary (the holy tent according to Diodorus Siculus (XX:65, 1) was always present with the Carthaginian army) which was placed in the fortress bastion when the garrison was present. In the post-military stage of the fortress, when it was an inner city, the bastion was structurally altered and became a temple shrine (Barreca et al. 1965-67; Barreca 1981a:387-88) (fig. 11.10).

The dimensions of the M. Sirai acropolis (approximately 300 x 60m) suggest a garrison composed of five hundred foot soldiers and a hundred mounted soldiers in the ratio of one to five (Barreca 1975b:30-36). This hypothesis takes into consideration that part was occupied by the road system, the storehouses and other structures. Similar numbers are assumed for garrisons placed in other acropoleis of similar dimensions (Santadi - Pani Loriga, Genoni - S. Antini, Bonorva - S. Simeone and so on), while proportionally smaller garrisons were surely in the smaller fortresses (Furtei - S. Biagio, Bolotana - Mularza, Noa and so on), which we can compute at least approximately, according to the strengthened surface.

It is still impossible to specify the composition of the civil population in the inner settlement; they never reached the demographic level of the big coastal cities even though they counted among their inhabitants many of mixed blood, foreigners, officers of Phoenician extraction and Libyans banished to Sardinia by Carthage (Barreca 1979a: 73-82).

Many inner settlements clearly derive from fortresses and outposts colonized at the same time by Carthaginians or their Phoenician forerunners according to the evidence of defensive areas. These are real fortified systems (Middle Eastern system by the Nuorese mountains and middle northern system on the Campeda), expressed according to the principles of mobile war and accomplished by active defense of the boundaries by moving garrisons, placed on fortified positions, monitoring roads and fixed crossings, that were interconnected by roads which would allow speedy movement. Obviously those roads, along with others connecting the inner settlements with the coastal ones, were utilized not only by exponents of the military and political Phoenician-Punic world, but also by those of the economic world (farmers, shepherds, miners, craftsmen and merchants) who were surely in touch with the natives, not only in the occupied and colonized areas, but in the mountains outside the fortified systems, as the Nuragic objects of Punic influence and the Punic coin hoards found in the Nuoro district prove.

There has been an impressive and extended circulation of men and objects to support the idea of the phenomenon of Sardinian-Punic integration, contributing aspects of the civilization of Carthage in its spread throughout the island.

2.   Private Institutions

Archaeological excavations have given full documentation for the typology of the Phoenician-Punic houses in Sardinia both in its urban and its rural translation. The urban house (such as at Karali, Nora, Tharros; there are very clear examples in Monte Sirai - see fig. 11.11) had a four-sided plan, was furnished with a decentralized hallway and had other areas of use such as bedrooms, kitchen, workroom and domestic shrine. These areas were placed in one or two storeys and covered by a roof made with wooden beams and planks, without tiles, waterproofed by pitch and lime-plaster (Barreca 1979a:233-238; 159-166). This same lime-plaster also covered the walls, one cubit thick, constructed by various techniques: thick stones connected by mortar and reinforced by squared blocks here and there and especially at the corners; also squared pillars placed at regular intervals (loom-walls) or irregular (pseudo loom-walls) in masonry made by thick stones connected by mortar, or green bricks upon a thick stone baseboard. The floors were made of beaten earth or (in later Punic period) in the cocciopesto technique, sometimes enriched by white mosaic tesserae arranged in magic-religious symbols.

The water supply was assured with wells and cisterns (generally the extended "bathtub" type), sometimes also with a modest public channel in masonry of which the only well known example was in Nora (Patroni 1904:17). Obviously the short stone drains for removing the waste water from single houses were private. They followed the entry passageway and discharged on the road, running in a partly covered canal to reach public collecting basins (M. Sirai).

There is no evidence of the existence of urban houses beyond the first floor, such as was found at Carthage and in Phoenician settlements. Otherwise the analogy is clear between the Phoenician- Punic Sardinian houses and the Israelite Praesilich ones (Albright 1962:fig. 46 showing examples from Tell Beit Mirsim).

The urban house had a modest middle area (70 mq.); the rural one, a considerably greater area with the presence of a large courtyard containing carts, agricultural tools and cattle (Barreca 1979a:260-263) (fig. 11.12). The most common house pattern is the Mediterranean archaic house, expressed with the typical functionality and asymmetry of the Phoenician-Punic world, housing families androcratically and monogamously.

The Phoenician-Punic tomb in Sardinia is today well known through thousands of examples which document a varying typology, even to a greater extent than the houses. There are pit graves, small containers, large containers, and underground chamber tombs accessible through a vertical shaft and containing steps or notches in the walls in order to permit the grave digger's descent. In the inner chambers, there are generally niches in the walls, or in the floor. Outside, the presence of the grave is marked by a little rectangular tumulus of crude stone or by a cone, shaped like a house with a roof with double sloping sides, with the ridge serving as an altar at the top; also by a conical or pyramidal or pillar-shaped cippus, sometimes placed in a complex monument, and whenever possible with steps furnished in the base (fig. 11.13).

The funerary depositions are either cremations or inhumations. The recent excavation at Pani Loriga (Barreca 1971:20-27; 1982a:183-184; Bartoloni and Bondì 1981; Bartoloni et al. 1982), Bithia (Barreca 1982a) and Monte Sirai (Bartoloni and Bondì 1981; Bartoloni et al. 1982), have revealed the greatest use of cremation in the Phoenician age (7th-6th centuries) and its impressive renewal in the late Punic age (4th-3rd centuries), while between the end of the sixth and the beginning of the fourth century B.C. inhumation was practiced exclusively. Wall paintings (Barreca 1982a:182, pl. 21), inscriptions and funerary finds provide ample documentation for the Phoenician-Punic faith in the personal survival of the soul,

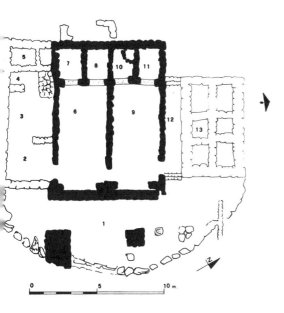

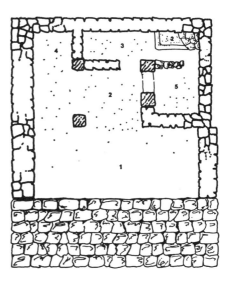

Figure 11.9 Monte Sirai (Carbonia): Plan of the shrine (sacellum) in the fortification of the acropolis

Figure 11.10 Monte Sirai (Carbonia): Plan of the tophet shrine

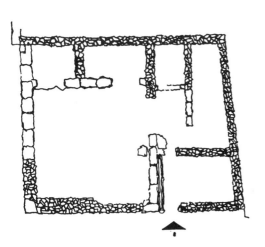

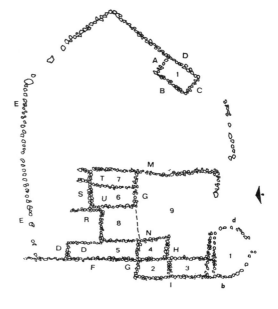

Figure 11.11 Monte Sirai (Carbonia): Plan of a typical urban Punic house

Figure 11.12 Monte Sirai (Carbonia): Plan of a typical rural Punic house

that after death returns to a new existence as on earth, through divine intervention and the help of magic. To this afterlife belong the profane objects of practical use (lamps, plates, jugs, and amphorae) and luxury goods (jewelry, perfume bottles). There is eloquent documentation for faith in divine help in painted pictures and sculptures (figurines and male or female busts), astral symbols (star, sphere and crescent) and geometric symbols (baetylic pillars, "Tanit's mark") of the Phoenician-Punic divine persons; while magic amulets of Semitic or Egyptian type, placed in the graves, are used in order to obtain a quiet and speedy death, revival, a quiet repose and happiness in the hereafter. Surely, the huge majority of these amulets are ambivalent, because they are designed to work in man's favor either during or after his life on earth.

During life, the Phoenicians and Carthaginians surely expected amulets to defend them against any demons, the evil eye and pernicious animals (fearful eyed masks, ostrich egg eyes; scapulars and medals with appeals to divinity or its symbols in pictures; hands with fingers to exorcise; Ra's eye or ugiat; sun scarabs with magic inscriptions; figured metallic sheets with the engraving of a long series of Egyptian gods; amulets such as cobras or urei; sphinxes, lions, crocodiles; talismen representing mighty and charitable Egyptian gods like Isis, Osiris, Horus, Knum the ram, Nefertum the lotus, Min the long phallic one, Ptah-Pateco the embryo), health (pictures of healer Egyptian gods Thoth and Konsu, the lioness goddess Sekhmet able to rule the negative force of diseases) fecundity (pictures of mother goddesses Isis, Hathor, Nut, gods of marriage, family, pregnancy and labor, wet nurses, protectors like Bes, Toeri and Mut; amulets reproducing the phallus too,

or the cyprea moneta sea shell, alluding to female sex), joy, love and wealth (pictures of Egyptian goddesses Bastit and Hathor, and the Uaz amulet in its vegetable shape). After death, in contrast, the Phoenicians and Carthaginians had to expect of those same amulets not only indefinite support through the divine presence and the fear that the frightful masks, the urei snakes, the sphinxes and the lions were able to inspire in the demons; but a quiet sleep inside the grave (watched by Bes) with copious food and drink, a merry life in the hereafter through the favor of Hathor and Bastit and especially the foundation for perpetual happiness: revival after death. We may imagine that they expected this supreme gift through the presence of pictures of gods and goddesses in the tomb, to which the Egyptian religion imputed giving life because they were either makers, fertilizers, resurrection givers or mothers (Isis, Hathor, Nut, Horus, Ptah - Pateco, Knum, Thoth, Nefertum, Min, Sebek), divine expressions of revival and rebirth (Osiris, Konsu), life symbols (Shu) or life protectors in its first moments (Bes, Toeri, Mut). The presence in the grave of other ambivalent amulets alluded to the life source and its secret renewal: these were the phallus and cyprea moneta pictures, the sun scarab (the-return-to-life pledge through self regeneration, analogous to that ascribed to such an insect in Egypt), and the Ra's weeping eye, from whose tears the human species was born according to Egyptian mythology. But there are other amulets too, surely needed by man only after earth life, therefore definable exclusively as amulets for the dead: small bronze hatchets commonly known as razors, which facilitated to men the passage to the hereafter, cutting the hidden thread from which dying was considered to be fastened to life; the ostrich egg, able to renew in favor of the dead, the first moment of cosmic life; the pictures of the Egyptian god Anubis the soul-weigher in the judgement of deeds, whose good will evidently was sought after; and the image of the vessel of life portrayed by the frog, a rebirth pledge analogous to the metamorphosis of this animal.

In conclusion, the Phoenician-Punic man in Sardinia, too, hoped to enjoy a new life in the hereafter, characterized by a long, untroubled repose and everlasting pleasure of the basic things, such as those possessed by him or at least desired on the earth. In order to attain these, he depended upon divine intervention, attempting to reach it through the plentiful use of magic means. The quantity of Egyptian or Egyptianizing amulets in the Phoenician-Punic graves of Sardinia is surely significant for the favor possessed by Egyptian magic in Sardinia between the 7th and 3rd centuries B.C. It is not possible to say the same about Egyptian religion, which never predominated in the Phoenician western world; even in spite of appearances, not even a cult of the Greek goddess Demeter prevailed: the western Phoenician religion was, and remained, forever Semitic.

3. Religious Institutions

Archaeology has, for the moment, proven the existence in Sardinia of at least 35 shrines (Barreca 1979a: 146; 249-259) in which ten divine Phoenician persons and two foreign "Phoenicianized" gods were revered: Baal Hammon, Baal Addir, Baal Shamem, Melqart, Sid, Eshmun, Horon, Shadrafa, Ashtart, Tanit, Bes (whom the Phoenicians received from Egypt) and Demeter (who, together with Kore, her daughter, came to Carthage from Greek Sicily and then was "Punicized" to such an extent that the Romans, after the acquisition of Punic Africa, named the pair 'Africanae'). Moreover, two funerary inscriptions found in Karali (Cagliari) document in this settlement the belief in Hut (Taramelli 1912:165-166); while an honorary inscription found in Sulcis (S. Antioco) attests to the belief in Elat, who was perhaps analogous to Ashtart or Tanit, because her name is an appellative and merely means "Goddess" (Guzzo Amadasi 1967:129-131).

Unfortunately we do not know all the cults and shrines to the same extent (Barreca 1979a:146); it is possible, however, to say that, in this situation, Sardinian documentation has a determining weight for the knowledge of Phoenician-Punic religion and its influence on architecture and on figurative art, not only on the island itself, but in the whole Carthaginian world as well. So, through the interpretation and integration of the archaeological data previously illuminated by the archaeological finds in Sardinia from 1958 to the present (Barreca 1973; 1974), and especially through the Antas finds (Barreca 1975), we are able to say that the Phoenician-Punic religion recognized the existence of numerous male and female divine persons, with fatherly, motherly, and filial characteristics, in pairs and especially grouped in triads; present in the skies (Baal Shamaim or Shamem), in the stars, on the earth and in the waters (the divine persons named in the fourth and fifth triad of Hannibal's famous oath), with supreme privileges (Baal Hammon, Baal Addir, Ashtart as Baalat or Lady of Sidon, Tanit like Rabat, or Lady of Carthage and especially Melqart, with the name of City King), beneficial in life on earth and the hereafter (Sid, Eshmun, Shadrafa, Horon, Hut), the creators of universal life (Reshef, Ashtart) or life-renewers in the annual cycle of vegetation (Sid and Eshmun), whose personalities fused and mingled in Adon of Byblos (Moscati 1972: 522-528; Barreca 1973:10-12 bis; 16-21). All those divine persons, furnished with personal characteristics, privileges and functions, could otherwise change, and exchange between themselves, all of these (Moscati 1958:133), appearing reciprocally equal, as manifold appearances of the spiritual and noncorporeal, supreme maker, king and universal rescuer, the God (Barreca 1973:40-62; 1977; 1979b). "Baal's name," appellative to Ashtart (Moscati 1972:520), and "Baal's face" to Tanit (namely manifestation or presence) (Gsell 1924:244-247), together with the fact that the various divine Phoenician names are all simple appositions (except for the foreign "Phoenicianized" gods), attributes and specifications always referable to the same god, are all, I think, impressive arguments in favor of this interpretation, that considers Phoenician-Punic spirituality based on the idea of divinity, unique in essence and various in shape or manifestation: a well known idea in the Near East and in Egypt at the end of the third millennium B.C., and in Israelite mystics from the remotest age, and in Zoroastrian Persia in the first millennium B.C., namely in those religious societies that have had extended and intimate connections with early Phoenician civilization.

Naturally, Bes and Demeter too, were worshipped through cults based upon this same notion: Bes as a healer (Pesce 1965; Uberti 1973; Gsell 1924:332-333; Caquot 1952:74-88; Sznycer 1969-70:69-74; Uberti 1978:315-319), perhaps like Shadrafa the Phoenician healer spirit, and Demeter as the expression of divine female fertility in the annual cycle of vegetation, as Ashtart (Gsell 1924:251-277; Barreca 1979a:152) or the Phoenician divine female person present on the earth according to Hannibal's oath. Both had numerous temples in Sardinia among which are worth mentioning the temples to Bes at Bithia (Taramelli 1933-34:288-291; Pesce 1961:37, 58, 77, 108-110; 1968:

331-337) and near the hot springs at Fordongianus (Taramelli 1903:482-85), the temples to Demeter at Terreseu – Narcao (Barreca 1979a:146-147) and in the bastion at Monte Sirai (Barreca 1965; 1966; 1967; 1979a:139). Most important for knowledge of Phoenician-Punic religion are the Sid temple at Antas, the tephatim at Sulci (Pesce 1961:68-71; Barreca 1979a, passim; 1979b:83-85; Tronchetti 1979: 201-205), M. Sirai (Barreca 1964b:20-36; Barreca and Bondì 1980:143-145; Bartoloni and Bondì 1981:217-230; Bartoloni et al. 1982:273-299), Tharros (Acquaro et al. 1975-1982), Nora (Patroni 1904) and Bithia (Barreca et al. 1965:145-152; Barreca 1979a:154, 250, 256-257), that prove by their Phoenician pattern, Baal and his providential manifestation of Tanit's creed. The excavations performed in the Phoenician/Punic/Sardinian shrines have proven to us how the covered shrine, not yet a necessary element in the temple structure, was always present in the holy area, generally having very modest dimensions, placed with a northern orientation and presented normally in a tripartite plan, with the Penetrale cut in two small spaces containing an altar in the right hand space and a statue or baetyl in the left.

The presence of shrines in perishable material such as wood is conjectured in the Archaic tophet at Bithia (Barreca 1979a:256) and in the M. Sirai acropolis for as long as the Carthaginian garrison with its holy tent remained (Barreca 1981b). The contents of the urns found in the various tephatim have proven the practice of the first-born sacrifice but at Tharros, have revealed traces of animal sacrifices consumed together with human ones (Fedele 1978; 77-78; 1979:67-88; Acquaro 1979: 53). Epigraphy confirms the existence in Sardinia of a Punic hierarchically organized clergy with the mention of "princes of priests"

(Guzzo Amadasi 1967:116-120), and the study of Sardinian folklore provides us with even more documentation related to ancient celebration of festivals glorifying Phoenician Adon, even if worshipped by various names at different places (Barreca 1973, passim; 1975a:10-12; 1979a:144-145; Cinus et al. 1981). The Antas finds have revealed the existence of a Punic myth of human deliverance from evil through divine intervention, declared by the triumphant armed Sid struggling against a monster; it has been possible to recognize this myth in Punic representations of Tharros (Barreca 1979a:19, 142), Karali (Barreca 1979a:141-142) and Carthage (Barreca 1979a:19-20) despite some iconographic variations.

4.   Epigraphy

Votive and funerary inscriptions provide the greater part of Phoenician-Punic epigraphy. In Sardinia their numbers have increased in the last twenty-five years through the finds in the tophet at Sulci (unpublished), in the temple "of the Punic inscriptions" at Tharros (Uberti 1976:53-55; Inedite), in the bastion-shrine at Monte Sirai (Barreca et al. 1965:79-92; Guzzo Amadasi 1967:121-123) and in the Sid-temple at Antas (Barreca et al. 1969:47-93). These inscriptions are generally short and pithy with the dedicator's name, sometimes followed by those of his forefathers and by the name of his home settlement. They are generally preceded by the name of the divine person to whom the offering is dedicated, with a final stereotyped formula indicating the reason for the offering. These Phoenician Punic inscriptions clearly resemble those found previously in the western Phoenician world, with letters, which are generally small and gracefully slender, producing a rather calligraphic effect.

5.   Arts and Handicrafts

The excavations from 1958 to the present have greatly extended the documentation of Phoenician and Punic art and handicrafts in Sardinia, architecture and building, monumental stone sculpture, wall and vase painting, pottery, terracotta and bronze sculpture, coinage, industrial metallurgy, jewelry, gem cutting, glyptics, glasswork, ivory and bone carving, and woodworking. Since the space available does not permit more than a mention of this most important aspect of the Phoenician-Punic civilization, it can only be treated as a synthesis of the characteristics that I think can be considered the essential common elements of its production according to the archaeological evidence. Reference is therefore made to the existing general studies and monographs on this subject (Bibliography in Moscati 1972:709-712 and in RSF 1973-1983). Here I have expressed in a schematic way, the positive and negative aspects of Phoenician and Punic art and handicraft production on Sardinia:

1) Absolute and firm functionality, always leading to technically vigorous and aesthetically modest workmanship, except when production pretends to high artistic rendering (jewelry).

2) Emphatic conservatism in technical, typological and stylistic aspects (similar to the conservatism documented by both ideology and institutions).

3) Lack of symmetry in architecture (clear examples in house and shrine plans).

4) Lack of realism and harmony in the figurative arts (the cult statue found in the bastion shrine at Monte Sirai (Barreca et al. 1965:53-54, pls. 28-29; 1979a:227, fig. 49) is a typical example).

5) Lack of movement in space, always producing static figures, except for the fighter-figure painted in a Karalis grave (Barreca 1982a:182, pl. 21) and clearly produced under the influence of Greek art; and also in the two reliefs of the Tharros area named "The Sacred Dance" and "The Fighter Overthrowing a Winged Monster" (Barreca 1979a:142, 159, 231-2, figs. 55-6; here fig. 11.14), in which a different native artistic sensitivity exists.

6) Distinct propensity for the aniconic shape, favored otherwise by Phoenician-Punic spirituality, but attenuatd by Greek influence as the stable and common presence of baetyls during the entire history of Phoenician-Punic civilization on the island proves.

7) Preference for "minor arts," producing little monumentality in Phoenician-Punic art in Sardinia; this phenomenon is nevertheless weakened by the influence of monumental native art, today well-known through the architecture (Lilliu 1962) and stone sculpture (Lilliu 1977; see Tronchetti, chap. 4 above).

8) Impressive decorative taste, expressing itself through line (jewelry and plastic modelling examples) or color (the oil bottles and the polychrome moulded glass necklaces).

9) A form of drawing favoring the production of bas-reliefs in stone sculpture and pictures expressed by engraving (Barreca 1979a:230-231, fig. 54) at the expense of "tondo" workmanship.

10) Absence of encomiastic emphasis, either in sculpture (except for portraits, honorary statues and historical-narrative reliefs), or in epigraphy which does not present any human glorification comparable to Classical epigraphy.

It is interesting to note that dilution of this character may be perceived only in Punic workmanship of the Roman period (Guzzo Amadasi 1976:129-131), during which ideas and lifestyles quite foreign to that of the original Semitic colonization started to infiltrate the Sardinian-Punic world.

Conclusion

Concluding this brief excursus, it seems to me that archaeological documentation in Sardinia to date not only illustrates and explains the Phoenician-Punic civilization by adding new information to that already known, but also confirms that something deeply alien to the Classical world is visible. This is so even in those cases where superficial influence from the Greek world on Punic workmanship, especially from the 4th century B.C. on, has been recognized. The reason that this is an obvious fact, however, is because Phoenician civilization was formed far earlier than the Greek, was an expression of people with a different origin, and the result of an ethnic and cultural structure that was divergent from the Hellenic world (Harden 1962, passim; Barreca 1964, passim; Moscati 1972, passim).

I think it has been proven at last that Phoenician-Punic colonization in Sardinia gave impetus to the island's evolution towards the patterns of historical civilization by being the very first to introduce town planning, an open economy first of a civic and then of a national nature, the use of coins, the written word; and finally, one of the highest expressions of religious thought in antiquity.

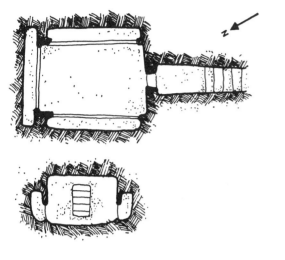

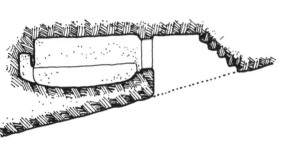

Figure 11.13 Monte Sirai (Carbonia):
Plan and sections of a Phoenician-
Punic tomb with an underground
chamber (left)

Figure 11.14 Tharros area: Relief of
combatant felling winged monster
(right). Cagliari, Museo Archeologico Nazionale

APPENDIX

The excavations conducted at Antas by the Soprintendenza Archeologica of Cagliari and Oristano between 1966 and 1968 have shown that: the Roman temple of Severan date ca. 215 A.D. (fig. 11.10) was dedicated to Sardus Pater Baby; a Punic temple of the 6th/5th century, rebuilt in the 3rd century B.C., is under the Roman one, and was dedicated to Sid Addir Babay; and that both temples were dedicated to the same divine person of Nuragic origin in ancient Sardinia, in a Mediterranean cultural context and therefore pre-Indo-European and pre-Semitic. In fact, both the Punic and Roman temples were dedicated to a divine person with the same name, Babay, rooted in a Nuragic substratum. The Roman temple was constructed according to the Punic canons of religious architecture, with a double inmost recess and northern orientation; Sardus and Sid were therefore equivalent, obviously being the Roman and Punic interpretations of the same Nuragic Babay.

It follows then that whatever applies to one, applies also to the other. With this understood, we observe that: Sardus is called the son of the Libyan Hercules, Macerides, that is, of Melqart, so Sid is therefore the son of Melqart. The divine double name Sid Melqart, documented in Carthaginian inscriptions of the 4th/3rd century B.C., literally translated "Sid of Melqart," therefore has to mean "Sid, son of Melqart." Similarly, the other double name, Sid Tanit, that appears in inscriptions of the same date in Carthage, must be taken to mean "Sid, son of Tanit." The Carthaginians, therefore, worshipped a divine triad: Melqart, Tanit and Sid. This explanation clarifies the triple divine iconography at Antas.

In like manner, all the double names of the Phoenician-Punic ono-mastica (lists of names) are names of divine persons with filial relationships, followed by names of divine fathers or mothers. It follows, therefore, that Melqart Reshef, attested at Tyre is also meant to be "Melqart, son of Reshef"; while Reshef Melqart, attested at Ibiza (that is to say in a Tyrian cultural context, because Ibiza was a colony of Carthage) means "Reshef, son of Melqart." The exchange between the two parts of the double name, clearly attributes to each both paternal characteristic (with all its implications, including royalty), and the filial characteristic (with implications of fertility and salvation), even though these characteristics may be acting theologically antithetical.

The facts that these opposing characteristics can coexist in the same divine person is demonstrated (still in a Tyrian context) by the figure of Sid who, undoubtedly also the "son" at Antas, was at the same time the "father" when he was designated "Babay," the precise meaning of which is "father." The coexistence, however, of these same contradictory characteristics in each of the three divine persons specified (Sid, Melqart, Reshef), seems inexplicable to me unless we concede that they are distinct epiphanies of one and the same divinity, in whom a complex expression must be considered a fusion of many, even antithetical, characteristics, all simultaneously present by virtue of a suspension of mundane logic. This is not really significantly different from what has long been recognized in the complex expression of the Great Goddess of fertility, worshipped by the pre-Semitic and pre-Indo European populations of the Mediterranean.

The same can be said of Adon and Eshmun, whom ancient sources write of as equivalents, while the discoveries at Antas have revealed that Adon is in substance the equivalent of Sid, both as young male divine persons, hunters, and conveyers of salvation, associated with springs, as well as with a great feminine divine person: Ashtart in the case of Adon, and Tanit in the case of Sid. Even these feminine divine persons, however, were in reality manifestations of the unique divinity Baal. As a matter of fact, Ashtart was already called "name of Baal" as early as Ugaritic literature and later at Sidon and Carthage; this means that she furnished one way of symbolizing Baal. Tanit was called at Carthage and in the Punic world "countenance of Baal," that is his "Personification" or "Presence" (1). In addition, her name always appears with a verb in the singular when it is associated with the name of Baal in votive inscriptions. This implies that the two names were officially considered a single entity because they belonged to a single divinity. Besides, if the divinity referred to by her feminine expressions Ashtart and Tanis is indicated by the masculine name Baal, it would appear, in my opinion, that use of differeng genders, (masculine and feminine) for divine manifestations, reflects the belief in the existence not of a god and goddess referred to by these expressions, but of a single divinity in whom is combined not ony the masculine concepts of father and son, but also feminine, maternal characteristics. One single divinity, in other words, could be conceived of as differeing divine persons, some masculine, others feminine, according to their worldly functions.

I maintain that the first, perceptible, all inclusive manifestation of that single divinity was Mot for the Phoenicians (and the Carthaginians): the Cosmic Egg, from which was attributed not only the origin of light, water and heaven with its sun, moon and stars, but also the two divine personifications, Heaven and Earth, whom the Greek versions of Phoenician mythology call Ge and Uranus. It seems to me a logical hypothesis that "Baal" was the name of this sole divinity as the following ideas suggest:

1) the designation, already mentioned, of Ashtart and Tanit; and

2) the divine names, Baal Addir, Baal Hammon, Baal Shamaim, Baal Saphon, Baal Lebanon, Baal Rosh, all consisting of the name of the same divinity, combined with an attribute or an identification that indicates the aspect or sphere of activity of some other of his expressions.

Note 1: Cf. the biblical use of the term sm ("Name") and pnh ("Countenance") referring to God, both expressing His "Personification" and "Presence."

REFERENCES

ACQUARO, E.
  1971   I rasoi punici. Rome: C.N.R.

  1980   Tharros: un centro dell'antico Mediterraneo. Atti del Convegno sulla Preistoria - Protostoria - Storia della Daunia (San Severo, 23-24 novembere 1979). San Severo s.a.

ACQUARO, E. ET AL.
  1975-82 Tharros I, II, III, IV, V, VI, VII, VIII. RSF 3(1); 3(2); 4(2); 6(1); 7(1); 8(1); 9(1); 10(1).

ALBRIGHT, W.F.
1962   The Archaeology of Palestine. Baltimore: Penguin.

BARRECA, F.
1961a   La città punica in Sardegna. Bollettino del Centro Studi
        per la Storia dell'Architettura 17:27-47, Rome.

1961b   Su alcune epigrafi puniche di Nora. RendLinc 16:298-305,
        figs. 1-4.

1964   La civiltà di Cartagine. Cagliari: Fossataro.

1968   L'architettura fenicio-punica (Dispense del Corso
        Universitario per l'Anno Accademico 1967-68). Cagliari.

1970   Ricerche puniche in Sardegna. Ricerche puniche nel
        Mediterraneo centrale. Rome: C.N.R.

1971   Sardegna. L'espansione fenicia nel Mediterraneo. Rome:
        C.N.R.

1973-74 I culti della Sardegna fenicio-punica. (Dispense del
        Corso Universitario biennale per gli Anni Accademici
        1972-73 e 1973-74). Cagliari.

1975a   Il tempio di Antas e il culto di Sardus pater. Iglesias
        (Cagliari): Associazione Culturale "Lao Silesu."

1975b   Istituzioni militari e fortificazioni fenicio-puniche
        (Dispense del Corso Universitario per l'Anno Accademico
        1974-75). Cagliari.

1976   Le fortificazioni settentrionali di Tharros.   RSF
        4(2):215-223, pls. 59-65, fig. 10.

1977   A proposito di una scultura aniconica rinvenuta nel Sinis
        di Cabras (Oristano). RSF 5(2):165-180, figs. 1a-b, 2a-d,
        pls. 37-39.

1978   Le fortificazioni fenicio-puniche in Sardegna. Atti del
        1° Convegno Italiano sul Vicino Oriente Antico (Roma 22-24
        Aprile 1976):116-128, figs. 27-36.

1979a   La Sardegna fenicia e punica[2]. Sassari: Chiarella.

1979b   La spiritualità fenicio-punica e le sue analogie con
        quella giudaica. La Rassegna mensile di Israel, ed. a
        cura dell'Unione delle Comunità israelitiche italiane,
        Roma, 45, n. 1-3 (3rd series) 79-97, figs. 1-6.

1979c   L'archeologia fenicio-punica in Sardegna (un decennio di
        attività). Atti del I Congresso Internazionale di Studi
        Fenici e Punici. Rome.

1980   Contatti fra Protosardi e Fenici. Atti della XXII
            Riunione Scientifica del IIPP (21-27 ottobre 1978):
            475-486.

1981a   La Sardegna e i Fenici. Ichnussa:349-418.

1981b   Monte Sirai (quindici anni di scavi e ricerche). Atti del
            I Convegno Nazionale Sulcis, Carbonia (in press).

1982a   Nuove scoperte fenicio-puniche in Sardegna. Phönizier im
            Westen. Madrider Beitrage 8:181-184, pls. 19-21.

1982b   L'età punica. Ricerche archeologiche nel territorio di
            Sanluri. Sanluri (Cagliari): Concu.

1982c   Stato attuale della ricerca sulla Sardegna fenicio-punica.
            Atti del Convegno di Studio della Deputazione di Storia
            Patria sullo stato attuale della ricerca storica in
            Sardegna. Cagliari (in press).

1983a   Magia egizia nelle tombe fenicio-puniche di Sardegna.
            Sardigna Antiga. Nuoro.

1983b   Gli amuleti nel mondo fenicio d'Occidente (dispense del
            Corso Universitario triennale per gli anni Accademici
            1980-81, 1981-82, 1982-83). Cagliari.

BARRECA, F. AND S.F. BONDI
    1980   Scavi nel tophet di M. Sirai, campagna 1979.   RSF
                8(1):142-145.

BARRECA, F. ET AL.
    1964-67 Monte Sirai I, II, III, IV. Studi Semitici 11; 14; 20;
                25.

BARRECA, F. ET AL.
    1969   Ricerche puniche ad Antas. Studi Semitici 30.

BARTOLONI, P.
    1981   Contributo alla cronologia delle necropoli fenicie e
                puniche di Sardegna. RSF 9:13-29.

BARTOLONI, P. AND S.F. BONDI
    1981   Monte Sirai 1980. RSF 9(2):217-230.

BARTOLONI, P. ET AL.
    1982   Monte Sirai 1981. RSF 10(2):273-299.

CANEPA, M.
    1983   La tomba dell'ureo nella necropoli punica di Tuvixeddu
                (Cagliari). Atti dell'Incontro di Studio "Lettura ed
                interpretazione della produzione pittorica dal IV sec.
                A.C. all'Ellenismo," Acquasparta (TR) - 8-10 aprile 1983
                (in press).

CAQUOT, A.
  1952   Chadrapha, à propos de quelques articles recents. Syria
          29:74-88.

CINUS, A. ET AL.
  1981   Su Beranu Quatesu, Osservazioni sulle analogie tra sagra
          di S. Giovanni a Quartu S. Elena e Rito di Adone.
          Cagliari: Trois.

COSTA, A.
  1980   Santu Teru - Monte Luna (campagne di scavo a Senorbì,
          1977-1979). RSF 8(2):265-270.

CROSS, F.M.
  1974   Leaves from an Epigraphist's Notebook. The Catholic
          Biblical Quarterly 36(4):486-494.

FANTAR, M.
  1970   Eschatologie   phénicienne-punique.   Tunis: Institut
          National d'archéologie et d'arts.

FEDELE, F.
  1978   Antropologia fisica e paleoecologia di Tharros - Campagna
          1977. RSF 6:77-78.

  1979   Antropologia e paleoecologia di Tharros - Ricerche sul
          tophet (1978) e prima campagna territoriale nel Sinis.
          RSF 7:67-88.

GSELL, S.
  1924   Histoire Ancienne de l'Afrique du Nord 4:243-250; 332-333;
          244-247. Paris; Hachette.

GUZZO AMADASI, M.G.
  1967   Le iscrizioni fenicie e puniche delle colonie in
          occidente. Studi Semitici 28:83-136.

HARDEN, D.
  1971   The Phoenicians.[2] Harmondsworth.

LEVI, D.
  1949   L'ipogeo di S. Salvatore di Cabras in Sardegna. Rome: La
          Libreria dello Stato.

LILLIU, G.
  1962   I Nuraghi: Torri preistoriche di Sardegna, "La Zattera."
          Cagliari: Cocco.

  1966   Sculture della Sardegna nuragica, "La Zattera." Cagliari-
          Verona.

  1967   La civiltà dei Sardi.[2] Torino: E.R.I.

1977   Dal "betilo" aniconico alla statuaria nuragica. StSar
24:1975-76.

1982   La civiltà nuragica. Sassari: Delfino.

MOSCATI, S.
1958   Le antiche civiltà semitiche. Bari: laterza.

1968   Fenici e Cartaginesi in Sardegna. Milano: Mondadori.

1972   I Fenici e Cartagine. Torino: U.T.E.T.

PADERI, M.C.
1982a   La necropoli di Bidd'e Cresia e le tombe puniche.
Ricerche archeologiche nel territorio di Sanluri. Sanluri
(Cagliari): Concu.

1982b   L'insediamento di Fundabi de Andria Peis - Padru Jossu e
la necropoli di Giliadiri. Reperti punici e romani.
Ricerche archeologiche nel territorio di Sanluri. Sanluri
(Cagliari): Concu.

PAIS, E.
1881   La Sardegna prima del dominio romano. AttiLinc 7.

PATRONI, G.
1904   Nora, colonia fenicia in Sardegna. MonAnt 14:col. 17.

PESCE, G.
1961   Sardegna punica. Cagliari: Fossataro.

1965   Statuette puniche di Bithia. Rome: Centro Studi Semitici.

1968   Chia (Cagliari) - Scavi nel territorio. NSc:331-337.

SZNYCER, M.
1969   Note sur le dieu Sid et le dieu Horon d'aprés les
nouvelles inscriptions puniques d'Antas (Sardaigne).
Karthago 15:69-74.

TARAMELLI, A.
1903   Fordongianus - Antiche terme di Forum Traiani. NSc
482-485.

1910   Il nuraghe Lugherras presso Paulilatino. MonAnt 20:cols.
153-234.

1912   La necropoli punica di Predio Ibba a S. Avendrace,
Cagliari (scavi del 1908). MonAnt 21:cols. 165-66.

1933-34 Scavi nell'antica Bitia a Chia (Domus de Maria). BdA
27:288-291.

TORE, G.
    1973-74   Ricerche puniche in Sardegna, b) San Giuseppe - Padria
              (Sassari). StSar 23(1):374-379.

    1982   Corredi da tombe puniche di Bidd' e Cresia. Ricerche
              archeologiche nel territorio di Sanluri. Sanluri
              (Cagliari): Concu.

TRONCHETTI, C.
    1979   Per la cronologia del tophet di S. Antioco. RSF
              7:201-205; pls. 67-68.

UBERTI, M.L.
    1973   Figurine fittili di Bitia. Rome: C.N.R.

    1976   Tanit in un'epigrafe sarda. RSF 4(1):53-55.

    1978   Horon ad Antas e Astarte a Mozia. Annali dell'Istituto
              Orientale di Napoli 38:315-319.

USAI, E.
    1981   Su alcuni gioielli della necropoli di Monte Luna -
              Senorbì. RSF 9:39-47.

PART FOUR:
SARDINIA AND THE GREEKS

Introduction

In these two articles, the authors deal with the importance of material associated with Sardinia and found elsewhere, and the significance of Greek material found on Sardinia. In assessing the importance of Sardinia in the Mediterranean of the early first millennium B.C., David Ridgway uses the evidence of finds on the island of Pithekoussai (Ischia) to suggest that the presence of metal made Sardinia well- known, and that perhaps Pithekoussai was a staging point for trade for entrepreneurs from the Near East. Cyprus is singled out for particular 'contact' as it was earlier in the Bronze Age (see chap. 16 below and Epilogue), again in some kind of association with metals.

It may come as a surprise to some that there should still be so much unknown about the Greeks, even the Greeks of the sixth and fifth century B.C., but the speculations about colonization, pottery, metal and history in these two articles show that there are still problems, and that evidence to approach these problems is sought in written texts of myth as well as history, and material ranging from ceramic to metal.

Defining the nature of the association of Sardinia with Greece is yet another unsolved problem not only for the Bronze Age (see chap. 16 below) but for the Archaic and Classical periods as well. The material found on the island that can be identified as Greek does not tell us directly whether it came through trade or presence, or from an actual Greek settlement. Olbia, Neapolis and Villagreca are the names of Sardinian towns today that some use as evidence to postulate ancient Greek settlement; other evidence is suggested by the presence of Greek pottery, although most of it may come from tombs. Jean Davison was able to identify pottery as Attic that had long been attributed to Greek Southern Italy, thereby proposing some variations of the manner in which imports arrived. By using both myth and history as well as excavated material to reconstruct evidence for settlement, she has supplied an analysis of the foundation myth that would legitimatize Greek presence in Sardinia.

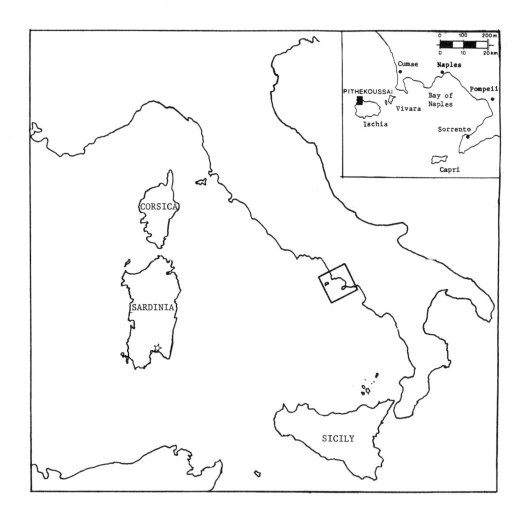

Figure 12.1 Map of Tyrrhenian Sea with inset of
Pithekoussai on Ischia and the Bay of Naples.
After D. Ridgway (1984:51, fig. 5).

12. SARDINIA AND THE FIRST WESTERN GREEKS

David Ridgway

Introduction

The first Greeks who ventured Westwards at the end of the Dark Age were Euboeans (Coldstream 1977:221-45; Boardman 1980:161-224). They were trading with the indigenous Iron Age peoples of the west-central Italian mainland by the beginning of the eighth century B.C., and their pre-colonial exchanges were soon put on a firmer footing with the establishment ca. 770 of a permanent trading station (emporion) at Pithekoussai on the island of Ischia at the northern end of the Bay of Naples (fig. 12.1). During the past few years, it has become increasingly clear that Pithekoussai acted as a clearing house for the advanced technology and the new ideas of all kinds brought to Italy from Greece and the Near East: Euboeans - probably from the recently excavated center of Lefkandi (Popham, Sackett et al. 1979-80) - had had a stake in the multinational emporion of Al Mina at the mouth of the Orontes since the late ninth century. The Pithekoussan operation thus contributed much to the "Orientalizing" appearance of the local cultures in Campania, Latium vetus and Etruria (Buchner 1979). The story continues with the foundation of the Euboean colony (apoikia) of Cumae on the Campanian coast opposite (and within sight of) Pithekoussai, an event that seems to have taken place around 725 (Buchner 1977). Cumae suffered from none of the notorious logistic disadvantages associated with Pithekoussai, and its position indeed offered the combined possibilities of further commercial expansion and wider territorial exploitation. "The rest is history": and this is not the place to write of

the Hellenization of Etruria in the seventh century, the consequent selection of Tarquinia as a place of refuge by Demaratus of Corinth after 656, and the adoption by the Etruscans (alone among the non-Greek Mediterranean peoples) of the city-state (polis) concept (Ridgway 1981a). My purpose in this paper is rather to review some of the circumstances that attracted the Euboeans to the West in the first place. My principal conclusion can be anticipated here: it is no longer reasonable to compile an account of western attractions that does not include Sardinia and its natural resources. That such accounts have been compiled in the past may be explained in terms of the political history of the nineteenth century A.D.: Marshall Becker (1980) has shown how, and why, Nuragic metallurgy acquired a "peripheral" reputation that was already unjustified a century ago, and is even more unjustified now - as will be clear from Fulvia Lo Schiavo's magnificent survey (chap. 16 below).

My starting point is the impressive bronze hoard from Santa Maria in Paulis near Uri (SS), acquired by the Trustees of the British Museum in 1926 and entrusted for publication to Ellen Macnamara, Francesca R. Ridgway and myself (1984) on the occasion of the Sixth British Museum Classical Colloquium held in London in December 1982 (see chap. 7 above).

We have found no reason to suppose that any of the pieces in this hoard were manufactured outside of Sardinia, and this conclusion receives a welcome measure of con-firmation from the analysis (by atomic absorption spectrometry) of 31 pieces carried out by P.T. Craddock and M.S. Tite of the British Museum Research Laboratory. We believe that the Santa Maria hoard is "votive" in character, in the diluted sense recently suggested by Fulvia Lo Schiavo: collective accumulation of the wealth of an entire village, from which the sacred aspect may not be absent. The process of accumulation makes the possibility of chronological similarity even more unlikely, adding to the already horrendous problems of dating individual Nuragic bronzes; Santa Maria is not a closed find, and its component parts thus cannot be dated by association. In our view, the minimal range during which the Santa Maria bronzes could have been accumulated consists of the four centuries between the beginning of the twelfth and the end of the ninth. A terminus ante quem between ca. 850 and ca. 775 is suggested by the comparison of two rattles with the incomplete example hitherto defined as a "miniature stool" in a Villanovan grave in the Cavalupo cemetery at Vulci in Etruria (Lilliu 1966:no. 263). A terminus post quem between 1230 and 1050 is provided by Ellen Macnamara's derivation of the Santa Maria tripod-stand (fig. 12.2) from the metalworking tradition of the Late Cypriot III period in Cyprus. It does not follow that the Santa Maria hoard represents four centuries' worth of accumulation. Were it to represent two centuries' worth, we would see no prima facie case for promoting the claims of the tenth-ninth at the expense of the eleventh-tenth or even of the twelfth-eleventh.

As far as the (newly restored and previously unpublished) Santa Maria tripod-stand is concerned, it will be apparent by now that we do not feel able to follow the chronological preference displayed by Professor Lilliu in assigning a date

between the second half of the ninth and the early years of the eighth century to another local Late Cypriot III-derived piece: the fine miniature tripod-stand from the votive deposit discovered in 1968 in the Grotta Pirosu, Su Benatzu (south of Santadi (CA); Lilliu 1973). In our view, Professor Lilliu's brilliant treatment of the Grotta Pirosu tripod needs to be reviewed in the light of two subsequent and startling discoveries, both of which have Cypriot implications. I refer firstly to Fulvia Lo Schiavo's comparison of two locally made hook-tang weapons in the Ottana (NU) hoard with examples of Late Cypriot I type (Lo Schiavo 1980: 355); and, secondly, to Maria Luisa Ferrarese Ceruti's brief mention of the stylistic affinities apparent in the Mycenaean III B/C pottery she excavated at the Nuraghe Antigori in Sarroch (CA). Ottana indicates a terminus post quem well before 1400 for the manufacture of Sardinian products in a Cypriot tradition; Antigori suggests that a connection with "l'arcipelago di Rodi, il Levante e Cipro" (Ferrarese Ceruti 1981:606) was maintained during the thirteenth-eleventh centuries not only by "trade" but in the context of peaceful cohabitation indicated by an alien cult place inside the Antigori fortress, and by the more homely presence of imported domestic pottery.

This new perspective enables us to contemplate more seriously than ever before the possibility that craftsmen capable of making copies of Late Cypriot III stands reached Sardinia during the twelfth, eleventh or tenth centuries - during, that is, the actual floruit (1230-1050) of the stands themselves in Cyprus. After all, the cargo of the merchantman wrecked ca. 1200 off Cape Gelidonya in southern Turkey (Bass 1967) included not only ox-hide ingots of a form attested in both Cyprus and Sardinia but also elements of Late Cypriot III tripod- and other stands.

Several items in the Santa Maria hoard bear witness to the outstanding feats of lost-wax casting achieved by Sardinian bronzesmiths; we are no longer compelled to explain them exclusively in terms of the presence and example of Phoenician prospectors and colonists of the ninth and eighth centuries. Earlier stimuli from the East Mediterranean are now more clearly perceptible, and their effect was deeper and more long lasting in Sardinia than it was on the Italian mainland. There, we have to wait until the Orientalizing - or even the Archaic - period for the technical mastery displayed long before by the many Nuragic "barchette" and "bronzetti", and by hapax legomena like the Santa Maria jug, cast in one piece (fig. 12.3). The variety no less than the quality of Sardinian metallurgy sets it apart from the metallurgical koinè that Professor Peroni (1969) has detected in the European and Aegean worlds during the period corresponding to the Italian Recent Bronze Age (thirteenth century); this phenomenon rises and falls with the Mycenaean commercial empire, while Nuragic metalworking continues undeterred. Sardinia's on-going affinities and contacts in the post-Mycenaean period were with the indigenous peoples of the Levant, which never had a Dark Age; with that "outside world," in fact, into which the Euboeans pioneered the Greek re-entry around the middle of the ninth century (Desborough 1976; cf. Frey 1982).

The awakening of Greece at the end of the Dark Age has been reviewed on a number of recent occasions, and there is no need to do so again here. The early contact with the Levant that is its hallmark emerges clearly from the distribution of Middle Geometric pottery, most notably of pendent semicircle skyphoi (Coldstream 1977:94, fig. 29, whence fig. 12.4), a type developed in Euboea (most probably, on present evidence, at Lef-kandi). From this, it is evident that the Euboeans soon realized that Cyprus was an ideal base for the investigation of Asia Minor; by 825, they were operating out of Al Mina; by the early eighth century a growing western commitment is signalled by the appearance of Middle Geometric chevron skyphoi on the native sites of mainland Campania, southern Etruria (Veii: Ridgway 1967; Descoeudres and Kearsley 1983) - and at Pithe-koussai (Ridgway 1981b). Meanwhile, there is plenty of evidence at home in Euboea for increasing contact of one sort or another with Cyprus and the Levant (Coldstream 1982; Riis 1982). It remains obstinately true, alas, that we have no real idea as to the precise nature of the exchanges sought and obtained by the Euboean pioneers either in the East or in the West. We may be sure, however, that it did not consist solely of skyphoi being bartered for Eastern luxury items and western raw materials - important though such transactions may well have been. Additionally, more complex and more elusive mechanisms were at work, involving the acquisition of ideas and information. As early as the late tenth century, craftsmen at Lefkandi were decorating bronze tripods in the Cypriot style; earlier still, a group of seventeen copper ingots of the "pillow" type (dated by Buchholz to ca. 1500) were lost at sea off Kyme in Euboea (Sackett et al. 1966:75, note 125; not Chalcis, as Pigorini 1904; and not Aeolian Kyme, as Lorimer 1950: 57). Euboeans with an eye to the main chance in the Near East must have heard - in Cyprus, say, or at Al Mina - of the rich pickings to be had in the Far West, which at this time consisted to a significant extent of metal-rich Sardinia and its far from tenuous relationship with the Levant. I suspect, in fact, that news of the West may well have been the most valuable commodity that the Euboeans acquired in the East - where "news of

Figure 12.2 Bronze hoard from Santa
Maria in Paulis: Tripod-stand. From
Macnamara et al. (1984:39, fig. 2).

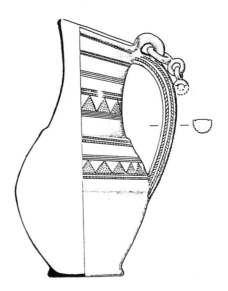

Figure 12.3 Bronze hoard from Santa
Maria in Paulis: Jug. From Macnamara
et al. (1984:38, fig. 1).

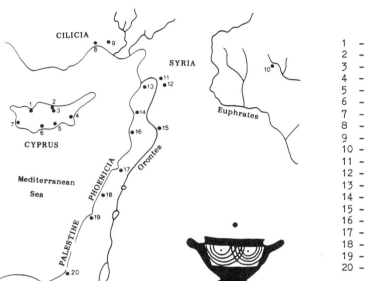

1 - Soli
2 - Kazaphani
3 - Palekythro
4 - Salamis
5 - Kition
6 - Amathous
7 - Paphos
8 - Mersin
9 - Tarsus
10 - Tell Halaf
11 - Tell Tayinat
12 - Tell Judaidah
13 - Al Mina
14 - Tell Sukas
15 - Hama
16 - Tabbat al Hammam
17 - Khaldeh
18 - Tyre
19 - Tell Abu Hawam
20 - Askalon

Figure 12.4   Levantine distribution
of Greek Middle Geometric skyphoi
with pendent semicircles.   From D.
Ridgway (1984:33, fig. 4).

the West" must often have meant "news of Sardinia."

Notoriously, however, there are no "pre-colonial" Middle Geometric skyphoi in Sardinia - although there is a Cypriot elbow fibula from Barumini (Lo Schiavo 1978:42, no. 20) that belongs to the same family as an example found with a pendent semicircle skyphos at Kouklia in Cyprus. It seems to be generally agreed that the Euboean pioneers established their first western base on Ischia because, in the first instance at least, the indigenous Iron Age communities of the Italian mainland did not feel able to accord them more than protected access to the raw materials they sought in the Colline Metallifere of northwestern Etruria (Colonna 1975). Although I will not go so far as to suggest that the first western Greeks were really aiming for Sardinia, were deflected to Etruria - and finally had to make do with Ischia; nevertheless, if there is a good case for supposing that the Euboeans were "not allowed" to settle in Etruria, there is an even better one for supposing that a far more formidable obstacle awaited the less than casual visitor to contemporary Sardinia. I am thinking of Frank Cross' (1972; 1984) interpretation of the inscription on the Nora Stone, and the very real possibility that this controversial artifact commemorates a victory won by Phoenician forces sent (at the end of the ninth or beginning of the eighth century) to acquire or to protect important mining and industrial interests in the highlands of the Sulcitano, rich in argentiferous lead and iron ore. It is tempting to conclude that by the mid-eighth century a division of interests was being consciously observed in the exploitation of western mineral resources: Phoenicians in Sardinia, and Euboeans along the Tyrrhenian coast of the Italian peninsula. There are good arguments for and against this: I suspect that our impression of a demarcation agreement is explicable in terms of the differences in identity and interest between the Levantines who preceded the Euboeans in western waters and those who - literally - accompanied them on their early voyages. At all events, it has now been established beyond reasonable doubt that, from a very early stage in its known history, the residents of Euboean Pithekoussai included Orientals.

The evidence for Oriental residents at Pithekoussai in the middle of the eighth century is partly direct and partly indirect (Buchner 1982). The clearest piece of direct evidence comes from the cemetery. A coarse and singularly unphotogenic amphora used to contain an infant burial (a sadly common feature) was deposed around 740, shortly before the erection of an adjacent tumulus over the comparatively rich cremation of an adult female. Together, these two depositions form part of a "family plot," typical of Pithekoussan funerary practice (in which, by and large, cremations under stone tumuli, inhumations in trench graves and inhumations in large pottery containers correspond respectively to adults, children and new-born babies). This particular amphora is of Greek shape, and had been inscribed on two quite separate occasions before being buried. A four letter word and a numerical sign (fig. 12.5) were originally identified as Aramaic, the language of the North Syrian hinterland beyond Al Mina (Garbini 1978): and that is how I defined them when I read this paper to the Tufts Colloquium in 1983. Frank Cross has since drawn my attention to an authoritative diagnosis of this writing as Phoenician (Teixidor 1979:387, no. 137), adding his own comparison with the script used on the Kition Bowl from Cyprus (ca. 800 B.C.; Guzzo Amadasi and Karageorghis 1977:149-160). The possibility of adding a Cypriot dimension to the early western Greek story is exciting. Cyprus is one of the very few major centers with which Pithekoussai has not hitherto been connected. In sharp contrast, the Cypro-Sardinian rapport that led to the manufacture in Sardinia of some of the components of the Santa Maria hoard cited above was in full working order before the beginning of the tenth century, and long before the rise of Euboean Greek interest in the West at the end of the ninth/beginning of the eighth. In addition, Alan Johnston (1983) has recently argued strongly for the recognition of Cyprus as the cradle of the Greek alphabet (see Cross, chap. 9 above, for the same argument for Sardinia). Less controversially, a second and later sign on the Pithekoussai amphora has been interpreted as an all-purpose religious symbol widely attested in funerary contexts all over the Semitic world. The person who incised this latter sign on the amphora at the time of its deposition in a Pithekoussan family plot was surely not a Euboean. There is food for thought, too, in the primary inscriptions - the four letter word and the numerical sign. Whether they are Aramaic or Phoenician, they must surely relate to the amphora's original function as a container in which liquid could be stored and transported. They were presumably made at the dispatch point in the Levant, by someone who had reason to suppose that they would be understood when the amphora reached its destination in the West.

The indirect evidence for close Oriental connections at Pithekoussai in the third quarter of the eighth century, during which the above amphora was deposed, consists of numerous Egyptian scarabs and North Syrian "Lyre-Player Group" seals, and a few Levantine aryballoi (fig. 12.6). Just over one third of all the graves that can be assigned to this quarter century contain at least one of these imported Oriental arti-facts. How many of the graves in question also contained Oriental residents is quite another matter, of course; perhaps the safest pointer is the presence of the Levantine aryballoi, representing a specific funerary ritual observed by 15% of the population at this time (Ridgway 1978). It is worth noting, incidentally, that the type of Levantine aryballos involved - the earliest in the whole of Magna Graecia - is also found on the island of Rhodes, where Coldstream (1969) has postulated a Phoenician community resident at Ialysos; they were engaged in the manufacture and export of unguents before the Corinthians flooded the market with their Early Protocorinthian globular aryballoi in the last quarter of the eighth century.

I should like to end by pointing to two pieces of intriguing evidence for "contact" between Sardinia and the Euboean emporion of Pithekoussai at the end of the eighth century. My first piece is the well known painted urn found in the Sulcis tophet during the 1960 excavations. Eight years later, Coldstream (1968:388, 429) defined the affinities of its decoration as Euboean Late Geometric, pointing to a close parallel for the main motif - facing birds and filling ornaments in the handle zone - on an amphora from Eretria, now in the Athens National Museum (Åkerström 1943:65, fig. 26). Next, I myself suggested that the ancillary decoration had at least one feature in common with that branch of Euboean Late Geometric now accepted as "Made in Ischia," in any case the nearest source of Euboean characteristics (Ridgway 1976:213) - and also the home of an amphora similar in shape and syntax to the example from Eretria mentioned above (Buchner 1971: 63, fig. 1). More recently, Carlo Tronchetti has extracted the surviving pieces of the Sulcis urn's lid from its interior; the lid's shape and decoration lead him to accept my discreetly veiled hypothesis of Pithekoussan manufacture (Tronchetti 1979:205), although not to answer my somewhat rhetorical question as to the identity of the painter: was he "a Phoenician who had learned to paint at Pithekoussai, or...a Pithe-koussan who had settled at Sulcis?" (Ridgway 1976:213). Finally, as I have recently had the pleasant duty of reporting elsewhere (Ridgway 1982: 65), the Sulcis urn and its lid were examined in September 1981 by the excavator of Pithekoussai, Dr. Gior-gio Buchner, who pronounced them both to be Pithekoussan products, exported to Sardinia. It could be that the form is a local version of imported Corinthian Late Geometric pyxides with facing birds in the handle zone: examples from Syracuse and Naxos in Sicily and from Francavilla Marittima in Calabria have recently been pub-lished by Pelagatti (1982:131, pl. 31; 145, pl. 49) and Zancani Montuoro (1983:34, fig. 13,b; pl. 13,a). The fact that the shape of the urn, un-like that of the lid, is not attested at Pithekoussai presents no problems: each new campaign of excavation there has added to the range of forms and shapes represented. The second piece of evidence for Sardo-Pithekoussan "contact" is more tantalizing (fig. 12.7): it is Lo Schiavo's identifica-tion of an incomplete bronze artefact found in the fill of Pithekoussai tomb 700 (most probably of the last quarter of the eighth century) as an Iberian fibula "a doble resorte" (Lo Schiavo 1978:40, fig. 7, 2). The only other example of the type in Italy comes from the votive accumula-tion in the Grotta Pirosu, Su Benatzu (Santadi, CA; Lo Schiavo 1978:39, no. 19) - already mentioned in connection with its Late Cypriot III-derived local miniature tripod-stand.

It would be patently absurd to postulate the existence and define the nature of a relationship on the evidence of an enigmatic urn and two broken fibulas. We are still at the stage where the questions are more important than the answers. And one question that has been on my mind for a long time is this: what is the source of the really quite surprising quantity of silver in the tombs of Euboean (ca. 750-700) Pithekoussai - particularly in those tombs that may conceivably have contained the Orien-tal residents described in above? The possibilities are not infinite, and until recently were derived from:

(1)   the Euboean interest attested by the ancient written sources in southern Illyria, rich in silver (Strabo 10, 449C; Pausanias 5, 22, 3-4); and

(2) the Pithekoussan parallels for Oriental material found in the excavation of the remains of a Phoe-nician or Phoenicianizing community of silver miners at Rio Tinto in Spain - an area on which Brian Shef-ton has recently (1982) written so helpfully for our present purposes.

Of these two sources, (1) is an unknown quantity archaeologically, at least to me; but (2) implies a route that cannot possibly have bypassed Sardinia. And even before the 1983 Tufts Colloquium, R.F. Tylecote (Tylecote, Balmuth and Massoli-Novelli 1984) added substance to a third possibility, hitherto regarded as little more than theoretical: the silver of Sardinia itself, knowledge of which could well have ensured a warm welcome at the first West Greek establishment for prospective Orien-tal residents.

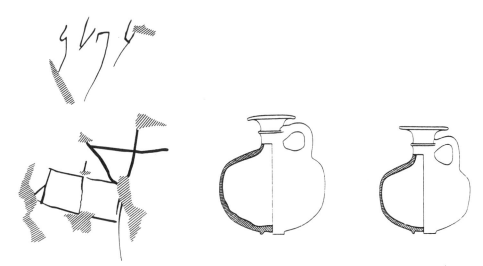

Figure 12.5 Pithekoussai, San Montano cemetery: Semitic graffiti on amphora 575-1. Upper: four letter word, once identified as Aramaic K P L N ("double"). Lower: numerical sign with funerary symbol superimposed. From Buchner (1978:133, fig. 2 - which was printed upside down).

Figure 12.6 Pithekoussai, San Montano cemetery: Levantine aryballoi. From Buchner (1982:278, fig. 2).

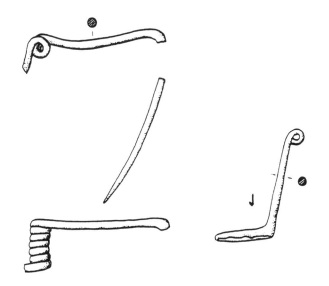

Figure 12.7 Iberian bronze fibulas "a doble resorte." Pithekoussai, San Montano cemetery, tomb 700 (left); Grotta Pirosu, Su Benatzu di Santadi (right). From Lo Schiavo (1978:40, fig.7).

REFERENCES

AKERSTROM, A.
     1943   Der geometrische Stil in Italien. Lund-Leipzig.

BASS, G.
     1967   Cape Gelidonya: a Bronze Age shipwreck = TAPS n.s.
                    57(4).

BECKER, M.J.
     1980   Sardinia   and   the   Mediterranean   Copper   Trade:
                    Political Development and Colonialism in the Bronze
                    Age. Anthropology 4(2):91-117.

BOARDMAN, J.
     1980   The Greeks Overseas: their early colonies and trade.
                    London; new and enlarged edition.

BUCHNER, G.
     1971   Recent   work   at   Pithekoussai   (Ischia),   1965-71.
                    Archaeological Reports for 1970-71:63-67.

     1977   Cuma   nell'VIII   secolo   a.C.,   osservata   dalla
                    prospettiva di Pithecusa. I Campi Flegrei nell'
                    archeologia e nella storia = Atti dei Convegni
                    Lincei 33:131-148.

     1978   Testimonianze epigrafiche semitiche dell'VIII secolo
                    a.C. a Pithekoussai. ParPass 33:135-147.

     1979   Early   Orientalizing: Aspects   of   the   Euboean
                    Connection. Ridgway and Ridgway 129-144.

     1982   Die Beziehungen zwischen der euböischen Kolonie
                    Pithekoussai   auf   der   Insel   Ischia   und   dem
                    nordwestsemitischen Mittelmeerraum in der zweiten
                    Hälfte des 8. Jhs. v. Chr. Niemeyer 277-298.

COLDSTREAM, J.N.
     1968   Greek Geometric Pottery. London.

     1969   The Phoenicians of Ialysos. BICS 16:1-8.

     1977   Geometric Greece. London.

     1982   Greeks and Phoenicians in the Aegean.   Niemeyer
                    261-272.

COLONNA, G.
     1975   Basi   conoscitive   per   una   storia   economica
                    dell'Etruria. AIIN Supplement 22:3-23.

CROSS, F.M.
    1972   An interpretation of the Nora Stone. BASOR 208:
                        13-19 (reprinted in SSA 53-59).

    1984   Phoenicians in Sardinia: The Epigraphical Evidence.
                        SSA 53-66.

DESBOROUGH, V.
    1976   The Background to Euboean Participation in Early
                        Greek   Maritime   Enterprise.   Tribute   to   an
                        Antiquary: Essays presented to Marc Fitch by some of
                        his friends 25-40. London.

DESCOEUDRES, J.-P. AND KEARSLEY, R.
    1983   Greek pottery at Veii: another look. BSA 78:9-53.

FERRARESE CERUTI, M.L.
    1981   Documenti   micenei   nella   Sardegna   meridionale.
                        Ichnussa 605-612.

FREY, O.-H.
    1982   Zur Seefahrt im Mittelmeer während der Früheisenzeit
                        (10.   bis   8.   Jahrhundert   v.   Chr.).   Zur
                        geschichtlichen Bedeutung der frühen Seefahrt =
                        Kolloquien   zur   Allgemeinen   und   Vergleichenden
                        Archäologie 2:21-43.

GARBINI, G.
    1978   Un'iscrizione aramaica a Ischia. ParPass 33:148-55.

GUZZO AMADASI, M.G. AND KARAGEORGHIS, V.
    1977   Fouilles de Kition III: Inscriptions phéniciennes.
                        Nicosia.

JOHNSTON, A.
    1983   The extent and use of literacy: the archaeological
                        evidence. The Greek Renaissance of the Eighth
                        Century BC: Tradition and Innovation = Proceedings of
                        the Second International Symposium at the Swedish
                        Institute in Athens, June 1981 63-68. Stockholm.

LILLIU, G.
    1966   Sculture della Sardegna nuragica. Cagliari-Verona:
                        La Zattera.

    1973   Tripode bronzeo di tradizione cipriota dalla Grotta
                        Pirosu, Su Benatzu di Santadi (Cagliari). Estudios
                        dedicados al Prof. Dr. Luis Pericot 283-313.
                        Barcelona.

LORIMER, H.L.
    1950   Homer and the Monuments. London.

LO SCHIAVO, F.
1978   Le fibule della Sardegna. StEtr 46:25-46.

1980   Wessex, Sardegna, Cipro: nuovi elementi di
              discussione. Atti della XXII Riunione Scientifica
              IIPP 341-358.

MACNAMARA, E., D. RIDGWAY, AND F.R. RIDGWAY
1984   The bronze hoard from Santa Maria in Paulis,
              Sardinia = BMOP 45.

PELAGATTI, P.
1982   I più antichi materiali di importazione a Siracusa, a
              Naxos e in altri siti della Sicilia Orientale. La
              céramique grecque ou de tradition grecque au VIII
              siècle en Italie centrale et méridionale = Cahiers du
              Centre Jean Bérard 3:113-180.

PERONI, R.
1969   Per uno studio dell'economia di scambio in Italia nel
              quadro dell'ambiente culturale dei secoli intorno al
              Mille a.C. ParPass 24:134-160 /⁻ English translation
              = Ridgway and Ridgway eds. 7-30_7.

PIGORINI, L.
1904   Pani di rame provenienti dall'Egeo scoperti a Serra
              Ilixi in provincia di Cagliari. BPI 30:91-107.

POPHAM, M., L.H. SACKETT ET AL.
1979-80   Lefkandi I. The Iron Age (two vols.) = BSA Supplement
              11.

RIDGWAY, D.
1967   'Coppe cicladiche' da Veio.   StEtr 35:311-321
              /⁻English translation = Ridgway and Ridgway eds.
              ⁻13-27_7.

1976   Review-discussion of PCIA I-III. JRS 66:206-213.

1978   Fra Oriente e Occidente: la Pithecusa degli Eubei.
              Magna Graecia 13 (fasc. 11-12):14-18.

1981a   The Etruscans. Edinburgh (pre-print: = CAH²,vol. IV
              forthcoming).

1981b   The   foundation   of   Pithekoussai.   Nouvelle
              contribution à l'étude de la société et de la
              colonisation eubéennes 45-56. Naples.

1982   Archaeology in South Italy, 1977-81. Archaeological
              Reports for 1981-82:63-83.

1984   L'Alba della Magna Grecia. Milan.

RIIS, P.J.
    1982   Griechen in Phönizien. Niemeyer 237-55.

SACKETT, L.H.
    1966   Prehistoric Euboea: contributions toward a survey.
                    BSA 61:33-112.

SHEFTON, B.B.
    1982   Greeks and Greek imports in the south of the Iberian
                    peninsula.   The archaeological evidence.   Niemeyer
                    337-370.

TEIXIDOR, J.
    1979   Bulletin d'épigraphie sémitique 1978-79.   Syria 56:
                    353-405.

TRONCHETTI, C.
    1979   Per la cronologia del tophet di Sant'Antioco.   RSF
                    7(2):201-205.

TYLECOTE, R.F., M.S. BALMUTH AND R. MASSOLI-NOVELLI
    1984   Copper   and   Bronze   Metallurgy   in   Sardinia.   SSA
                    115-162.

ZANCANI MONTUORO, P.
    1983   Necropoli e Ceramico a Macchiabate: fornace e bot-
                    teghe antecedenti: Tombe T. 1-54.   Atti e Memorie
                    della Società Magna Grecia n.s. 21-23 / 1980-1982 /:
                    7-129.

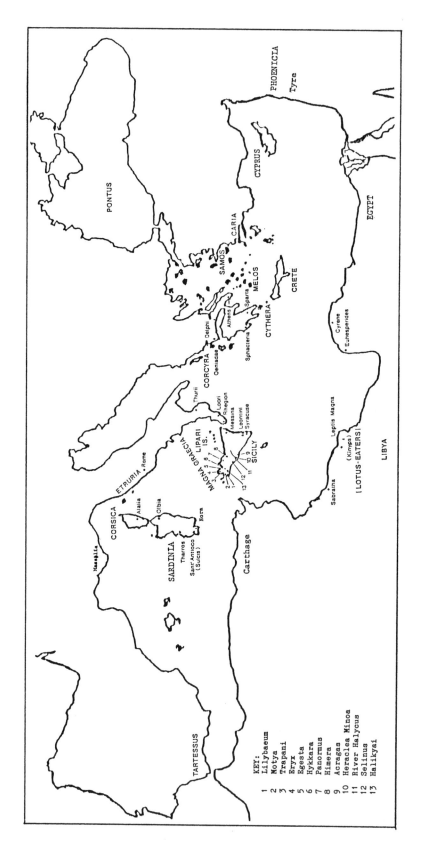

Figure 13.1 Map of Mediterranean sites mentioned in text of chapter 13

Jean M. Davison

The terms 'myth' and 'speculation' in my title are intended to be considered from both an ancient and a modern perspective. Greek speculation upon the past (their own and every area of the Mediterranean with which they had contact) (fig. 13.1) resulted in the creation of a mythic prehistory which blended experience, memory and legend and from which they derived justification for political actions during the historical period.

The focus of the speculation here is on Athenian aspirations in the West during the second half of the fifth century and the extent to which these aspirations involved Sardinia (fig. 13.2). On the basis of evidence, which in most cases is limited to the fifth century or earlier, and thus representative of the current attitudes of contemporary Athenians, a picture emerges which at the very least seems to include Sardinia.

Sardinia in Legend

Sardinia does not appear in our oldest references to the several legendary voyages which converge upon the western Mediterranean (Pearson 1975:182-183). Although Odysseus' adventures are not localized by Homer in the eighth-century epic, by the fifth century Sicily is recognized as the site of the Cyclops' cave (Euripides, Cyclops), and the Lotus-Eaters are at home along the coast of Libya southeast of Carthage (Hdt. 4.177-178). The Argonauts also visit this area of Africa, on their way home with the fleece according to Pindar (Pyth. 4.), on their way to Delphi before the trip acording to Herodotus (4.179). It is Herakles whose adventures bring him into contact with the greatest number of regions in the West. His tenth labor takes him to Spain to fetch the cattle of Geryon (a legend attested at least as early as the first half of the sixth century: Stesichorus, Geryeis). On his way home he passes through Italy and crosses over to Sicily, to its westernmost corner, where he claims the area of Eryx for his descendants (Hdt. 5.43; Pearson 1975:188-191). From here he makes his way to Libya where he seizes the three Golden Apples from the Garden of the Hesperides (Diod. Sic. 4.26.2), and where the Argonauts catch a last glimpse of him (Ap. Rh. 4:1473ff.). Herakles is the only one in these early tales to lay claim to any actual territory: Eryx in western Sicily. Although his adventures and settlements in Libya are attested only in later literature (Diod. Sic. 4.17.4; 26.2), Herodotus mentions an oracle which says that Lacedaemonians should send settlers there (4.178; see also Pindar, Pyth. 4).

Our earliest literary evidence for these various voyagings in the West appears between the late eighth and early fifth centuries. The dramatic date for these activities lies in Hesiod's Age of Heroes (Herakles, the Argonauts) and the immediately following generation, that of the Trojan War. Sardinia plays no part in any of the activities attested by our oldest sources and ascribed to the major heroes. When the island does appear, it is in a cluster of stories which belong dramatically to the same periods as the earlier tales but whose literary existence cannot be proved before the third century and whose heroes belong to the second rank (see Nicosia 1981 for the most recent discussion of the literary evidence). Aristaeus abandoning Thebes brings the blessings of agriculture to the island, and two generations later Iolaus, the nephew of Herakles, comes to settle with a band of Thespians and Athenians. A generation after Iolaus some Trojans, separated from Aeneas' fugitive band, take shelter there. Thucydides gives us some fifth-century support for the legend of Trojan refugees in the area when he equates them with the Elymians of Sicily (6.2.3), but otherwise, while the individuals themselves appear in earlier literature, their identification with Sardinia does not.

Even if we contend that the story of Iolaus is rooted in older legends, the Greek attempt to enfold a Hellenic strain into Sardinian prehistory seems half-hearted at best. The Greeks had long accepted the assumption that the Phoenicians had preceded them in the West. Thucydides states flatly (although he is not yet supported by archaeological evidence) that the Phoenicians had already settled in eastern Sicily and were pushed to the western end of the island when Greek colonization began (6.2.6). The Greek story of settlement in Sardinia yields pride of place to what is clearly a Phoenician version: The Libyans under Sardus, son of Melkart, and later the Iberians under Norax, the grandson of Geryon, form the first major settlements. The Greeks insert Aristaeus (as a civilizer, not as a colonizer) between Sardus and Norax, and then Iolaus appears, as the first Greek colonizer and city-builder. Iolaus is placed fourth in the series, but in Greek legendary chronology he cannot really be later than Norax, the grandson of Geryon, since he himself is the nephew of Herakles, Geryon's contemporary.

Iolaus seems to represent the Greek response to the Phoenician story of Sardus and his Libyans: Since the Greeks recognize in the Phoenician Melkart an analogue to their own Herakles, Melkart's son Sardus must therefore be the equivalent of Herakles' nephew/son, Iolaus. Thus the insertion of Iolaus into Sardinian prehistory can be satisfactorily explained, from the Greek point of view, as a recognition of a parallel relationship to the Phoenician original foundation story. It also gives a logical reason for not connecting a Sardinian episode to the wanderings of Herakles in the West: It is not that the story must have developed after the canonization of Herakles' exploits during the sixth century (although this may also be true); it is simply that the story is based on, and must therefore accord with, a Phoenician original version which ascribes the foundation to Sardus and not to Melkart.

Historical Background

When the historical adventuring in the West is considered (or at least those voyages which are described in our sources as occurring within the historical period), we notice some interesting overlapping of itineraries with those of legend. Equally interesting is the fact that the areas of permanent colonization, in eastern Sicily and southern Italy, show no such overlapping. The inference is that the travels of Herakles and the Argonauts and the western wanderings after the Trojan War reflect the voyages of exploration and trade which preceded the period of colonization of the mid eighth to early sixth centuries, while the isolated ventures which are historically attested are either a continuation of the earlier activity or an attempt to expand colonization in a world of dwindling opportunity. The overlapping with the legendary itinerary is therefore no accident in such cases, for the exploit of the earlier hero (i.e., Herakles) can be used as the justification for the later endeavor (Pearson 1975:192-3) although Pearson (ibid. 193) uses this as justification for colonization in Magna Graecia - in places where in fact Herakles was not). With or without such justification, the historically attested travelers to the West seem to be following in the footsteps of Herakles.

We hear first of the Samian merchant Kolaios, who while sailing to Egypt was blown off course all the way to Tartessos in Spain (the original site of Herakles' confrontation with Geryon). According to the evidence of Herodotus (4.152), this episode can be placed ca. 638 B.C. In the early sixth century, ca. 570 B.C. (though attested only in a late source: Diod. Sic. 5.9), Pentathlos of Cnidus with a group of Cnidians and Rhodians attempted a reprise of Herakles' assault upon the region of Eryx. When they formed a settlement at Lilybaeum, opposite the Phoenician port-of-call on the island of Motya, they were driven out by the Phoenicians and the local Elymians. They went on to settle on the Lipari Islands off the north coast of Sicily, where they carried on piracy against the Phoenicians and the Etruscans.

The case of the Phocaeans and their ouster by the Carthaginians and Etruscans from their settlement of Alalia on the island of Corsica does not fall into quite the same category as the other adventurers of the seventh and sixth centuries. Their colony was founded under the auspices of nearby Massilia and lasted for a generation, from ca. 565 to 535 (Hdt. 1.165-166). It does serve, however, as a useful indication of the apparent intention of Carthage to control the waters around Corsica and Sardinia, if not the islands themselves.

The latest and clearest example of a replication of Herakles' journeys is the failed attempts by the Spartan Dorieus to found colonies in Libya and in the territory of Eryx. Herodotus (5.41-66) informs us that Dorieus set out to found a colony in Libya in the region of the river Kinyps (now identified from air photographs as lying about 40km east of Leptis: Boardman 1980:279, n. 203; How and Wells 1912:161 on Hdt. 4. 175.2; Schenk 1960:184-185). When this venture failed, he went on to Sicily and founded the city of Heraklea by Mt. Eryx, relying on his Dorian origin and the legend that the land of Eryx was held in trust for Herakles' descendants (Hdt. 5.43). The Carthaginians and the natives destroyed the settlement and killed Dorieus; some of his followers later founded Heraklea Minoa, between Selinus and Acragas. These events have been dated between 520-510 B.C., and mark the end of expeditionary efforts into western Sicily until they are renewed by Athens during the last quarter of the fifth century.

A retaliatory action planned by Gelon of Syracuse to avenge the death of Dorieus apparently came to nothing because of the lack of cooperation from the mainland (Hdt. 7.158; Schenk 1960:190-191). This operation may also have been aimed at Libya, for Gelon's intentions included freeing what Herodotus calls 'the emporia.' It has been suggested that these emporia should be interpreted as settlements along the Libyan coast below and to the east of Carthage (Schenk 1960:197-198; cf. Boardman 1980:216; Gelon planned to open Africa to Greek trade). This could well be the case, if Dorieus' original endeavors in both Africa and Sicily are thought of as representing an imperial design initiated by Sparta to weaken or at least to limit Carthage by a flanking movement on both sides of the Sicilian Sea. The reaction of Carthage resulted in the appearance of a Punic settlement at Leptis Magna by 500 B.C. (Stillwell 1976:499), apparently designed to scotch any further exploration along the coast between Cyrene and Carthage (see, however, Whittaker (1974:66), where Leptis Magna and Sabratha are dated to the seventh century).

Archaeological evidence offers little support for including Sardinia in the itineraries of these wandering Greeks, whether legendary or historical. A Greek 'presence' in Sardinia can be identified from the late eighth century in the form of a scattering of pottery and a growing influence upon sculptural forms. But of actual Greeks on the ground there is scarcely a trace. The few inscriptions are late, and there are none of the monumental remains which could be expected of any permanent settlement. The closest possibility occurs in a single grave at Nora filled with fifth century Athenian pottery, perhaps to be recognized as the burial of an Athenian commercial agent or of a Punic proxenos looking after Athenian interests (Davison 1984:75-76; see also Nicosia 1981:35; who notes the amount of Attic pottery found at Neapolis near Tharros).

Athenian Involvement in the West

Athens' involvement in Sicilian affairs during the second half of the fifth century invites speculation concerning her intentions toward Sardinia as well. Thucydides ascribes to Alcibiades, and reports Alcibiades as ascribing to Athens, the real policy underlying the Sicilian Expedition of 415: to take over Sicily, Magna Graecia, the imperial possessions of Carthage, and finally Carthage herself (6.15; 90.2). Sardinia is not specifically identified, but as the 'imperial possession' lying closest to Sicily, the island would be the first objective after the subduing of the Carthaginian portion of western Sicily. And that Athens had designs on both western Sicily and Carthage (and by inference Sardinia) is betrayed both by her actions during the Peloponnesian Wars

and in the literature of the period in addition to Thucydides. Nicosia (1981:474) suggests that Athens' commercial interests in the West in the early fifth century may have been encouraged by Carthage herself, in preference to the nearer rivalry of Etruria.

Aside from the stories of Herakles in Africa, Pentathlos at Eryx, and Aristaeus and Iolaus in Sardinia, all our sources concerning legendary and historical Greek contacts in the western Mediterranean date no later than the fifth century, and thus were already part of Greek tradition at the time of the Peloponnesian Wars. This is especially the case with Herodotus, who was resident in Athens for some years before 444/3 and who was a member of the Athenian group which colonized Thurii after that date. Herodotus gives new currency to the colonizing efforts of Dorieus (if he is not in fact relaying the story for the first time), and he may well have whetted Athenian ambitions by his description of the fertility of Libya (4.198) and Sardinia (1.170; 5.106, 124; 6.2).

During the fifth century Athens has been showing signs of intending to usurp certain 'Dorian' (i.e., Argive and Theban) traditions and prerogatives, both culturally and politically. Theseus, the legendary king of Attica, had already been emphsized from the mid sixth century as an Ionian hero modeled after the Dorian Herakles. Both are represented as among the heroes who accompany Jason in his quest of the Golden Fleece, though neither plays any active role, and in fact Herakles leaves almost immediately to continue his Labors (notably in the West, where he is seen by the Argonauts on their way home via Libya). Two plays by Euripides (dated before the Sicilian Expedition of 415) indicate the absorption of the Theban Herakles into Athenian tradition. In the

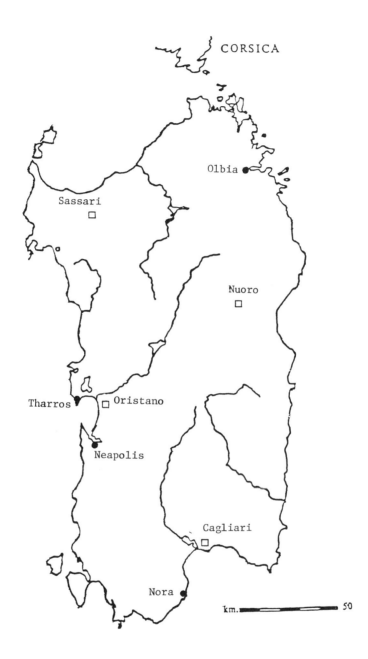

Figure 13.2 Map of Sardinia showing provincial capitals
and sites mentioned in text of chapter 13

Herakles, the hero himself (fresh from having saved Theseus from his captivity in Hades) is offered absolution and refuge in Attica by Theseus after he has killed his wife and children in a fit of madness induced by Hera. In the Herakleidai it is Iolaus and the Thespian children of Herakles who gain sanctuary in Attica at the hands of Theseus' son and successor in return for help in fighting off the attack of Herakles' former master, Eurystheus. This same tendency toward absorption of Theban/Argive legend is still operative at the end of the century, in Sophocles' Oedipus of Colonus, where the blind old king is welcomed by Theseus to a final resting place in Athens.

Less subtle evidence of a more political nature is offered by Thucydides, Aristophanes, and again Euripides. Aristophanes makes several allusions to overseas interests which fuel our speculation concerning Athenian designs in the West. In the Knights, produced in 424, he ascribed to Hyperbolus, a political rival of Alcibiades, the intention of sending 100 triremes to Carthage (1300-1304). Since the Greek preposition eis can mean either to or against, there is some ambiguity in the phrase. The large number of triremes, however, implies something more momentous than a diplomatic mission, especially since in the continuation of the passage, the personified triremes express horror at the possibility of such an expedition.

There are also two provocative references to the boundaries of Athenian expansion, one in the Knights, the other in the Wasps. In the Knights (164-178) a sausage-seller is being urged to take over control of the state and is offered a seductive view of the extent of the realm: from Caria to Carthage (173). In the Wasps, produced in 422, the people are complaining that they are not receiving the appropriate profits

from an imperial enterprise that extends from Pontus to Sardinia (698-701). These references are usually interpreted as representing a set of internal east-west parentheses for the Athenian empire - 'as far as but not including.' Even this interpretation puts some strain upon the facts, for Athenian claims in the West reach barely to Thurii in southeastern Italy. However, since the areas used to mark the eastern limits, Caria and Pontus, are regions in which Athens had already established or was attempting to establish a measure of control (Thuc. 2.9.4: Caria a member of the Delian confederacy; Mattingly (1966:195; n. 12): Pontus on the tribute list for 425/4), there is every reason to suggest that Aristophanes' remarks imply an equally active intent in the other direction. It should be noted, too, that Aristophanes shows a familiarity with geographical relationships that is not usually expected in fifth-century Greece. In the Knights he pairs Caria with Carthage, and both lie, with Athens, on the 38th parallel. Pontus and Sardinia are equally well matched in the Wasps, for Sardinia stretches across the parallels which include the Hellespont and the Bosporus.

Euripides, in his Trojan Women and Phoenician Women, again reminds us of the current interest in matters Carthaginian. In the Troades (415) the Trojan captives who are about to be shared out among their captors speculate on the future homes. They welcome the possibility of going to Athens or to Thessaly; and then, in what must be a deliberately anachronistic reference (and one which is unnecessary to the dramatic content), agree that southern Italy, too, or Sicily, 'opposite Phoenicia,' would be surely preferable to Sparta. In the Phoenissae the focus is even more marked, for the chorus of Phoenician women has no real connection with war-torn Thebes except to serve as a reminder of its origin from Phoenician Kadmos. The women are on their way to serve Apollo in Delphi, having been sent as a victory-offering from a 'Phoenicia' which, like the reference in the Troades, is clearly in the West and must therefore represent Carthage (Troades 220-229; Phoenissae 202-260; Powell 1911:156; Méridier 1950:129-130). This 'victory' has often been interpreted as referring to the sack of Selinus by Carthage in 409 and thus as a means of dating the play to the same year. It is clear that the reference to the destructive effects of internecine war are a reflection on the current situation in Athens (Vellacott 1972:56-68), but the peculiar composition of the chorus may be intended by Euripides to point out an even subtler irony: had the recent Sicilian Expedition been successful in all its purposes, there might have been real 'Phoenician' women devoted to Apollo as booty from an Athenian, not a Carthaginian, victory.

These references to Carthage (and rarely to Sardinia) in literary contexts which are current but not historial (Aristophanes, Euripides) or historical but not current (Herodotus) bring us to Thucydides and his contemporary account of Athenian intentions and activities in the West. Even before the sending of the Sicilian Expedition in 415, Athens had shown interest in Sicily to the extent of alliances with non-Dorian or native cities. It was in response to the pleas of one of these signatories (Leontini) that she had sent an earlier expedition in 427; and the weakest and most western of these allies (Egesta) which served as her pretext for action in 415. Athens' military activities during the course of the war before 415 already indicate the laying of a path to the West: Corcyra (432: Thuc. 1.44); Sphacteria (425: Thuc. 4.31-39); Cythera (424: Thuc. 4.54-55; 7.57.6);

Oeniadae (424: Thuc. 4.77.2); Melos (416:5: Thuc. 5.84-116); the earlier foundation of Thurii along the eastern coast of South Italy; then the attempts during the expedition of 427-424 to control Locri, Rhegion, Messina, the Lipari Islands - all point to efforts (of varying success and duration) to control a route not just to Sicily but beyond.

In the Wasps Aristophanes refers to the expedition of 427 in a parody of the actual trial of two of its generals. He presents a mock trial in which one of the generals (though not in fact one of the two involved in the real trial) is represented as a dog and is accused of stealing a cheese and retiring to a corner to eat it all by himself. I have suggested in an earlier paper (Davison 1984) that a play on words may be involved in ho tyrós (cheese) and the stem tyr- (Tyrian = Phoenician), and that the corner could refer to the northwestern segment of Sicily (Eryx and its vicinity) long under the control of Carthage. Thucydides concentrates his description mainly on the northeastern corner, in the area around Messina, but he notes one action which goes farther afield: an apparently unsuccessful attempt made upon the territory of Himera (3.115).

The Wasps also contains an allusion to the possible activity of the fleet. The defendant dog is described as 'coasting round and round the mortar and snapping up all the rind off all the cities' (924-925; Rogers tr.). Whatever it was that was collected from the cties, the implication of embezzlement is clear. The use of the word peripleuo for 'coasting around' seems a sure indication that the fleet is thought to have sailed around the island, or at least a large part of it. The word thueia (mortar) has been taken to mean in this context a platter or receptacle for the stolen cheese, but its usual meaning is in fact <u>mortar</u> – a utensil which may be used to crush cheese, but whose immediate identification would be with the grinding of wheat. All of this implies that the Athenians were aware of ramifications of the expedition which were considerably more extensive than anything we learn from Thucydides.

One of the early acts of 415, even before Syracuse is attacked, indicates a focus which is determinedly aimed at the western Mediterranean and thus inescapably at Carthage and her possessions (or more accurately, at her possessions if not at Carthage herself). Nicias takes part of the fleet along the north coast, past Panormus; he captures the port of Hykkara, renews friendly relations with Egesta and Halikyai, and returns; another part of the fleet was to sail along the south coast to Selinus. Even without any intended control of Selinus, Nicias' success in the northwestern corner accomplished at least diplomaticaly what Pentathlos and Dorieus had failed to do in the previous century. With a friendly foothold on the north coast west of Panormus, and with the alliance of Egesta and Halikyai, which controlled the land routes leading to Trapani and Lilybaeum and Motya on the western coast, Nicias had prepared a useful springboard for future sallies either against Motya or the southern coast of Sardinia and thus into the western Mediterranean.

Nothing further may actually have been intended; control of western Sicily and southern Sardinia would have ensured to Athens an access at source to her two most pressing needs, grain and timber (Green 1970:chap. II). Aside from Herodotus, who mentions the general fertility of Sardinia, we have no early reference to the grain production of the island. Diodorus Siculus, however, tells us that Carthage sent for supplies of grain from Sardinia (and Libya) on two

occasions during the fifth century: at the time of the assault upon Himera in 480 (11.20.4) and during her own attempts at the end of the century to defend western Sicily against Dionysios I of Syracuse (14.63.4:77.6). If we can trust Diodorus, then, we can understand an Athenian interest in Sardinia, buttressed as it could well be by the recollection (if not the actual creation, suggested by Euripidean drama) of the story of an earlier settlement there by Athenians under the leadership of Iolaus. Usurpation of the legendary and historical travels originally belonging to Dorian adventurers would thus be complete, and Athens, having followed in the footsteps of Herakles, Pentathlos, and Dorieus into western Sicily, would be poised to emulate Iolaus. And having carried speculation thus far, she might easily see in Sardinia, whose ancient name of Ichnoussa signified footprint (Paus. 10.17.1), an actual stepping-stone on the way to Herakles' most distant adventure, Spain itself.

We may suggest a further clue to Athenian policy, uncertain and fluctuating as it was, in the actions of Carthage herself. In two major treaties with Rome, one in 510 and one in 348 (Heurgon 1973:250-254), she reflects a political development and experience which seem the result not of current relations with Rome but of previous relations with Greeks. The treaty of 510 permits Rome to trade with Sardinia only through Carthaginian agents, presumably on the same terms as apply to any other state. This provision assumes Carthaginian control of the island by the end of the sixth century, a situation which could already have existed after 540, upon the abandonment by the Phocaeans of their settlement of Alalia in Corsica (Hdt. 1.166).

The treaty of 348, however, has far harsher conditions. Neither trade nor settlement shall be permitted either in Sardinia or in North Africa. This emphasis on the isolation of North Africa and Sardinia can have no possible reference to suspected <u>Roman</u> encroachment in these directions. It seems rather to reflect Carthaginian suspicions after her experiences with Athens at the end of the fifth century and with Dionysios I during the fourth. But even her various treaties with Dionysios do not contain provisions warding him off from such overseas expansion; they merely name the River Halycus as the boundary between their respective spheres of influence in Sicily.

By 348 Carthage has had time and opportunity to acquire a belated but enlightening familiarity with Greek history and cultural propaganda as the result of her series of victorious campaigns against the Greek cities of Sicily at the end of the fifth century, and after the establishment of the cult of Demeter and the importation of Greek priests at the beginning of the fourth (Xella 1969). She would by now perhaps have heard of the earlier excursions of Pentathlos and Dorieus and their legendary precursors, and would be aware of how readily the Greeks tended to use such tales to justify political actions. And she would be mindful of the comparatively recent, though temporary, presence of the Athenians in that very corner of Sicily which had been the object of those earlier exploits. Small wonder, then, if she now specifies in her treaty with Rome in 348 restrictions which are no longer appropriate to the time, the circumstances, nor the present signatory.

Conclusion

By the middle of the fifth century the Greeks had inherited or reconstructed a legendary past which not only authenticated their presence in the western Mediterranean but guaranteed their right to be there. Aside, then, from those areas in which they already had colonies in place - Cyrene, Southern Italy, Sicily, and Massilia, the Greeks could honestly enough claim even earlier 'interests' in regions now colonized or claimed by others: North Africa between Cyrene and Carthage, western Sicily, Sardinia, and Spain. Historical attempts to implement these claims - during the sixth century by settlers relying on their descent from Herakles - had met with failure. But during the second half of the fifth century Athens can be seen to be carrying out deliberate efforts to become the leader of the Greek world both politically and culturally. She developed a naval empire which ensured her own independence while threatening that of others, and in her art and literature so borrowed and interpreted the mythology of Argos and Thebes that it became entwined with that of Athens. Thus, when she turned her attention to the West (or when economic need forced her attention to the West), she was able to consider herself, and represent herself to others, as an appropriate and legitimate claimant to the inheritance of Herakles.

SELECTED REFERENCES

The following bibliography is designed to include not only the references mentioned in the text but also material which will indicate the direction of continuing research. (For a good general biblography, including archaeological reports, see Boardman below.)

Texts and Commentaries

GOMME, A.W., A. ANDREWS AND K.J. DOVER
    1970   Historical Commentary on Thucydides IV. Books V.25-VII.
            Oxford: Clarendon Press.

HOW, W.W., AND J. WELLS
    1912   A Commentary on Herodotus. I;I-IV; II:V-IX. Oxford:
            Clarendon Press.

LEE, K.H.
    1976   Euripides. Troades. St. Martin's Press.

MACDOWELL, DOUGLAS M.
    1971   Aristophanes. Wasps. Oxford: Clarendon Press.

MERIDIER, LOUIS
    1950   Les Phéniciennes. Budé text: Euripide V. Paris: Société
            d'Edition "Les Belles Lettres."

POWELL, JOHN U.
    1911   The Phoenissae of Euripides. London: Constable and
    Company Ltd. (repr. 1979 Arno Press Inc.).

ROGERS, B.B.
    1910   The Knights of Aristophanes. London: G. Bell and Sons,
    Ltd.

    1915   The Wasps of Aristophanes. London: G. Bell and Sons, Ltd.

DE SELINCOURT, AUBREY
    1972   Herodotus: The Histories. Baltimore: Penguin Books.

VELLACOTT, PHILIP
    1972   Euripides: Orestes and Other Plays. Baltimore: Penguin
            Classics.

    1975   Ironic Drama. A Study of Euripides' Method and Meaning.
            Cambridge University Press.

WARNER, REX
    1972   Thucydides: History of the Peloponnesian War. Baltimore;
            Penguin Books.

ZUNTZ, GUNTHER
    1955   The Political Plays of Euripides. Manchester University
            Press.

(for other translations, see the Loeb Classical Library or Penguin
Classics series)

General

BENGTSON, H.
  1962   Die Staatsverträge der griechisch-römischen Welt von 700
          bis 338 v.Chr. II. Munich and Berlin.

BOARDMAN, JOHN
  1980   The Greeks Overseas: Their Early Colonies and Trade. New
          and enlarged edition. London: Thames and Hudson; the 2nd
          edition (Penguin 1973) is also still useful.

BONDI, SANDRO F.
  1981   Qualche appunto sui temi della più antica colonizzazione
          fenicia. Egitto e Vicino Oriente 4:343-348.

BREGLIA PULCI DORIA, LUISA
  1981   La Sardegna arcaica tra tradizioni euboiche ed attiche.
          Nouvelle contribution à l'étude de la société et de l
          colonisation eubéennes. Cahier du Centre Jean Bérard
          61-95. Naples.

BRUNT, P.A.
  1966   Athenian Settlements Abroad in the Fifth Century B.C.
          Ancient Society and Institutions. Studies Presented to
          Victor Ehrenberg on his 75th Birthday:71-92. Ernst
          Badian ed. Oxford.

CAPOVILLA, G.
  1925   Eracle in Sicilia. Lombroso Festschrift 178-199.

DAVISON, JEAN M.
  1984   Greeks in Sardinia: The Confrontation of Archaeological
          Evidence and Literary Testimonia. SSA 67-82.

  forth- Catalogue of Greek Pottery, Appendix IV, Nuraghe Ortu
  coming Comidu (Sardara - CA) Preliminary Report of Excavations
          1975-1978, M.S. Balmuth et al., NSc.

FRANKENSTEIN, SUSAN
  1979   The Phoenicians in the Far West: A Function of
          Neo-Assyrian Imperialism = Mesopotamia 7:263-94. Power
          and Propaganda. A Symposium on Ancient Empires. M.T.
          Larsen, ed. Copenhagen.

FREEMAN, E.A.
  1891-94 A History of Sicily. Oxford.

FREYER-SCHAUENBERG, G.
  1966   Kolaios und die westphönizischen Elfenbeine. Mitteilung
          des deutschen archäologischen Instituts, Madrider
          Abteilung 7:89-108.

GREEN, PETER
  1970   Armada from Athens. New York: Doubleday and Company.

LURIA, S.
    1964   Zum Problem der griechisch-karthagischen Beziehungen.
            Acta Antiquae Academiae Scientiarum Hungaricae
            12(1):53-76.

HEURGON, JACQUES
    1969   The Rise of Rome to 264 B.C. University of California
            Press.

MANNI, EUGENIO
    1974   Sémites et Grecs en Sicile jusqu'au Ve siècle avant J.-C.
            Assoc. Guillaume Budé. Bulletin sér. 4:63-84.

MASTRUZZO, G.
    1977   Osservazioni sulla spedizione di Dorieo. Sileno 3:
            129-147 (Rivista di Studi Classici e Cristiani. Catania).

MATTINGLY, H.B.
    1966   Periclean Imperialism. Ancient Society and
            Institutions (cf. under Brunt) 193-224.

MERANTE, V.
    1972-73 La Sicilia e Cartagine dal V secolo all conquista romana.
            Kokalos 18-19:77-103.

    1970   Sui rapporti greco-punici nel Mediterraneo occidentale nel
            VI secolo a.C. Kokalos 16:98-138.

MOMIGLIANO, A.
    1936   La lotta per la Sardegna tra Punici, Greci e Romani.
            Studia et Documenta Historiae et Iuris (SDHI) II:373-398
            (=Quarto contributo alla storia degli studi classici e del
            mondo antico (1969:352ff.)). Rome.

NICOSIA, FRANCESCO
    1981   La Sardegna nel mondo classico. Ichnussa:420-476.

PEARSON, L.
    1975   Myth and Archaeology in Italy and Sicily. Timaeus and his
            Predecessors. YCS 24:171-195.

RAMIN, J.
    1979   Mythologie et géographie. Paris: Les Belles Lettres.

RAUBITSCHEK, A.E.
    1944   Athens and Halikyai. TAPA 75:10-14.

ROWLAND, ROBERT J. JR.
    1975   The Biggest Island in the World. CW 68(7):438-439.

SCHENK, ALEXANDER, GRAF VON STAUFFENBERG
    1960   Dorieus. Historia 9:181-215.

SJOQVIST, E.
    1962   Heracles in Sicily. Acta Instituti Romani Regni Sueciae
              22:117-123.

SMART, J.D.
    1972   Athens and Egesta. JHS 92:128-146.

STILLWELL, RICHARD, ED.
    1976   The Princeton Encyclopedia of Classical Sites. Princeton
              University Press.

STROHEKER, KARL FR.
    1954-55   Die Karthagergesandtschaft in Athen 406 v. Chr. Historia
              3:163-171.

THIMME, J., ED.
    1980   Kunst Sardiniens.

TORE, G.
    1978   Nota sulle importazioni in Sardegna in età arcaica. Les
              céramiques de la Gréce de l'Est et leur diffusion en
              Occident. Cahier du Céntre Jean Bérard 206-210. Naples.

TREU, MAX
    1954/55   Athen und Karthago und die Thukydideische Darstellung.
              Historia 3:41-57.

TRONCHETTI, C.
    1983a   La presenze della ceramica attica nella Sardegna
              fenicio-punica. Atti 1° Congresso Internazionale di Studi
              Fenici e Punici - 1979 II. Rome: Consiglio Nazionale
              delle Ricerche:501-507; pls. 89-110.

    1983b   Ceramica greco-orientale e attica arcaica da Tharros nel
              Museo Nazionale Archeologico di Cagliari e
              nell'Antiquarium Arborense di Oristano. Atti del Convegno
              Internazionale Ceramiche Arcaiche di Tharros - Nuoro 1980.

TUSA, V.
    1964-65   Testimonianze fenicio-puniche in Sicilia. Kokalos
              10-11:589-602; figs. 1-32.

    1967   La questione fenicio-punica in Sicilia. Eretz-Israel
              8:50-57 (E.L. Sukenik Memorial Volume).

VIAN, F.
    1982   Les navigations des Argonautes; Elaboration d'une légende.
              Assoc. Guillaume Budé. Bulletin sér.4(3):273-285.

WENTKER, HERMANN
    1956   Sizilien und Athen. Heidelberg: Quelle and Meyer.

WHITTAKER, C.R.
    1974   The Western Phoenicians: Colonization and Assimilation.
            Proceedings of the Cambridge Philological Society
            20:58-79.

    1978   Carthaginian Imperialism in the Fifth and Fourth
            Centuries. Imperialism in the Ancient World, P.D.A.
            Garnsey and C.R. Whittaker, eds.   Cambridge University
            Press:chap. 3:59-90; notes 297-302.

WICK, TERRY E.
    1976   Athens' Alliances with Rhegion and Leontinoi.   Historia
            25:288-304.

XELLA, P.
    1969   Sull'introduzione del culto di Dimetra e Kore a Cartagine.
            Studi e Material di Storia delle Religioni 40:215-228.

ZEVI, F.
    1979   Il mito di Enea nella documentazione archeologica.   Atti
            XIX Convegno di Studi sulla Magna Grecia.   Taranto.

PART FIVE:
EVIDENCE FOR TRADE AND CONTACT

Introduction

Peter Wells

The following chapters complement each other to provide an overview of trade in ancient Sardinia. The first deals with trade early in the settlement history of the island, the second with commerce at the end of Sardinian independence during the Roman period. Both papers emphasize the strong commercial links between Sardinia and mainland Europe that persisted throughout the culture history of the island.

The two studies illustrate the variety in Sardinia's commerce. The first concerns trade from Sardinia to the mainland, the second trade from the mainland to Sardinia. Obsidian was traded principally as raw material, whereas amphoras were imported as finished products. Obsidian was desired for its inherent properties as a material for tools; amphoras served as containers for wine, garum, and oil. The societies trading obsidian were small-scale and simple politically and economically, whereas commerce in amphoras was carried on in the context of complex states and empires.

Already in the 4th millennium B.C. we find Sardinian obsidian comprising substantial proportions of the tool assemblages on Neolithic sites in southern France and northern Italy, implying that the obsidian trade from Sardinia to the mainland was a regular and planned venture, not a series of chance meetings and exchanges. Many questions come to mind for future archaeological investigation of this commerce.

Was the trade carried on year-round or seasonally?

What goods were exchanged for obsidian?

Who did the traveling across the sea, Sardinians or mainlanders?

Were full-time specialists involved in mining and trading Sardinian obsidian, or was the commerce carried on by farmers or fishermen at times when food production did not demand their undivided attention?

The abundance of traded obsidian suggests that some degree of occupational specialization may have been involved. This instance might be compared with the Neolithic flint mining industries in southern Britain and Denmark in terms of specialization and societal complexity.

What we need most to study further such aspects of the obsidian trade is extensive settlement excavation, as Phillips states. Besides seeking more information about quantities and forms of obsidian extracted, used, and traded, we need to know more about the context of the trade, about subsistence, settlement size and organization, distribution of wealth among members of communities, and commerce in other materials.

The trade in wine, garum, and oil transported in amphoras was certainly a highly organized and planned activity. In the Roman world there is no question about the existence of full-time specialist producers of wine and other goods, makers of amphoras, and merchant-sailors. Since we have extensive written records from the Roman period, we can fill in much of the political and economic background of the trade. Yet, in an environment such as Sardinia where the records are very incomplete, the amphoras themselves yield abundant information about changes in commerce over time. Since each product was transported in its own particular type of amphora, and a reliable amphora chronology in the Mediterranean world has been established, the trade history of these three products can be reconstructed on the basis of the amphoras alone. Beside the directions and chronology of the trade, the amphoras permit a reconstruction of the broader commercial history of Roman Sardinia, as Will so clearly illustrates. Because we are so well informed by historical sources about politics and trade in the Roman-dominated Mediterranean, the archaeological evidence offered by the Sardinian amphoras permits us to make a detailed reconstruction of the character and changes in the trade. We really know very little about how societies worked during the Neolithic Period, however, and hence for the obsidian trade we need to compare the archaeological evidence with documented ethnographic trade systems in order to reconstruct probable mechanisms of exchange.

For both the obsidian trade and commerce in amphoras, these two papers show what we have to work with and what that information can tell us. The two cases offer exciting prospects for further research into ancient Mediterranean trade.

14. SARDINIAN OBSIDIAN AND NEOLITHIC EXCHANGE IN THE WEST MEDITERRANEAN

Patricia Phillips

Trace element analysis of obsidian represents a success story in one field of scientific archaeology: source determination. However, lack of advance in another field of archaeological science, dating, still prevents complete understanding of the ways in which obsidian was exploited on Sardinia during the Neolithic period (6th to 3rd millennia bc).

Obsidian, a black glossy material formed under volcanic conditions (Cann 1983), breaks with a conchoidal fracture. It thus made excellent cutting tools, arrowheads and scrapers for early man.

Our knowledge of the exploitation of obsidian in Sardinia in the Neolithic period stems from pioneer research around the obsidian mountain of Monte Arci by Cornelio Puxeddu in the 1940's and 1950's (Puxeddu 1955-7). This identified various obsidian flows and noted prehistoric quarrying activities. During the same time period the classic sequence of the Arene Candide cave in Liguria was defined and published by L. Bernabò Brea (1946; 1956), a sequence which contained 39 obsidian artifacts in the Neolithic levels (Williams Thorpe, Warren and Barfield 1979).

Trace element analysis of obsidian followed other less successful characterization methods in the 1960's and was able to distinguish between many of the Mediterranean sources (Cann and Renfrew 1964). Subsequent work, principally by neutron activation analysis, but more recently also by X-ray fluorescence and palaeo-magnetism, has shown that four different Sardinian sources may be involved - SA, SB, SC, and SD (Hallam, Warren and Renfrew 1976:92; 95-97; Mackey and Warren 1983). The West Mediterranean is now regarded as one of the best zones for obsidian sourcing in the Mediterranean-Near East area (Dixon 1976).

On Sardinia itself, fieldwork by geologist M. Mackey has located three definite sources in the Monte Arci area, two of which correspond closely to the analytical results, and one less closely (Conca Cannas = SA, Pedras Urias = SC, possibly Santa Maria Zuarbara = SB). The Santa Maria Zuarbara obsidian bears small white flecks, and can be distinguished visually from the other source material. Pedras Urias obsidian is matte, and formed in relatively small blocks. Conca Cannas' modern perlite quarry produces the best quality obsidian, in relatively large nodules (Mackey and Warren 1983).

Trace element analysis has identified the area covered by the Sardinian obsidian "market" as Corsica, Elba, North Italy and Southern France (Hallam, Warren and Renfrew 1976). Hallam et al. (1976:fig. 4) illustrate "interaction zones," with Sardinian obsidian being the most frequently represented in the areas cited above. However, the analyses cover obsidian found in all contexts from the 6th millennium to the late 3rd millennium bc, and Lipari appears to have been the dominant source for obsidian in the "Sardinian" interaction zone in the early and middle phases of the Neolithic (5th millennium to mid 4th millennium bc).

The few available radiocarbon dates for Neolithic Sardinia are indicated in table 14.1. The earliest evidence for use of Sardinian obsidian comes from Basi, Corsica, in the early 6th millennium bc; the obsidian only forms a small part of the lithic assemblage. Unfortunately there is no radiocarbon date for the Sardinian Early Neolithic rock-shelter site of Su Carroppu, Carbonia (Atzeni 1980) 100km to the south of Monte Arci, where obsidian is the only lithic raw material. It should date to the late 6th or 5th millennium bc. Somewhat surprisingly, obsidian forms only about 25% of the raw material used 200km to the north of Monte Arci at the Filiestru cave at Sa Korona, and the Thiesi Cave (Trump 1982; Foschi 1982). The two latter caves are relatively near to good flint resources at Perfugas, Gallura, while the Filiestru people could also exploit local jasper. At the Cave of Curracchiaghiu in Corsica, in levels probably dating ca. 4750 bc there is much greater use of obsidian than at Basi (Lanfranchi 1980). Lanfranchi has remarked on the incidence of white-spotted obsidian at this site, and at several of the north Sardinian Early Neolithic sites: this type of obsidian seems to have been popular in Early Neolithic contexts, together with the fine translucent obsidian from the Conca Cannas source. White-spotted Sardinian obsidian reached the Ligurian cave of Arene Candide towards the end of the 5th millennium bc, together with Liparian obsidian, which is also found on two sites in Southern France.

Students of Sardinian archaeology are indebted to David Trump and Renato Loria for the first publication of in situ Middle Neolithic ceramics, type-named Bonu Ighinu after the northern Sardinian comune

in which their cave site of Sa Ucca de su Tintirriolu was situated (Loria and Trump 1978) (see above, chap. 2). Bonu Ighinu pottery has now been identified, with regional variants, at 31 sites all over Sardinia; there are two major sites and numerous smaller ones to the north of Monte Arci on the shores of the Cabras lagoon. By comparison, Cardial Early Neolithic pottery has been reported from 16 sites, and Ozieri pottery from 127 (Tanda 1980: figs. 11, 12; Atzeni 1975-77:fig. 1).

Two radiocarbon dates were run on charcoal from the Bonu Ighinu level at Sa Ucca cave, only one of which was acceptable to the excavators, a date of 3730 ± 160 bc (R882). This date has been used in recent summaries of the Sardinian culture sequence to initiate the Middle Neolithic around 4000 bc (Atzeni 1980; Contu 1980). More recently, Trump has published a preliminary account of excavations at another cave in the same comune, Grotta Filiestru, where the Bonu Ighinu level 5 is again dated ca. 3700 bc, while the Filiestru phase (a type of Epicardial) in level 6 has dates of around 4000 bc (Trump 1982; 1983). It therefore seems likely that Bonu Ighinu started rather later than 4000 bc, perhaps nearer the 2nd quarter of the 4th millennium b.c.

In the 4th millennium bc a larger percentage of obsidian occurs in the Bonu Ighinu levels at Filiestru (personal observation and personal communication, David Trump). Huge numbers of obsidian artifacts and waste have been obtained via surface collection and excavation at Bonu Ighinu and at Ozieri settlement sites just north of Monte Arci; Puxeddu has recorded 5890 obsidian tools from the comune of Cabras, most of them deriving from the rich sites of Cucurru S'Arriu and Conca Illonis (Puxeddu 1975:122). There also seems to be a greater emphasis on blade production, a feature shared by other West Mediterranean groups.

Puxeddu's most recent work (1975) has concentrated on the Monte Arci exploitation and settlement sites. At the four sources (these include Sonnixeddu, which Mackey regards as a collecting site, with material derived from higher sources), 11 collecting centers, 84 workshops and 192 settlements which he recognizes in the Ales diocese, Puxeddu has collected 1360 implements, including 661 (48%) blades. At the most extensively studied site, Puisteris, he has suggested that most of the cultural debris dates to the Late Neolithic-Chalcolithic Ozieri period, although Middle Neolithic Bonu Ighinu potsherds and transverse arrowheads do occur (Atzeni 1975-7: fig. 18). Other authors have interpreted the numerous finds of obsidian artifacts and waste on Ozieri sites as evidence for the major obsidian exportation taking place during this cultural phase (e.g. Tanda 1977:151). I would suggest, however, that there is evidence for Sardinian obsidian being used outside the island in the earlier phases of the Neolithic, and that its major distribution probably coincided with the Bonu Ighinu phase.

About 1200 pieces of obsidian have been found in North Italian contexts, with over half coming from Sardinia, if we can extrapolate from the analytical results (31 out of 57 samples were Sardinian - Williams Thorpe, Warren and Barfield 1979). Recent analytical results have been particularly interesting in that they seem to demonstrate a gradual changeover from use of Liparian obsidian to use of Sardinian obsidian in North Italy and Southern France (Williams Thorpe, Warren and Barfield 1979). The majority of samples tested from Po Valley Late Neolithic Lagozza contexts come from Sardinia, including the four pieces from the huge obsidian assemblage of 950 items found at Pescale; Lagozzan sites probably date from ca. 3300 bc.

In Southern France the majority of the 160 pieces of obsidian are found in Chasseen Middle Neolithic contexts (ca. 4000/3500 bc - ca. 2600 bc, Phillips 1982). Most of the samples tested are of Sardinian origin, with a few Liparian pieces at the earliest sites (Williams Thorpe, Warren and Courtin 1984). There may have been direct contact between Sardinia and southern France, but the fall-off pattern of numbers of obsidian artifacts from East to West suggests that movement by land was more likely, both along the Ligurian coastline and from the Po Valley across the Alps into Provence. The role of Corsica is by no means clear at this time period; presumably Corsican societies acted as "middlemen" in the Early Neolithic, but they may have been by-passed later.

On the West Mediterranean mainland the 4th millennium bc saw the culmination of changes initiated by the development of cereal farming a half millennium earlier - changes in settlement location, group size and site assemblages (table 14.2). Analysis has shown that artifacts in raw materials such as flint, green-stone and marble were exchanged in greater numbers than in the Early Neolithic, and the movement of the relatively small numbers of pieces of Sardinian obsidian can be seen as part of complex exchange relationships set up both for acquisition of necessary resources and to modify relationships with neighbors.

Why was Sardinian obsidian preferred - even the good quality Conca Cannas type - to the excellent Liparian obsidian, by the late 4th millennium bc? Social factors, and the attraction of the strongly ritualistic Bonu Ighinu culture must have played a part.

Ethnography teaches us that people seek as exchange partners those who have desirable exchange items themselves. By expanding our knowledge about Neolithic culture and subsistence in Sardinia, and perhaps examining the impact of the strong ritual focus of Sardinian society in the 4th and 3rd millennia bc on neighboring groups, we may be able to explain Sardinia's increasing attraction as an exchange partner.

Conclusion

Trace element analysis of obsidian has provided a range of new data for the archaeologist to interpret. Even though all three main sources at Monte Arci may have been used by local groups throughout the Neolithic, trace element analysis seems to indicate that whereas white-spotted Santa Maria Zuarbara obsidian and the poorer quality Pedras Urias obsidian might have been exported in the earlier part of the Neolithic, most of the later exports derived from the top quality Conca Cannas source.

We now need to increase the precision of dating of the various cultural phases of the Sardinian Neolithic, to appreciate the true relationships of island and mainland during the Bonu Ighinu and Ozieri periods. We also need to identify the uses to which the obsidian blades and flakes were put both on Sardinia itself and on the mainland.

Obsidian use-wear studies are now under way at Sheffield University and may ultimately provide some answers (Linda Hurcombe, personal communication). Obsidian seems to have been exported to the mainland as cores, usually blade cores, and the role of the rare pieces of obsidian here as against flint or other stone materials may similarly be derived eventually by use-wear studies.

Ultimately the focus will have to widen to the whole West Mediterranean basin, and the results of analyses on obsidian and other stone raw materials used to derive a sophisticated model of trade and exchange processes in the West Mediterranean throughout the Neolithic period.

Table 14.1 Sardinian Chronology (years bc)

a) Classic (Atzeni 1980; Contu 1980)

6000-5000	Early Neolithic
5000-4000	Early Neolithic
4000-3100	Middle Neolithic (Bonu Ighinu)
3100 +	Late Neolithic-Chalcolithic (Ozieri)

b) Revised (Trump 1983; Phillips this paper)

6000-41/4000	Early Neolithic
41/4000-38/3700	Final Early Neolithic or Middle Neolithic (Filiestru)
38/3700-3200	Middle Neolithic (Bonu Ighinu)
3200-3100	Final Middle Neolithic? (Cabras lagoon sites - Santoni 1982)
3100 +	Late Neolithic-Chalcolithic (Ozieri)

Table 14.2 Sardinian Obsidian Usage (years bc)

6000 - 5000   ? S. Sardinia
                     ? N. Sardinia
                         x Corsica

5000 - 4000   X S. Sardinia
                     X N. Sardinia
                         x Corsica
                         x Liguria

4000 - 3000   X Central Sardinia
                     xx N. Sardinia
                         ? Corsica
                         ? Elba
                         x Liguria
                         x Po Valley
                         x S. France

        Key   ? assumed use of obsidian, but no dated sites
                     x small quantity obsidian in lithic assemblages
                     xx greater quantity obsidian in lithic assemblages
                     X majority of lithic raw material = obsidian

REFERENCES

ATZENI, E.
    1973-4   Nuovi idoli della Sardegna prenuragica. StSar 23:3-51.

    1975-7   La dea madre nelle culture prenuragiche. StSar 24:1-69.

    1980   Prima del nuraghe. NUR 80-101.

BERNABO BREA, L.
    1946,   Gli scavi nella Caverna delle Arene Candide 1-2.   1956
              Bordighera.

CANN, J.R.
    1983   Petrology of obsidian artifacts. The Petrology of
              Archaeological Artifacts, D.R.C. Kempe and A.P. Harvey
              eds. Oxford.

CANN, J.R. AND C. RENFREW
    1964   The characterisation of obsidian and its application to
              the Mediterranean region. PPS 30:111-133.

CONTU, E.
    1980   La Sardegna preistorica e protostorica. Aspetti e
              problemi. Atti XXII Riunione Scientifica IIPP. 21-27
              ottobre 1978:13-39. Firenze.

COURTIN, J.
  1967   Le problème de l'obsidienne dans le Néolithique du Midi de la France. RStLig 33:93-109.

DIXON, J.E.
  1976   Obsidian characterization studies in the Mediterranean and Near East. Advances in Obsidian Glass Studies, R.E. Taylor ed. Park Ridge, N.J.: Noyes Press.

FOSCHI, A.
  1982   Il neolitico antico della Grotta Sa Korona di Monte Maiore (Thiesi, Sassari), Nota preliminare. Le Néolithique Ancien Méditerranéen, Archéologie en Languedoc no. spécial 1982:339-46.

HALLAM, B.R., S.E. WARREN AND C. RENFREW
  1976   Obsidian in the western Mediterranean: characterisation by neutron activation analysis and optical emission spectroscopy. PPS 42:85-110.

LANFRANCHI, F. DE
  1980   L'obsidienne préhistorique corso-sarde: les échanges et les axes de circulation. BSPF 77(4):115-122.

LONGWORTH, G. AND S.E. WARREN
  1979   The application of Mössbauer spectroscopy to the characterisation of western Mediterranean obsidian. JAS 6: 179-93.

LORIA, R. AND D.H. TRUMP
  1978   Le Scoperte a 'Sa'Ucca de su Tintirriolu' e il neolitico sardo. MonAnt II-2.

MACKEY, M.P. AND S.E. WARREN
  1983   The identification of obsidian sources in the Monte Arci region of Sardinia. Proceedings of the 22nd Symposium on Archaeometry, Bradford 1982:420-431.

MICHELS, J.W.
  1982   Bulk element composition versus trace element composition in the reconstruction of an obsidian source system. JAS 9:113-123.

PHILLIPS, P.
  1982   The Middle Neolithic in Southern France: Chasseen farming and culture process. BAR Int. Ser. 142.

PUXEDDU, C.
  1955-7 Giacimenti di ossidiana del Monte Arci in Sardegna e sua irradiazione. StSar 14-15:10-66.

  1975   La preistoria. Diocesi di Ales-Usellus-Terralba. Aspetti e valori 69-122. Cagliari.

SANTONI, V.
    1977   Cucurru Arrius. RSP 32:350-357.

    1982   Il mondo del sacro in età neolitica.   Le Scienze
                170:70-80.

TANDA, G.
    1977   Gli anelloni litici italiani.   Preistoria Alpina 13:
                111-155.

    1980   Il neolitico antico e medio della Grotta Verde.
                Alghero.   Atti XXII Riunione Scientifica IIPP, 21-27
                ottobre 1978:45-94.   Firenze.

TRUMP, D.H.
    1982   The Grotta Filiestru, Bonu Ighinu, Mara (Sassari).   Le
                Néolithique Ancien Méditerranéen, Archéologie en Languedoc
                no. spécial 1982:333-338.

    1983   La Grotta di Filiestru a Bonu Ighinu, Mara (SS). Quaderni
                13.

WILLIAMS THORPE, O., S.E. WARREN, AND L.H. BARFIELD
    1979   The sources and distribution of archaeological obsidian in
                Northern Italy.   Preistoria Alpina 15:73-92.

WILLIAMS THORPE O., S.E. WARREN AND J. COURTIN
    1984   The distribution and sources of archaeological obsidian
                from Southern France.   JAS 11:135-46.

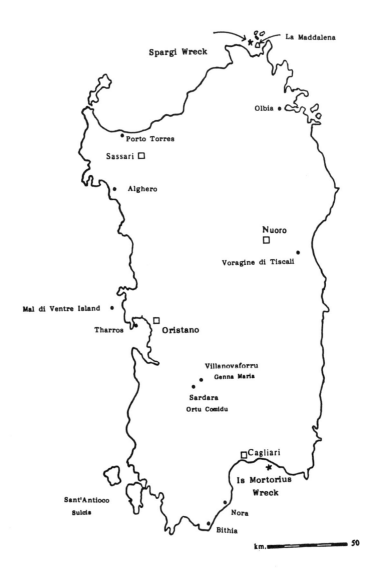

La Maddalena

Spargi Wreck

Olbia

Porto Torres

Sassari

Alghero

Nuoro

Voragine di Tiscali

Mal di Ventre Island

Tharros   Oristano

Villanovaforru
Genna Maria

Sardara
Ortu Comidu

Cagliari

Is Mortorius
Wreck

Sant'Antioco
Sulcis

Nora

Bithia

km. ▬▬▬▬▬▬ 50

Figure 15.1   Map of Sardinia showing sites mentioned
in text of chapter 15

15. AMPHORAS AND TRADE IN ROMAN SARDINIA

Elizabeth Lyding Will

The Roman shipping amphoras found in Sardinia tell a story of the island's importation of wine, garum, and olive oil during eight centuries, from the 3rd century B.C. to the 5th century A.D. It is a rich and complicated story, about which little has been published. In June of 1983, with the aid of a grant from the American Philosophical Society, I undertook a survey of the Roman amphoras in the major Sardinian collections, hoping thereby not only to fill a gap in my own knowledge of ancient trade but also to add to the sum of general knowledge on the subject. It is a pleasure to have the opportunity to present my observations and initial conclusions at this colloquium, which is such a persuasive demonstration of the importance that is increasingly being attached to the study of Sardinia's role in the history of the ancient Mediterranean. Much of the current interest in Sardinia stems from its function as a hub of trade and of that offspring of trade, culture. The island's pivotal geographical position facilitated contact with all parts of the Mediterranean, and the Roman amphoras illustrate that centrality for a period of many centuries. It is of interest to note that the realization of the importance of amphoras reflects the same kind of awareness that has led to renewed attention to Sardinia. As methods of investigating the past have matured, as political, military, and artistic perspectives on history have accommodated themselves to viewpoints that are based also on economic and social discoveries, shipping amphoras, which

are found in abundance on Roman sites and can now be dated quite closely, have come to be recognized as valuable historical documents. The same interest in the past as it was actually lived underlies some of the present focus of attention on Sardinia; an understanding of the island's central economic and cultural role is essential to a balanced view of the history of the Mediterranean in antiquity (fig. 15.1).

Not only is Sardinia a crucial piece in the Mediterranean puzzle but study of the island serves another important purpose. It miniaturizes and thereby helps to clarify the economic history of Italy itself, especially of the western coast, in the Roman period. I say the western coast, because the western and eastern coasts of the country faced in different directions, not only geographically, but also economically. We see in the Sardinian amphora finds the story chiefly of western Italian exports during the Late Republic and of western Italian imports during the Empire, and Sardinia documents that sending and receiving. During the Late Republic, especially after the First Punic War, wine from Campania and Etruria was in most of the many shipping containers that reached Sardinian shores from Italy. A little olive oil came to Sardinia from the Adriatic coast of Italy and from Istria, but wine was the peninsula's chief export to the island. With the end of the Republic, Italy's exportation of wine and oil to the West was sharply curtailed, and the result in Sardinia was a cessation of almost

211

all importation of wine. Very few non-Italian wine amphoras have been found on the island. Italy had dominated the western wine trade so totally that the island may have had no choice but to begin to produce enough wine for its own use. The effect on oil production was probably soon felt. As in Italy itself, so in Sardinia when farmers turned to cultivation of the vine, the need for oil grew, particularly since such oil as had been imported from the Italian peninsula was no longer available. Stepping in to fill the gap, and perhaps thereby further discouraging oil production in Sardinia and in Italy, were the energetic Spanish oil distributors along the Guadalquivir river in Baetica, whose boats were taking oil in huge ball-shaped amphoras as far afield as Egypt and the Aegean by at least the second quarter of the 1st century A.D. Another Spanish import also proves that Sardinia quickly replaced trade with Spain for the former trade with Italy. As early as the Augustan Age, masses of amphoras with garum, a salted fish sauce, began to reach Sardinia, as they did Italy itself, from southern Spain. Garum became, in fact, the chief import into Sardinia from Spain, as was apparently the case with all of Italy except for the city of Rome, where the existence of the dole made the importation of oil a matter of urgency. As the city absorbed more and more of the oil of Spain, Sardinia turned increasingly for its oil to Africa, as did the cities of the peninsula itself outside of Rome. Sardinia thus reflects the heyday of exportation of wine from Italy during the Republic and the situation that ensued when the mainland ceased to export and became a more leisure-oriented, consumer society. Like Italy, Sardinia demanded garum and olive oil from foreign markets, emphasizing at the same time production of enough wine for domestic use. Such are the outlines

of the story told by the amphora finds.

Let me try to clarify my remarks by looking next at some of the material in the chief collections of amphoras in Sardinia. I saw or examined over 460 amphoras in museums and private collections in Cagliari, Sassari, Sant' Antioco, Oristano, and La Maddalena, and I made visits also to smaller museums such as those at Nuoro and Villanovaforru. I studied the rather sparse published references to Roman amphoras found in Sardinia, and I made my own observations at the sites of Nora and Tharros. The survey was thus as comprehensive as the availability of finds and time allowed, and it was much more informative than I had dared to hope.

Starting my amphora odyssey at Oristano, I found in the Antiquario there a collection in which Republican wine jars preponderate. Of the 22 amphoras on display, over half are so-called Greco-Italic amphoras (fig. 15.3). Two belong to my Type 1a (Greco-Italic Form a in Will 1982, passim), a wine jar probably chiefly manufactured in Sicily and southern Italy, according to our present information, and datable chiefly to the first quarter of the 3rd century B.C. Ten other Greco-Italics at Oristano belong to Type 1d (Greco-Italic Form d in Will 1982), which dates from the first half of the 2nd century B.C. and originated in Campania and in Etruria. These later jars at Oristano bear marine deposits, and it seems likely to me that they are from the cargo of the same wrecked ship, one doubtless located off Oristano. The Type 1a amphoras, however, lack marine accretions, and it seems logical to associate them with the excavations of Tharros. Other finds in the Oristano Antiquario are known to be from Tharros; and, although there seems to be no record of where any of the Oristano amphoras were found, the fact that recent excavations in Tharros have uncovered amphoras of the same type (Acquaro 1979; 1983; Rodero Riaza 1981a; 1981b; 1982; Righini Cantelli 1982) leads me to associate the Oristano pieces of Type 1a with Tharros, at least provisionally. In all, two-thirds of the material at Oristano consists of Republican wine jars. In addition to the Greco-Italic types, there are three larger wine jars of my Type 4a (Will 1956; 1979; a type ancestral to Form 1 in Dressel 1889 and termed Dressel 1A by Lamboglia 1955), dating chiefly from the late 2nd and early 1st centuries B.C., when export of wine from Italy was at its height.

Early amphora material far outweighs late at Oristano, and since that ratio is not characteristic of the other major collections on the island, except for La Maddalena, I believe that, as at La Maddalena, a shipwreck best explains the imbalance and accounts for the unusual number of Greco-Italic amphoras of Type 1d at Oristano. We do not, moreover, lack knowledge about later types of amphoras from the area. A large group of amphora stamps certainly belonging to South Spanish olive oil jars of Type 20 (Will 1983a; Dressel 20) is reported by Sotgiu (1967 (1971)), and another published stamp from Tharros (CIL X.8051.42) probably comes from a 1st century A.D. Spanish wine jar of Type 12b (Dressel 2; cf. Tchernia and Zevi 1972). Imperial amphoras on display in the Antiquario at Oristano, and possibly also from Tharros, include four Spanish garum jars (varieties of my Type 16; Dressel 7-14, etc.); an African oil jar of the middle of the 3rd century A.D. (Type 21a, called "African I" by Zevi and Tchernia 1969); a "chimaera" jar, in which a neck of Type 21a has been incorrectly restored on a base of Type 16 (fig. 15.4); and finally a (Massaliote ?) wine jar of Type 18a

(similar to Dressel 30), a variety of amphora manufactured in southern France from the Flavian period to the end of the 2nd century A.D. These later pieces permit us to see the Oristano collection in somewhat better perspective.

More characteristic of the material in other parts of Sardinia is the large group of amphoras in the National Archaeological Museum in Cagliari. There are 96 amphoras from a variety of sites, including the Is Mortorius wreck, in addition to 11 jars or large fragments from Nora, one from Bithia, and at least five pieces from Ortu Cômidu (Sardara). While many of the amphoras in the museum are of unknown provenance, the collection, surely amassed from a number of sites, can be assumed to be representative of the island as a whole, perhaps particularly of the southern part. At Cagliari, by my count, and excluding the sites of Nora, Bithia, and Ortu Cômidu, to be discussed below, the numbers of wine, garum, and olive oil amphoras are roughly equal: 36 for wine, 33 for garum, 27 for oil. The number of garum jars would be greater if six pieces published as from the Is Mortorius wreck east of Cagliari (Pianu 1981) were now in the museum. Of that group of 13, however, I was able to identify only seven. The collection as a whole includes, for wine jars, two examples of the very early Greco-Italic Type 1a (fig. 15.5), two examples of Type 1d, one of Type 1e (some of these pieces may be the Greco-Italics referred to by Zucca 1981 as found in Cagliari; and 24 of the later, larger wine jars of Type 4a (fig. 15.6) and its descendant, Type 4b (Dressel 1, also reported from Cagliari by Zucca 1981), a category dating from the second through the fourth quarters of the 1st century B.C. Of Imperial wine jars, there are five examples of Type 12b and two of Type 18a, which have already been discussed. They are among the few instances of imported wine containers in Sardinia after the fall of the Republic.

The 33 garum amphoras seen in Cagliari comprise six subvarieties of Type 16, including 14 examples of Dressel 7/8, datable as early as the Augustan Age (fig. 15.7); three jars of Dressel 14 (to which I have added in computing the totals two jars now in a private collection in Cagliari and found off the island of Mal di Ventre); a jar of Dressel 17; and three jars of a type identified by Beltrán (1970) as Form III. All of those amphoras date from the first century and a quarter of the Empire. Somewhat later are three amphoras of Beltrán II A and II B. Also well represented in Cagliari are jars for olive oil, which include five examples of the ball-shaped South Spanish Type 20 (fig. 15.8); nine cylindrical African jars of Types 21a and 21b, one of them cut for reuse as a coffin (fig. 15.9); five amphoras (called spatheia) that are probably 5th century A.D. descendants of the African containers; and an example of Type 23, known as Tripolitanian. African jars clearly outnumber Spanish, especially for the later Empire. Only one Republican oil jar was noted, an example of the Italian Type 7 (Will 1970), datable to the first quarter of the 1st century B.C. Miscellaneous types, mostly for oil, make up the remainder of the 96 amphoras at Cagliari. Except for a dearth of early Italian oil amphoras, then, Cagliari provides a picture of many of the chief types of Roman amphoras and at the same time well reflects the history of the importation of wine, garum, and olive oil during the Roman period of Sardinia.

Eleven pieces from Nora are also stored in the Cagliari museum. They are illustrative especially of the later Imperial period at that site, although a 1st century B.C. Italian

wine jar of Type 4b is in the group. There are five Spanish garum amphoras of Type 16, a French wine jar of Type 18a and an African wine jar of Type 18b, a Spanish oil jar of Type 20, and an African oil container of Type 21b, as well as one of its 5th century A.D. descendants. At the site of Nora, too, a large pile of amphora sherds is mute testimony to the African oil jars that came to Nora during the 3rd century A.D. Reuse of such jars as coffins was common during the later Empire, and Patroni (1901) graphically describes the finding of the extensive cemetery at Nora in which such jars were used for burials in the 3rd century A.D.

The site of Bithia is also represented in the Cagliari museum by a Spanish garum jar of the type called Beltrán II B. From published evidence (Tronchetti 1981), we learn that oil amphoras from Africa have also been among recent finds at that excavation. They are said to include Types 21a and 21b, from the province of Africa, and the Tripolitanian Type 23.

While the Cagliari museum's collection of finds from Nora and Bithia chiefly reflects later trading activity at those coastal sites, the amphora fragments from the inland settlement of Ortu Còmidu in Sardara (Balmuth, forthcoming), also stored in the museum, document by chance several centuries of Roman economic history, from the 3rd century B.C. to the 3rd century A.D. At the same time, they illustrate how important fragments can be in the reconstruction of history. The base of a rare wine amphora of Type 1b (no. OC 75/E II/925; here below, fig. 15.10) can be dated in the latter 3rd century B.C. (Will 1982), and there is also a rim of an Italian oil amphora of Type 10, of the first quarter of the 1st century B.C. (no. OC 75/Surface/23). This type of jar is rarely found in Sardinia, although it is one of the

two chief types of Italian oil amphoras in the eastern Mediterranean
(Will 1970). The fragmentary rim of
an Augustan garum jar of Dressel 7/8
(no. OC 75/E III/810; OC 75/E IV/800)
has also been discovered at Ortu
Cŏmidu, and there is a toe of an
Early Imperial South Spanish oil jar
of Type 20 (no. OC 76/Surface/2141).
A handle of a 3rd century A.D. African oil container of Type 21b (no. OC
75/E IV/1009) completes the group,
which provides an insight into the
nature of the Roman presence in the
interior of Sardinia.

Another rich group of Roman amphoras, carefully chosen, well displayed, and accessible for study, is
in the National Archaeological Museum
at Sassari. Here, 41 jars are again,
as at Cagliari, drawn from a variety
of sites and therefore probably provide us with a reliable general picture of trade in the northern part of
the island, as Cagliari does particularly for the southern part. At Sassari, however, wine and oil jars outnumber containers for garum (I counted 19 wine jars, 16 for oil, and six
for garum). The relative lack of
garum jars and also of Spanish oil
amphoras may indicate that the southern, not the northern, part of the
island was on the direct route between the south of Spain and the
chief ports of mainland Italy. A
difference from the Cagliari collection can also be seen in the several
examples of early Italian oil jars.
These are: a jar of Type 10, already
noted at Ortu Cŏmidu; two examples of
Type 11b (Will 1977), which was an
olive oil container of the last half
of the 1st century B.C.; and a still
later variant of the same type. An
important amphora for Istrian oil,
found in May of 1983 off Alghero, is
also stored at Sassari. This piece
is the only example known to me in
Sardinia of Type 14 (Dressel 6),
which was the type of jar used to
export the famous olive oil of Istria
all over the Mediterranean during the

early Empire. The amphoras at Sassari are otherwise representative of
types frequently observed in the island's collections: Italian wine jars
of Types 4a (fig. 15.11) and 4b (fig.
15.12); Spanish garum jars of, for
example, Beltrán II A (fig. 15.13)
and III; oil jars of Type 21b, with
their 5th century descendants, and of
Type 23. The Sassari museum also has
the only example I saw in Sardinia of
a widespread Late Roman amphora of
which we do not yet know either the
source or the contents, a type called
Kapitän 2 (Kapitän 1972; Panella
1973:596-599; fig. 15.14).

The dangerous coast of northeast
Sardinia must have witnessed many
shipwrecks in antiquity. One ill-
starred ship went down off the island
of Spargi. It was carrying a cargo
of wine amphoras, a small number of
jars of olive oil, and other objects,
the retrieval of which commenced in
1958. The finds from the underwater
site are now housed in the exciting
new Nino Lamboglia Museum of Naval
Archaeology at La Maddalena. The
museum contains in my view the best
display of commercial amphoras visible anywhere in the world. As one
enters the building, one looks down
on a group of over 200 amphoras that
are arranged to represent the upper
layer of the amphora cargo in the
hold of the original ship, before it
sank. Following down some stairs the
sides of the reconstructed hull, one
turns to face a restored cross-
section of the three layers of jars
as they were superimposed in the
original packing of the cargo (fig.
15.2). Surely, bringing antiquity to
life in this manner should be the
goal of all museums. At La Maddalena, the goal is achieved imagina-
tively but also simply. Coarse wares
become both dignified and exciting.
The amphoras stand out as almost
anthropomorphic reminders of all the
unnamed, forgotten humans who made
and handled them: the potters, farm
workers, sailors, longshoremen, and

business people, not to forget the consumers. The effect of such a display is very moving, especially in the context of the sudden tragedy of a shipwreck. The La Maddalena exhibit is cause for hope that similar means will be found to show other collections of amphoras that are not yet on display in Sardinia. I have mentioned already the useful display at Sassari, and I am told that a stimulating amphora exhibit is being made ready at Porto Torres. I regret that the material there was not available for study during the summer of 1983. Sardinia has a richly varied heritage of Roman amphoras. For the scholar, they will serve in the future as documents bearing on the island's economic history. For the layman, they can serve as tangible links with the past. I have myself had many occasions to observe that both students and museum-goers in the late 20th century want to know how life was really lived in the past. Simple objects well displayed say as much to the modern world as million-dollar red-figure vases.

The amphoras of Sardinia as a whole are little known, but the island is leading the way in innovative amphora exhibits. The shipload of jars on display at La Maddalena consists chiefly of wine containers, and the ship apparently began its final voyage in Etruria or Campania. Study of the stamps and the clay of the jars should make it possible to determine the port of origin. The wine jars in the cargo are a mixture of Types 4a and 4b, a fact which leads me to feel the wreck dates from about 75 B.C. or perhaps as early as the mid-80's B.C., although the date usually assigned it is 120-100 B.C. Type 4b (fig. 15.15) was beginning to evolve out of Type 4a in the 80's B.C. By the second quarter of the century the evolution is complete. That is the date of the Albenga wreck, the wine amphoras of which belong solely to Type 4b. The very

beginning of the evolution is illustrated by a fragment found in a Sullan destruction context (86 B.C.) at the Athenian Agora (no. SS 6814; cf. Will 1956). Jars of Type 4b are especially abundant, however, throughout the Mediterranean world in contexts of the last half of the 1st century B.C. Type 4a, on the other hand, was the chief type of Italian wine amphora in the latter 2nd and early 1st centuries B.C., although it was in use down to about the middle of the 1st century. The Spargi wreck must date from the years when one type was succeeding the other; and although Type 4a seems to preponderate in the cargo, the presence of quite a few jars of Type 4b leads me to feel at the present time that a date of about 75 best fits the evidence provided by the amphoras (cf. Will 1983/84).

Also part of the Spargi cargo were oil jars of Type 11a, manufacturing sites for which I rediscovered some years ago near Brindisi (Will 1962). Such jars apparently served as export containers for Venafran oil and are found in many parts of the Mediterranean but especially in the East. The floruit of the type was the first quarter of the 1st century B.C., on the basis of Sullan destruction contexts at the Athenian Agora. An Italian oil jar of Type 10, also apparently part of the cargo, must be given the same date. All the amphora evidence thus argues for a later date than the one proposed by the excavators of the wreck (Roghi 1965). From the Spargi cargo should be excluded, however, several other amphoras which are on display in the La Maddalena museum. These are both earlier and later in date than the Spargi wreck itself: a jar of Type 1b (late 3rd century B.C.); four examples of Type 20, the South Spanish oil jars which date no earlier than the second quarter of the 1st century A.D., according to present information; and a neck of the African Type 21b, of the

3rd century A.D. These pieces must be intrusive, and they suggest that the Spargi site became over the centuries a kind of graveyard for ships. The site is, in other words, not a closed context. Its amphoras reflect several stages of Sardinian economic history during the Roman period.

A similar miniaturization of the island's Roman trade, and also of Roman economic history in the western Mediterranean as a whole, is provided by the amphoras that have been found in and near Sant' Antioco. I refer to the exciting Biggio Collection and also to the amphoras in the Antiquario at the site of the excavations of Sulcis. The strategic position of Sulcis at the southwest corner of the island enhanced, of course, the likelihood that the city would be a witness to trading activity in all periods. In the Biggio Collection, 40 or more amphoras represent a wide spectrum of dates. They include an example of Type 1a, the earliest form of Greco-Italic wine amphora; another of Type 1d, a later Greco-Italic shape (fig. 15.16); still later wine jars of Type 4; Republican oil jars of Types 10 and 11; and several types of Spanish garum jars of the early Empire (fig. 15.17). It was of great interest to me, too, to discover in the collection five examples of an amphora form that is clearly related to Tripolitanian amphoras (Type 23) and may even be ancestral to them (fig. 15.18). Many questions remain unanswered about this category, but a date as early as the Republican period may be suggested by the occurrence of several fragments in the "Punic ship" off Marsala (Frost 1976). On the other hand, a late date may be indicated by other known pieces (Beltrán Forms 59-60). Whole jars of this shape are very rare, and the jars in the Biggio Collection are of more interest for that reason.

Supplementing the Biggio Collection, the amphoras which are said to have been found partly at Sulcis and partly in the sea nearby, are four jars on display in the Antiquario located beside the excavations of Sulcis. African jars of Types 21a and 21b and Tripolitanian jars of Type 23 have been found in the necropolis (Tronchetti 1981), and an example of each shape can be seen in the Antiquario. Other, similar amphoras are said to be stored in the magazines, but they were unfortunately not available for study during the summer of 1983. A fourth amphora on display in the Antiquario is of special interest as the only example I saw in Sardinia of Type 13, an Adriatic oil jar of the latter half of the 1st century B.C. and a type commonly found in the Aegean area. The amphora at Sant' Antioco was covered with marine deposits. The finding of this jar near Sulcis adds to our understanding of the history of the site and of Sardinia as a whole.

In addition to the larger amphora collections visited during my survey, material in two smaller collections added useful supplementary information. Two fragments of Type 1d have been found in Villanovaforru and are on display in the fascinating new Museo Genna Maria. And at the Museo Civico Speleo-Archeologico in Nuoro, a toe of Type 1b from Voragine di Tiscali (Dorgali; Lo Schiavo 1978) closely resembles a similar toe, described above, from Ortu Cómidu (Sardara). This is perhaps the place to mention other recently published fragments from the Dorgali area but apparently not on display at Nuoro: a toe of Type 1c from Balu Birde (Boninu 1980), a rim of Type 4b from Voragine di Ispinigoli (Moravetti 1980), and a neck of Type 18b from S'Abba Meìga (Boninu 1980). All of these pieces show the importance of fragments to our understanding of ancient trading practices and patterns.

Publications of amphora finds in Sardinia have been, at least until recently, scattered and infrequent. That fact underlines the need for a survey such as the one I undertook. I do not doubt that some of the pieces I saw have been published; for example, amphoras from Olbia are said to be in the collections at Cagliari and at Sassari, and some of the profiles of Olbia finds published by Levi (1949 (1950)) are reminiscent of jars now stored in those museums. More recent Olbia finds are referred to by Acquaro (1980). In addition, Rowland's useful and informative compendium (1981), mentions finds which may also now be part of the groups of amphoras examined by me, as may objects reported in, among other publications, the Notizie degli Scavi, Studi Sardi, and the several helpful volumes of reports recently published by the Soprintendenza for Sassari and Nuoro. My survey indicates that the process of publishing or republishing all this material will be exacting but also richly rewarding. It would be especially useful if, in addition to the whole amphoras and large fragments which comprised the collections studied by me, any future research on Sardinian amphora finds should seek to include as much fragmentary evidence as possible, both what may be in museum collections and what still lies on the surface of the ground at unexcavated sites. A survey of private collections on the island would also be informative. When a thorough study of the Roman amphoras of Sardinia has been made, a step will have been taken toward a much more complete understanding of the economic history of the island, one in which imports of wine, garum, and olive oil will be seen both in the light of our knowledge of Sardinian export of grain and in the light also of the study of other kinds of everyday commercial and domestic objects. Meloni (1975: 163) foresaw that such a study could provide the basis for the writing of a new page in Sardinian economic history during the Empire. My survey has, I believe, demonstrated

that Meloni's prediction holds true for the history of trade during the Republic as well.

The Roman amphoras illustrate for us an important chapter in the story of Sardinian imports during the Roman period. It is a homogeneous picture, sketched in similar terms throughout the island. An emphasis on the importation of wine during the Late Republic gave way to an emphasis on bringing in foreign garum and olive oil during the Empire. While the Republic lasted, Sardinia had been a market for Italy. During the Empire, the island shared with the mainland a need for imported garum and oil. The island therefore provides a mirror in which we can see reflected the ebb and flow of trade in Italy itself. As far as Sardinia's own trade is concerned, the centrality of its commercial role in the western Mediterranean can be seen in the fact that the chief kinds of shipping containers found elsewhere in the Roman world were also sent to the island. The locations of shipping lanes may well explain the apparent presence of more Spanish garum jars and African oil jars in the southern part of Sardinia than in the north, whereas more oil amphoras from Italy seem to occur in the north than in the south. Throughout the island, however, in the interior as well as on the coasts, the amphora finds reflect the popularity of the same kinds of products used in other parts of the Mediterranean. And they reflect Sardinia's very real dependence on imports, although, as I have suggested, they also indicate that wine-production on the island during the Imperial period apparently solved the shortage of wine that had occurred during the Republic. An insight into that shortage of wine, certainly of good wine, is provided us by Plutarch, who tells us (Caius Gracchus 2.5) that Gracchus reported to the Censors in Rome in 124 B.C. that his fellow officials in Sardinia brought their own wine with them from Italy and, incidentally, took the amphoras home filled with gold and silver. They were probably amphoras of Type 4a. If they had not been taken back to Italy, the numerous finds of Republican wine amphoras in Sardinia would be even more numerous, and museums on the island, already plentifully supplied with amphoras, would have even greater storage problems. Enough material remains, however, to provide us with suggestive new insights into trade in Roman Sardinia.

Acknowledgments

I should like to take this opportunity to express my thanks to the American Philosophical Society for its grant (no. 9455) from the Penrose Fund in support of my trip to Sardinia in 1983. See the report on that trip (Will 1983b). I owe a debt of gratitude, also, to the following: Miriam S. Balmuth, who suggested that I make the amphora survey and provided me in Sardinia with invaluable aid and encouragement; Ferruccio Barreca, Signora Biggio, Lionel Casson, Fulvia Lo Schiavo, Raniero Massoli-Novelli, Anna Marguerite McCann, Robert J. Rowland, Jr., Carlo Tronchetti, Barbara Will, and Samuel Wolff.

Note on Illustrations

The amphoras shown are approximately 1/10 actual size.

CATALOG OF SHIPPING AMPHORAS FOUND IN SARDINIA

1. Greco-Italic amphora of Will Type 1d (fig. 15.3, left)

2. Greco-Italic amphora of Will Type 1a (fig. 15.3, right)

3. "Chimaera" amphora (fig. 15.4)

4. Amphora of Will Type 1a (fig. 15.5)

5. Amphora of Will Type 4a (fig. 15.6)

6. Amphora of Dressel Forms 7/8 from the Is Mortorious shipwreck (fig. 15.7)

7. Amphora of Will (and Dressel) Type 20 (fig. 15.8)

8. Amphora of Will Type 21a ("African I"), cut for reuse as a coffin (fig. 15.9)

9. Base of amphora of Will Type 1b, from Ortu Còmidu, no. OC 75/E II/925 (fig. 15.10)

10. Amphora of Will Type 4a (fig. 15.11)

11. Amphora of Will Type 4b (fig. 15.12)

12. Amphora of Beltrán Type II A (fig. 15.13)

13. Amphora of Kapitän Type 2 (fig. 15.14)

14. Amphora of Will Type 4b (fig. 15.15)

15. Amphora of Will Type 1d (for wine) (fig. 15.16, left)

16. Amphora of Beltrán Type II A (for garum) (fig. 15.16, right)

17. Two amphoras of Beltrán Type II B (fig. 15.17a, left;
18. fig. 15.17b, right)

19. Amphora of early (?) Will Type 23 (fig. 15.18)

Figure 15.2   Restored cross-section of Spargi shipwreck
La Maddalena, Nino Lamboglia Museum of Naval Archaeology

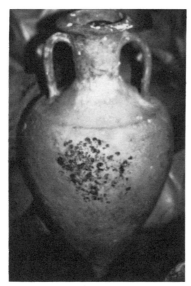

Figure 15.3 Greco-Italic amphoras of Will Type 1d (upper left)
and Will Type 1a (upper right)
Oristano Antiquarium

Figure 15.4 "Chimaera" amphora (lower left)
Oristano Antiquarium

Figure 15.5 Amphora of Will Type 1a (lower center)
Cagliari, National Archaeological Museum

Figure 15.6 Amphora of Will Type 4a (lower right)
Cagliari, National Archaeological Museum

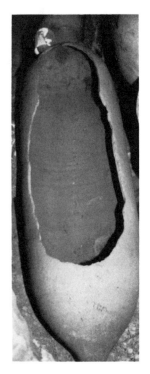
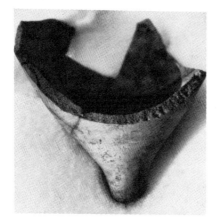

Figure 15.7 Amphora of Dressel Forms 7/8 from the
Is Mortorius shipwreck (upper left)
Cagliari, National Archaeological Museum

Figure 15.8 Amphora of Will (and Dressel) Type 20 (upper center)
Cagliari, National Archaeological Museum

Figure 15.9 Amphora of Will Type 21a ("African I"),
cut for reuse as a coffin (upper right)
Cagliari, National Archaeological Museum

Figure 15.10 Base of Amphora of Will Type 1b, from
Ortu Còmidu, no. OC 75/E II/925 (lower left)
Cagliari, National Archaeological Museum

Figure 15.11 Amphora of Will Type 4a (left)
Sassari, National Archaeological Museum: no. 7714

Figure 15.12 Amphora of Will Type 4b (left center)
Sassari, National Archaeological Museum: no. 2808

Figure 15.13 Amphora of Beltrán Type II A (right center)
Sassari, National Archaeological Museum: no. 34

Figure 15.14 Amphora of Kapitän Type 2 (right)
Sassari, National Archaeological Museum: no. 30

Figure 15.15 Amphora of Will Type 4b.
La Maddalena, Nino Lamboglia Museum
of Naval Archaeology.

Figure 15.16 Amphora of Will Type 1d
(for wine, left); amphora of Beltrán
Type II A (for garum, right). Sant'
Antioco, Biggio Collection.

Figure 15.17   Two amphoras of Beltrán
Type II B.   Sant' Antioco, Biggio
Collection.

Figure 15.18   Amphora of early (?)
Will Type 23.   Sant'Antioco, Biggio
Collection.

REFERENCES

ACQUARO, ENRICO
    1979   Tharros-V. Lo scavo del 1978. RSF 7(1):49-59.

    1980   Olbia-II (Campagna 1978). RSF 8(1):71-77.

    1983   Tharros-IX. Lo scavo del 1982. RSF 11:49-70.

BALMUTH, M.S.
    forth-   Nuraghe Ortu Cōmidu (Sardara-CA).   Preliminary Report
    coming   of Excavations (1975-1978). NSc.

BELTRAN LLORIS, MIGUEL
                Las ánforas romanas en España.   Zaragoza: Institución
                Fernando el Católico.

BONINU, A.
    1980   Testimonianze di età romana nel territorio di Dorgali.
                Dorgali. Documenti archeologici, A. Boninu et al.
                eds. 221-239. Sassari: Chiarella.

DRESSEL, HEINRICH (ED.)
    1889   CIL 15: 2.   Inscriptiones Urbis Romae Latinae.
                Instrumentum Domesticum. Berlin: Georg Reimer.

FROST, HONOR
    1976(1981) The Punic Ship: Final Excavation Report.   Lilybaeum =
                NSc Supplement.

KAPITAN, GERHARD
    1972   Le anfore del relitto romano di Capo Ognina (Siracusa).
                Recherches sur les amphores romaines, Paolo Baldacci et
                al. eds. 243-252. Rome: Ecole française de Rome.

LAMBOGLIA, NINO
    1955   Sulla   cronologia   delle   anfore   romane   di   età
                repubblicana (II-I secolo A.C.). RStLig 21:241-270.

LEVI, DORO
    1949   Le necropoli puniche di Olbia. StSar 9.

LO SCHIAVO, FULVIA
    1978   Sardegna Centro Orientale.   Voragine di Tiscali, Oliena
                95-96. Sassari: Dessì.

MELONI, PIERO
    1975   La Sardegna romana. Sassari: Chiarella.

MORAVETTI, ALBERTO
    1980   Nuovi materiali dalla voragine di Ispinigoli. Dorgali.
                Documenti archeologici, A. Boninu et al. eds. 165-171.
                Sassari: Chiarella.

PANELLA, CLEMENTINA
   1973   Appunti su un gruppo di anfore della prima, media e tarde età imperiale (secolo I-V d.c.). StMisc 21: Ostia III. Rome: De Luca Editore.

PATRONI, G.
   1901   Nora. NSc 1901:365-381.

PIANU, GIAMPIERO
   1981   Un carico di anfore romane proveniente dalla località 'Is Mortorius'. Annali della Facoltà di Lettere e Filosofia, Università degli Studi di Cagliari, n.s. II (39): 5-10.

RIGHINI CANTELLI, V.
   1982   Una marca anforaria di MAHES da Tharros. RSF 10(1): 87-95.

RODERO RIAZA, A.
   1981a   Anforas de la Campaña de 1980. RSF 9(1):57-67.

   1981b   Anforas del Tofet de Tharros. RSF 9(2):177-185.

   1982   Anforas de la campaña de 1981. RSF 10(1):79-86.

ROGHI, GIANNI
   1965   Spargi. Marine Archaeology, Joan du Plat Taylor ed. London: Hutchinson (New York: Crowell, 1966), 103-118. (A translation of "Note tecniche sul rilevamento e lo scavo della nave romana di Spargi." Bollettino e Atti (Centro Italiano di Ricercatori Subacquei, 1958-1959), 9ff.)

ROWLAND, ROBERT J. JR.
   1981   I ritrovamenti romani in Sardegna. Rome: "L'Erma" di Bretschneider.

SOTGIU, GIOVANNA
   1971   Instrumentum Domesticum della Sardegna. Acta of the Fifth International Congress of Greek and Latin Epigraphy, Cambridge, 1967. Oxford: Oxford University Press:247-251.

TCHERNIA, ANDRE, AND FAUSTO ZEVI
   1972   Amphores vinaires de Campanie et de Tarraconaise à Ostie. Recherches sur les amphores romaines, Piero Baldacci et al. eds. 35-67. Rome: Ecole française de Rome.

TRONCHETTI, CARLO
   1981   Domusdemaria - Torre di Chia (Bithia), S. Antioco. ArchSarda (December 1981):82-85.

WILL, ELIZABETH LYDING
    1956   Les amphores de Sestius. Revue archéologique de l'Est et du Centre-Est 7:224-244.

    1962   Latin-stamped Amphoras in the Eastern Mediterranean Area. Year Book of the American Philosophical Society 647-650.

    1970   Les timbres amphoriques latins. L'Îlot de la Maison des Comédiens. Exploration archéologique de Délos 27, Philippe Bruneau et al. eds. 383-386. Paris: Editions E. de Boccard.

    1977   Two Amphoras from Populonia. A.M. McCann, et al., Underwater Excavations at the Etruscan Port of Populonia. JFA 4:293-296.

    1979   The Sestius Amphoras: a Reappraisal. JFA 6:339-350.

    1982   Greco-Italic Amphoras. Hesperia 51:338-356.

    1983a   Exportation of Olive Oil from Baetica to the Eastern Mediterranean. Producción y comercio del aceite en la antigüedad (II Congreso Internacional), J.M. Blázquez Martínez et al. eds. 391-440. Madrid: Universidad Complutense.

    1983b   A Survey of the Roman Amphoras Found in Sardinia. Yearbook of the American Philosophical Society: 273-274.

    1983/84 The Spargi Wreck: a Reconsideration. Archaeological Institute of America Abstracts 8:32 = AJA 88:264.

ZEVI, FAUSTO AND ANDRE TCHERNIA
    1969   Amphores de Byzacène au bas-Empire. Antiquités Africaines 3:173-214.

ZUCCA, RAIMONDO
    1981   Cagliari - S. Gilla. ArchSarda (December 1981):82.

PART SIX:
SARDINIAN METALLURGY

Introduction

The evidence for metallurgy in Sardinia is critical for under-standing the relationship of Sardinia to other areas of the Mediter-ranean. Since there is still no complete agreement on the origin of all the metals used in the Sardinian products, but no doubt that the island was clearly a rich source of metals itself, the search for these sources is accompanied by a quest to determine which metal products on the island are local and which imported. The present limitations in source determination plus the dependence on style for judging origins combine to generate a lively debate on these matters. Further work on the subject continues with new finds appearing so frequently that metallurgy in Sardinia constitutes one of the most dynamic of archaeological subjects.

One problem that has attracted widespread interest was created by the discovery in Sardinia of oxhide ingots of copper that weigh about 30kg and were shipped as bullion throughout the Mediterranean. These ingots have been found either whole or cut-up in at least fourteen different sites on Sardinia alone. They are associated with Cyprus and Crete and other areas during the Late Bronze Age, but their appearance so far west in such volume affords an opportunity for multiple hypotheses about the place of the mining of ore, the smelting of ore, the mixing of smelted metals and the casting of the mixture.

Fulvia Lo Schiavo reminds us, quite appropriately, that ancient Sardinia consists of more than those curious Nuragic towers and the charming little bronze figurines. The extent to which the development of Sardinian metallurgy has been clarified through her work with its emphasis on typological series, can be seen in the emerging order in chronology and in regional studies that promise to be a key to the solution of some of the metallurgical problems associated with Sardinia, particularly the question of the sources of metal ore and of fabricated metal objects in the Mediterranean. Her account of the archaeological background of Sardinian metallurgy details the pre-Nuragic finds of metal and the history in Sardinia of the oxhide ingot, with additional emphasis on parallels in tools and weapons elsewhere, especially Cyprus.

In a presentation of the technical background of Sardinian metal-lurgy, R. F. Tylecote reiterated some of the information he treated in SSA (1984:115-162) about the sources of metals in Sardinia, with an emphasis on copper. Through study of a hoard of ancient bronze and tin that was found in 1882 and housed in the National Archaeological Museum in Cagliari, Tylecote discovered the first real evidence for ancient smelting on the island in the form of highly cupriferous tin slag. Since slag is the waste extracted from ores while separating the metal, the implication here is that the tin was present for mixing with extracted copper to produce bronze. The metalwork associated with the Nuragic population shows that they were much involved with mining, smelting, and casting, but Tylecote's find marks the first appearance of proof that the smelting was actually done on the island. In addition, he identified the earliest known tuyere on the island from the tomb material in the Chalcolithic necropolis of Anghelu Ruju. As the first scientist to make a metallographic analysis of some oxhide ingots from Sardinia (Balmuth and Tylecote 1976), he has been conservative about the source of the ore from which the oxhide ingots found in Sardinia might have come, pending more definitive information on trace elements, but found Lo Schiavo's firm conviction that Sardinian oxhide ingots found in Sardinia were also made in Sardinia attractive, even persuasive, but not yet fully documentable.

John Merkel, who experimented with the technology for producing ingots, reproduced their construction with remarkable results. Merkel also conducted the discussion on the ingots that followed. Newly developed analytical techniques are being applied to the problem, as the colloquial discussion indicated. In fact, the purpose of the colloquial discussion was to assemble the foremost experts in the field to discuss the problem. While the results of new analyses are eagerly awaited, the replication of the processes involved in smelting and casting of ingots is revealing some unexpected results.

16. SARDINIAN METALLURGY: THE ARCHAEOLOGICAL BACKGROUND

Fulvia Lo Schiavo

Introduction

For the last five years, ancient Sardinia has increasingly been the focus of a great deal of study and research. As a result, our general knowledge has gone far beyond the commonplace view of the Sardinia of Nuragic towers and interesting bronze figurines. In fact, the small bronzes should be considered only one aspect of a very rich range in metallurgical production, even if one of the most fascinating.

This presentation is meant to trace the development of metallurgy in ancient Sardinia from its very beginning, based solely on the archaeological data, with an attempt to trace all the possible influences, interferences and imports, and leaving to other specialized scholars the technical discussion. My feeling is that, sooner or later, the results of both approaches will combine to fill the gap and join in one conclusion.

Pre-Nuragic Chronology

It is appropriate to give a brief summary of the cultural development of Sardinian prehistory: in general, I agree with Enrico Atzeni's chronology for the pre-Nuragic period (Atzeni 1980a; 1981); the few slight differences are due to the results of the excavations in the cave at Fili-estru (Trump 1983). This scheme is obviously useful as a general indica-tion and not as a rigid framework, particularly now in Sardinia where new discoveries determine important changes yearly (table 16.1).

Ozieri

The earliest metal-using culture of Sardinia was the Ozieri culture, though for the moment this is sug-gested by meager evidence. The recent excavations of Enrico Atzeni in the huts of the village at Cùccuru Arrìus, Cabras (OR), brought to light fragments of a flat copper dagger and of some pins with a square section, in stratigraphic association with

Table 16.1 Chronology of Pre-Nuragic Sardinia

Dates b.c.		Culture
100,000 ?	Lower Paleolithic	?
///		
6000	Early Neolithic	Su Carroppu
5000		Grotta Verde
		Filiestru
4000	Middle Neolithic	Bonu Ighinu
3100	Late Neolithic	Ozieri (Gallurese)
2800	Early Eneolithic	Late Ozieri
		Abealzu – Filigosa
2400	Late Eneolithic	Monte Claro
2000		Beaker
1800	Early Bronze Age	Bonnannaro A

pottery of typical Ozieri style. Two silver rings have been found, again by Atzeni, at Pranu Mutteddu, Goni (CA), where, again, objects of the Ozieri culture were present (Atzeni 1981:40, NIO5-7). Although few, these elements are of extreme importance because they demonstrate that in Sardinia, as in mainland Italy and Sicily, the first appearance of metal can be referred to the Late Neolithic from the end of the 4th to the beginning of the 3rd millennium B.C., at least according to recent radiocarbon dates, (Bernabò Brea and Cavalier 1980).

It must not be forgotten, however, that in Aléria in Corsica at the site of Terrina IV, fragments of crucibles, slag and tuyéres, and an awl with two sharpened ends were found. Analyses demonstrated that the awl is of arsenical copper; traces of metallic copper (97.30%) on one of the crucibles and traces of copper, iron and magnesium oxide on another crucible suggest that the provenance of the ores worked at Terrina is the small local mine of Linguizetta. This can easily be considered evidence of primary smelting on the site. The shapes and decoration of that pottery and the radiocarbon dating indicate a Chalcolithic culture, datable to about the end of the first half of the 3rd millennium (2540-2480); in Sardinia, this would be represented by Late Ozieri and Abealzu - Filigosa (Jehasse 1978; 1980). The metal objects and the crucibles of Monte D'Accoddi (Sassari) (Contu 1982:n. 16) should also be referred to this period (fig. 16.1).

Abealzu - Filigosa

The use of silver objects is also certain in the succeeding cultures of Abealzu - Filigosa: a silver spiral ring was found in the 1981 excavations of a rock-cut tomb at Filigosa (Macomer-NU) (Foschi 1981) and a silver cylindrical spiral ring in a dolmen at Sa Corte Noa (Laconi-NU) in 1982, together with a few simple rings (Atzeni 1982: personal communication).

The use of copper undoubtedly continued, even if it may not now be possible to indicate any specific object found in a closed context. The problem of context is widely known in Sardinian rock-cut tombs, the so-called "domus de janas," in which

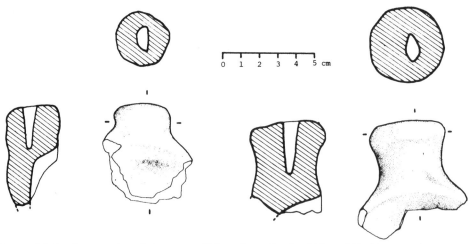

Figure 16.1 Fragments of two crucibles from Monte d'Accoddi (Sassari)

burials begin in the Ozieri culture and continue to the Bonnanaro culture in the Early Bronze Age, and where every inhumation generally removes the former, mixing the grave goods; such is the case, for example, of the famous necropolis of rock-cut tombs at Anghelu Ruju (Alghero-SS). Tyle-cote recently recognized a tuyére in the Cagliari Museum from tomb XIV of Anghelu Ruju and suggested the possibility that it was a part of the grave goods of a smith in analogy to other European burial customs. This hypothesis is interesting but the tuyére cannot specifically be related to the Beaker culture: in that tomb only Ozieri and Late Ozieri or Abealzu-Filigosa seem to be repre-sented, while the whole necropolis can be dated from about 3100 to about 1600 B.C. (Taramelli 1909:43-47; Tylecote, Balmuth, and Massoli-Novelli 1984).

Monte Claro
The use of lead for pottery repairs is first documented in the Chalcolithic culture of Monte Claro in a beautiful bowl showing the most typical southern Monte Claro decora-tion, found in the cave of Cuccuru Tiria or S. Lorenzo at Iglesias (CA),

in the middle of the mining district of Sulcis-Iglesiente (Atzeni 1981: fig. 22, N124). Atzeni also mentions that some awls came from that cave, but they are of widespread occurrence in Monte Claro as well as in Beaker and Early Bronze Age contexts.

A specific type of tanged dagger furnishes the first recognizable shape for metal weapons during the Monte Claro phase, one of the most interesting and rich pre-Nuragic cultures distinguished by a variety of regional aspects. These daggers were found in the tombs of Cresia Is Cuccurus (Monastir-CA), from Via Basilicata (Cagliari) and from Serra Is Araus (S. Vero Milis-OR) (Atzeni 1981;43, fig. 22; 44, fig. 24, pl. N124).

Another blade (fig. 16.2) of characteristic shape was found in the huge fortification of Monte Baranta (Olmedo-SS) (Moravetti 1981), and an awl (fig. 16.3) in the village of Biriai (Oliena-NU) (Castaldi 1982).

Elaborate double daggers are carved on the statue-menhirs (fig. 16.4) of Laconi and Nurallao in the Sarcidano region of the province of

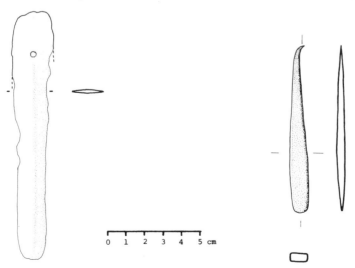

Figure 16.2 "Bronze" blade from Monte Claro sanctuary Village of Biriai (Oliena-NU)

Figure 16.3 "Bronze" awl from Monte Claro site of Monte Baranta (Olmedo-SS)

Figure 16.4   Menhirs from Genna Arrele and Perda Iddocca (Laconi-NU)
with double daggers carved on the statue

Nuoro, only a few miles from the copper mines at Funtana Raminosa. These are worth mentioning even though the chronology and the cultural context of these monuments are still in discussion (Atzeni 1980a).

Beaker

Fortunately, there is a good recent synthesis of the Beaker and Bonnanaro cultures, covering the end of the 3rd and the beginning of the 2nd millennium, where the few metal weapons and implements so far known are collected and discussed (Ferrarese Ceruti 1981a:62; 73). To the Beaker culture are attributed an arrow-head, eight daggers and two axes, all apparently made of copper. The copper arrow-head of Tomb XX of Anghelu Ruju is very unusual in a culture where they were still generally made of flint; the shape is convincingly attributed to the Beaker culture since it is identical to the barbed-and-tanged arrow-head, so common in Beaker contexts all over Europe. Ferrarese Ceruti refers the weapon to a late phase of the Beaker culture. Characteristic Beaker Palmela points of the type known in Portugal have not yet been found in Sardinia.

The shape of the daggers, however, is also quite typical with a large and triangular butt, mostly with indented edges and without holes. The appearance of the blades suggests a production in a mould with a hammered finish (Tylecote 1973). One of eight daggers from Su Crucifissu Mannu is very short in comparison with the general length, and resembles a small votive dagger found in a pure Beaker context in Hungary (Ferrarese Ceruti 1981a:63). The other blades have been found at Anghelu Ruju, Su Crucifissu, Serra Is Araus and at the cave of San Bartolomeo (Cagliari). A copper flat axe with a round blade also comes

from San Bartolomeo and compares well to one in the Foix Museum in Ariège; another flat axe with straight edges was found at Su Crucifissu. In the rock-cut tomb of Cuguttu (Alghero-SS) there are two open ring bracelets, two rings and a small cylindrical spiral, all made of a thin metal sheet and attributed to a Late Beaker context. The most recent metallic objects to have been found are a round silver sheet pendant and a small copper dagger from a typical rock-cut tomb at Padru Jossu (Sanluri-CA), dated on a stratigraphical basis to Phases A and B, respectively, of the Beaker culture (Ugas 1982:XVI, 18; 35).

Bonnanaro

The problem with the Bonnanaro culture is the difficulty in identifying dwelling sites, in contrast to the increasing number of rock-cut tombs, rich in pottery and other grave goods; recently Ferrarese Ceruti suggested recognizing two facies A and B, that can be distinguished with respect both to typology and chronology (Ferrarese Ceruti 1981a:75).

Only one village has been found, at Sa Turricula (Muros-SS); a small dagger with a round butt and two rivets (fig. 16.5), very similar to two blades from the Polada culture, was discovered there. Two other small daggers referred to Bonnanaro come from Frommosa Cave I at Villanovatulo (NU).

Appearing more frequently are the awls with two sharpened ends and a square section in the middle, a type well known all over Europe in the Early Bronze Age. A group of awls has been found in the Aiodda tomb at Nurallao (NU). This tomb, built up with anthropomorphic statue-menhirs can be considered an ancestor of the "giants' tombs." (Atzeni 1980a:100-101).

The SAM analyses of Anghelu Ruju awls gave a composition close to Remedello material, "mostly copper with a variable content of As, Sb, and Ag, which is a fairly typical composition from the EBA. This material compares well in composition with the Remedello material from the Italian mainland" (SAM I: 1960; Tylecote, Balmuth and Massoli-Novelli 1984), stressing the direct connections of Sardinia with the Italian mainland and southern France during this period.

The extraordinary El Argar sword from southern Sardinia, still unpublished is reminiscent of the western connections of the island and of the plausibility of the hypothesis that at any moment technical innovations might have reached Sardinia in the currents of trade.

Nuragic Chronology

Research and study of the Nuragic culture is proceeding, with particular interest in the early phases. The following chronology (table 16.2) was proposed by Lilliu in 1980 and recently again well illustrated in his book La Civiltà Nuragica (Lilliu 1980:47; 1982).

It must be stressed that, though still in discussion, Lilliu's hypotheses should not be undervalued. The two main innovations are:

1. The suggestion that the Early Bronze Age, represented in Sardinia by the Bonnanaro culture, can be a real first stage in Nuragic evolution as well, based on the high chronology of the earliest Nuragic towers, and of the "giants' tombs" where vessels with elbow handles characteristic of the Bonnanaro repertoire were found. This means raising the date of the early development of Nuragic civilization to the beginning of the 2nd millennium, that is, from the 18th century B.C. on; and

2. The subdivision of the whole evolution into five phases and the admission that even a unique culture such as the Nuragic had vital relationships with the other Mediterranean people.

With respect to metallurgy, a change occurred between Phase I and Phase II, that is, during the Middle Bronze Age and the beginning of the Late Bronze Age, that produced a rise

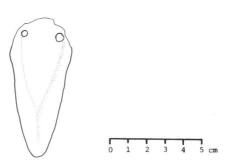

0 1 2 3 4 5 cm

Figure 16.5 Bronze dagger from Bonnanaro culture
village of Sa Turricula (Muros-SS)

Table 16.2   Chronology of Nuragic Sardinia

BRONZE AGE
  Phase I   1800 - 1500 B.C.

  Phase II   1500 - 1200 B.C. Archaic or Proto-Nuragic (the period
             of the simple round towers)

  Phase III 1200 - 900 B.C. Middle Nuragic I or First Lower
             Nuragic of Barumini (the beginning of the nuraghi
             with complex plans)
IRON AGE
  Phase IV   900 - 700 B.C. Middle Nuragic II or First Upper
             Nuragic of Barumini (the development of Nuragic
             structures with various additions of walls and
             towers)

             700 - 500 B.C. Late or Recent Nuragic or Second
             Upper Nuragic of Barumini

  Phase V   500 - 238 B.C. (the period of Sardo-Punic koinè)

---

in technical skill and production from a very simple level, with imports and influences from the west, central Europe and mainland Italy, to a more sophisticated level and therefore to the growth of a prosperous local production, profiting both from experience and from models of undeniable eastern origin.

My personal opinion is that this "high tide" began in the Middle Bronze Age, perhaps on the stream of the important cultural and technical changes that were taking place all over Europe: for documentation there are daggers and axes that can be dated to the middle of the 2nd millennium, with good comparisons to well known types from mainland Italy (Lo Schiavo 1978b:85, XXVII, 1-3; 1978c:54, 1; Carancini 1982a; 1982b).

As a consequence of the beginning of the "high tide" (and I am aware that other scholars would pre-fer to think that this was a cause rather than an effect; I invite them to provide the evidence), the Mycenaeans appeared in Sardinia.

Cypriot Daggers

Cyprus seems to have played a particular and perhaps privileged role with regard to Sardinia from a very early date: a first and striking item is represented by two unusual forms of "Cypriot dagger" from an unknown site in central Sardinia, with no exact parallels in Cyprus or anywhere else, but undoubtedly with a "family likeness" that cannot be underestimated. A plausible opinion is that these weapons were made in Sardinia, between the Middle and the Late Bronze Age, imitating Cypriot models. The intriguing presence in the same group of weapons of other blades of western tradition can be explained only by considering Sardinia as a halting place along the "tin route" (Lo Schiavo 1978d).

One problem with "Cypriot dag-gers" in Europe is that they have never been found in regular excava-tions; again this is the case with this Sardinian "hoard" and with another important group of bronze implements from Sansueña (Zamora) in the northwest of the Iberian Penin-sula (Delibes De Castro 1980:figs. 3-5) where there are two blades very similar to the ones associated with "Cypriot daggers." The present position of scholars with respect to this problem is to wait for further evidence.

Mycenaeans

From the time of the first dis-covery of Mycenaean pottery in Sar-dinia in 1976, a great deal has been done and written on this subject, so that it can now be considered sufficiently familiar (Lo Schiavo and Vagnetti 1980; Ferrarese Ceruti 1979; 1980; 1981a; 1981c).

The pottery seems to be mostly Myc. IIIB and IIIC in date, with many shapes and types represented. Only thirty fragments of the hundreds found have been published, and the study is far from complete. It seems, however, that they come from various places: mainland Greece, the Aegean Islands, Cyprus and the Le-vant; some even appear to be of local production.

In Sardinia (fig. 16.6), Myce-naean pottery was discovered on the eastern coast, for the most part in Nuraghe Antigori, with two sherds in Nuraghe Sa Domu'e S'Orku, both at Sarrok near Cagliari in the south; other sherds were found at Barumini in the interior; still others, it seems, at Tharros in the Sinis Peninsula; and one sherd of a pictorial style with a good parallel in a kylix from Rhodes (Vermeule and Karageorghis 1982:153-154, XII, 13) has been found by D.H. Trump in June 1983 in the Mara region, quite in the interior in the north: it is not a presumption to expect that much more is going to be found. It is important to stress the fact that the location of Nuraghe Antigori, rising at one end of the Gulf of Cagliari, is in direct connection with a route leading to the mining district of the Sulcis, the richest area of metal ores of southern Sardinia.

Lead

In a small rocky shelter proba-bly used as a tomb in the Nuragic complex of Antigori, an object first interpreted as a votive double axe made of lead was found, a miniature reproduction of the most typical Sardinian version of this class of tools, that has both blades curving towards one side. The votive use of the object should have been proven by the fact that the perforation is not complete; evidently a stick was in-serted to hold it up for worship (Ferrarese Ceruti 1979:pl. I; 1981b: M 1; 1982a:176, 28, pl. 61, 2; Lo Schiavo 1982b), but more careful examinations have suggested the pos-sibility that it represents a mini-ature boat with the hole for the mast; it is also possible that the small object (gr. 46.1) was used as a weight or a clamp.

Lead clamps for repairs of pottery are normally associated with Mycenaean and Nuragic sherds, and it should be remembered that the use of lead for this purpose began in Sardinia, in the Copper Age in the second half of the 3rd millennium.

Only a few other bronze frag-ments, of mostly indeterminate shape, have been discovered in the Mycenaean levels at Nuraghe Antigori.

Oxhide Ingots

The most impressive element of the connection between Sardinia and the Aegean, particularly to Cyprus, as pointed out by earlier scholars, was the oxhide shape of copper ingots (fig. 16.6), discovered first

1 - Arzachena (SS)
2 - Ossi (SS)
3 - Ozieri (SS)
4 - Ittireddu (SS)
5 - Mara (SS)
6 - Orosei (NU)
7 - Dorgali (NU)
8 - Nuoro
9 - Teti (NU)
10 - Ortueri (NU)
11 - Belvì (NU)
12 - Tharros (OR)
13 - Lanusei (NU)
14 - Nuragus (NU)
15 - Barumini (CA)
16 - Villanovaforru (CA)
17 - Tertenia (NU)
18 - Assemini (CA)
19 - Cagliari
20 - Capoterra (CA)
21 - Sarrok (CA)

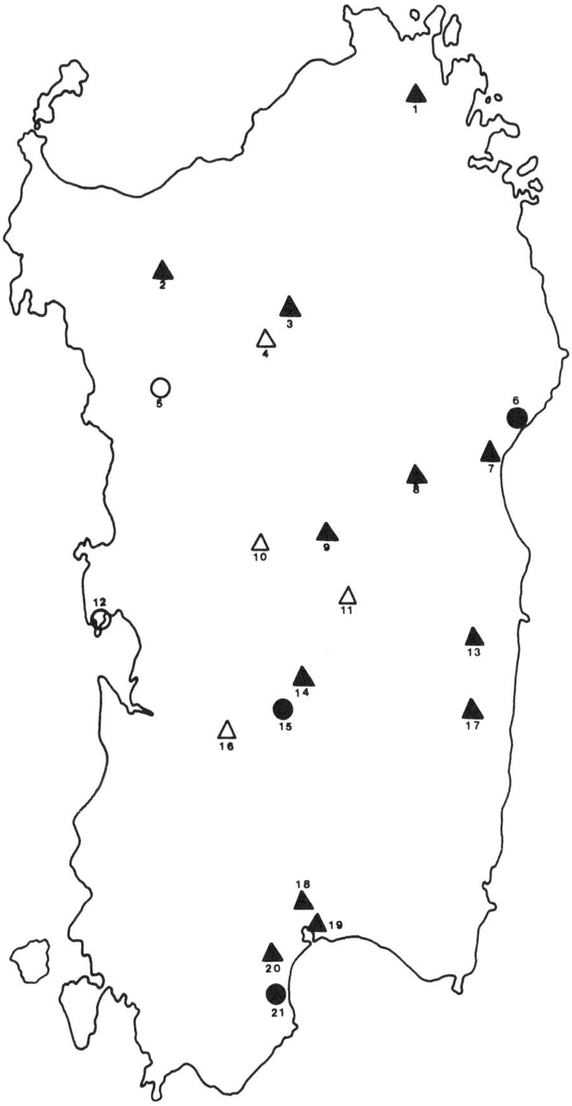

Figure 16.6 Map of Sardinia showing distribution of
Mycenaean pottery (circles) and oxhide ingots (triangles);
white symbols indicate recent finds

in Sardinia in 1857, forty-six years before those of Haghia Triada in 1903, and soon related by Pigorini to eastern trade, not only because of the shape but also because of the Cypro-Minoan marks impressed and incised on them.

Buchholz' work on oxhide ingots and his list of Sardinian examples (Buchholz 1959) are well-known, but some sites must be removed from that list because of a misunderstanding of Italian mid-eighteenth century texts. Many other discoveries have also been made since his first list. To date, fourteen sites are known where oxhide ingots have been found (apart from the fragments in the Nuoro and Cagliari Museums with no indication of association or findspot).

Chronology remains a problem, and so far there is not enough evidence to solve it. According to the associations at Arzachena, Tertenia and Teti, fragments of oxhide ingots continued in use until the Early Iron Age. This by no means designates the period of production since two complete oxhide ingots were dug out from under the pavement of a Nuragic tower at Bisarcio (Ozieri), but unluckily not in a regular excavation. The use of ingot fragments continued later as scrap metal (Lo Schiavo and Vagnetti 1980).

As to the site of production, my personal and firm conviction, based on all the archaeological documents I am trying to present here, is that Sardinian oxhide ingots were made in Sardinia, at the beginning of the Late Bronze Age, under the influence and perhaps the technical supervision of eastern traders, metal prospectors and metalsmiths.

Cyprus
Let us now consider Cyprus again. All the evidence seems to indicate that the main period of contacts with Cyprus was in the 12th

century B.C., in the currents of Mycenaean navigation and after the fall of the Mycenaean empire; my opinion is that in Cyprus itself, an affinity between the two mining islands of the Mediterranean might have been created, because of the extraordinary richness of metals; but it cannot be excluded that a Cypriot component was present from the beginning in the Mycenaean wave. Also, the coasts of Palestine and the Levant must have been involved in the movement of people, merchandise and ideas; in brief, we are dealing with east-west cultural contact. The problem is that not very much is known of the Late Bronze Age contexts of Palestine, and particularly it is not always easy to distinguish what is uniquely Cypriot from the Levantine imports and influence; for example, the nationality of the cargo and of the ship of Cape Gelidonya is still being discussed.

While new and careful studies and analyses are needed before finding a solution to these problems, it may be that knowing the provenance of Mycenaean pottery in Sardinia will hasten that solution. Let us now consider briefly some striking evidence: double axes, smithing tools, tripods and a handle of unusual shape.

Double Axes
In this general frame of eastern connections, the double axe is yet another much discussed theme, from the time of Hawkes' work in 1937 onward (fig. 16.7). It is not possible here and now to summarize the whole problem, which includes the remote origin as well as the direct provenance of the few tools of this type scattered in Europe. Five of them come from Britain though, as the "Cypriot daggers," never, as far as I know, from recent excavations. In contrast, in Sardinia we are not dealing with a few isolated pieces, but with a whole class of two-edged

instruments of varying size, from big picks to small axe-adzes. They present two typical characteristics in common: a round hole, and the prominence of the socket, when present, on one side only. These characteristics are shared by all the Cypriot tools of this class that, as in Sardinia, includes flat double axes, concave-sided double axes, socketed double axes and axe-adzes.

The number of these different kinds of tools rises to the hundreds, found in nuraghi, in hoards and in sacred wells; the matrices of many of them are seen in the stone moulds. It also needs to be said that in Italy double axes are practically nonexistent, with very few exceptions, some of which are of Sardinian provenance.

To conclude, the connection between the Aegean and Sardinia for the use of the double axe, practical and votive, is not a hypothesis in my mind; more precisely, Cyprus and Sardinia share the shapes and the round shaft of these tools (Lo Schiavo 1982b).

Smithing Tools

The next evidence is provided by smithing tools (fig. 16.8). The Sardinian examples show striking similarities to the bronze tongs, hammers and shovels from the Enkomi Foundry Hoard and from other Cypriot hoards.

Big fire tongs with broad shoulders are known from Siniscola, from Fertilia, from the Nuragic village of Serra Orrios (this one much smaller in scale) and from two private collections.

Two square-shaped hammers from Nuchis and from an unknown provenance, now in the Oristano Museum, and a small cylindrical hammer from Perfugas closely resemble Cypriot tools, while the hammers of Surbo on the Italian continent and from the Montagnana hoards have the typical oval hole of Aegean tools.

A splendid charcoal-shovel comes from a private collection and a steatite mould for a shovel (or a furnace spatula) and two daggers were found

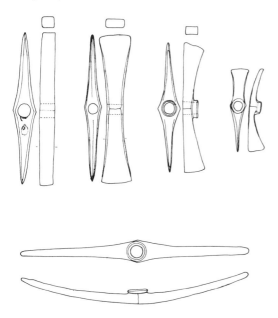

Figure 16.7 Nuragic double axes

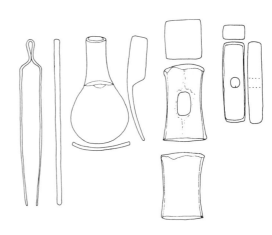

Figure 16.8 Smithing tools

at Irgoli. Another socketed shovel, very similar to the big ones from the Gunnis Hoard in Cyprus, is illustrated in Zervos (1954) from the mining district of the Sulcis (Lo Schiavo 1980b:fig. 110a-c, III 1981b: 276; 1982a; 1982b).

Again, the typological connections of this particular class of tools with Cyprus cannot be a coincidence: "they provide in themselves indirect evidence for some of the industrial processes associated with the foundry and the forge, including casting in both one- and two-piece moulds" (Catling 1964).

Tripods
Bronze tripods are the third and perhaps the most impressive body of evidence of connections with Cyprus. The first to be discovered was the small tripod from the Pirosu-Su Benatzu cave (Santadi-CA); rightly supposed to be a local copy after Cypriot models (Lilliu 1973). In 1982 an extraordinary example of a Cypriot tripod (fig. 16.9) was recognized in a Sardinian private collection. Here Cypriot manufacture and an ancient import to Sardinia can be suggested (Lo Schiavo 1982b; for a comparison see Karageorghis 1971:fig. 23). At the end of the same year, the tripod from Santa Maria in Paulis near Ittiri (SS), now in the British Museum, was thoroughly illustrated by Macnamara et al.(1984), who suggested Sardinian manufacture under the influence of Cypriot models). A fragment of a tripod almost identical to this last comes from the Nuragic sanctuary of S. Vittoria di Serri (NU); other possible fragments and pendants of tripods had been found here and there in the province of Nuoro.

The tripod from the private collection confirms the hypothesis of an early date in the Late Bronze Age (ca. 12th century) for a strong Cypriot technical influence on Sar-

dinian metallurgy, undoubtedly supported by trade.

Cypriot Handles
Another element pointing to Cyprus is a characteristic type of handle-attachment (fig. 16.10) found in the Nuragic village of Serra Orrios: it is shaped in a figure-eight with a rising handle, sometimes with a lotus flower in the middle and with two supporting rods from the handle to the attachment (Lo Schiavo 1980b:pl. 41, 6).

Handles of this kind are quite frequent in Cyprus on hemispherical bowls and cauldrons, from the earliest examples from the Paphos tombs of the 11th century onward (Karageorghis 1971:fig. 24).

The presence in the same village of Serra Orrios of a couple of bronze firé tongs of a Cypriot type is very interesting, and perhaps significant.

Further consideration should be given to many other elements of metal working found in Sardinia: bronze mirrors, bronze hemispherical bowls, decoration with cable bands bordered by plain bands either cast in one piece or composed of various rods joined together, and a fragment of a small bronze statue inspired by the Horned God of Enkomi (Lo Schiavo 1983b). Here there is also evidence of later date that can be attributed to the Phoenicians.

Archaeological Evidence For Smelting
In Sardinia, archaeological evidence for smelting of copper ores is almost totally lacking so far (Tylecote, Balmuth and Massoli-Novelli 1984). Huge deposits of slag were reported near Funtana Raminosa by the engineer who directed the mine at the beginning of this century. He also sketched a plan indicating working sites that he attributed to the Nuragic period, but it seems that no trace of them is now detectable and

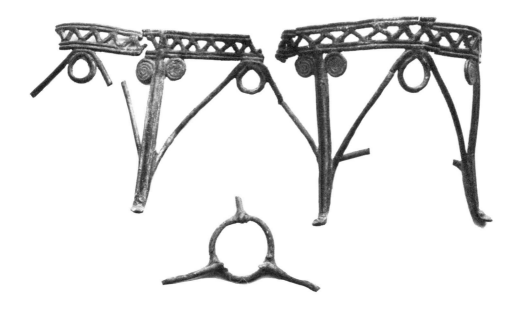

Figure 16.9   Cypriot tripod from a Sardinian private collection

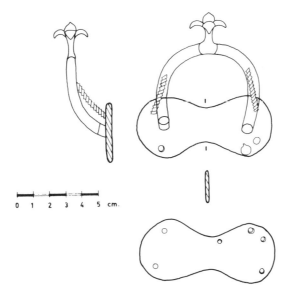

Figure 16.10   Fragment of bronze attachment from Nuragic village of
Serra Orrios (Dorgali-NU) and reconstruction of the handle

careful new studies are required. Another accumulation of slag was seen by Ceruti and Virdis at the Nuragic site of Nieddiu (Nurallao-NU), where they collected samples, recently analyzed by Zwicker et al. (1980: 138); unfortunately, the site has been almost destroyed by a bentonite quarry. Other slags collected here and there (Villanovaforru and Oliena, for example) are insufficient to prove primary smelting of copper ores.

This need not mean that such metallurgical operations did not take place on the island - a statement very hard to maintain - but simply that, for various reasons, traces of the smelting of ores have not been found so far. An assumption of primary metallurgy is supported by the evidence of the secondary processes in the smelting and refining of copper, and also by the evidence of the production and repair of all kinds of tools and weapons such as stone moulds and plano-convex ingots. The number and quality of bronze objects gives yet another clue (Lo Schiavo 1981b).

Stone Moulds

After a short study by Taramelli, who simply made a list of all the moulds in the Cagliari Museum in 1918 on the occasion of the discovery of the big mould from Urzulei, attention has been drawn to this class of tools by Marshall Becker, who carried out a study, not only on the moulds in the Sassari and Cagliari Museums, but also on the soft stones of which they were made, steatite and chlorite (Becker 1978a; 1978b; 1984).

Rich deposits of steatite are known and still worked in the Orani Mountains in the Barbagia; we can therefore assume that stone moulds as well as other objects of common use in Nuragic villages, like the decorated stone polishers or the small Nu-

ragic models carved in the same stone, were produced locally.

What must be stressed is the number and the distribution of stone moulds: Taramelli counted 14 of them in the Cagliari Museum; Becker 16 in Cagliari and another eight in the Sassari Museums. Now seven more moulds are known in the Sassari Museum, seven in Nuoro and two in the Dorgali Museum; a stone mould for a gamma-hilted dagger has been found in the excavation of a nuraghe near Fonni (NU).

The wide distribution clearly shows that it is impossible to hypothesize a metallurgical district and itinerant coppersmiths, for every important nuraghe seems to have had its local foundry on the spot (Balmuth and Tylecote 1976:196). Some of these moulds were collected in what early authors referred to as foundries; this is the case of Urzulei, Irgoli, "Setti Nuraxi," Ittireddu, Tula, and now Genna Maria in Villanovaforru.

A research project is currently under way, designed to examine the typology of Sardinian moulds: monovalves either simple or multiple, and bivalves. Bronze and clay moulds are unknown on the island (Lo Schiavo 1981a).

Secondary Foundries

A secondary foundry is considered to be a site where, according to the authors, evidence of some kind of metallurgical work can be detected: stone moulds, ashes, coal and/or fragments of raw metals and implements.

Almost every big nuraghe with a village seems to have had its own workshop where tools and weapons could be made and mended. A distribution map, elaborated only from the bibliography, would give an impressive overview, but the references need to be verified wherever possible before we can make further hypotheses or conclusions.

Plano-convex Ingots and Hoards

Eusebio Birocchi (1934) published a comprehensive study of the "panelle" (Italian for "bun ingots") or plano-convex ingots. Their number in closed finds, hoards, nuraghi, or sporadic finds is not exactly known, but it is in the hundreds.

Important closed finds are the Flumenelongu hoard (1967) with 32 plano-convex ingots, four axes and two bracelets, and the Torralba hoard (1965) with 16 plano-convex ingots and two axes. The number, however, is increasing, and a complete survey is now in progress (Lo Schiavo 1976).

Attention should be given to the different shapes of the ingots. The plano-convex shape can be either high and regular or flat. A truncated/conical shape is known. There are fragments and descriptions in the literature that suggest a certain number of slab ingots.

The problem of chronology is particularly interesting. The use of plano-convex ingots earlier than oxhide ingots in Sardinia remains to be proven, and the consequences are of great importance: it is absolutely inconceivable to me that bun ingots were imported or that they were smelted from imported metals. Likewise, it is very hard to accept the assumpaion that thousands of tools and weapons in the roughly 50 hoards and in many nuraghi and Nuragic villages were made from imported raw metal on an island rich in copper ores.

A complete edition of all the bronzes from old excavations in the Cagliari and Sassari Museums is in preparation. Then perhaps it will be possible to determine the exact chro-

nology of many types of weapons and instruments of typical Sardinian shapes (Lo Schiavo 1980a; 1982b).

Iron Working and the Phoenicians

There are two subjects that need further investigation: the degree of technical skill involved in the production of bronze figurines and the use of iron. In a way, these two subjects are connected. Iron was certainly used in the same period and in the same workshops in which bronze figurines and other common objects were made. This can now be shown with increasing evidence: iron elements in the votive boats, iron clasps in bronze basins, bronze pins with iron rods, and the attempt at a votive boat made of iron, now in the Museo Civico Speleo-Archeologico in Nuoro.

The presence of a Sardinian bronze figurine in the Cavalupo tomb at Vulci, from a datable context of the second half of the 9th century B.C., places the bulk of the production, and consequently the use of iron, at least as early as the Early Iron Age (9th - 8th c. B.C.). This high chronology has been recently supported by the discovery, made by Prof. Lilliu himself, of an iron ring bracelet in the chamber of the "Giants' Tomb" at Bidistili (Fonni-NU) (Lilliu 1980:abb. 48; 1982:figs. 105-107).

It would not be extreme to suggest oriental influence for the earliest iron working and a Sardinian intermediary for the beginning of the exploitation of the iron mines of Tuscany, now that both Phoenician "trade before the flag" at the end of the second millennium B.C., and the strong interrelations between Sardinia (mostly in the north) and Populonia and Vetulonia have been confirmed (Barreca 1971; 1979:11-28; 1980; Lo Schiavo 1978a; 1979; 1983a).

Conclusion

At the Larnaca Symposium in June 1981, I concluded my paper with a quotation from a recent work by Wheeler, Muhly and Maddin (1979:142), "Mediterranean Trade in Copper and Tin in the Late Bronze Age," where I substituted Sardinia for Cyprus:

"There is no proof that the evidence for the working of copper in Late Bronze Age times, ingots and moulds, and tools, clearly marks Sardinia as a source of copper ore. It is conceivable that all the copper being worked in second millennium Sardinia was imported from sources outside the island, although it is difficult to imagine what foreign source of copper would have been exploited. As Sardinia has produced more evidence for the working of copper in the second millennium B.C. than any other area in the western Mediterranean and as Sardinia also has more copper ore than any other country in that part of the world, it seems only reasonable to connect the two bodies of evidence and assume that Sardinian metalsmiths were working Sardinian copper."

At that time I thought that the same argument used for Cyprus could be applied as successfully to the western island of Sardinia, since it is the only one that could explain the arrival of Mycenaean prospectors, the choice of the international shape of oxhide ingots and the close contacts between Sardinia and Cyprus through Mediterranean metal trade (Lo Schiavo 1982a).

Now, after more than two years of study and research, I am even more convinced that archaeological evidence identifies Sardinia as a land where fully developed metallurgy took place from a very early date, on the basis of the presence of very rich metal ores, under both western and eastern influence, and on the stream of advanced trade.

Figure 16.11 Sardinia in the Mediterranean showing directions of trade and communication in the Late Bronze/Early Iron Ages in the Mediterranean

REFERENCES

ATZENI, E.
  1980a   Menhirs antropomorfi e statue - menhirs della Sardegna.
             Annali del Museo Civico La Spezia II:9-62.

  1980b   Prima del nuraghe. NUR 81-120.

  1981   Aspetti e sviluppi culturali del neolitico e della prima
             età dei metalli in Sardegna. Ichnussa XXI-LI. Many
             thanks are due to E. Atzeni for his kind communications.

  1982   Notiziario: Laconi. RSP 37.

BALMUTH, M.S. AND R.F. TYLECOTE
  1976   Ancient Copper and Bronze in Sardinia: Excavation and
             Analysis. JFA 3(2):195-201.

BARRECA, F.
  1971   L'espansione fenicia nel Mediterraneo: Sardegna. Studi
             Semitici 38:7-27.

  1979   La Sardegna fenicia e punica.^{2} Sassari: Chiarella.

  1980   Contatti tra i protosardi e i fenici. Atti XXII
             Riunione Scientifico IIPP. 21-27 ottobre 1978:475-486.
             Firenze.

BECKER, M.
  1978a   Stone   Moulds   in   Sardinian   Museum   Collections:
             Indications of Bronze Age Metallurgical Technology, MS.
             February 1978.

  1978b   Stone   Moulds   in   Sardinian   Museum   Collections:
             Indications of Bronze Age Metallurgical Technology, MS.
             March 1978.

  1984   Sardinian Stone Moulds: An Indirect Means of Evaluating
             Bronze Age Metallurgical Technology. SSA 163-208.

BERNABO BREA, L. AND M. CAVALIER
  1980   Meligunis-Lipàra IV. Palermo.

BIROCCHI, E.
  1934   I ripostigli nuragici e le panelle di rame grezzo.
             StSar I:37-108.

BUCHHOLZ, H.G.
  1959   Keftiubarren und Erzhandel in Zweiten Vorchristlichen
             Jahrtausend. PZ 37:1-40.

CAMPS, G.
  1979   Préhistoire dans la Région d'Aléria. Archeologia Corsa
             4:1-21.

CARANCINI, G.
1982a   Su alcuni problemi della protostoria della Calabria.
            Temesa e il suo territorio, Perugia-Trevi, 30-31 maggio
            1981:153-165. Taranto.

1982b   Metallurgia e territorio: tipi e cerchie officinali.
            Problemi teorico-pratici. DialAr n.s. 2:92-98.

CASTALDI, E.
1982   Terza campagna di scavi a Biriai (Oliena, NU). RSP 37.

CATLING, H.W.
1964   Cypriot Bronzework in the Mycenaean World. Oxford.

CONTU, E.
1983   Alcuni problemi cronologici della preistoria sarda nel
            contesto mediterraneo.   La ricerca storica sulla
            Sardegna (Cagliari 27-29 Maggio 1982), Archivio Storico
            Sardo 38.

DELIBES DE CASTRO, G.
1980   Un presunto deposito del bronce final del Valle de
            Vidriales (Zamora). Trabajos de Prehistoria 37:221-246.

FERRARESE CERUTI, M.L.
1979   Ceramica micenea in Sardegna (notizia preliminare). RSP
            34:1-2; 242-253.

1980   Micenei in Sardegna! RendLinc 35:5-6; 391-393.

1981a   La cultura del vaso campaniforme - Il Primo Bronzo.
            Ichnussa 55-77.

1981b   Documenti micenei nella Sardegna meridionale. Ichnussa
            605-612.

1982a   Il complesso nuragico di Antigori, Sarroch (CA). Magna
            Grecia e Mondo Miceneo. Nuovi documenti 167-176.

1982b   Nuraghe Domu 's Orku (Sarroch). Magna Grecia e Mondo
            Miceneo. Nuovi documenti:176-179.

FOSCHI, A.
1981   Notiziario: Filigosa (Macomer). RSP 36:1-2, 360.

HAWKES, C.
1937   The Double Axe in Prehistoric Europe. BSA 37:141ff.

JEHASSE, J.
1978   Informations archéologiques.   Circoscription de la
            Corse. Gallia Préhistoire 21:723-726.

1980   Informations archéologiques.   Circoscription de la
            Corse. Gallia Préhistoire 23:549-554.

JUNGHANS, S., E. SANGMEISTER AND M. SCHRODER
   1960   SAM I.

KARAGEORGHIS, V.
   1971   Chronique des fouilles á Chypre en 1970. BCH 95:344.

LILLIU, G.
   1973   Tripode bronzeo di tradizione cipriota dalla Grotta
           Pirosu - Su Benatzu di Santadi (Cagliari). Estudios
           dedicados al Prof. Luis Pericot 283-313. Barcelona.

   1980   Die Nuraghenkultur. Kunst Sardiniens 44-84.

   1982   La civiltà nuragica. Sassari.

LO SCHIAVO, F.
   1976   Il ripostiglio del Nuraghe Flumenelongu (Alghero-
           Sassari). Considerazioni preliminari sul commercio
           marittimo nel mediterraneo occidentale in età
           protostorica. Quaderni 2. Sassari.

   1978a   Le fibule della Sardegna. StEtr 46:25-46.

   1978b   Armi ed utensili da Siniscola. Sardegna Centro-
           Settentrionale.

   1978c   La Collezione Cabras. Bronzi d'uso di età nuragica.
           Sardegna Centro-Settentrionale.

   1980a   Wessex, Sardegna, Cipro: nuovi elementi di discussione.
           Atti XXII Riunione Scientifico IIPP. 21-27 ottobre
           1978:341-358. Firenze.

   1980b   Waffen, Werkzeuge und Schmuck aus Bronze. Kunst
           Sardiniens 134-142.

   1980c   Il villaggio nuragico di Serra Orrios: i bronzi.
           Dorgali. Documenti archeologici 145-154. Sassari.

   1981a   Osservazioni sul problema dei rapporti fra Sardegna ed
           Etruria in età nuragica. L'Etruria Mineraria. Atti XII
           Convegno di Studi Etruschi ed Italici, Firenze-
           Populonia-Piombino 16-20 giugno 1979:298-314. Firenze.

   1981b   Economia e società nell'età dei nuraghi. Ichnussa 255-
           347.

   1982a   Copper Metallurgy in Sardinia during the Late Bronze
           Age: new prospects on its Aegean connections. Early
           Metallurgy in Cyprus 4000-5000 B.C. Larnaca Symposium,
           1-6 June 1981. Nicosia.

1982b   Le componenti egea e cipriota nella metallurgia della
             tarda età del bronzo in Italia. XXII Convegno Studi
             sulla Magna Grecia. Taranto, 7-11 ottobre 1982, in
             press.

1983a   Il primo millennio avanti Cristo. La Provincia di
             Sassari - I secoli e la storia 37-49. Sassari.

1983b   Un bronzetto da Galtellí. Atti I Congresso
             Internazionale di Studi Fenici e Punici. Roma 5-10
             Novembre 1979:463-469.

LO SCHIAVO, F. AND L. VAGNETTI
1980   Micenei in Sardegna? RendLinc 35:5-6; 371-391.

MACNAMARA, E. AND D.F. RIDGWAY
1984   The Bronze Hoard from Santa Maria in Paulis, Sardinia.
             Aspects of Italic Culture. BMOP No. 45.

MORAVETTI, A.
1981   Nota agli scavi nel complesso megalitico di Monte
             Baranta (Olmedo, Sassari). RSP 36:1-2; 281-290.

PIGORINI, L.
1904   Pani di rame provenienti dall'Egeo scoperti a Serra
             Ilixi. BPI 91-107.

TARAMELLI, A.
1909   Alghero. Nuovi scavi nella necropoli preistorica a
             grotte artificiali di Anghelu Ruju. MonAnt 91, 93, 104.

TYLECOTE, R.F., M.S. BALMUTH AND R. MASSOLI-NOVELLI
1984   Copper and Bronze Metallurgy in Sardinia. SSA 115-162.

UGAS, G.
1982   Padru Jòssu - Tomba ipogeica ed elementi di cultura
             materiale delle fasi campaniforme A e B. Ricerche
             archeologiche nel territorio di Sanluri 19-26. Sanluri.

WHEELER, T.S., J.D. MUHLY AND R. MADDIN
1979   Mediterranean Trade in Copper and Tin in the Late Bronze
             Age. AIIN 139-152.

VERMEULE, E. AND V. KARAGEORGHIS
1982   Mycenaean Pictorial Vase Painting. Cambridge, Mass.:
             Harvard University Press.

ZERVOS, C.
1954   Sardaigne.

17. ANCIENT SMELTING AND CASTING OF COPPER FOR "OXHIDE" INGOTS

John F. Merkel

Oxhide-shaped copper ingots from the Late Bronze Age have become a lively topic in archaeo-metallurgy as important contributions have been made over the years by several research groups. The term "oxhide" is used for this type of copper ingot in order to suggest a similarity to the tanned hide of an ox, with the four corners representing legs. Much recent progress has come from the technical examination of these ingots, which are unalloyed and very "pure" in composition. Nevertheless, there remain problems with the interpretations of the analytical results, especially concerning possible modes of production for the ingots. The difficulties arise from the assumption that the oxhide ingots were the result of copper smelting, and thus represent "raw" or primary, smelted copper. Considerable evidence now supports the alternative theory, that oxhide ingots represent a final, refined product in the sequence of ancient copper production. To supplement the fragmentary archaeological evidence and to better investigate the steps of ancient copper production, a series of simulation experiments were undertaken at the Institute for Archaeo-Metallurgical Studies (IAMS), London. Each step of the ancient, primitive process was replicated; the objective was to duplicate the various Late Bronze Age copper ingot types, including an oxhide ingot.

Experimental work toward the reconstruction of Bronze Age copper smelting has contributed significantly to our present understanding. Although experimental simulations cannot "prove" the archaeological evidence, the results are especially relevant since modern metallurgical analyses and thermodynamic principals are involved. In copper smelting, certain chemical reactions must take place, and conditions under which these reactions occur in turn affect other reactions in known ways. The study of ancient copper smelting has become quite technical.

The laboratory experiments on copper smelting and refining, which I will summarize, were completed during 1979-1981 as part of my doctoral research at the Institute of Archaeology, London. The work was funded by the Institute of Archaeo-Metallurgical Studies. I would like to acknowledge and thank my advisors on this project, Professor R.F. Tylecote and Professor Beno Rothenberg.

The copper smelting experiments were set up in hope that they would shed light upon the operational parameters of the furnaces found at Timna Site 2, in southern Israel, from excavations directed by Professor Rothenberg. These furnaces, which date to the mid 12th century B.C., are believed to have been shaft furnaces, approximately 30cm in diameter and 70 to 100cm high (Tylecote et al. 1976). Although the furnaces were found to be in a fairly good state of preservation, many questions arise from the fragmentary evidence concerning how they were operated.

The metallurgical remains at Site 2 have been previously studied. On the basis of chemical analyses of the metallurgical products, Tylecote et al. (1976) concluded that local iron ore was used as a flux for smelting. Additionally, a reconstruction of the smelting furnace was suggested, with features which included a slag tapping pit, one or possibly two tuyeres, and the formation of a plano-convex copper ingot in the furnace bottom.

Simulation of the copper smelting process for this Late Bronze/ Early Iron Age furnace type has also been attempted before. Tylecote and Boydell (1978) conducted eleven smelting experiments, but with limited success, in that, in no instance was molten slag tapped from the furnace. Subsequent efforts were redirected to experimentation with the more primitive bowl type furnace and toward understanding the "prill extraction" smelting process that possibly represents the Chalcolithic period at Timna (Tylecote et al. 1977; Tylecote 1980a).

The present series of experiments started where the previous research by Tylecote and Boydell had ended. These experiments are classified as simulations. Modern materials were used. For example, the furnace was built from modern firebrick and operated with three tuyeres (fig. 17.1). Both horizontal and inclined tuyeres were tested. Air was blown through the tuyeres into the furnace from an industrial blower. The airflow rate was constantly measured and kept at about 350 liters per minute. The furnace measured 30cm in diameter and 100cm in height. The bottom could also be adjusted to control the height of the furnace for experimentation. For heat flow calculations, temperatures were measured using thermocouples placed throughout the furnace. Additional thermocouples were used to determine internal furnace temperatures. Charcoal was the fuel. The charcoal was screened and sized for better furnace

operation. During a typical experiment, about 50-60kg of charcoal would be burned.

In some of the preliminary experiments, a simulation copper ore was prepared from sand and copper turnings. The sand was used to represent unwanted material mixed with the malachite copper ore found at Timna. Copper ore shipped from Timna was used in later experiments. Iron ore from Cumbria in England was used as flux. The purpose of the flux was to produce a mineral phase with the unwanted sand in the ore that would have a relatively low melting point. The desired slag phase was fayalite, which melts at approximately 1150 $^\circ$C. The composition of the experimental slags was slightly richer in iron, but lower in manganese, than slag from Timna as reported by Bachmann (1980) and other researchers. The experimental slags were 40-50% FeO with less than 0.2% MnO, while the Timna slags were 35-45% FeO with 1-10% MnO. The iron ore flux used in the experiments did not contain the same concentration of manganese as the Timna iron ore, so to produce a free-running slag, essential for the Late Bronze Age smelting process, the difference was compensated for with more iron. This correction would not have affected the quality of the products from the experiments, since the observed differences are slight, and the slags were in both cases predominantly fayalite.

During a typical experiment, the furnace was first preheated with charcoal for several hours. To begin smelting, the furnace would then be filled to the top with charcoal and layers of copper ore mixed with iron ore flux were charged. To monitor the reducing atmosphere in the furnace, the exhaust gases were analysed periodically. During the combustion of charcoal, carbon monoxide is formed which reduces the ore to metallic copper. The ratio of CO to

CO_2 was approximately 5 to 1. Similar measurements have been made during other smelting experiments by Tylecote, Ghaznavi and Boydell (1977) and Hetherington (1980). Over-reducing conditions, such as observed experimentally, in the smelting furnace adversely affect the quality of the recovered copper product. Under primitive conditions it is not possible to control the ratio of carbon monoxide to carbon dioxide to the degree necessary to produce a "pure" copper product from smelting, while still producing sufficient heat from the combustion of charcoal to melt the slag and copper. It may be better to think of the various chemical reactions as consisting of some independent and dependent variables. Although difficult to control, the ratio of carbon monoxide to carbon dioxide is a very important independent variable in copper smelting. The resulting quality of the copper product represents one of the dependent variables.

During the experiments, when the tuyeres were observed to become irreparably blocked with molten slag, a hole was made in the section of the furnace. The molten slag was drained into a circular channel to copy a common type of tapped slag found at Site 2. The furnace had to be broken down to recover the smelted copper.

Typical copper products recovered from the simulation smelting experiments occurred as flat ingots resting directly upon the furnace bottom. In the experiments using Timna copper ore, the impure smelted copper was recovered as small flat ingots, usually positioned under each tuyere. With about 30% copper in the ore, relative to furnace volume, slag requirements and copper lesses in the slag, insufficient copper was input to form a single copper ingot across the furnace bottom. The shape of the bottom, or hearth, of the experimental furnace closely matched the shape

and dimensions of the Site 2 furnace remains. The copper smelted from Timna copper ore in the simulation experiments contained roughly 10-20% iron. As noted by Tylecote (1980) for other smelting experiments, the copper which collected in the bottom of the furnace contained less iron than the filaments of copper entrapped in the slag at higher levels in the furnace. This reflects further variation in reducing conditions throughout a primitive smelting furnace.

In a single smelting experiment using copper ore from Calabona in Sardinia (Merkel and Tylecote 1983), the composition of the copper product was: 89.1% Cu, 9.0% Fe, 0.98% S, 600 ppm As, 350ppm Sb, 200ppm Zn, 300ppm Pb with additional traces of Co, Sn, W, Ag and Cr at levels under 100ppm. Analysis also showed 0.28% Ni. However, compared to input ore and flux quantities, this value is inappropriate, and resulted from the loss of a thermocouple in the furnace during the experiment. The partial contamination of the copper by the metal from the thermocouple serves as a warning that all input materials must be accounted for in the products. A strict mass balance for the input and output elements is required for a meaningful comparison of the trace element patterns from smelting experiments. As has been emphasized repeatedly by other researchers, the composition of smelted copper is affected by numerous variables, such as additions from the copper ore, flux, fuel ash and furnace lining, as well as furnace operation procedures.

The modern firebrick was highly susceptible to slagging. It was estimated that about 2kg of firebrick was slagged away during an experiment. Slag attack was especially severe around the tuyeres where the temperatures were the highest. The downward flow of molten slag in the furnace is correspondingly greatest around the tuyeres. After 22 experiments and rebuilding the firebrick furnace numerous times, a more authentic furnace was built from clay to be used for further experimentation (fig. 17.2). To provide a more refractory material, the clay was mixed with sand and charcoal dust (see Smith and Wallraff 1974). The furnace was built by simply coiling the clay mixture into a pit in the sand. With this furnace construction, arrangements of 3, 2 and 1 tuyeres were compared.

Generally, the same operating procedures were used with the clay-built furnace as with the firebrick furnace. Fuel and ore/flux were charged in the same ratio (1:1). The largest tapped slag from a single batch weighed 25.9kg. Using multiple taps, the maximum weight of tapped slag reached 45.9kg. However, the clay-built furnace rapidly deteriorated from extensive slagging during these experiments, while the actual quantity of copper in the bottom of the furnace was not significantly increased by the greater charge weights. The longer the furnace was operated, more lining was slagged away. As a result, the slag became more viscous and copper losses in the slag increased. Furthermore, the different layers of slag tapped from the furnace, at intervals of about 30 minutes, did not adhere to form a single massive block in the tapping pit outside the furnace. Rather each cycle of tapped slag solidified as separate plates. The large tapped slag circles from Timna are evidently formed from a single tapping cycle. Even so, due to pervasive deterioration and slagging over long periods of operation, the experience with the experimental furnace also suggests that the ancient furnaces were used only in a single batch process, with the copper being recovered after a single large tap, once the furnace was cool enough.

After each experiment with the clay-built furnace, the front was broken down to recover the smelted copper. This is approximately the same condition in which the furnace remains at Timna were found. A hammer was used to break off the slag from the copper product. In Experiment 23, a single flat copper ingot of 2.2kg was recovered. It roughly conformed to the dimensions of the furnace bottom, but it was not plano-convex. The dimensions of Late Bronze Age plano-convex copper ingots do not match the dimensions of the furnace bottom remains found at any of the Timna sites. Neither was the experimental ingot very "pure." In Experiment 27, a reconstruction experiment using Timna copper ore, the copper product contained 22% iron as the chief impurity with additional concentrations of 0.4% S, 0.15% As, 670ppm Sb, 660ppm Pb, 690ppm Ag, 190ppm Ni and 80ppm Co. Other elements were detected at lower levels.

To test the experimental furnace under more realistic conditions, demonstrations were conducted at Timna in September 1981. Authenticity was the emphasis of the experiments. The experimental furnace built at Timna operated with three tuyeres, each connected to a set of pot bellows. The pot bellows had leather tops with two valves. The maximum airflow rate for such a set of bellows was estimated experimentally at about 350 l/min. No bellows have been found at Timna (see Davy 1979). However, from other Late Bronze Age sites, pot bellows were the most efficient type in use. The experiment was only moderately successful; many new values for operating variables were encountered that were very different from those in the laboratory. Only a small amount of slag was tapped. The furnace was broken down to recover 1.1kg of impure copper. The copper was recovered as large prills that

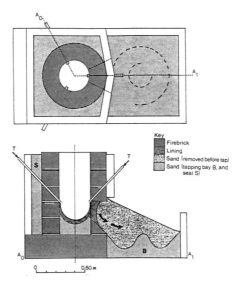

Figure 17.1   Schematic section and plan of the experimental furnace built from modern firebrick.   The section is drawn through two of the three tuyeres.   For tapping the molten slag, the sand insulating the front of the furnace was simply moved away and a circular channel made to receive the slag.

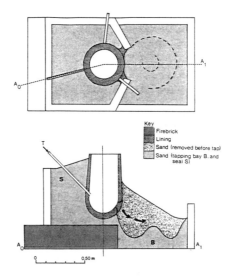

Figure 17.2   Schematic section and plan of the experimental furnace built from a coiled mixture of clay with sand and charcoal dust.   This structure is based on the archaeological evidence for Furnace IV found at Timna Site 2.

needed to be collected by hand and refined.

To refine the smelted copper, a reconstruction crucible furnace was built. It was operated with one tuyere and a set of pot bellows. Further remelting and refining experiments were conducted on the impure smelting product back in the laboratory. For example, the impure black copper smelted from Timna ore in Experiment 27 contained 22% iron. By simply remelting the copper in a shallow, lined put using charcoal, the iron content was decreased to 6%. The second remelting experiment decreased the iron to 3% and the third remelt decreased the iron to 2%. A plano-convex shaped ingot was the product of each refining experiment. These values for iron in the copper fit in closely with the other analyses of copper-based objects from the Timna Temple at Site 200 (Craddock 1980).

Deliberate fire-refining with a gentle airblast on the top surface of the molten copper from Experiment 27 further decreased the iron content to under 200ppm. Based on the composition of the copper products from these refining experiments, 99% of the iron was removed, as was 100% of the Zn, 96% of the S, 59% of the Pb, 26% of the Ni, 75% of the Co and only 7% of the As. The observed losses in concentration were accounted for in the analysis of crucible slag from the experiments. Based on the analysis alone, it appears that the concentration of Ag was increased in the refined copper, the final value being 730ppm. The molten copper was also stirred with a wooden stick to remove copper oxide that formed during refining. This process is called "poling" and is very effective under primitive conditions. The reconstruction refining experiments, using charcoal as fuel, resulted in a more complete removal of impurities than for other laboratory experiments

using an electric furnace (Tylecote 1980a). These refining experiments emphasize the complexity of trying to identify ore sources from the trace element patterns of ancient copper ingots or objects. Primitive fire-refining is very effective.

A few of the conclusions from these copper smelting and refining experiments may be summarized:

1. A plano-convex copper ingot is not formed under slag in the bottom of a furnace as a direct product from smelting. The production of about 2kg copper seems to be associated with about 30-40kg smelting slag.

2. The copper ingots produced from smelting were flat and very impure. The composition is explained thermodynamically, based on the observed CO/CO_2 ratios in the experimental furnaces. The experimentally produced copper ingots most nearly resembled the specimen of impure copper with adhering slag found at Beer Ora, Site 28, near Timna (Tylecote 1976a).

3. The smelted copper needed to be refined to approximate the quality of copper ingots dated to the Late Bronze Age. Fire-refining may have been done inadvertently in steps through remelting. The observed compositions of the experimental products offer an explanation for the analytical results for copper-based objects found at the Timna Temple (Craddock 1980). Other trace elements were followed from the ore, through smelting and refining using mass balances. With fire-refining, it is impossible to identify copper smelted from Timna ores, Sardinian ores or ores from other locations in the Late Bronze Age, based on composition alone.

4. Reconstruction, simulation and laboratory experiments do not always result in similar quality pro-

ducts. Thus, conclusions may also differ.

5. It must be stressed again that an experimental reconstruction cannot "prove" the archaeological evidence. The rules given by Coles (1979) for experimental archaeology pertain, of course, to archaeo-metallurgy as well. Successful reconstruction serves only to delimit the possibilities. Although the experimental furnaces have been successfully operated with several different arrangements of multiple or single tuyeres, based on the archaeological evidence, the furnace remains at Timna seem to have been operated with one or possibly two tuyeres as originally proposed by Tylecote, Lupu and Rothenberg in 1976.

The results from the copper smelting experiments may now be extended to the interpretation of other ingot types, such as the oxhide ingots. A brief overview of the previous theories and technical work on oxhide ingots is pertinent to this discussion.

In the catalogue of oxhide ingots published by Buchholz in 1959, it was assumed that the ingots originated from areas of copper ore deposits and thus copper smelting. This view has dominated and developed in the many publications on the subject. A copper smelting furnace capable of producing oxhide ingots was proposed by Tylecote (1976b; 1980b). It was developed from a reconstruction of a copper smelting furnace used in Roman Britain that could have produced tapped plano-convex copper ingots up to about 7kg in weight (Tylecote 1962). With extended operation, the same furnace type could also have been used to tap copper into an oxhide-shaped mold of clay or sand.

To allow sufficient molten copper to collect in such a smelting furnace - up to 30kg of copper or more - the furnace would have to be run continuously with the molten slag tapped at intervals from a level above the level of the accumulating copper. With adequate temperatures and an appropriate slag composition, the molten copper would settle down through the slag and fill the bottom of the furnace. When the desired quantity of copper had been reached, the copper could be tapped into an oxhide-shaped mould. From mass balances of the input materials, it has been estimated that the production of 30kg copper would result in approximately 300kg of slag. Since the maximum weight of known Late Bronze Age slag blocks is usualy well under 50kg, this quantity of copper would require at least six slag tapping cycles. Based on the known remains of Late Bronze Age copper smelting furnaces, at Timna for example, thirty kilograms of molten copper would fill such a primitive furnace practically up to the level of the tuyeres. Thus, operation of the furnace for smelting and tapping 30kg of copper would be extremely difficult and leave very little margin for error. This reconstruction is too sophisticated for what is currently known about operating parameters for Late Bronze Age shaft furnaces used for smelting.

Several researchers have previously expressed doubts that oxhide ingots are a direct product from copper smelting. For example, Catling (1964) in Cypriot Bronzework in the Mycenaean World viewed the production of oxhide ingots relative to Late Bronze Age international trade in copper. Rather than from smelting, the size and shape of the oxhide ingots were attributed to convenience for trade. A suggested weight around 29kg for the oxhide ingots remains controversial. Catling assigned the ancient production of oxhide ingots to the casting foundry alone - and thus explained the observed distribution of ingots generally in coastal Late Bronze Age sites. Although the initial chronological sequence for the oxhide ingots is no longer valid (Bass 1967), the archaeological evidence indicates the earliest examples come from regions without major copper ore deposits. However, of course, the argument over distribution vs. production is complicated for such trade items.

To date, all of the oxhide ingots that have been analyzed or rechecked have been unalloyed copper. Ony one specimen has been reported with about 10% Fe by Maddin and Muhly (1974). Generally, the iron concentrations are well under 0.5%. The results of smelting and refining experiments with copper suggest that the concentration of iron is a possible means with which to evaluate the degree of refining. Certainly more information is required on the intermediate and final products for matte smelting of copper sulfide ores and subsequent copper converting under primitive conditions.

Comparison of analytical results between laboratories using different techniques may be often misleading, as demonstrated in the study by Chase (1974). For oxhide ingots, sampling is an important factor in the problem. Notwithstanding, a few general trends seem apparent for the bulk compositions of oxhide ingots from Sardinia (Balmuth and Tylecote 1976). The iron was less than 0.02%. In concentrations less than 50ppm were the elements: zinc, cobalt, nickel, arsenic and manganese. Less than 20ppm were: silver, tin, antimony and lead. From the experimental evidence, these impurity levels are reasonable only for fire-refined copper.

Oxygen and sulfur concentrations are usually not determined in the analyses of copper-based objects of ingots (Tylecote 1976a). Slag in-

clusions have been noted, but rarely analyzed. The microscopic inclusions of copper sulfide, copper oxide, and slag are extremely important aspects of the composition of oxhide ingots and provide further evidence for how the ingots may have been produced. Detailed work on seven oxhide ingots or fragments from Sardinia by Zwicker et al. (1980) well documents such inclusions. However, comparing their analytical results using microprobe to results by other techniques for bulk compositions is most difficult. In the study by Zwicker et al., it was noted that a trend existed between the degree of surface blistering on the ingots and the presence of copper oxide inclusions. The two ingots with copper oxide inclusions exhibited the greater degree of blistering. The other five Sardinian specimens contained more numerous sulfide inclusions, many with concentrations of sulfur up to 30% for point analyses. Perhaps this line of investigation may lead to a satisfactory distinction between copper products smelted from copper sulfide ores. Quantitative results, however, are needed on bulk samples, since copper smelted from oxide ores has been shown experimentally to contain often up to approximately 2% sulfur (Tylecote et al. 1977).

Concerning the composition of the slag inclusions in the oxhide ingots from Sardinia, Zwicker et al. (1980) concluded that the observed concentrations of As, Ni and Co as oxides in the slag indicated that the copper was smelted under final oxidizing conditions. Evidence from copper smelting and refining experiments, however, suggests another interpretation. These elements are also characteristic of crucible slag produced in the refining experiments. Tylecote (1976b) stated that complex crucible slags may be differentiated from smelting slags by a relatively lower concentration of iron and higher concentrations of the nonferrous oxides, such as Co, Ni, Ca, etc. The compositional trends for the complex slag inclusion in the Sardinian ingots more closely match the characteristics of refining slags.

As a related project with the smelting and refining experiments for the Timna furnaces, the experimental approach was also used to cast an oxhide ingot in order to evaluate some of these operating variables better. A shaft furnace was built of clay in the laboratory (fig. 17.3). It measured 50cm in height and measured 30cm internal diameter. It was operated with one tuyere and had an average airflow of about 700 liters per minute. This airflow rate is approximately equal to two sets of pot bellows, which was estimated from additional testing. Charcoal and scrap copper were charged in layers into the furnace at a ratio of 1:2. During melting, the total input weight of copper was 28kg against 14kg charcoal. The observed burning ratio was about 14kg charcoal per hour, so the experiment proceeded very quickly, with few difficulties. No special tapping arrangement was needed, a hole was simply pushed through the furnace wall near the bottom and the molten copper splashed into a dry sand mould in the shape of an oxhide. The steep side of the mould prevented the formation of a runner; no launder was used. The copper ingot was allowed to cool in place. It weighed 25.1kg and measured roughly 50 x 25 x 4cm (fig. 17.4). The remainder of the input copper was recovered from the furnace with a small amount of slagged lining. Molten copper does not react with the lining in the same manner as the iron-rich slag, so the furnace sustained very little damage and could have been reused for melting and casting more ingots.

Since modern electrode scrap copper was remelted in this casting

experiment, the refining capability of the furnace could not be estimated (see Gowland 1895). From the metallographic examination of a sample cut from the ingot, gray-colored copper oxide inclusions were observed to be greatest near the top surface (penetrating down 1-4mm) and at grain boundaries (figs. 17.5-17.6). The structure of the ingot was typical of cast copper and is comparable to the photomicrograph published by Muhly et al. (1979) for a fragment of an oxhide ingot from Cape Gelidonya, labelled Gelidonya 3. There was a "chill margin" of fine grains (with diameters about 0.1-0.25mm) along the bottom and edges. The grains in the center of the ingot were the largest (equiaxes with diameters around 1.0mm). Only a slight tendency toward columnar crystallization was observed, near the bottom of the section, suggesting that the molten copper was not appreciably 'superheated' prior to casting. The average Vickers hardness was 45Hv, which is comparable to values for two of the Sardinian ingots examined by Balmuth and Tylecote (1976). However, the porosity of the experimental ingot was much greater, with the point count estimate around 20%. This level of porosity was judged several times too great, when compared to ancient castings. The reason the porosity of the experimental ingot was so high was that no attempt had been made to decrease the oxygen content of the molten copper. The input fuel-to-copper ratio was 1:2 for two reasons: both to save fuel, and because an extreme reducing atmosphere was not required. The microstructure implies that the copper evidently absorbed a great deal of oxygen. 'Poling' the molten copper with a wooden stick prior to casting would have effectively decreased the oxygen content to produce a less porous structure. Along with refining, this would be an ideal area for further experimental work on oxhide ingots.

The archaeological evidence, the composition, inclusions and micro-structures, and the experimental results all must be incorporated into a reconstruction of a method by which the oxhide ingots were produced.

To summarize:

1.   The distribution of oxhide ingot finds suggest that they may be associated with trade.   There is no direct spatial relationship with copper ore deposits.

2.   Smelted copper is "impure" and needs refining in order to approach the quality of the oxhide ingots.

3.   Oxhide ingots are unalloyed and relatively free of minor element concentrations. Muhly et al. (1977) concluded that no compositional patterns were evident for distinguishing groups of ingots.

4.   More evidence is still required for primitive copper converting, oxidizing copper-iron sulfide matte to produce copper metal. Reconstruction experiments on an appropriate scale would indicate the quality of products to be expected for these steps in ancient copper extraction.

5.   The presence of copper oxide inclusions in the ingot microsections is better explained by refining or remelting, than by postulating a final oxidizing atmosphere in a primitive smelting furnace.

6.   The remelting of copper in contact with slag decreases the quality of the copper product.   Usually remelting is done to decrease copper losses in the slag, but it has been shown experimentally that copper actually picks up iron during this process (Opie et al. 1979).   This means that for a primitive smelting furnace, the tapping of molten slag would have had to be nearly complete and perfect to allow for the possi-

bility of a successful final oxidizing or refining stage.   Perhaps as the level of fuel burned down in the furnace, there might be a slight chance of this occuring, but not while in contact with appreciable quantities of slag.   Smelting slag left in the furnace would be detrimental and would lower the quality of the recovered copper.   Slagged lining, additional fuel ash and slagged tuyeres would further complicate such a possibility.   Experimentally, it proved better to let the furnace slag and copper cool before separating it by hand and refining.

7.   The previously accepted reconstruction of a smelting furnace for the production of a 30kg oxhide-shaped ingot is too sophisticated for the Late Bronze Age.   It would demand inordinate skill to produce such quantities of copper and slag from a primitive shaft furnace.   The available refractories would not be suitable.   Furthermore, sufficient control over the reducing atmosphere cannot be achieved to produce good quality copper in one step from smelting.   Here, a couple of side notes are relevant.   In the southwest United States in the late 19th century, the quality of "black" copper smelted from copper oxide ores was considered acceptable with roughly 1-4% iron (Peters 1907).   Ethnographic evidence for primitive copper smelting in Africa, still practiced at the turn of the century, also produced impure copper which needed refining (Rickard 1935).

8.   In conclusion, the most straightforward interpretation of oxhide ingots - which has been proposed before by Catling (1964), among others - is that oxhide ingots were simply a convenient form in which to consolidate and transport large quantities of copper during the Late Bronze Age.   Oxhide-shaped copper ingots were items of trade, most easily produced by melting, not smelting.

Figure 17.3   The molten copper was tapped from the clay-built furnace into a sand mould.   No channel system was used to direct the molten copper into the mould.

Figure 17.4   The experimental oxhide ingot weighed 25.1kg.   A wedge section measuring about 6cm in depth and 2cm wide was cut from the edge of the ingot for microscopic examination.

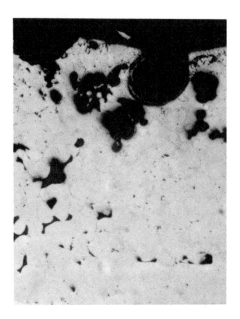

Figure 17.5 Photomicrograph of the experimental oxhide ingot at 64x magnification (unetched). This is the section at the top surface of the ingot showing the copper-copper oxide eutectic and porosity.

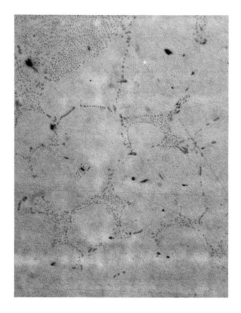

Figure 17.6 Photomicrograph of the ingot at 256x magnification. This view of the eutectic structure at greater magnification better shows the copper oxide inclusions at grain boundaries.

REFERENCES

BACHMANN, H.-G.
    1980   Early copper smelting techniques in Sinai and the Negev as
                deduced from slag investigations. BMOP 20.

BALMUTH, M.S. AND R.F. TYLECOTE
    1976   Ancient Copper and Bronze in Sardinia: Excavation and
                Anlysis. JFA 3:195-201.

BASS, G.F.
    1967   Cape Gelidonya: A Bronze Age Shipwreck. TAPS 57/8.

BUCHHOLZ, H.G.
    1959   Keftiubarren und Erzhandel im zweiten vorchristlichen
                Jahrtausend. PZ 37:1-40.

CATLING, H.W.
    1964   Cypriot Bronze Work in the Mycenaen World.   Oxford
                University Press.

CHASE, W.T.
    1974   Comparative   Analysis   of   Archaeological   Bronzes.
                Archaeological Chemistry, C.W. Beck ed. Washington D.C.:
                American Chemical Society.

COLES, J.
    1979   Archaeology by Experiment. London: Academic Press.

CRADDOCK, P.T.
    1980   The composition of copper produced at the ancient smelting
                camps in the Wadi Timna, Israel. BMOP 20.

DAVY, C.J.
    1979   Some Ancient Near Eastern Pot Bellows. Levant XI:101-111.

GOWLAND, W.
    1895   The Art of Casting Bronze in Japan. Journal of the
                Society of Arts, May. London: William Trounce.

HETHERINGTON, R.J.
    1980   Investigations of primitive lead smelting and its
                products. BMOP 17.

MADDIN, R. AND J.D. MUHLY
    1974   Some notes on the copper trade in the ancient Mid-East.
                Journal of Metals 26(5):1-7.

MERKEL, J.F. AND R.F. TYLECOTE
    1983   Appendix: The smelting of copper ore from Calabona.
                Historical Metallurgy 17(2):77-78.

MUHLY, J.D., T. STECH WHEELER, AND R. MADDIN
       1977   The Cape Gelidonya Shipwreck and the Bronze Age Metals
                Trade in the Eastern Mediterranean. JFA 4:353-362.

OPIE, W.R., H.P. RAJCEVIC, AND E.E. QUERIGERO
       1979   Dead Roasting and Blast-Furnace Smelting of Chalcopyrite
                Concentrate. Journal of Metals 31(7):17-22.

PETERS, E.D.
       1907   Modern Copper Smelting. New York: Hill Publishing.

RICKARD, T.A.
       1935   The Primitive Smelting of Copper and Bronze. Transactions
                of the Institution of Mining and Metallurgy 44:227-254.

SMITH, C.S AND B. WALLRAFF
       1974   Notabilia in Essays of Oars and Mettals. A 17th Century
                Manuscript. Historical Metallurgy 8(1):75-87.

TYLECOTE, R.F.
       1962   Metallurgy in Archaeology. London: Arnold.

       1976a   Properties of Copper Ingots of Late Bronze Age Type.
                Festschrift für Richard Pittioni. ArchAustr 14(2):
                157-172.

       1976b   A History of Metallurgy. London: The Metals Society.

       1980a   Summary of results of experimental work on early copper
                smelting. BMOP 17.

       1980b   Furnaces, Crucibles and Slags. The Coming of the Age of
                Iron, T.A. Wertime and J.D. Muhly eds. New Haven: Yale
                University Press.

TYLECOTE, R.F., A. LUPU, AND B. ROTHENBERG
       1976   A Study of Early Copper Smelting and Working Sites in
                Israel. Journal of the Institute of Metals 95:235-243.

TYLECOTE, R.F., H.A. GHAZNAVI AND P.J. BOYDELL
       1977   Partitioning of Trace Elements Between the Ores, Fluxes,
                Slags and Metal During the Smelting of Copper. JAS
                4:305-333.

TYLECOTE, R.F. AND P.J. BOYDELL
       1978   Experiemnts on Copper Smelting Based on Early Furnaces
                Found at Timna. Archaeo-Metallurgy, IAMS Monograph no. 1.

ZWICKER, U., P. VIRDIS AND M.L. CERUTI
       1980   Investigations on copper ore, prehistoric copper slag and
                copper ingots from Sardinia. BMOP 20.

18. COLLOQUIAL DISCUSSION ON COPPER "OXHIDE" INGOTS

John F. Merkel

List of Participants:

Miriam S. Balmuth	Tufts University
Elie Borowski	Toronto
John Dayton	London
Moshe Dothan	University of Haifa
Fulvia Lo Schiavo	Museo Archeologico Nazionale 'G.A. Sanna'
Robert Maddin	University of Pennsylvania
John F. Merkel	University of Pennsylvania - MASCA
Patricia Phillips	Sheffield University
Cyril Stanley Smith	Massachusetts Institute of Technology
Ronald F. Tylecote	University of London

Cyril Stanley Smith: Do you have a slide of the microstructure of this oxhide sample? (These have been added in the publication).

John Merkel: I do not have a slide of this, the micrographs and microstructures are being prepared right now for publication. Professor Tylecote and I are working on this together...

Smith: Is the one he showed typical?

Merkel: The copper that I used in my experiment was purer than that; it did not have...it was scrap electrode copper so the only thing I could base conclusions on for the microstructure was the orientation and sizes of the grains, because there was no coring of impurities and other materials in there, and the inclusion of oxygen as CuO_2 particles at the grain boundaries. In that sense the photomicrograph he showed is very similar.

Smith: I haven't studied these things in any detail but I have been quite fascinated by them nevertheless. I am quite convinced that it's not primary smelting but something that has happened afterwards (referring to surface blistering of oxide ingots). But there are three things which continue to bother me: one is the fact that the edge of the oxhide ingot is raised above the average level. It looks as if there has been something splashed up against the side and frozen there and then settled down. Secondly, the coarsely granular structure of the surface of the ingot, both top and bottom, does not look like the cast ingot that you showed us last (Merkel fig. 17.4 above). Thirdly, a cast copper with oxygen in it just as cast, does not look like this micrograph we have before us. You have primary crystals of copper and you have puddles of eutectic following the intercrystalline interstices. This (Balmuth and Tylecote 1976: fig. 4) (fig. 18.1) is not that way. Something has happened to the oxide eutectic before this photo was taken.

Merkel: Briefly, in the microstructure of the sample (Merkel's experiment) from the oxhide ingot, I observed large quantities of copper-copper oxide eutectic only near the top surface of the ingot (Merkel

265

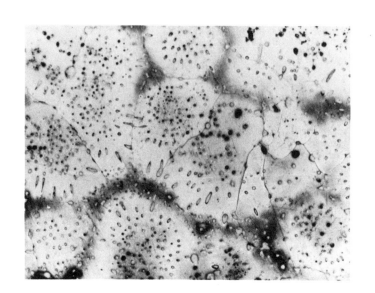

Figure 18.1 Oxhide ingot from Cagliari: Section CA1.
Magnification 80x. From M.S. Balmuth and
R.F. Tylecote, _JFA_ 3(1976):198, fig. 4.

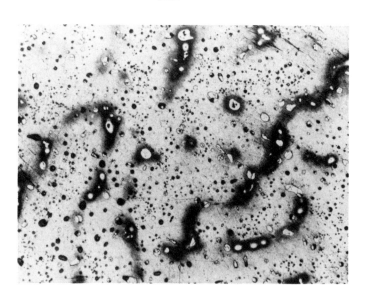

Figure 18.2 Oxhide ingot from Cagliari: Section CA2.
Magnification 80x. From M.S. Balmuth and R.F.
Tylecote, _JFA_ 3(1976):198, fig. 5.

figs. 17.5-17.6). However, relative to this slide, there seems to be less overall.

Smith: I think that any number of those who have looked at copper a lot will say that this is not a normal structure of a copper-copper oxide alloy. It is unwise to make a suggestion five minutes after you have thought of it, but your presentation brought something to my mind which I will suggest anyway, namely that the initial reduction produced rather irregular blobs of copper; then that these were put together in something like the mould that you showed, in a furnace that was not a blast furnace but was essentially a ceramic kiln. Can someone say what temperature was used in the firing of ceramics at that time? Were ceramics regularly fired at temperatures of 1200 $^{\circ}$C or so? It's rather hot isn't it?

Merkel: It's closer to 800 or 900 $^{\circ}$C. The problem now with moulds for oxhide ingots is that only one has been found. Generally it has been assumed that oxhide ingot moulds were usually sand, that there was a sand casting of copper. There are recent reports of one mould of sandstone being found at Ibn Hani near Ras Shamra, but this is unpublished and few details are available. We are having trouble finding evidence for other types of moulds and moulding materials for oxhide ingots and it seems the most likely candidate would probably be sand casting - something that would leave no evidence or very few remains in the archaeological record. For example, when I removed the (experimental) ingot (fig. 17.4) from the sand the level of induration around the side, the discoloration, didn't penetrate very far at all; a few centimeters at the most. The rest of the sand was more or less unaffected. You can see some parting of the copper from the mould along the side, where it contracted upon cooling. Some of it splashed along the side.

Smith: You would agree that the surface texture of the ingots is quite different from your sample? I think that is a very important point.

Merkel: Yes indeed. The experimental oxhide ingot was made from electrode scrap copper. Trying to sort out the production of copper from copper converted from matte is very difficult. We have few experimental data. How is the sulphur actually removed from the primitive converting of the matte? Slag production? - There is evidence that suggests the ingots with the rougher, more bubbly surface texture, blister texture, (the evidence strongly supports the fact), that those oxhide ingots were produced from another quality of copper; possibly from a matte smelting technique for sulfide ores.

Smith: Still, the blisters do not look like modern blister copper.

Merkel: Composition is a difficult problem. Any suggestions?

Robert Maddin: Regarding the ridge that you talked about, Cyril, on the edge. The largest collection of oxhide ingots on display are in the Numismatic Museum in Athens and to the best of my recollection (it has been nine years since I have seen them) not one has that ridge and the only time I have seen the ridges are on the Sardinian ingots. Can someone add any further information to that point?

Merkel: All of the ridges that I have seen on oxhide ingots are on the bottom surface and are cast in the mould, but on the top surface?

Ronald Tylecote: May I tell Cyril what that slide was before - that was a plano-convex ingot that was cast fairly rapidly in a sand mould and froze from the top and the bottom. It was just pure electrolytic remelted.

Smith: Would you put on the previous slide (Balmuth and Tylecote 1976:fig. 5) (fig. 18.2) from Tylecote's presentation please. Look at the grain belt, look at the dark areas of segregation which are the last parts to solidify and look at the relation of the oxide particles to it – totally different.

Tylecote: This is one of the ingots from Serra Ilixi (Sardinia).

Merkel: It has a very complex composition.

Maddin: That is not typical of all of the ingots. I have looked at a piece of that that Ronnie sent me, but the ones that we have looked at from some 20 ingots from other places do not have a structure like that.

Smith: Would you say the ones that you have looked at have had a normal cast copper structure?

Maddin: The two – one from Enkomi in the British Museum and the other from the Cyprus Mines office in Los Angeles – do have a typical cast structure, a very pronounced cored structure over a long period.

Merkel: What is the view of the audience toward a standard unit of weight for oxhide ingots – it has been proposed that 29kg or a talent seems to represent a standard weight for the ingots.

Miriam Balmuth: I have more information. If this ingot in fact was from Serra Ilixi, and I recall that it was, I would like to point out that that is not a coastal site and that Dr. Lo Schiavo's map shows that most of the oxhide ingots found in Sardinia were found not on coastal sites but rather inland and many of them near the Barbagia where there is some evidence for mining. I would also like to explain where we get the name "oxhide." It is one of those classi-

cal derivations from testimonia. The concept that there might have been a Bronze Age coinage, and that it would have an ox on it or be represented by an ox, derives not only from Plutarch's Life of Theseus (and in Theseus we see a symbol for Bronze Age Athens), but also from a scholion to Aristophanes' The Birds, quoting the 4th century B.C. antiquarian Philochorus and also 2nd century A.D. Ephorus. These tell us that the first coinage had an ox; and in 1924, in Athens Its History and Coinage, Charles Seltman put this testimonia together to suggest that what was in Athens (what Bob Maddin has just told us about) were the earliest coins, were ingots to which he gave the name "oxhide" with which we have been stuck ever since.

Merkel: Yes, the use of the word "oxhide" is very unfortunate in presentations such as this, as we are talking about oxhide shape and oxide inclusions.

Maddin: Let me respond to the question about whether the unit 29kg could have been a standard measurement. I speak as a metallurgist and not as an art historian or an archaeologist. The oxhide ingots range in size from as little as 16kg to almost 40kg. Every time the oxhide ingots have been found, for example on the Cape Gelidonya shipwreck, they have been found with bun ingots, with slab ingots, and the unpublished ingots found off the coast of Israel by the Haifa group, also contain segments of oxhide ingots along with slab ingots, along with bun ingots. So how then could oxhide ingots have been a unit of measurement or a unit of exchange? I can't buy that Catling hypothesis and I'm surprised it's being resurrected.

Merkel: Catling did not claim there was a certain unit – I'm referring to a recent article by Muhly in the Reallexikon der Assyriologie und vorderasiatischen Archäologie (1983: 353) with 29kg in there. Concerning the production of oxhide ingots on Sardinia, is there further discussion on that?

Patricia Phillips: It just struck me that these were not for further melting, these particular ingots, but were a finished product as such and they had some role like that - is that what you have been saying?

Merkel: No, not at all. There are so many fragments, especially of handles, from the ingots, that were obviously cut or removed somehow, possibly broken, from the ingots and reused. Weights of 16-40kg of copper breaking down into smaller objects, it's very difficult to handle those quantities, without a larger, shaft furnace to melt that quantity of copper. The 1-2kg bun ingots are much easier to remelt or possibly to cast. Even again, the smaller bar or slab ingots are another breakdown for transport of copper.

Maddin: I would like to bring up a point brought up by Prof. Smith many years ago, when I first started to look at ingots. If you consider, let's say a 30kg oxhide ingot, how would you remelt it? Would you have a furnace big enough to remelt that size? Suppose you were trying to break it apart. Has anyone every tried to break apart a piece of refined copper?

Tylecote: We have not had the pleasure of trying to break apart an oxhide ingot, but we have tried to break apart a plano-convex ingot. The scheme is that you heat them as hot as you can get them and hit them as hard as you can. We hope they break at the grain boundaries. It seems to work. We have knocked pieces off, but I agree with you that it is jolly difficult.

Merkel: With this experimental ingot that we cast, part of the continued research on that ingot was to try to break it, using such techniques, but it seems that the Institute of Archaeology people do not want to break it up.

Balmuth: In fact, the finds in Sardinia are mostly broken or cut up ingots; on view in the Sassari Museum from Nuraghe Albuicciu, are very clearly fragments of oxhide ingots. Dr. Lo Schiavo has given me the weights of the small pieces and apparently there is no premeditated weighing. Either by handful or by hunk, must have been the way they were transacted, but how they were cut up I don't know.

Fulvia Lo Schiavo: I only want to recall the bun ingots displayed in the Sassari Museum from hoards, for instance Flumenelongu. These have been cut in half and in thirds in very well-decided pieces, and not by chance, and so the problem of cutting applies here. Some very heavy double axes have also been found cut. I also want to recall the work of N. Parisi, in the 1960's in Studi Micenei ed Egeo-Anatolici, who has dismissed very clearly the opinion that the oxhide ingots can be of a well-decided weight and have been used as an early type of coinage.

Borowski: I believe that the so-called "oxhide" was a finished product as currency, because I have evidence from several objects that were donations brought to temples in the end of the 2nd millennium B.C., ca. 1200 or 1100. Among these donations, instead of currency, there were the seven replacements often mentioned in the Bible like large cattle, small cattle, silver, gold, and copper as well as oil and wheat. One of the representations there is carrying a sheep and carrying an ingot (oxhide) and then larger cattle. In the time of Abraham, we know he paid in Hebron with large and small cattle. I would suggest that instead of oxhide ingot, it should be "sheephide." Now the question of the weight depends on the time of the currency. What the currency was at the beginning and what was it at the end of the second millennium B.C.? The weight of the talent, i.e. how many shekels, varies from time to time. Therefore, my opinion is that the oxhide was a currency, before money was introduced, and the "oxhide" should actually be "sheephide."

Merkel: Well, "sheephide" would make a metallurgical discussion easier. But, on the other hand, Prof. Maddin was correct on the range of observed weights of the ingots and the distribution. It's possible there is some mode weight around 29kg, or a unit weight, but certainly if you're basing that theory on observed weights of complete ingots, that is problematic.

Borowski: What was the value of a sheep at a given time?

Merkel: There seems to be too much variation in weight of ingots from single hoards, such as Cape Gelidonya, no whether these represent possible values of sheep with slight variation, seasonally or otherwise, is tenuous.

Moshe Dothan: I would like to come a little to the history of the ingots. Some conclusions may be drawn from all you said. If we all agree that the oxhide ingots found in Sardinia were made in Sardinia, not talking about export, who were the people who made them and why couldn't this people be the same people who brought in Mycenaean pottery and later imitated Mycenaean pottery in the 13th century B.C. In the matter of the great trade and immigration, we talk about Mycenaeans, Cypriots, Sea Peoples, all kinds of people, who came to Sardinia; it could be immigration, it could be settlement, it could be just for trade, and they came and they came with the knowledge of making the

ingots, that we know from Cyprus, and they are so similar why couldn't they be the same kind of production, as long as we don't know exactly when they were made. I don't know if thermoluminescence could say more, but everybody agrees that the end of the 13th century was the time of the great catastrophes, but also the time of the great trade still along the Mediterranean.

Merkel: I understand there is recent evidence for Sardinian ingots and ores from lead isotope studies.

John Dayton: As Prof. Massoli-Novelli said yesterday, Sardinia is extremely interesting, as it is a Cambrian or pre-Cambrian or very old element of rock in Europe. In fact, it is a part of Europe before Europe broke away from America. Now lead isotope dating, which was pioneered by Brill some years ago, and has been carried on by me and Gale and other people, which is a geological dating technique which uses the lead isotopes very much like carbon 14 work. We are very fortunate indeed in that the ore deposits - the first thing that we had to do was find ore deposits from all over the world, and 10-20,000 samples have now been analyzed. Now, Sardinia is extremely distinct and the first thing that I found, I was looking at a spear from Beth Shean in 1972, which is in Philadelphia, and has a cartouche of Amenophis III from 1400 B.C., and is made of Sardinian copper. Now, this is when the Sherden are mentioned in Egyptian records. At the same time, we have another dagger from Beth Shean from the same date which is coming from Laurion copper in Greece. Blue frit, absolutely distinct, but coming from Mycenae from Schliemann's excavations which are coming from Cyprus ore. Of all the objects that I have had analyzed, this is the only one (mind you, we could use some more) that comes from Cyprus, which is extremely interesting. The Isili slag falls into this ratio which is between Sardinia and somewhere else which I think is probably Spain, which supports Cole's idea that copper was coming from Spain and was remelted in Sardinia and sent onwards. Now coming back again, we have a very interesting thing here, Stewart Fleming has done some Etruscan bracelets from Vetulonia, which fit exactly an MBII axe from Megiddo (tomb 911) dated to 1600-1650. Therefore, I'm not saying this is coming from Etruscan ore, because one of the things we have not yet done is we haven't got a good sample of copper ore from Tuscany. I think we now have evidence for the Sherden around in the Mediterranean. Now finally we have the Haghia Triada oxhide ingots which have Linear A signs, dated again to 1600 and they are absolutely, definitely coming from Sardinian ore. Therefore, when I said earlier the movement is coming from the metal, it is not Mycenaean prospectors going over to, it's like the Sumerian prospectors of Gordon Childe getting off their backsides in Baghdad and going up the Danube. I mean, the thing went the other way, and the people went the other way. The reason there is so little Mycenaean pottery is because once they reached the Levant, they didn't go home again. This I think is very interesting proof and if we can now get more objects we've now got a framework and we can fingerprint the things and see where they're coming from. Of course, you always have mixing problems.

PART SEVEN:
EPILOGUE

Miriam S. Balmuth

The island of Sardinia occupies a central position in the western Mediterranean that belies its consideration - until recently - as an ancient backwater. In addition to its location, the fact that it is an island with rich mineral resources has left its imprint on the archaeological record in a way that has formerly been almost inaccessible to archaeologists. The stated intention in the preface of this book is that the colloquium, "Sardinia in the Mediterranean," was meant to emphasize Sardinia's relationship to the rest of the Mediterranean and at the same time to illuminate those unique aspects of the island whose archaeological shape is just emerging. This stated intention has been more than amply rewarded by the proceedings and their written account.

The phenomenon of Sardinian archaeology in the fourth quarter of the twentieth century resembles a sleeping giant that, upon awakening, produces an outpouring of information and problems. Any contemporary treatment of ancient Sardinia can only be dealt with by understanding how far and fast the results of the most recent research are moving, by consulting those active in the field, and by bringing them together to discuss, question and argue their points. The colloquium was planned in just that way and Sardinia in the Mediterranean as a book offers the presentations of the colloquium with the additional benefit of being able to incorporate the results of the discussions and arguments.

Synthesis and analysis alternated with hypothesis in the reconsideration of known material, the presentation of new material and the formulation of new ideas. Material published for the first time can be found in many of the articles, with catalogs of objects that help to put them in a coherent order for further study. Material known for a longer time was reassessed in the light of more recent knowledge or newly developed scientific techniques. Phoenician bronze figurines and their putative heirs, Nuragic bronze figurines; the unpredictable large stone Nuragic statues, in fact, probably descended from Nuragic bronze figurines; and Roman shipping amphoras, found in Sardinia, but of origins that reflect Mediterranean trade: these catalogs constitute contributions to art history as well as to archaeology and history, and place in an even closer focus the relationship of Sardinia to the rest of the Mediterranean. The planned accumulation of subject matter, attractive in theory, came together in a way that was most successful in execution. The presentation of synthesis, analysis and hypothesis produced new problems, new ideas, and even new speculations and plans for further research.

The disciplines of geology, history, prehistory, art history, anthropology, philology, epigraphy, and metallurgy mingled as archaeological companions in the unfolding of the tangled problems created by new finds and illuminated by new ideas. Why are so many other disciplines required in studies that are basically archaeological? The answer is that archaeology has become basically multidisciplinary:

considerations of metal figurines, for example, cannot any longer be made without the study of the metal; and studies of metal cannot be fully made without studies of ore; studies of ore cannot be made without studies of the geological environment. Even with these technical studies, the expertise of the art historian, still remains necessary for the understanding of style and its development through time.

The chronological range of material and ideas treated extends from before the first settlements on the island - around 6000 b.c. - and concentrates on a period between 1500 and 500 B.C., when the large stone towers, nuraghi, were built, modified, added to, destroyed, rebuilt and reused, in a variety of combinations. The dynamic nature of the archaeology of Sardinia, can be seen in the constant refining of dates allowed by new discoveries or interpretations. This is vividly illustrated by the dating of the Neolithic: Patricia Phillips in discussing 'Classic' and 'Revised' chronology (p. 206), makes use of the latest available radiocarbon dates from David Trump (p. 10) and adds two typesites to develop more precise definitions in the development of the cultures within those millennia; Fulvia Lo Schiavo (p. 231) adds even other typesites within the 'Classic' chronology. There is no large distance between the dates, but a finer and finer accuracy becomes visible.

Dating by inscriptions provides another surprise by way of the presence of Phoenicians on the island as early as the eleventh century B.C. This was demonstrated by Frank Moore Cross (chap. 9) in an analysis of the letter forms on Phoenician inscriptions found on Sardinia. The earlier date for the presence of Phoenicians, in turn, allows for an earlier date for the presence of Phoenician material, such as the bronze figurines shown by Ferruccio Barreca from the Nuragic village of Santa Cristina (chap. 10). These include unpublished pieces, which will create a springboard for the consideration of the relationship of Phoenician to Nuragic figurines. Surely the second item in Barreca's catalog of these figurines reflects the very moment of transition from Phoenician to Nuragic Mediterraneanizing in style!

The physical description of the island anticipates treatments dependent on rock, ore, and metal. Raniero Massoli-Novelli (chap. 1) explains the possibility of change in the early coastal environment that would allow for Paleolithic presence, but might well insulate Sardinia later in prehistory. It is nevertheless the place of Sardinia in the Mediterranean that is emphasized here; the idea of Sardinia as an isolated entity does not last beyond the appearance of Cardial Impressed Ware in the Early Neolithic, although there may have been periods of introspection as well as those in which she rode the Mediterranean mainstream. The early obsidian trade defined by Patricia Phillips (chap. 14) confirms the appearance of island material beyond the island as early as the 6th millennium b.c.

David Trump (chap. 2) offers an exemplary treatment of the relation of landscape to settlement in his synthesis of the successive phases in one discrete area through seven millennia. With new interest and discoveries from the Neolithic Age, and always copious discussion on the period instituted by the building of the nuraghi, the intervening cultures are also treated here, by both James Lewthwaite (chap. 3) and

Fulvia Lo Schiavo (chap. 16). Lewthwaite adds an analysis of settlement patterns and consideration of the economy to define the succession of the post-Neolithic, pre-Nuragic cultures that range from the Chalco-lithic phase of Ozieri to the Early Bronze Age Bonnannaro. These are given chronological definition by Fulvia Lo Schiavo (p. 231) along with the known extent of metallurgy for each.

From early in the second millennium onwards, the island began to take on a new look, provided by the building of large stone towers, nuraghi. They represent only one defining aspect of that complex culture, but are the most widely known. Yet, even their function is still being argued. The distribution of nuraghi within a relatively small, circumscribed area prompts Trump's suggestion of different dates for their existence (p. 14), a restricted length of occupation, and varying functions. Trump's explanation for the coexistence of juxtaposed towers by a multiplicity of function represents one of the few reasonable solutions to the problem of such large numbers in such close proximity. Their architectural origins, a much discussed problem, are given new insights here by virtue of an analysis of their earliest known predecessors and a glimpse of extrainsular similarities by Lewthwaite. His discussion of the development of Nuragic architecture speculates with the social structure of the Nuragic population.   Of the architectural variety, Lewthwaite (p. 25) explains that while the corridor form of nuraghe may be simpler and earlier, both corridor and corbelled forms coexisted throughout the Nuragic era, and that each can be derived from a separate Copper Age (= Lo Schavio's Late Eneolithic) prototype.

The 'material culture' of the nuraghi is of special importance in demonstrating that Sardinia, while now better understood to have been often in the mainstream of the Mediterranean, was an innovator as well as a borrower. In Carlo Tronchetti's presentation (chap. 4), the first exposition in English, we have not only a revelation of the newly found sculpture, but an interpretation for understanding their form and function within the society of the 7th century. In the presence of prosperity (perhaps due to trade in metals) and of a resulting class situation, the large-scale stone sculpture reflects a need to construct monumental memorials.

An interpretation of the statues as inspired by Phoenician or Punic predecessors, might make good geographical and cultural sense, and the analyses and comparisons that follow Tronchetti's exposition seem to place them accurately in a world associated with one kind of Oriental-izing or another. In complying to a request to provide a larger Medi-terranean setting for the sculptures, Brunilde Ridgway (chap. 5) has illuminated their uniqueness by placing them against a general back-ground and showing possible sources of inspiration. The criteria of medium, technique, style and iconography for comparisons have the effect of excluding the possibility of influence from Near Eastern hard stone colossal statues. She finds the Monte Prama statues almost a cross between a naturalistic Aegean current and the stylized Italic approach. Conversely, the production of such monumental memorials 'from scratch,' according to the analysis of Larissa Bonfante in supplying an Etruscan connection (chap. 6), represents a 'blowing up' of the bronze figurines, the magnification of the miniature, and can be documented in similar transitions within the Tyrrhenian area, one of which is the well known Warrior from Capestrano. While earlier production in the western Mediterranean may have been of small-scale sculpture, the seventh century as the period of the introduction of large size sculpture and as an age of experimentation provides the right time and place to allow that the Monte Prama sculptures might not be so unpredictable after all, even though they were unpredicted.

Bronze figurines and nuraghi, both famous for centuries, are generally the first things that come to mind when considering the material culture of Nuragic Sardinia and both are considered in the realm of 'primitive' by some classically-oriented art historians whose standards are firmly crystallized by a narrow appreciation of familiar work. Other aspects of production are little-known and less appreciated. The ceramic material associated with the appearance of the nuraghi presents a range from homely household objects to unusual shapes with more elegant treatments. The structures themselves are now being studied with a view to the architectural refinements and the use for visual effect of different colors and patterns in the stone.

Metal working reappears throughout this book as a subject for different kinds of treatment. The Nuragic bronze figurines represent the fusion of techniques characteristic of a metal-rich island that has communications with the outside world and local independence in craft traditions. Through an analysis of bronzes in the British Museum, some only recently published for the first time, some receiving their introduction here, Francesca Ridgway (chap. 7) was able to hypothesize a date of the late ninth century as the latest rather than the earliest for one specific regional workshop; this represents an even earlier date than the widely held eighth century associated with most of the non-Mediterraneanizing types. In addition to her suggestion for a timely re-examination and reassessment of all Sardinian bronze figurines, she points out the need for a re-evaluation of contacts between Sardinia and Cyprus and the East Mediterranean.

Cyprus too reappears throughout this book, almost always in connection with metalworking. It is in another connection, however, that Moshe Dothan (chap. 8) cites the appearance of a kind of Mycenaean pottery, IIIC:1, at some Cypriot sites, and also at Akko in northern Israel, at the crossroads of the ancient coastal road from Egypt to Syria. In these eastern sites, it has been associated by some with the tribes of the so-called Sea Peoples. It is its appearance as well at Nuraghe Antigori in Sardinia (see map p. 246) that allows the reinvoking of the hypothesis that one of the tribes, whose name can be translitered from Egyptian inscriptions as 'Shardina,' may somehow be connected with the island. Oxhide ingots, present as well in the areas under discussion, may furnish yet another link.

Is it possible that a route from the Near East to Sardinia may have been pioneered by Sea Peoples and continued by Phoenicians? In a close analysis of the Phoenician inscriptions found on Sardinia, Frank Cross (chap. 9) was able to redate their first presence to as early as the 11th century B.C. and to support the date with other early Phoenician inscriptions from Crete and nearby islands. The 9th century is his date for the systematic colonizing of the West Mediterranean by the Phoenicians, with metal resources as the goal.

Ferruccio Barreca uses Cross' early dating to interpret the Phoenician figurines (chap. 10) and their subsequent development on Sardinia. He makes a distinction between the Phoenician work on the island and the Phoenicians as carriers of material from other eastern sources, in parallel with Francesca Ridgway (chap. 7), and is also in accord in citing Phoenician inspiration for only one group of figurines.

Barreca's masterly synthesis of Phoenician and Punic civilization (chap. 11) and its impact on the island - appearing for the first time in English - underlines, in fact, the rarity of those studies in our time and place. The Punic-Nuragic symbiosis is especially significant for understanding the conservative continuity on the island. The testimony of Punic religion, however, points to one instance of their ethnic and cultural divergence.

Looking at old material in new ways, and benefitting immediately from the direct exchange of information at the colloquium, allowed David Ridgway to make connections between the silver in the tombs of Pithekoussai on the island of Ischia and the silver resources from Sardinia (chap. 12). He also learned from Frank Cross that an inscription, formerly thought to be Aramaic, on an amphora used for holding an infant burial, was, in fact, Phoenician; and perhaps even expected to be recognized at Pithekoussai. This inscription, plus some fragments of material he presented, was combined to suggest that Pithekoussai was a staging point for Phoenicians or others from the Near East going to and coming from Sardinia. Metal from Cyprus is once more a catalyst, here in the account that puts together evidence for the westward movement of Greeks, in particular Euboeans, in the eighth century B.C.

Any historical account of Greek colonization is certain to contain the components that the literature of mythology supplies: the hero, the foundation, and probably some trace of Herakles. In assembling the tools for assessing the possibilty of Greek presence on Sardinia, Jean Davison (chap. 13) was already armed with the knowledge of archaeological evidence. Her use of history, mythology and literature enable a keen analysis of Athens' ability to rationalize a Greek relationship to Sardinia as the legitimate claimant to the inheritance of Herakles.

Peter Wells points out how trade in the Mediterranean, documented in the Early Neolithic and then again in Roman times, provides a demonstration of the island as both exporter and importer. Patricia Phillips (chap. 14) shows Sardinia's Early Neolithic extrainsular involvement as confirmed by the obsidian from Monte Arci that is found in Corsica, Liguria and Southern France. The problem of preference on the part of trading partners is introduced by illustrating the use of more Sardinian than the superior Liparian obsidian in some areas.

The Roman shipping amphoras collected for publication by Elizabeth Will (chap. 15) are essentially a catalog of this kind of vessel, and have been treated as such in the text. By understanding their style and

contents, she has been able to show the centrality of Sardinia's commercial role in the western Mediterranean over a period of time, and
even trace another preference - for imported or domestic wine - at
different times among the Romans on Sardinia. Combining the knowlege of
the material with that of the history and literature produces once more
the ability to reconcile the archaeological evidence with documentary
evidence.

Metal working has emerged as an outstanding characteristic of the
island by virtue of the large number of finds not only of weapons,
tools, stands, vessels and jewelry, but also of moulds for casting them,
and especially of metal hoards, often containing ingots, which suggest
that they were founders' hoards. Fulvia Lo Schiavo (chap. 16) presents
here a valuable account of the earliest appearing metal objects on
Sardinia plus a discussion of the various metal objects from the Bronze
Age, and their extrainsular associations. It is in her arguments of the
presence of Mycenaean prospectors and the Sardinian source for oxhide
ingots that she contributes the hypotheses for further testing.

Once more that interaction, only partly defined, between Sardinia
and Cyprus from the 14th century B.C. on is mentioned. It seems to imply
some kind of contact, whether it be trade, immigration, the visitation
of craft specialists or some other means that singly, or in any combination, resulted in the presence of Cypriot material and ideas on the
island. This includes metal work, such as weapons, tripods and ornaments. It also means some connection in the idea, the metal or the
actual production of copper oxhide ingots. It is even sensed by some in
ceramic shapes. It is worth repeating here that if any mathematical
formula could be created to express the relationship between Sardinia
and the East Mediterranean in the Late Bronze and Early Iron Ages, then
Cyprus would surely emerge as a constant.

The repeated treatments of ingots makes John Merkel's work in their
experimental reconstruction (chap. 17) especially appropriate. His
account of the technology of ingot fabrication shows that the plano-
convex form of the traditional ingot was not the result of the shape of
the bottom of the furnace, but created by other means, thereby shatter-
ing yet one more long held assumption.

The colloquial discussion was valuable for refining ideas on the
oxhide ingots of copper and on the problem of their appearance in such
great number in Sardinia. The interdisciplinary nature of the studies
involved in the archaeology of Sardinia was again vividly illustrated.
The discussion brought out several opinions but the consensus was that
the material does not yet lend itself to the definitive solution of the
ultimate provenience of either the ore or the metal. That goal, however
is closer in sight.

In sum, the colloquium on Sardinia in the Mediterranean, and this
publication of it, can be considered the beginning of a series of
effects. Metals and metal working; Cyprus; the involvement within the
Mediterranean long before and far more widely than previously understood: these are some of the subjects treated, related to Sardinia, that
provided new information as well as new ways of thinking. The study of

<u>nuraghi</u> gained additional insights in the area of function as well as architecture. There was no ultimate solution to the mystery of copper oxhide ingots, now known throughout the Mediterranean, but appearing in Sardinia in the greatest number. This may represent yet another Cypriot connection, either by importation of material and/or ideas; a great deal of evidence was collected to help unravel the knotty problem.

Catalogs with unpublished material that can act as a point of departure for further study contributed yet one more dimension to this collection. The bibliographies, too, are all essentially tools of research; those by Bonfante and Davison went even further to supply additional information. Suggestions for future investigation have been explicitly as well as implicitly expressed, promising the emergence of more and more information and ideas. Much of this research is already under way, and some is already in print. For all these reasons, the colloquium may be thought of as a moment, but it also stands as a monument to Sardinian archaeological research, not longer lasting than bronze, but nevertheless timely, necessary, and fruitful.